Krishna Bista, *Executive Editor*
Morgan State University, USA

Chris R. Glass, *Editor-In-Chief*
Old Dominion University, USA

I0022967

Vol. **11** No **1** February **2021**

JOURNAL OF INTERNATIONAL STUDENTS

A Quarterly Publication on International Education

Access this journal online at: http://ojed.org/jis

Print ISSN 2162-3104
Online ISSN 2166-3750

Disclaimer
Facts and opinions published in *Journal of International Students* (JIS) express solely the opinions of the respective authors. Authors are responsible for their citing of sources and the accuracy of their references and bibliographies. The editors cannot be held responsible for any lacks or possible violations of third parties' rights.

Special Issues

Special Issue on
Reflection and Reflective Thinking (2020)
Special Issue Co-Editors:
Georgina Barton, University of Southern Queensland, Australia
Mary Ryan, Macquarie University, Australia

Special Issue | *Bahasa Indonesia* on
International Students and COVID-19 (2020)
Special Issue Co-Editors:
Handoyo Puji Widodo, King Abdulaziz University, Saudi Arabia
Sandi Ferdiansyah, Institut Agama Islam Negeri, Indonesia and
Lara Fridani, Universitas Negeri Jakarta, Indonesia

Special Issue | *Chinese* on
International Students in China (2020)
Special Issue Co-Editors: *Mei Tian and Genshu Lu*
Xi'an Jiaotong University, China

Special Issue on
Fostering Successful Integration and Engagement Between
Domestic and International Students (2018)
Special Issue Co-Editors: *CindyAnn Rose-Redwood and Reuben Rose-*
Redwood, University of Victoria, Canada

Special Issue on
The Role of Student Affairs in International Student Transition and
Success (2017)
Special Issue Co-Editors:
Christina W Yao, University of Nebraska-Lincoln, US
Chrystal A. George Mwangi, University of Massachusetts Amherst, US

Special Issue on
International Student Success (2016)
Special Issue Editor: *Rahul Choudaha, DrEducation, United States*

Emerson is a campus without borders.

We believe producing inspired work requires a global perspective, which is why the Emerson experience isn't limited to one city or even one country. As a global hub of arts and communication in higher education, we strive to provide our students, faculty, and staff with opportunities to connect and collaborate across countries and cultures. From our Global Pathways Programs to our castle in the Netherlands and beyond, we offer more than opportunities for students to study abroad—we provide access to enriching cultural experiences that will guide you on the path to becoming a global citizen.

Our newest global degree programs:

- **Global BA in Business of Creative Enterprises: Australia**
  Our accelerated Global BA in Business of Creative Enterprises (BCE) is powered by a rich management-focused curriculum; immerses students in the life of companies and organizations across two continents through intensive internship programs; and spans venues in **Sydney**, **Boston**, and **Los Angeles**.

- **Global BFA in Film Art**
  Our intercontinental joint Global BFA in Film Art spans venues in **Paris**, **the Netherlands**, and **Boston**. In this one-of-a-kind degree program, students will not only study visual and media arts in the City of Light itself, but will also receive a foundation in the liberal arts and French language.

Learn more at **emerson.edu/global**.

Routledge
Taylor & Francis Group

Routledge Studies in Global Student Mobility Series

This Routledge Series offers a scholarly forum for original and innovative research to understand the issues and challenges as well as share the best practices related to international student mobility in K-12 and beyond, education abroad, and exchange programs globally that creates a professional network of researchers and practitioners. Submit your proposal via emails.

Series Editors
Dr. Chris R. Glass & Dr. Krishna Bista,
For questions and submission, email at crglass@odu.edu

Published Titles

Inequalities in Study Abroad and Student Mobility

The Experiences of International Faculty in Institutions of Higher Education

International Students in Community Colleges

Critical Perspectives on Equity and Social Mobility in Study Abroad

Online Teaching, Learning and Virtual Experiences in Global Higher Education

International Student Support and Engagement

Impact of COVID-19 on Global Student Mobility and Higher Education

Cross-Cultural Narratives
Stories and Experiences of International Students
Edited by Ravichandran Ammigan (2021)

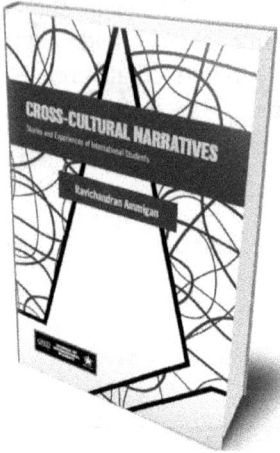

Praise for this book

Through rich and engaging stories, *Cross-Cultural Narratives* offers important personal accounts of the challenges and triumphs of international students navigating diverse and foreign academic and cultural landscapes. This inspiring and thought-provoking collection adds to other noble qualitative documentation of the international student experience.

Anthony L. Pinder, EdD
Associate Vice President for Academic Affairs –
Internationalization & Global Engagement
Emerson College, USA

***

This is a great resource for researchers, university staff, and students to (re)-situate themselves in the day-to-day reality of international students at U.S. universities. In our data driven world abounding with echo chambers, it is critical that we as humans continue to nurture and attend to diverse individual narratives of challenge, success, failure, humor, learning, shock, community, belonging, and resiliency. Let us listen to the next generation as they share the ties that bind us across differences.

Nelson Brunsting, PhD
Director, RAISE Center
Research Associate Professor, International Studies
Wake Forest University, USA

***

This edited collection of stories offers insight into the concrete details of US life that international students find confounding: that bread is soft and sweet, that everyone asks, "How are you?" but no one wants to know the answer, that fellow students don't know the metric system, and that people are startled if you kiss them on the cheek in greeting. All of these examples, in the students' own voices, will be valuable to practitioners and faculty who want to understand how life on and off campus appears from multiple perspectives.

Martha C. Merrill, PhD
Associate Professor, Higher Education
Kent State University, USA

OJED
OPEN JOURNALS IN EDUCATION

ISSN: 2162-3104 Print/ ISSN: 2166-3750 Online
2021 Volume 11, Number 1
© *Journal of International Students*
http://ojed.org/jis

Editorial Team

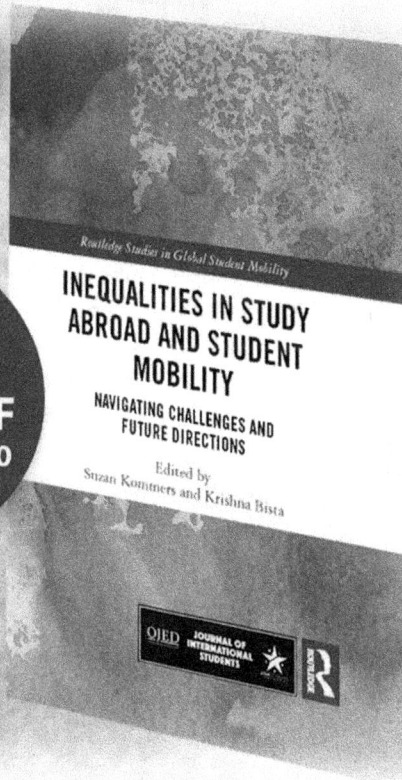

Routledge Studies in Global Student Mobility

INEQUALITIES IN STUDY ABROAD AND STUDENT MOBILITY

NAVIGATING CHALLENGES AND FUTURE DIRECTIONS

Edited by
Suzan Kommers and Krishna Bista

OJED JOURNAL OF INTERNATIONAL STUDENTS

Routledge
Taylor & Francis Group

Reviews

"This book is a valuable addition to our understanding of the relationship between inequalities and international education – both at home and abroad. Besides offering insights from cases around the Western world, all chapters also offer useful implications for daily practice."
Christof Van Mol, Assistant Professor, Tilburg University, Netherlands

"Inequalities in Study Abroad and Student Mobility presents a remarkable set of voices that, taken together, provide a deep, critical, and valuable analysis of some of the most pressing issues for international higher education."
Gerardo L. Blanco, Associate Professor, Boston College, USA

"The COVID-19 crisis made the risk of growing inequalities in higher education even more visible. *Inequalities in Study Abroad and Student Mobility* is a must-read book addressing the topic of inequalities in internationalization and study abroad in a holistic manner.
Giorgio Marinoni, Manager, International Association of Universities, France

"An impressive and important collection. The editors have assembled twelve strong contributions that not only lay out the challenges inherent in study abroad access in an unbalanced and vulnerable world, but offer well-reasoned prescriptions for greater equity, effectiveness, and sustainable positive impact.
James E. Callaghan, Assistant Vice-President, Georgia College & State University, USA

Open Journals in Education (OJED) publishes high quality peer reviewed, open access journals based at research universities. OJED uses the Open Journal System (OJS) platform, where readers can browse by subject, drill down to journal level to find the aims, scope, and editorial board for each individual title, as well as search back issues. OJED journals are required to be indexed in major academic databases to ensure quality and maximize article discoverability and citation. Journals follow best practices on publication ethics outlined in the COPE Code of Conduct. Explore our OJED Journals at www.ojed.org

***

A. Noam Chomsky Global Connections Awards celebrate the power of human connections. The awards recognize distinguished service to the global mission of the STAR Scholars Network. Several individuals with a deep impact on advancing global, social mobility are recognized every year.

For more information, visit https://starscholars.org/global-connections-award/

Indexing

ISSN: 2162-3104 Print/ ISSN: 2166-3750 Online
Journal of International Students
http://ojed.org/jis

OJED
OPEN JOURNALS IN EDUCATION

All articles published in the *Journal of International Students* are indexed and listed in major databases and sources:

SUBJECT: EDUCATION – HIGHER   DEWEY # 378

CEDROM SNI
- Eureka.cc, 01/01/2017-
- Europresse.com, 01/01/2017-

Directory of Open Access Journals
- Directory of Open Access Journals, 2011-

EBSCOhost
- Education Source, 03/01/2012-

Gale
- Academic OneFile, 09/01/2011-
- Contemporary Women's Issues, 09/01/2011-
- Educator's Reference Complete, 09/01/2011-
- Expanded Academic ASAP, 09/01/2011-
- InfoTrac Custom, 09/01/2011-

Multiple Vendors
- Freely Accessible Social Science Journals, 2011-

ProQuest
- Education Collection, 10/01/2011-
- Education Database, 10/01/2011-
- Education Database (Alumni Edition), 10/01/2011-
- ProQuest Central, 10/01/2011-
- ProQuest Central - UK Customers, 10/01/2011-
- ProQuest Central (Alumni Edition), 10/01/2011-
- ProQuest Central (Corporate), 10/01/2011-
- ProQuest Central (US Academic Subscription), 10/01/2011-
- ProQuest Central China, 10/01/2011-
- ProQuest Central Essentials, 10/01/2011-
- ProQuest Central Korea, 10/01/2011-
- ProQuest Central Student, 10/01/2011-

- ProQuest Research Library, 10/01/2011-
- ProQuest Research Library (Corporate), 10/01/2011-
- ProQuest Social Sciences Premium Collection, 10/01/2011-
- ProQuest Social Sciences Premium Collection - UK Customers, 10/01/2011-
- Research Library (Alumni Edition), 10/01/2011-
- Research Library China, 10/01/2011-
- Research Library Prep, 10/01/2011-
- Social Science Premium Collection, 10/01/2011-

Clarivate Analytics
- Web of Science
- Emering Sciences Citation Index
- Higher Education Abstracts

Source: Ulrichsweb Global Serials Directory

Google My Maps

You may access the print and/or digital copies of the *Journal of International Students* from **586 libraries** worldwide (as of Nov 8, 2020).

The *Journal of International Students* (Print ISSN 2162-3104 & Online ISSN 2166-3750) is a member of the STAR Scholars Network Open Journals in Education (OJED), a OJS 3 platform for *high-quality, peer-reviewed* academic journals in education.

JIS is a Gold Open Access journal and indexed in major academic databases to maximize article discoverability and citation. JIS follows best practices on publication ethics outlined in the COPE Code of Conduct. Editors work to ensure timely decisions after initial submission, as well as prompt publication online if a manuscript is accepted for publication.

Upon publication articles are immediately and freely available to the public. The final version of articles can immediately be posted to an institutional repository or to the author's own website as long as the article includes a link back to the original article posted on OJED.

None of the OJED journals charge fees to individual authors thanks to the generous support of our institutional sponsors.

For further information

Editorial Office
Journal of International Students
URL: http://ojed.org/jis
E-mail: contact@jistudents.org

OJED
OPEN JOURNALS IN EDUCATION

ISSN: 2162-3104 Print/ ISSN: 2166-3750 Online
2021 Volume 11, Number 1
© *Journal of International Students*
http://ojed.org/jis

CONTENTS

Research Articles

Research in Brief

Study Abroad Reflections

Book Reviews

Peer-Reviewed Article

© *Journal of International Students*
Volume 11, Issue 1 (2021), pp. 1-23
ISSN: 2162-3104 (Print), 2166-3750 (Online)
doi: 10.32674/jis.v11i1.1955
ojed.org/jis

OJED
OPEN JOURNALS IN EDUCATION

The Synthesis and Future Directions of Empirical Research on International Students in the United States: The Insights from One Decade

Masha Krsmanovic
University of Southern Mississippi, USA

ABSTRACT

The purpose of this systematic review was to identify the trends in empirical research on international students in the United States produced between 2010 and 2019. After reviewing and synthesizing the characteristics of 334 research articles published over the past decade, I identify the areas that have been overly researched and the domains that have not yet been adequately explored. The overall findings of this review indicate that recent scholarly efforts have not always been aligned with the international student representation on U.S. campuses. Consequently, I provide eight critical recommendations for future research in the field in the context of over- and underresearched institutional sites (e.g., institutional type and control), international student populations (e.g., academic level, field of study, and country of origin), research methods employed, and research questions examined.

Keywords: international students, international student mobility, systematic review

INTRODUCTION

According to the U.S. Department of Homeland Security, an international student is defined as a "nonimmigrant ... foreign student coming to the United States to pursue a full course of academic study" (2019, para 2). In the academic year 2018–2019, more than 1 million students in U.S. colleges and universities were classified as international (Institute of International Education [IIE], 2019). Of

1

this number, 39% were undergraduates, 35% were graduate students, 20% were enrolled in optional practical training, and 6% were nondegree seekers.

Reasons why international applicants decide to pursue their higher education degree in the United States are multifold and complex. Exploring prospective students' attitudes about possible study abroad destinations, IIE (2015) identified main pull factors that motivate them to choose a particular destination. In that regard, 77% of prospective international students believed that the quality of U.S. education was superior to that of global competitors, 78% were attracted by the variety of schools and educational programs, and 68% believed that the United States is welcoming toward international students.

In some cases, these predeparture perceptions prove to be warranted. For instance, the recent survey of international students in the United States, conducted by World Education Services (2019), revealed that 89% felt satisfied with the quality of academic programs and teaching. Additionally, 83% found it easy to adjust their educational experiences to new environments, while more than 90% perceived faculty and staff as welcoming. At the same time, however, the survey also revealed that students' positive perceptions and enthusiasm often became moderated by a wide range of challenges and barriers they encountered upon the transition. Thus, approximately 60% of respondents shared not being actively involved in activities and events at their host institutions, while more than 80% disclosed that their social relationships included either students from their home countries or other international students. Consequently, more than half of the respondents reported difficulties in forming close relationships with domestic students. Other roadblocks moderating their positive experiences included a lack of campus networks, cultural and language barriers, academic stress, and barriers to community integration (World Education Services, 2019).

Many of these perceptions have already been identified by the past empirical findings. In that regard, scholars have already noted that international students report lower levels of satisfaction with undergraduate experience than their domestic peers (Kim et al., 2017; Kim et al., 2015). This, in turn, has been found to negatively affect students' self-efficacy and create additional barriers to their academic adjustment (Poyrazli et al., 2002). Similarly, the literature has also repeatedly supported the argument that international students remain highly reluctant toward initiating out-of-class communication with professors, establishing relationships with faculty members, or seeking academic advising, mentorship, or support (Kim et al., 2017; Kim et al., 2015; Leong, 2015; Mamiseishvili, 2012a, 2012b).

With regard to international students' social experiences, the unfamiliarity with American culture emerges as the most prevalent barrier to their successful integration (Andrade, 2005; Kim et al., 2017; Kim et al., 2015). Moreover, scholars have identified numerous cases of international students' inability to form friendships with their domestic peers and community (Leong, 2015; Wu et al., 2015). As a result, international students resort to voluntary and involuntary separation, social isolation, and loneliness (Krsmanovic, 2020; Leong, 2015; Wu et al., 2015). Ultimately, low levels of acculturation and high levels of acculturative stress have been found to be strongly associated with students' psychological distress and depression (Shadowen et al., 2019).

This adverse evidence supports the need for a comprehensive understanding of the complexity of international student experience in the U.S. institutions of higher education. Providing deeper and systematic insights into the prior research in this area is necessary for the work of higher education institutions, faculty, and student affairs professionals tasked with supporting this student population and aiming to enhance their cultural, social, and academic experiences. A systematic analysis of prior literature can help produce a comprehensive overview of critical areas in international student experiences so that future research and practical efforts can be directed toward supporting these students more strategically and efficiently.

Therefore, the purpose of this systematic review was to gain a comprehensive understanding of current trends in empirical research on international students in American higher education. To achieve this objective, the following research question was investigated: What trends can be identified in empirical research on international students in the United States during the period between 2010 and 2019 in regard to (a) research productivity; (b) research questions; (c) research methods; (d) institutional types and control; and (e) participants' academic level, the field of study, and country of origin?

LITERATURE REVIEW

The first half of the last decade was characterized by a steady annual growth in international student enrollments in U.S. colleges and universities, which ranged from 4.7% in 2010 to 10% in 2015. Even though the number of international students continued to increase in the remaining 5 years, the annual growth percentages declined (from 7.1% in 2016 to 0.5% in 2019). The distribution between undergraduate and graduate students was fairly comparable over the last decade. The percentages of international students pursuing an associate or bachelor's degree ranged between 39% and 47% per academic year while graduate enrollments fluctuated between 34% and 46% (IIE, 2019)

The analysis of the top places of student origin revealed considerable consistencies over the past decade. China, India, South Korea, and Saudi Arabia remained the four countries with the highest student representation over the past decade, followed by Canada, Vietnam, Taiwan, and Japan. In the beginning of the past decade, the leading field of study for international students was business and management, which, even though it still remains among the top 10 majors, became less appealing to global learners. Education and humanities, on the other hand, lost its place among the leading 10 disciplines by the end of the decade. Instead, the fields with increased international enrollments became communication and journalism, health professions, fine and applied arts, physical and life sciences, social sciences, and math and computer science. Not surprisingly, engineering has maintained its position among the top 10 majors over the past decade and its leading position since 2015 (IIE, 2019). Additional trends can be noted for institutional types, with 72% of all international students in 2019 attending doctorate-granting universities, 13% master's colleges and universities, 8% associate colleges, and 3% bachelor colleges and special focus institutions, respectively.

Prior Syntheses of Literature

Over the past decade, a limited number of scholars have conducted systematic literature searches for the purpose of establishing patterns and trends in the research on international students around the world (Alharbi & Smith, 2018; Click et al., 2017; Khanal & Gaulee, 2019; Tiwari et al., 2017). Moreover, despite the growing number of international students in the United States and the documented benefits of their presence, only a handful of studies have solely focused on synthesizing the research pertaining to global learners in the U.S. academic institutions. Among those that did, additional boundaries were noted in regards to the methods of inquiry, student subpopulation, research questions, or scholarly resources.

For instance, Araujo (2011) provided a valuable synthesis of the empirical research on international students in the United States, but limited such insights to only student adjustment and, consequently, to 21 peer-reviewed studies. On the other hand, Bista and Gaulee (2017) explored a variety of themes and patterns that occurred in the literature on international students in the United States, but limited their investigation only to theses and dissertations published in 2016.

Similarly, Zhang-Wu (2018) directed the focus of her review to international students in the United States but restricted the inquiry to Chinese students, thus producing the synthesis of 21 empirical studies related to students from this cultural group. Li et al. (2014) undertook a similar approach. Even though their systematic review was extended to all East Asian students in the United States, it remained limited to the issues of students' psychological well-being and a sample of 18 studies.

Even though these reviews produced critical insights into the literature on international students attending U.S. colleges and universities, none of them were conducted with the purpose of portraying a comprehensive picture of the general state of research in this field over a certain period of time. While trends in the representation of international students in the United States remain transparent and easily accessible through numerous channels (e.g., IIE), there are still no efforts that would evaluate if the empirical research in this area is representative of the recorded enrollment trends. Consequently, the vision, aim, and scope of future research in this important domain can only be speculated based on the known trends in students' enrollment and representation, but cannot be presumed to address the gaps and limitations of prior scholarship if such gaps remain unknown. In the effort to overcome such a conundrum, this study identified trends, patterns, and gaps in the empirical work pertaining to international students in the United States that were published over the past decade.

THEORETICAL FRAMEWORK

Higher education policymakers have already recognized that college access does not necessarily translate into opportunity unless it includes supportive tools for *all* students to achieve their educational goals (Heller, 2011; Pandit, 2007). Consequently, the concepts of college access and opportunity have evolved over time to incorporate an array of factors, such as cultural, social, geographic, and academic accessibility (Heller, 2011). With respect to international students, in particular, scholars and practitioners have already agreed on one common perspective—despite national efforts to attract and retain international students, positive outcomes are significantly diminished by the absence of a national strategy on internationalization of higher education or a coordinated set of initiatives for increasing college access and opportunity for this student group (American Council on Education, 2015; Helms, 2015; Hudzik, 2011).

Therefore, the conceptual underpinnings for this study were grounded in the theories of comprehensive internationalization (Helms, 2015; Hudzik, 2011) and universal access (St. John, 2013). Comprehensive internationalization is defined as "commitment, confirmed through action, to infuse international and comparative perspectives throughout the teaching, research, and service missions of higher education" (Hudzik, 2011, p. 1). Similarly, Helms (2015) defined comprehensive internationalization as "a broad, but well-coordinated set of well-funded initiatives that support comprehensive internationalization of U.S. higher education" (p. 1). Finally, St. John (2013) described universal access as the need for bridging large disparities between just promoting universal access and actively applying working mechanisms that would ensure the opportunity for every student to succeed academically.

The presented theories served as conceptual underpinnings for this research for several reasons. First, this study has already provided the evidence that, despite their growing access to U.S. higher education, international students' opportunity to succeed academically is often undermined by a wide array of underlying barriers (e.g., cultural, social, and academic). Thus, this research sought to provide a comprehensive insight into the contemporary scholarly contributions that investigated the experiences of international students in U.S. colleges and universities, along with the array of challenges they encounter. In doing so, the theoretical framework guided this research toward investigating if, and to what extent, the contemporary research is truly comprehensive and inclusive of international students from all institutional types, programs, academic levels, and countries of origin. Consequently, this research attempted to synthesize prior literature by providing a comprehensive description of its scope, directions, and prevalent patterns. Ultimately, this approach allowed for a universal examination of prior scholarly work for the purpose of generating more strategic, deliberate, and, ultimately, comprehensive empirical insights in the future.

METHOD

I designed this study as a systematic literature review with the aim of exploring empirical peer-reviewed research on international students in the United States in a comprehensive manner and through the implementation of an organized, transparent, and replicable process (Littell et al., 2008). I conducted the systematic review following a strict methodological protocol for choosing the literature. I present and discuss the protocol in detail to eliminate potential for author bias (Feak & Swales, 2009).

The central step in the protocol was to determine the study eligibility criteria or to decide what empirical studies will be included and excluded from the review. Detailed specification of inclusion criteria limited the opportunity for selection bias and prevented me from unintentionally selecting studies based on inherent ideological views, personal preferences, or convenience (Littell et al., 2008). Additionally, the rigorous selection criteria produced clear boundaries for other authors who wish to replicate this study in the future.

The selection criteria for this study were guided by the central research question: What trends can be identified in the empirical research on international students in the United States during the period between 2010 and 2019? Consequently, the following inclusion and exclusion criteria were used.

- Publication type: This review is limited to empirical peer-reviewed research articles. Consequently, nonempirical research was excluded (e.g., commentary, reflections, essays, literature reviews, book chapters, brief reports, reactions, and editor's notes). Students' papers, theses, and dissertations were also excluded.

- Publication date: The search was limited to peer-reviewed articles published between 2010–2019.

- Location: As determined by the central question of the study, the search was limited to research conducted at higher education institutions in the United States.

- Participants: The search was limited to undergraduate and graduate degree-seeking international students in 4-year universities and 2-year colleges in the United States. Therefore, the search excluded studies on international students in short-term English language programs and university pathway programs, as well as studies on international students' prearrival or postdeparture experiences. This criterion was developed due to the volume of research on internationals students and fact that the pool of studies that include all international students in the United States would be too large to effectively review in one research project.

6

Data Resources

In selecting possible data resources, researchers need to be cognizant of the fact that exhaustive and complete search of the literature is improbable because the total and exhaustive universe of prior scholarship in any field is unknown (Brunton et al., 2012). Thus, rather than attempting to search for every possible study related to international students in the United States, I decided to locate the pool of studies that would be most likely to answer the research question explored in this study. Consequently, the literature search for this review was undertaken thorough investigation of three online search engines: *ERIC*, *Academic Search Premier*, and *PsycInfo*. Guided by the research question of this study, I deemed these databases as the most appropriate because they specifically focus on educational research (*ERIC*), academic disciplines in colleges and universities (*Academic Search Premier*), and behavioral and social sciences (*PsycInfo*).

The keywords used included "international student" or "foreign student." The initial search resulted in 7,707 results. Applying the presented inclusion criteria reduced the number of results to 532 articles. I reviewed the titles and abstracts of all studies and removed those that did not meet the inclusion criteria as well as duplicate articles. This process resulted in obtaining the final sample of 334 eligible studies used for this review.

Data Analysis

I analyzed the 334 articles in two stages. The first stage involved a categorial coding process in which I developed and applied predefined codes to each study to produce a categorial representation of the data (Oliver & Sutcliffe, 2012). For the data to be categorized, I first needed to define codes and their unambiguous definitions that would be consistently applied. Thus, I used spreadsheet software (Excel) to develop the categories driven by the central research question (Brown et al., 2013; Brown et al., 2003). The coding spreadsheet included the following codes and their unambiguous categories: (a) publication year (2010–2019); (b) research site (single/multiple); (c) institutional type (2-year/4-year); (d) institutional control (public/private); (e) participants' academic level (undergraduate/graduate); and (f) research method (qualitative/quantitative/mixed-method). As presented in the previous section of this study, the operational definition for all codes and categories were developed as mutually exclusive and collectively exhaustive (Brown et al., 2003). Using the coding spreadsheet, I reviewed and coded each study using the same guidelines.

The second stage of the data analysis involved open-coding process for analyzing the data that were not suitable for categorical coding. These data included participants' country of origin, participants' field of study, and research questions examined in the reviewed studies. The process of open coding involved developing and assigning relevant codes during the review process and as I became more familiar with the content of each study (Oliver & Sutcliffe, 2012). Using the same spreadsheet software (Excel), I first extracted the verbatim content from the reviewed studies that pertained to the participants' country of origin, participants' field of study, and research questions examined. I then carefully reviewed the extracted content for the purpose of developing structural codes or content-based words and phrases that would best illustrate the content of the extracted data (Saldana, 2012). As such, these structural codes served as "labeling and indexing devices" (Namey et al., 2008, p. 141), which allowed me to systematically synthesize the data and examine the commonalities, differences, and relationships among the extracted segments (Saldana, 2012).

RESULTS

The review of 334 peer-reviewed articles used for this study revealed several patterns that have developed in the scholarship on international students in the United States over the past decade. These patterns are presented and discussed in alignment with the preestablished codes used for reviewing the studies.

Publication Year

The results revealed a continuous annual increase in the number of empirical peer-reviewed articles on international students in the United States. As illustrated in Figure 1, this increase ranged from 13 empirical studies published in 2010 to 60 articles published in 2018. Even though only 30 studies were published in 2019, this finding does not necessarily indicate a decrease in research engagement. Given that the search for this review was conducted in November of 2019, this number can be justified by the fact that not all studies from 2019 were yet available or published.

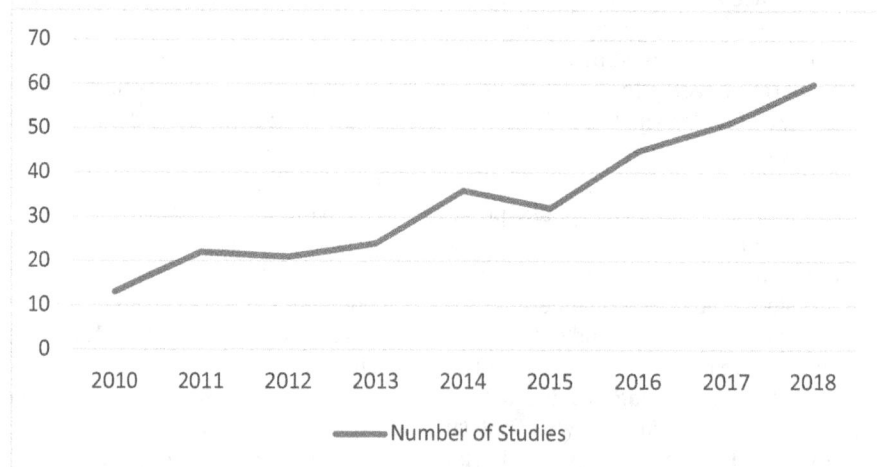

Figure 1: The Increase in Research Activity

Research Site

The examination of the research site in the reviewed studies revealed a much stronger preference for single-site than multi-site research. As illustrated in Table 1, 219 studies were conducted at a single higher education institution in the United States, while the remaining 115 articles examined international students enrolled in multiple U.S. colleges and universities.

Among these 219 single-site studies, the overwhelming majority of the studies ($n = 211$) were conducted at 4-year universities (e.g., bachelor degree-granting or higher), with only eight studies located within 2-year colleges. Additionally, 113 of these single sites were identified as public institutions, while only 19 were private colleges and universities. In 87 cases, the institutional control of the research site was not specified. Four research sites were identified as Historically Black Colleges and Universities and three as faith-based institutions (one as "a Catholic university," one as "a Christian university," and one as "a faith-based institution").

Table 1: Trends in Research Sites ($N = 334$)

Code	n	%
Research site		
Single	219	65.6
Multiple	115	34.4
Institutional type		
2-year	8	2.4
4-year	211	63.2
Multiple	115	33.4
Institutional control		
Public	113	33.8
Private	19	5.7
Multiple	115	34.4
Unspecified	87	26.1

Research Participants

The most prevalent pattern that emerged with respect to participants' academic level was that the majority of the reviewed studies ($n = 146$) examined both undergraduate and graduate learners simultaneously. Among the studies that differentiated between the two academic levels, no strong preferences were recorded for either of the groups. Undergraduate international students were investigated in 79 studies while their graduate counterparts served as participants in 82 articles. As many as 26 studies did not specify participants' academic level.

Interestingly, some studies focused on a particular subpopulation within either the undergraduate or graduate level. Thus, 13 studies specifically concentrated on undergraduate first-year students, and one study investigated

Table 2: Trends in Research Participants (*N* = 334)

Demographic	*n*	%
Academic level		
Undergraduate	79	23.6
Graduate	82	24.6
Professional	1	0.3
Both	146	43.7
Unspecified	26	7.8
Special population		
Athletes	2	0.6
Black	5	1.5
Nontraditional	1	0.3
Students with disabilities	1	0.3
Female	11	3.3
Male	1	0.3
No special population	313	937
Academic field		
Business	2	0.6
Counseling	10	3.0
Education	3	0.9
Law	1	0.3
Music	2	0.6
Nursing	1	0.3
STEM	10	3.0
Theology	1	0.3
Multiple	304	91
Origin		
Multiple	190	56.4
China	64	19.0
Korea	24	7.1
East Asia	16	4.7
Saudi Arabia	9	2.6
Africa	8	2.4
Arab states	4	1.2
India	3	0.9
Japan	3	0.9
Caribbean	3	0.9
Turkey	2	0.6
Brazil	2	0.6
Colombia	1	0.3
Dominican Republic	1	0.3
Greece	1	0.3
Indonesia	1	0.3
Nigeria	1	0.3
Nepal	1	0.3

Demographic	n	%
Rwanda	1	0.3
Taiwan	1	0.3

Note. The sum of studies for Origin code does not equal 334 as some studies included two cultural groups.

sophomores. On a graduate level, 17 studies limited the inquiry to doctoral students, while three studies focused on master's students.

With respect to participants' country of origin, the majority of the reviewed articles (n = 190) were conducted using the sample of students from varied cultures and countries of origin. The remaining 144, on the other hand, concentrated on only one international student population. Unsurprisingly, Chinese students constituted the participants in the majority of studies that examined a single student population (n = 64), followed by Asian students (n = 24) and Korean students (n = 16). Other countries of origin that were of interest to researchers are presented in Table 2. The table also includes the distribution of studies that examined special groups of international students, as well as the number of studies that investigated international students from specific majors and disciplines.

Research Design

Over the past decade, researchers displayed a stronger preference for using quantitative research methods in investigating the issues related to international students in U.S. colleges and universities. From the reviewed sample, 177 studies were conducted using quantitative methods and 136 applied qualitative approaches. Only 21 studies employed a mixed-method research design.

Research Questions

As previously explained, I analyzed research questions in the reviewed studies using the open-coding process. In the first step, I extracted the verbatim content of research questions from each study and pasted it into the spreadsheet software (Excel). I then developed structural codes that would most accurately illustrate the content of the extracted research questions. This process produced the codes presented in Table 3. As illustrated, almost one third of all sampled studies (n = 108) focused their research questions on the issues related to students' social and cultural integration, with particular interest devoted to participants' acculturation processes and acculturative stress. This phenomenon was followed by the scholarly intent to understand international students' academic experiences, which were examined in one quarter of the research articles published in the past decade (n = 82). On that subject, the authors were primarily interested in gaining insights into students' academic success, retention, and degree attainment (n = 17) and their overall academic experience (n = 10). Mental health and physical well-being of international students emerged as the third most prominent theme examined in 38 studies, which was followed by the simultaneous

11

investigation of students' academic and social experiences that was undertaken in 37 articles. The other themes noted included international student development ($n = 23$), transition and adjustment ($n = 18$), postgraduation and career outcomes ($n = 12$), language ($n = 10$), and destination choice ($n = 6$).

Table 3: Trends in Research Questions ($N = 334$)

Theme	n
Social and cultural experience	108
Acculturation	40
Acculturative stress	30
Social relationships and communication	22
Racialization, discrimination, and stereotypes	8
Sense of belonging and isolation	6
Campus involvement	2
Academic experience	82
Success, retention, degree attainment	17
Overall experience	10
Library use	8
Program experience	6
Academic anxiety and stress	5
Advising and mentoring	5
Interactions with faculty	4
Academic adaptation	3
Academic motivation	3
Class participation	3
Plagiarism and academic integrity	3
Writing practices	3
Group work and communication	2
Co-curricular learning experiences	2
Pedagogical preferences	2
Procrastination	2
Reading preferences	1
Physical and mental well-being	38
Mental health	24
Physical health	10
Health care communication	4
Academic and social experience	37
Adjustment and integration	20
Overall experience	11
Campus involvement and support	6
Student development	23
Identity	8
Leadership	4
Cognitive	3
Emotional	3

Theme	*n*
Psychosocial	2
Academic	1
Cultural	1
Personality	1
Transition and adjustment	18
Psychological	5
Overall experience	4
Undergraduate first-year students	4
Adjustment challenges	2
Graduate students	1
Doctoral students	1
Students with disabilities	1
Postgraduation and career outcomes	12
Career outcomes	6
Migration intentions	4
Degree value	2
Language	10
Oral and spoken English	3
Academic self-efficacy	3
Language challenges	2
ESL classes	1
Language adaptation	1
Destination choice	6
Influencing factors and motivators	5
Recruitment practices	1
Total	334

DISCUSSION

I conducted this systematic review to clarify the state of the existing research on international students in the United States and to provide implications for future scholarly pursuits in this area. Despite the easily accessible and up-to-date knowledge of international students' enrollment trends, the overall state of the empirical research in this domain remains unclear. Thus, undertaking new empirical studies on this student population without being unambiguously informed about previous research may result in unnecessary, inappropriate, or irrelevant research. In that regard, the main contribution of this review is providing findings that can serve as both a precursor for further research and a context for interpreting the results of future empirical studies. Specifically, clarifying the state of current research and empirical findings on international students in the United States generated several critical recommendations for future research.

Overall, the substantial growth in the number of international students who have pursued their higher education in America over the past decade was accompanied by an even greater increase in scholarly commitments to investigate the wide range of students' study abroad experiences. As an illustration, international student enrollments rose by 58% from 2010 to 2018, a phenomenon to which the scholarly community responded with 4.6 times more studies produced in 2018 compared with 2010. This finding further corroborated the need for classifying and systematizing the ever-growing volume of the research on international students so that future scholarly efforts can be more appropriately aligned with this student representation. In order to assist researchers with this task, I offer the following eight recommendations.

Recommendation 1: Increase research productivity in the domain of international students attending private institutions in the United States.

The examination of the top 25 enrolling colleges and universities in 2019, which welcomed one quarter of all international students, revealed that 59% of international students opted for public institutions, while 41% of their peers decided to attend private colleges and universities (IIE, 2019). Still, only 6% of the single-site studies published over the past decade were conducted at private institutions. In 2019 specifically, only 3% of the single-site studies took place in a private setting. Consequently, an important direction of future research on international students would be to increase the research activity in private colleges and universities.

Recommendation 2: Increase research productivity in the domain of international students attending 2-year community colleges in the United States.

According to the American Association of Community Colleges (2019), approximately 121,000 of community college students in 2017 were classified as international, which represented 11% of the total international student enrollments. On the other hand, the synthesis of the research presented in this review illustrated that only 8% of the empirical studies published over the past decade were conducted at community colleges, while none of the single-site studies published in 2017 took place in a 2-year setting. Therefore, the overall picture of the evidence in this area indicates the need for increased research efforts in examining the experiences of international students enrolled at 2-year community colleges in the United States.

Recommendation 3: Abandon the tradition of examining international undergraduate and graduate students as a single, homogenous group.

As many as 43.7% or 146 articles reviewed for this research investigated both undergraduate and graduate international students simultaneously. Equally concerning is the finding that 7.8% ($n = 26$) articles did not even specify the academic level of their international participants. At the same time, a comprehensive body of theoretical and empirical literature has been produced to demonstrate the importance of accounting for the range of developmental stages that students undergo while in college (see Pascarella & Terenzini, 2005; Patton et al., 2016).

Scholarly generalizations across students' academic levels become even more alarming after gaining further insights into the studies that investigated undergraduate and graduate participants simultaneously. Namely, 10 of these studies specifically examined the issues related to student development, thus generalizing the findings across both undergraduate and graduate learners. Six of the studies investigated international student transition and adjustment while, again, failing to account for the differences in the age and developmental levels between undergraduate and graduate participants. Moreover, 25 of the studies produced the results pertaining to both undergraduate and graduate students' mental and physical well-being, thus generalizing the findings across the students of different cognitive, emotional, psychosocial, psychological, or identity development levels. Therefore, the overall recommendations stemming from this review are twofold—the future direction of the research on international students' needs to (a) clearly account for students' academic level and (b) limit the investigation and generalizability of findings to either undergraduate or graduate students.

Further examination of the findings related to students' academic level indicated that only 14 articles investigated a particular subgroup of undergraduate students—13 studies focused on freshmen and one on sophomore students. Therefore, the scholars who seek to contribute innovative knowledge on international undergraduate learners should direct their inquires toward less frequently explored subgroups—sophomores, juniors, or seniors. On a graduate level, scholarly intents to understand a specific subpopulation were mostly directed to doctoral students (17 studies). As only three studies investigated the experience of graduate students in master's programs, focusing future research efforts in this direction can represent the novelty in the field.

Recommendation 4: Increase research productivity in the domain of special populations of international students.

The findings of this review illustrated that only 6.3% ($n = 21$) articles uncovered the issues pertaining to special populations of international students. In that regard, five studies (1.5%) investigated the experiences of Black international students, two studies (0.6%) sought to understand international student athletes, and one article (0.3%) investigated nontraditional students and students with disabilities respectively. Thus, an overall recommendation for future research would be to embrace the general trend of higher education research and increase awareness of the nuances shaping the educational experiences of special populations and diverse groups of international students. Diversity has been commonly defined in higher education literature (and taught on college campuses) as an intersection of students' race, gender, sexual identity, religion, age, and ability (see Cuyet et. al., 2016; Pascarella & Terenzini, 2005). Consequently, an originality in the future empirical work can be exhibited by attempting to uncover the intersection of international students' experiences and particular aspects of their diverse identities.

Recommendation 5: Increase the research productivity in the domain of international students from underinvestigated academic fields and disciplines.

Comparable with the enrollment trends, the experiences of international students in STEM programs attracted a lot of scholarly interest over the past decade as indicated by 10 articles published on this topic. These 10 articles accounted for 33.3% of all studies that focused on understanding international students within a particular academic field or 3% of all published studies. However, in 2019 alone, U.S. colleges and universities hosted an imposing number of 434,241 STEM students from around the world, which constituted almost half of all international student enrollments. Therefore, it is necessary for the research on this particular student population to increase further so that it would accompany the prevalence of both their enrollment and importance for American higher education institutions.

Another 10 articles (33.3%) of studies that focused on students within a particular discipline were dedicated to graduate students in counseling programs. On the other hand, in 2016, only 1% of all students in counseling and related educational programs were international students (Council for Accreditation of Counseling and Related Educational Programs, 2017). Therefore, it can be argued that this particular area represents an overly researched domain in the scholarship on international students and should yield to other underinvestigated fields such as business and management, social sciences, fine and applied arts, health professions, education, and humanities. Namely, all of these disciplines have been among the top 10 majors for international students over the past decade but have accounted for only 3% of the literature published in this period.

Recommendation 6: Abandon the tradition of examining international students from multiple cultures and counties of origin as a single, homogenous group.

As presented in the findings, more than half of the available studies (57% or 190 articles) examined the experiences of international students from multiple countries of origin and generalized the findings across a variety of cultural groups. This becomes even more concerning in the light of the fact that 53 of these studies specifically investigated students' acculturation and generalized the insights across the participants from multiple countries and cultural groups. Accordingly, the scholarly contributions in this domain need to be extended to more closely investigate the experiences of international students from culture-sharing groups and produce evidence of their acculturation (or other experiences) that is not moderated by the country of origin and prior cultural experiences.

At the same time, however, the results of this study revealed that the remaining 43% of articles ($n = 144$) focused the inquiry on international students of a particular nationality or cultural group. Not surprisingly, the scholars followed the national trends in student enrollments and were primarily interested in understanding the experiences of Chinese students attending U.S. colleges and universities. As students from China constituted 33.7% of all international enrollments in 2019, and have been maintaining the leading position over the past decade (IIE, 2019), 20% ($n = 64$) studies were dedicated to this student group. Another alignment of research and enrollment trends was reflected in the number of published studies related to international students from Asia (10%; $n = 31$), Korea (5%; $n = 16$), and Saudi Arabia (3%; $n = 8$ studies), all of which maintained their position among the top 10 sending countries over the past decade (IIE, 2019).

Still, a major disparity emerged regarding the students from India. Even though India has been the second top sending country from 2010–2019, Indian students served as participants in only 1% of studies ($n = 3$) published during this time period. Consequently, the most critical area where research on international students needs to be advanced is investigating the experiences of Indian students on U.S. campuses, primarily due to their ever-growing presence in American higher education. Other countries from the top 10 sending list whose students were underresearched over the past decade include Canada (no studies), Brazil (1 study), Taiwan (1 study), Vietnam (0 studies), and Mexico (0 studies).

Recommendation 7: Increase the investigation of international students in the United States using a mixed-method research design.

The conclusion of this review is that the examination of the issues pertaining to international students in the United States has been primarily relying on quantitative research design. Namely, 53% of the reviewed studies ($n = 177$) were conducted using quantitative methods while 40.7% ($n = 136$) applied qualitative research design. Therefore, mixed-methods have been underutilized in the research on international students, as indicated by 6.3% ($n = 21$) mixed-method studies published over the past decade.

On the one hand, these results can be justified by the fact that mixed methods represent a novelty in the research design and are often described as the "third methodological movement" (Tashakkori & Teddlie, 2010, p. xii) or the "third research paradigm" (Johnson & Onwuegbuzie, 2004, p. 15). On the other hand, the use of mixed methods has been rapidly expanding across disciplines and countries, as manifested by the growing number of articles, journals, books, professional associations, and special interest groups focusing on this method (Creswell & Clark, 2018). Accordingly, the research on international students needs to keep abreast of this trend and diversify its contributions to the literature by undertaking more mixed-method investigations.

Recommendation 8: Increase the research productivity in the domain of underinvestigated areas of inquiry.

Approximately one third of all studies reviewed (32.3%; $n = 108$) focused the investigation on international students' social and cultural experiences. In that regard, the greatest attention has been dedicated to students' acculturation processes and acculturative stress. Next, 24.5% articles ($n = 82$) were devoted to international students' academic experiences in the U.S. higher education, with particular emphasis on the issues related to their retention and degree attainment ($n = 17$) and overall academic experience ($n = 10$). The third area of interest that emerged over the past decade was students' physical and mental well-being (11.4%; $n = 38$), with a much stronger preference for understanding students' mental health than their physical well-being. This trend was followed by the simultaneous exploration of students' academic and social experiences, which was undertaken in 11.1% of studies ($n = 37$), as well as student development explored in 6.9% of studies ($n = 23$).

Even though the findings of this review identified several areas that were overly researched in the past decade, they do not undermine the need for continued scholarly exploration in these domains. Instead, the overall implication of this study is that scholars should focus on finding a niche that would provide a novelty in any area that has already been extensively explored. Such a goal can be best achieved by intersecting future scholarly investigations with any of the recommendations proposed in this review (e.g., focusing on underinvestigated research settings, student populations, or research methods). By doing so, scholars can ensure the originality of their work and avoid producing the knowledge that has already been offered to the readership.

CONCLUSION

Limitations

Even though this review helped provide a critical understanding of the breadth, purpose, and extent of research activity in the domain of international students in the United States, it remains characterized by a critical limitation. A general weakness of any systematic review is the fact that authors can never claim with certainty how many studies have addressed their subject of inquiry and, therefore, cannot claim to have identified all potentially relevant studies in their field (Brunton et al., 2012). Still, the purpose of this review was not to obtain an all-inclusive synthesis of all research in the field but, instead, to generate a detailed and comprehensive inquiry that would help understand the most current trends and directions of scholarly efforts. For that reason, I never sought to access all studies ever published on this topic, but to obtain a maximum sample of studies within a universe of potentially relevant resources.

Implications

Despite these limitations, this research produced several important findings, all of which translate into concrete implications for research and practice. The overall conclusion of this study is that contemporary research efforts do not effectively bridge the gaps in the empirical knowledge on international students' in the United States. As such, current research does not serve as "a broad, but well-coordinated set of initiatives" (Hudzik, 2011, p. 1) that would increase the opportunity for every international student to succeed—a goal envisioned by the frameworks of compressive internationalization and universal access (Helms, 2015; Hudzik, 2011; St. John, 2013). Thus, the following implications were developed with the hope of making this goal more attainable.

First, to begin developing a more comprehensive empirical understanding of the factors contributing to social, cultural, and educational experiences of international students in the United States, increased attention needs to be directed to the students attending private institutions and community colleges, both of which have been underresearched over the past decade. Second, a comprehensive research model also needs to include a clear differentiation between undergraduate and graduate students, as well as students from different academic levels. Similarly, in order for faculty, staff, and administrators to truly benefit from the future research findings, these investigations must no longer perceive international students from multiple cultures and counties of origin as a single, homogenous group. Further, to overcome current research limitations, more knowledge needs to be produced regarding the experiences of international students from nationalities and cultures who have been well-represented but underresearched, mainly India, Canada, Brazil, Taiwan, Vietnam, and Mexico.

Next, a more comprehensive and inclusive research model needs to be built by dedicating more attention to special student populations (e.g., nontraditional, first-generation, students with disabilities). Increased research heterogeneity is also needed with respect to students' academic fields and disciplines. In order for empirical investigations to be commensurate with student representation, more research is required for international students from underinvestigated majors, mainly business and management, social sciences, fine and applied arts, health professions, education, and humanities.

Additionally, to provide a methodologically comprehensive inquiry into international students' experiences, more mixed-method research is suggested because prior efforts have mainly relied on either qualitative or quantitative studies. The last implication includes a strategic commitment to addressing the identified underinvestigated research areas. With that respect, this study revealed that the greatest attention over the past decade has been dedicated to students' acculturation processes and acculturative stress, overall academic experiences, and physical and mental well-being. Therefore, future insights should be advanced by either investigating these areas in relation to underresearched institutional settings, student populations, and research designs, or by devoting the inquiries to other areas that have not been adequately explored.

Overall, this review elucidated the state of the existing research in the field and identified critical underlying implications (Feak & Swales, 2009). As such, it is helped promote the originality of future scholarly work related to international students in the United States. Critically exploring and methodologically synthesizing existing research in this area provided an opportunity for scholars to identify the domains where research has not yet been undertaken, the research questions which have not been adequately explored, and the best ways to avoid research approaches that will not lead to any significant or innovative insights in the field.

On a macro level, this synthesis can be used for designing new empirical undertakings in a manner that would support any culturally and linguistically diverse student, not just an international student. The value of synthesizing prior research in this domain is also reflected in advancing the scholarship on cultural diversity in U.S. higher education. Consequently, the implications of this research synthesis are not limited to only to the scholarship on international students but are also aimed at advancing the existing knowledge in the domain of higher education diversity, inclusion, and internationalization for the benefits of all parties involved—institutions, faculty, staff, and, primarily, their diverse students.

In conclusion, this review provided insights into 344 empirical research studies on the experiences of international students in the United States over the past decade. I conducted this review with the belief that understanding prior scholarly efforts would provide valuable recommendations for the direction of future empirical undertakings. As this review revealed, there is no doubt that the research on international students is claiming a vital position in the higher education scholarship. In order for that position to be sustained, however, future efforts need to be strategically and methodically envisioned. Only by dedicating continued effort to understanding the current trends and directions of research in this domain can authors ensure that their work will truly reflect the richness of global diversity within their academic communities.

REFERENCES

Alharbi, E. S., & Smith, A. (2018). Review of the literature on stress and wellbeing of international students in English-speaking countries. *Canadian Center of Science and Education, 11*(6), 22–44. doi:10.5539/ies.v11n6p22

American Association of Community Colleges. (2019). *Community college enrollment crisis: Historical trends in community college enrollment.* https://www.aacc.nche.edu/wp-content/uploads/2019/08/Crisis-in-Enrollment-2019.pdf

American Council on Education. (2012). *Mapping Internationalization of U.S. campuses.* http://www.acenet.edu/news-room/Documents/Mapping-Internationalizationon-US-Campuses-2012-full.pdf

Andrade, M. S. (2005). International students and the first year of college. *Journal of the First-Year Experience, 17*(1), 101–129.

Araujo, A. A. (2011). Adjustment issues of international students enrolled in American colleges and universities: A review of the literature. *Higher Education Studies, 1*(1), 2–8. doi:10.5539/hes.v1n1p2

Bista, K., & Gaulee, U. (2017). Recurring themes across fractal issues facing international students: A thematic analysis of 2016 dissertations and theses. *Journal of International Students, 7*(4), 1135–1151. doi:10.5281/zenodo.1035989

Brown, S. A., Martin, E. E., Garcia, T. J., Winter, M. A., Garcia, A. A., Brown, A., Cuevas, H. E., & Sumlin, L. L. (2013). Managing complex research datasets using electronic tools: A meta-analysis exemplar. *CIN: Computers, Informatics, Nursing 31*(6), 257–265.

Brown, S. A., Upchurch, S. L., & Acton, G. J. (2003). A framework for developing a coding scheme for meta-analysis. *Western Journal of Nursing Research, 25*(2), 205–222.

Brunton, G., Stansfield, C., & Thomas, J. (2012). Finding relevant studies. In D. Gough, S. Oliver, & J. Thomas (Eds.), *An introduction to systematic reviews* (pp. 107–134). SAGE.

Council for Accreditation of Counseling and Related Educational Programs. (2017). *Annual report 2016*. http://www.cacrep.org/wp-content/uploads/2019/05/CACREP-2016-Annual-Report.pdf

Cuyjet, M. J., Howard-Hamilton, M. F., & Cooper, D. L. (Eds.). (2016). *Multiculturalism on campus: Theory, models, and practices for understanding diversity and creating inclusion*. (2nd ed.). Stylus Publishing

Click, A. B., Wiley, C. W., & Houlihan, M. (2017). The internationalization of the academic library: A systematic review of 25 years of literature on international students. *College & Research Libraries, 78*(3), 328–358.

Creswell, J. W., & Clark, V. L. P. (2018). *Designing and conducting mixed methods research* (3rd ed.). SAGE.

Feak, C., & Swales, J. M. (2009). *Telling a research story: Writing a literature review*. University of Michigan.

Heller, D. E. (2011). *The states and public higher education policy: Affordability, access, and accountability*. Johns Hopkins University Press.

Helms, R. M. (2015). *Internationalizing U.S. higher education: Current policies, future directions*. Report of the American Council of Education. http://www.acenet.edu/news-room/Documents/Current-Policies-Future-Directions-Part-2-US.pdf

Hudzik J. (2011). *Comprehensive internationalization: From concept to action*. http://www.nafsa.org/resourcelibrary/Default.aspx?id=24045

Institute of International Education. (2015). *What international students think about U.S. higher education: Attitudes and perceptions of prospective students from around the world*. https://www.iie.org/Research-and-Insights/Publications/What-International-Students-Think-About-US-Higher-Education

Institute of International Education. (2019). *Open doors report*. Retrieved December 19, 2019 from https://www.iie.org/en/Research-and-Insights/Open-Doors/Data

Johnson, B. R., & Onwuegbuzie, A. J. (2004). Mixed methods research: A research paradigm whose time has come. *Educational Researcher, 33*(7), 14–26.

Khanal, J., & Gaulee, U. (2019). Challenges of international students from pre-departure to post-study: A literature review. *Journal of International Students, 9*(2), 560–581. doi:10.32674/jis.v9i2.673

Kim, Y. K., Collins, C. S., Rennick, L. A., & Edens, D. (2017). College experiences and outcomes among international undergraduate students at research universities in the United States: A comparison to their domestic peers. *Journal of International Students, 7*(2), 395–420.

Kim, Y. K., Edens, D., Iorio, M. F., Curtis, C. J., & Romero, E. (2015). Cognitive skills development among international students at research universities in the United States. *Journal of International Students, 5*(4), 526–540.

Krsmanovic, M. (2020). I was new and I was afraid: The acculturation strategies adopted by international first-year students in the United States. *Journal of International Students, 10*(4), 954–975.

Leong, P. (2015). Coming to America: Assessing the patterns of acculturation, friendship formation, and the academic experiences of international students at a U.S. college. *Journal of International Students, 5*(4), 459–474.

Li, J., Wang, Y., & Xiao, F. (2014). East Asian international students and psychological well-being: A systematic review. *Journal of International Students, 4*(4), 301–313.

Littell, J. H., Corcroran, J., & Pillai, V. (2008). *Systematic reviews and meta-analysis.* Oxford University Press.

Mamiseishvili, K. (2012a). Academic and social integration and persistence of international students at U.S. two-year institutions. *Community College Journal of Research and Practice, 36*(1), 15–27. doi:10.1080/10668926.2012.619093

Mamiseishvili, K. (2012b). International student persistence in U.S. postsecondary institutions. *Higher Education, 64*(1), 1–17. doi:10.1007/s10734-011-9477-0

Namey, E., Guest, G., Thairu, L., & Johnson, L. (2008). Data reduction techniques for large qualitative data sets. In G. Guest & K. M. MacQueen (Eds.), *Handbook for team-based qualitative research* (pp. 137–161). AltaMira Press.

Oliver, S., & Sutcliffe, K. (2012). Describing and analyzing studies. In D. Gough, S. Oliver, & J. Thomas (Eds.), *An introduction to systematic reviews* (pp. 35–64). SAGE.

Pandit, K. (2007). The importance of international students on our campuses. *Yearbook of the Association of Pacific Coast Geographers, 69*, 156–159. doi:10.1353/pcg.2007.0012

Pascarella, E. T., & Terenzini, P. T. (2005). *How college affects students, Vol. 2: A third decade of research.* Jossey-Bass.

Patton, L. D., Renn, K. A., Guido, F. M., & Quaye, S. J. (2016). *Student development in college: Theory, research, and practice.* Jossey-Bass.

Poyrazli, S., Arbona, C., Nora, A., McPherson, R., & Pisecco, S. (2002). Relation between assertiveness, academic self-efficacy, and psychosocial adjustment among international graduate students. *Journal of College Student Development, 43*(5), 632–642.

Saldana, J. (2012). *The coding manual for qualitative researchers* (2nd ed). SAGE.

Shadowen N. L., Williamson, A. A., Guerra, N. G., Ammigan, R., & Drexler, M. (2019). Prevalence and correlates of depressive symptoms among international students: Implications for university support offices. *Journal of International Students, 9*(1), 129–148. doi:10.32674/jis.v9i1.277

St. John, E. P., Daun-Barnett, N., & Moronski-Chapman, K. M. (2013). *Public policy and higher education: Reframing strategies for preparation, access, and success*. Routledge.

Tashakkori, A., & Teddlie, C. (2010). *Mixed methods in social & behavioral research* (2nd ed.). SAGE.

Tiwari, R., Sing, B. G., & Hasan, B. (2017). Acculturative stress and coping strategies of foreign students: A systematic review. *Indian Journal of Health and Wellbeing, 8*(7), 683–686.

U.S. Department of Homeland Security. (2019). *Who are F and M nonimmigrant students?* Retrieved January 23, 2020 from https://www.ice.gov/sevis

World Education Services. (2019). *Are U.S. HEIs meeting the needs of international students?* https://knowledge.wes.org/rs/317-CTM-316/images/research-report-are-us-hei-meeting-the-needs-of-international-students.pdf

Wu, H. P., Garza, E., & Guzman, N. (2015). International students' challenge and adjustment to college. *Education Research International, 2015,* Article 202753. doi:10.1155/2015/202753

Zhang-Wu, Q. (2018). Chinese international students' experiences in American higher education institutes: A critical review of the literature. *Journal of International Students, 8*(2), 1173–1197. doi:10.5281/zenodo.1250419

MASHA KRSMANOVIC, PhD, is an Assistant Teaching Professor in the Higher Education and Student Affairs program at the University of Southern Mississippi. Her major research interests lie in the area of international students, student development, academic and social integration, and first-year experience. Email: Masha.Krsmanovic@usm.edu

Peer-Reviewed Article

© *Journal of International Students*
Volume 11, Issue 1 (2021), pp. 24-40
ISSN: 2162-3104 (Print), 2166-3750 (Online)
doi: 10.32674/jis.v11i1.1356
ojed.org/jis

OJED
OPEN JOURNALS IN EDUCATION

The Relationship Between Perceptions of Multicultural Competence and Democratic Values: Examining Science Teachers Working with International Students

M. Said Doğru
İbrahim Demirbaş
Kastamonu University, Turkey

ABSTRACT

The present study aims to determine the perceptions of multicultural competence and democratic values of science teachers in schools where international students study and to find out whether there is a relationship between them. The study surveyed 436 secondary school science teachers in the Western Black Sea region in the 2018–2019 academic year. Data were collected using the Perceptions of Multicultural Competence Scale and the Democratic Values Scale. We found positive and moderate relationship between teachers' perceptions of multicultural competence and their democratic values. As teachers' democratic values increased, their perceptions of multicultural competence increased, and as their democratic values decreased, their perceptions of multicultural competence decreased as well. Understanding teachers' opinions about democratic values, justice, respect for differences, and equality reveals an important relationship between their multicultural competence and their democratic values.

Keywords: democratic value, multicultural competency, multiculturalism, science teachers

INTRODUCTION

To improve their social and economic situation and to have more positive expectations for their future, people move within or outside their country of origin (International Organization for Migration, 2019). This phenomenon, which is called migration, is one of the sources of cultural diversity in today's societies (Doytcheva, 2009). In countries receiving immigrants, workforce, economic, and cultural diversity grows, and multiculturalism takes root (Günay et al., 2017). Multiculturalism is defined as the ability of different societies with different cultures to live together with equal opportunities within the boundaries of a nation state (Say, 2013). Multiculturalism also refers to cultural diversity arising from the existence of two or more groups with beliefs and practices that often create a unique sense of collective identity linked to racial, ethnic, or linguistic differences (Heywood, 2013). Parker (2002) described the effects of multiculturalism on social unity as follows: "Unity without difference results in cultural repression and unrest. And difference without unity leads to the shattering of the nation-state. In a multicultural democratic nation-state, diversity and unity must coexist in a gentle balance" (p. 133). Living with different cultures creates a culturally open-minded and tolerant community (Gordon & Newfield, 1996). Kılıç and Kılıç (2016) stated that social peace and democracy can be achieved when society accepts that all humans are born equal, when they are not considered different in terms of race, color, gender, economic differences, religious beliefs, and social status, and when all people enjoy rights and freedoms equally. Respectful and tolerant societies where individuals live without marginalizing each other are a must for democracy (Akkaya et al., 2018). Democracy enables the adoption of human rights by society, the resolution of social conflicts, and the establishment of bridges between different cultural structures (Kaya & Aydın, 2014). In this sense, multiculturalism and democratic values overlap. Multicultural education is a democratic, participatory education that advocates for equal opportunities in education for all individuals, regardless of their language, religion, gender, race, ethnicity, social class, and cultural background. This educational approach is seen as a solution to some social and individual problems, wherein differences are considered as wealth (Aydın, 2013). Multicultural education opposes xenophobia, involving equality and social justice (Hidalgo et al., 1996; Nieto, 2017). The present article focuses on teachers' self-perceptions of their multicultural competence, their democratic values, and the relationship between them.

Culture and Multiculturalism

The concept of culture includes shared values, attitudes, behaviors, habits, aesthetics, language, belief, etc. that affect the individual's and society's behavior, sociological status, and understanding (Spencer-Oatey, 2012). Parekh (2002) defined culture as a system of meanings and beliefs created to understand, organize, and structure the individual and collective life of a group of people. Multiculturalism is the awareness and acceptance of the differences among people affirming each group's right to maintain its own language and culture, and to participate fully in the civic culture of the democratic state as long as each group conforms to a set of basic state values (American Psychological Association, 2002; Castles, 2004). Multiculturalism is diametrically opposed to the concept of assimilation, which expects ethnic and linguistic minorities to forsake their original culture and adopt the mainstream culture (Bennett 2001; Castles, 2004). It enables groups to express their differences and encourages the cultural appreciation of all individuals, regardless of their origin (Doytcheva, 2009). Multicultural education provides social justice for all students, using strategies that "[support] and [spread] the concepts of culture, diversity, equality, social justice and democracy in the school environment" (Gollnick & Chinn, 2009). Multicultural education makes significant contributions to community peace and democracy by seeing different cultures as sharing a common heritage of humanity rather than promoting one ethnic identity. It also ensures equality in all areas of education, providing students with critical thinking skills and reducing prejudices (Yazıcı et al., 2009). In a multicultural classroom, concepts such as culture, migration, racism, sexism, cultural assimilation, structural assimilation, ethnic groups, stereotypes, prejudice, and institutional racism are addressed. Teachers use their understanding of these concepts to help students identify their emotions and experiences, and to make connections between different topics (J. A. Banks, 2009). J. A. Banks (2009) regarded egalitarian pedagogy as one of the dimensions of multicultural education and emphasized the importance of implementing egalitarian pedagogy in multicultural classes. Egalitarian pedagogy is defined as employing effective and different teaching strategies and preparing appropriate classroom environments in order to provide students from different groups with the knowledge, skills, and attitudes necessary to be effective individuals in a fair, humanitarian, and democratic society (C. A. M. Banks & Banks, 1995).

Democratic Values in the Classroom

Values are the most fundamental elements that shape societies and differentiate them from others. Concepts such as equality, respect for life, freedom, justice, honesty, understanding, cooperation, self-confidence, tolerance, sensitivity, responsibility, accepting differences, security, and peace constitute democratic values (Y. R. Kıncal, 2007; R. Y. Kıncal & Işık, 2003; Kinnier et al., 2000). According to Irvine and Armento (2001), culturally responsive education focuses on creating positive classroom climates based on social justice, democracy, and equity. Schools are the places where principles of multiculturalism can be systematically delivered, as school life and culture have a significant impact on children's gaining democratic values (Doğanay & Sarı, 2004). Colombo (2006) stated that schools and teachers who see the world through an intercultural lens develop teaching and training skills through the focus of this lens, and creating safe classes where students can improve their academic achievement and express their cultural identity. Therefore, to facilitate the democratic values of multiculturalism, teachers should accept students' biological, sexual, racial, religious, cultural, economic, and political differences as natural and, when planning teaching-learning processes, highlight these differences and create a multicultural education environment to encourage positive attitudes toward differences (S. Aslan, 2017; Polat, 2009).

Teachers are agents of social change that empower their students and support democratic values (Banks, 2004). Therefore, teachers must be aware of the strong influence they have on the ways of thinking, decision-making, behaving, and defining events of students from different cultures. According to Washington (2003), teachers need to have skills of self-understanding, understanding the cultures of others, and academic-multicultural competences. Teacher competence is defined as the knowledge, skills, understanding, and attitudes that teachers should have to effectively fulfill the responsibilities required by the teaching profession (Şahin, 2007, as cited in Akdağ & Yıldız, 2011). Estimating one's self-efficacy as a teacher is understanding to what extent they can or cannot achieve a goal through their beliefs, attitudes, and experiences in situations where their competence cannot be directly observed (Akhtar, 2008; Bandura, 1997; Schunk, 1990). Gavora (2010) furthermore explained teacher self-efficacy as a teacher's personal belief in their skills of planning the lesson, achieving goals, and teaching their students effectively and efficiently in an educational environment. Previous studies (Buluç & Demir, 2015; Fackler & Malmberg, 2016; Günbayı & Tokel, 2012; Morgül et al., 2016; Wertheim & Leyser, 2002) have determined that teachers' high self-efficacy has a positive effect on their organizational commitment, job satisfaction, teachers and students' performance, and students' academic achievement.

Context of the Study

As a result of the war and humanitarian crisis that began in Syria in 2011, millions of people have been displaced. In Turkey, migration from neighboring countries has caused multiculturalism and diversity to come to the forefront in the curriculum renewed by the Ministry of National Education in 2018. Therefore, a teaching approach that considers the sociocultural differences of students has become inevitable with this new situation. According to the Grand National Assembly of Turkey (2018), as of the beginning of 2018, approximately 3.4 million Syrians lived under temporary protection status in Turkey, which has implemented a humanitarian asylum policy. In addition to Syrians, as of the end of 2017, 300,000 refugees from countries such as Iraq, Afghanistan, Iran, and Somalia had sought temporary protection in Turkey (Grand National Assembly of Turkey, 2018). Today, 5.7 million refugees (of whom 3.5 million are under temporary protection, 300,000 under international protection, and 600,000 with residence permit) from around 190 different countries live under different statuses in Turkey. Therefore, in our country, foreign children are encountered in schools in the provinces where asylum seekers have congregated. With this social change teachers must develop multicultural competencies and effective multicultural education in schools, promoting democratic values. According to Kesici (2008), to create democratic classrooms, teachers need to display behaviors such as openness to communication with an objective perspective, consistency, equal opportunities in the classroom, openness to criticism and innovation, guidance for students, and respect for differences. Teachers' efficacy in creating a supportive educational environment is closely related to their multicultural education competencies and democratic values. Thus, an evaluation of teachers' perceptions of their self-efficacy, multiculturalism, and democratic values in classrooms with international students stands out as a topic worth researching.

Based on the influx of international students in Turkey coming from countries like Iraq, Afghanistan, Iran, Somalia, and especially Syria, a study of teachers' adoption of democratic values and multicultural perceptions is warranted. These findings will shed light on the determination of policies for implementing multicultural education training programs for teachers. Therefore, the present study aims to determine science teachers' self-perceptions of multicultural competence and democratic values in schools where international students study, and to find out whether there is a relationship between perceptions of multicultural competence and democratic values. To this end, answers to the following questions were sought:

1. What is the level of perception of multicultural competence of science teachers who work in schools where international students study?
2. What is the level of democratic values of science teachers who work in schools where international students study?
3. Is there a significant relationship between the perceptions of multicultural competence and democratic values of science teachers who work in schools where international students study?

METHOD

Research Model

The purpose of the present study was to determine the perceptions of multicultural competence and democratic values of science teachers in schools where international students study and to find out whether there is a relationship between them. To this end, we employed the relational screening model in the study. The relational screening method is used to identify relationships and connections between variables and to predict possible results. The level of relationship between two or more variables is tried to be measured using statistical tests. The relational screening model aims to describe a situation that exists or existed in the past, and in this model, we try to describe the relationship between perceptions of multicultural competence and democratic values (Büyüköztürk et al., 2009).

Population and Sample

The universe of the study consists of 835 science teachers working in secondary schools where international students study in eight provinces of Turkey's Western Black Sea Region. Since it is not possible to reach all the teachers in the universe, sampling was been taken. It is suggested to select approximately 400 sample sizes from this universe in the amount of deflection and margin of error (Büyüköztürk et al., 2016). When sampling from the universe, we applied nonprobability sampling methods to teachers who could be reached. Teachers who filled out this sampling scale incorrectly, did not want to answer, or did not complete the survey were not included. On the basis of confidentiality, the names of these teachers were not taken. We determined the schools that have international students (nationals of Syria, Iraq, Iran, Afghanistan, and Turkmenistan) from information received from the school administrators. Of these 835 science teachers, 436 science teachers constituted the sample of the study. Of these 436 teachers, 210 (48.2%) were female, while 226 (51.8%) were male.

Data Collection Tools

Data were collected using the Perceptions of Multicultural Competence Scale, developed by Başbay and Kağnıcı (2011) to determine teachers' perceptions of multicultural competence, and the Democratic Values Scale, developed by Çermik (2013) to determine the democratic attitudes of teachers.

The Perceptions of Multicultural Competence Scale measures the levels of multicultural awareness, knowledge, and skill of teachers. The awareness dimension of the scale includes items reflecting teachers' attitudes toward different cultural structures. The knowledge dimension includes items aimed at revealing teachers' efforts to gain knowledge about the cultural characteristics of both themselves and the individuals around them. The skill dimension includes items that reflect the skills that a teacher is expected to have about multiculturalism both inside and outside the classroom. Cronbach's alpha coefficients obtained from the scale were as follows: .85 for the awareness dimension; .87 for the knowledge dimension; .91 for the skill dimension; and .95 for the total scale (Başbay & Kağnıcı, 2011).

It has been argued that the scale can also be used in research with teachers working in the field (Başbay & Kağnıcı, 2011). To use this scale in his research, Bulut (2014) first conducted a validity and reliability study for the usability of the scale for teachers. Bulut (2014) found the χ^2 value as 2263.72 ($p < .001$) in confirmatory factor analysis. The χ^2 value was significant as expected. The χ^2/d value was 2.91; the nonnormed fit index was .95; the normed fit index was .93; comparative fit index was .95, and the root mean square error of approximation was .068. For the reliability of the scale, Cronbach's alpha coefficients of the dimensions were calculated as follows: .84 for the awareness subdimension, .83 for the knowledge subdimension, .84 for the skill subdimension, and 0.93 for the total scale. The results of the confirmatory factor analysis showed that the scale was reliable and valid, and the scale was used in the thesis study titled "An of Teachers' Perceptions of Multicultural Competence" (Bulut, 2014).

The Democratic Values Scale was developed by Çermik (2013). The scale contains 5-point Likert-type items. The scale was applied to a total of 1,022 prospective teachers studying at Pamukkale University Faculty of Education. As a result of factor analysis, 24 items were excluded from the scale, and factor

29

analysis of the scale was conducted with 17 items. As a result of factor analysis, Kaiser-Mayer Olkin value was calculated as .848. Bartlett's Test of Sphericity of the data used in the study was found to be significant ($\chi^2 = 4971.442; p <.05$). The fact that the Kaiser-Mayer Olkin value was .848 indicated that factor analysis was applicable to the data. As a result of the analyses, we found that the scale had a one-dimensional and four-factor structure. The subfactors of the scale were named as (a) "claiming rights," (b) "respect for differences," (c) "justice," and (d) "equality." The first factor explained 27.97% of the total variance, the second factor 12.90%, the third factor 7.74% and the fourth factor 6.36%, and 17 items explained 54.97% of the total variance. Factor load values were found to be between .40 and .87 for all four factors. The Cronbach's alpha coefficient of the total scale was found to be .848 (Çermik, 2013). In this study, Cronbach's alpha coefficients were calculated as follows: .90 for the claiming rights dimension; .89 for the respect for differences dimension; .91 for the justice dimension; .71 for the equality dimension; and .94 for the total scale.

Data Analysis

To teachers working in schools in Kastamonu, Karabuk, and Sinop, we delivered and collected the surveys by hand. To teachers working in schools in other cities, we delivered and collected the surveys by mail. SPSS 20.0 package program was used for data analysis. Descriptive statistical techniques such as percentage, frequency, arithmetic mean, and standard deviation were used in the analysis of the research data. Pearson's correlation coefficient was used to determine whether there is a relationship between teachers' perceptions of multicultural competence and their democratic attitudes. To determine the strength of the relationships obtained in the correlation analysis, 0.70–1.00 high, 0.69–0.30 medium, and 0.29–0.00 low ranges were used. Data were tested at the .05 significance level (Büyüköztürk, 2002; Köklü et al., 2007).

RESULTS

Science Teachers' Perceptions of Multicultural Competence

The findings related to the question "What is the level of perception of multicultural competence of science teachers who work in schools where international students study?" are shown in Table 1.

Table 1: Study Science Teachers' Perceptions of Multicultural Competence ($N = 436$)

Subfactors	M	SD	Rating	Explanation
Awareness	3.81	0.48	Agree	Sufficient
Knowledge	3.75	0.62	Agree	Sufficient
Skill	3.69	0.51	Agree	Sufficient
Total scale	3.75	0.45	Agree	Sufficient

Table 1 shows the arithmetic mean of the scores of science teachers from the subdimensions of the perceptions of the multicultural competence scale. When we examine the arithmetic means we see that the highest mean belongs to the awareness factor ($M = 3.81$), followed by the knowledge ($M = 3.75$) and skill ($M = 3.69$) factors, respectively. The arithmetic mean of the total scale is $M = 3.75$. The findings show that science teachers "agree" with the items related to multicultural competencies.

Democratic Values of Science Teachers

The findings related to the question "What is the level of democratic values of science teachers who work in schools where international students study?" are shown in Table 2.

Table 2: Democratic Values of Science Teachers ($N = 436$)

Subfactors	M	SD	Rating	Explanation
Justice	4.63	0.63	Strongly agree	Well-adopted
Respect for differences	4.41	0.55	Strongly agree	Well-adopted
Equality	4.30	0.74	Strongly agree	Well-adopted
Claiming rights	4.11	0.59	Agree	Well-adopted
Total scale	4.35	0.48	Strongly agree	Well-adopted

Table 2 presents the arithmetic mean of the scores of science teachers from the democratic values scale. When we examine the arithmetic means, we see that the highest mean belongs to the "justice" factor ($M = 4.63$), followed by "respect for differences" ($M = 4.41$), "equality" ($M = 4.30$), and "claiming rights" ($M = 4.11$), respectively. The arithmetic mean of the total scale was found to be ($M = 4.35$) The findings indicate that science teachers agreed with the items related to the "claiming rights" dimension, while they strongly agreed with the items related to the "justice," "respect for differences," and "equality."

Relationship Between Science Teachers' Perceptions of Multicultural Competence and their Democratic Values

The relationships between the three dimensions of multiculturalism (awareness, skills, and knowledge) are examined. The awareness dimension has a high positive relationship ($r = 78$) with the skill dimension and a moderately positive ($r = 43$) relationship with the knowledge dimension.

When the relationships among the four subdimensions (claiming rights, respect for differences, justice, and equality) of democratic values are examined, there is a moderately positive relationship between claiming rights and respect for differences ($r = 59$), between claiming rights and justice ($r = 60$), and between claiming rights and equality ($r = 64$). Similarly, there is a high positive relationship between respect for differences and justice ($r = 69$) and between respect for differences and equality, while a moderately positive relationship between justice and equality ($r = 62$).

When we examine the relationships between the subdimensions of perceptions of the multicultural competence scale and the subdimensions of the democratic values scale, we see a significant positive relationship between all subdimensions. In Table 3 a moderately significant relationship between awareness and respect for differences is shown ($r = 39$), between awareness and justice ($r = 31$), and between awareness and equality ($r = 38$). There is a moderately positive relationship between skill and respect for differences ($r = 39$), between skill and justice ($r = 31$), and between skill and equality ($r = 37$). Again in Table 3, we see a moderately positive relationship between knowledge and respect for differences ($r = 40$), between knowledge and justice ($r = 32$), and between knowledge and equality ($r = 37$). Also, there is a low positive relationship between knowledge and claiming rights ($r = 28$), between awareness and claiming rights ($r = 22$), and between skill and claiming rights ($r = 25$). In conclusion, we found that there was a moderate positive relationship between science teachers' perceptions of multicultural competence and their democratic attitudes ($r = 41$).

Table 3: The Correlation Values between the Perceptions of Multicultural Competence and Democratic Values

	1	2	3	4	5	6	7	8	9
Multicultural competences									
1. Awareness		.78**	.43**	.22**	.38**	.31**	.38**	.81**	.32**
2. Skill		—	.63**	.25**	.39**	.31**	.37**	.86**	.33**
3. Knowledge			—	.28**	.40**	.32**	.37**	.71**	.33**
Democratic values									
4. Claiming rights				—	.59**	.60**	.64**	.38**	.92**
5. Respect for differences					—	.69**	.74**	.42**	.90**
6. Justice						—	.62**	.36**	.88**
7. Equality							—	.34**	.90**
8. Multiculturalism								—	.41**
9. Democratic values									—

Note. $N = 436$ *$p < .01$, ** $p < .05$

DISCUSSION AND CONCLUSION

The present study was conducted to determine the relationship between self-perceptions of multicultural competence and democratic values of science teachers in schools where international students study.

As a result of the data analysis, we found that the science teachers in schools where international students study agreed with the items related to the awareness dimension of the perceptions of multicultural competence scale ($\bar{x} = 3.81$). This finding shows that teachers' levels of awareness of different cultural structures are sufficient. Based on this finding, we conclude that teachers have embraced values and attitudes of different cultures, believe that cultures should be protected, and think that communicating with students from different cultures does not disturb them and that students are not culturally superior or weaker, showing a sufficient level of awareness.

These findings are consistent with those obtained in other studies. In the study conducted by Strickland (2018), it was found that teachers working in various American schools with different ethnic backgrounds had multicultural experience medium level close to high. Akyıldız (2018) determined that teachers' multicultural competencies and their scores from the awareness, knowledge, and skill subdimensions were sufficient. Bulut and Başbay (2014) found that teachers had sufficient awareness of multicultural competencies and the awareness, knowledge, and skill subdimensions. Similarly, in other studies conducted on teachers, it was determined that teachers' multicultural competence perceptions were sufficient in awareness, skill, and knowledge (Cırık, 2014; İsmetoğlu, 2017; Özdemir, 2018; Perkins, 2012; Yüksel, 2018). Sheets and Chew (2000) also found that prospective teachers generally adopted multicultural education, and they were aware that multicultural education provided for the development and change of the school environment. Gorham (2001) also revealed that teachers have multicultural competences. The findings indicate that science teachers who work in schools where international students study consider themselves sufficient in multiculturalism (Aslan & Kozikoğlu, 2017; Kaya & Söylemez, 2014; Taştekin et al., 2016; S. Yazıcı et al., 2009).

For teachers to prepare a multicultural education environment in schools and classrooms where students from different cultures study, their perception of multicultural competence should be much higher. However, as the findings of this study show, teachers' perceptions of multicultural competence are not at a "quite sufficient" level. The reason teachers do not consider themselves quite sufficient in terms of multicultural competence may be due to the lack of multicultural education in preservice and in-service training programs. A training program for teachers and prospective teachers on this subject may raise their perceptions of multicultural competence. In O'Byrne & Smith, (2015), Brady (2014), and Johnson Wells (2011), multicultural education practices had an impact on prospective teachers' attitudes toward and competences in multicultural education.

Prospective teachers agreed with the items related to the claiming rights dimension of the democratic values scale, while they strongly agreed with the items related to the justice, respect for differences, and equality dimensions. Teachers showed a high level of agreement ($M = 4.63$) with the items related to the justice dimension of democratic values, and a lower level of agreement ($M = 4.11$) with the items related to the claiming rights dimension. The justice dimension of democratic values includes items related to the exercise of democratic rights, the impossibility of progress without justice, equal application of the principle of justice to all, and the functioning of democracy based on the legal guarantee. The claiming rights dimension, on the other hand, includes items related to taking decisions voluntarily, the courage to challenge the opinions of high-status people, boldly expressing one's opinions even if they are contrary to the opinions of the group, never putting up with injustice, struggling for justice, and being undaunted in the struggle for justice.

While teachers showed a higher level of agreement with the items related to the justice, respect for differences, and equality dimensions of the democratic values, they showed a lower level of agreement with the items related to the claiming rights dimension. This finding is similar to the findings of other similar studies. Turnsek and Pekkarinen (2009) found that the democratic attitudes of teachers were above average. Almog and Shechtman (2007) found a positive relationship between teachers' democratic attitudes and their ability to use methods. Kesici et al. (2017) found that teachers had high perceptions of democratic behaviors in the classroom. Wang (2004) found that the democratic attitudes of teachers were positive. Similar to these findings, Demoulin and Kolstad (2000) found that prospective teachers had high democratic values.

In our study, we found a generally positive, moderate, and significant relationship between teachers' perceptions of multicultural competence and their democratic values. The most significant relationship was found between the respect for differences dimension of democratic values and the awareness, skill, and knowledge dimensions of perceptions of multicultural competence. Accordingly, as science teachers' level of agreement with the respect for differences dimension of democratic values increased, their level of agreement with the awareness, skill, and knowledge dimensions of perceptions of multicultural competence increased. Based on this, we concluded that teachers' high levels of perceptions of multicultural competence in a multicultural society are related to their adoption of democratic values. This can be interpreted as teachers' perceptions of multicultural competence increase as their democratic values increase, and their perceptions of multicultural competence decrease as their democratic values decrease (Akyıldız, 2018; F. Yazıcı et al., 2016).

Based on the findings of the research, the following suggestions can be put forward: In a multicultural society, teachers have an important role in providing multicultural education. The presence of students from different cultural backgrounds in the teachers' classrooms gives the experience of multiculturalism. In this context, the presence of students with differences can contribute to the development of multicultural education. Teachers should organize out-of-school educational activities for students of different cultural backgrounds to protect their culture and to integrate with the place where they live. In-service training related to the attitudes and values teachers should have in a multicultural education environment and the methods and techniques they should use can be organized for the teachers in schools where international students are located. The implementation of projects on multicultural education in higher education institutions and among teachers should be encouraged. In addition, within the scope of teaching practices, prospective teachers can gain awareness and democratic attitudes by visiting international students' schools, making observations and organizing activities in classrooms. Further qualitative research can be done on multicultural education and democratic values of teachers working in schools where international students are concentrated.

REFERENCES

Akdağ, M., & Yıldız, H. (2011). Primary first grade teachers' views about developing students' literacy skills proficiency. *Journal of Theoretical Educational Science, 4*(1), 50–70.

Akhtar, M. (2008). *What is self-efficacy? Bandura's 4 sources of efficacy beliefs.* Positive Psychology UK. http://positivepsychology.org.uk/self-efficacy-definition-bandura-meaning/

Akkaya, N., Kırmızı, F. S., & İşçi, C. (2018). Examining teacher candidates' perceptions of multiculturalism based on different variables. *Adiyaman University Journal of Social Sciences, 10*(29), 308–335. https://doi.org/10.14520/adyusbd.381005

Akyıldız, S. (2018). The relation between multicultural competency perceptions and democratic values of primary teachers at schools that foreigner students attend. *Education and Science, 43*(195), 151–165.

Almog, O., & Shechtman, Z. (2007). Teachers' democratic and efficacy beliefs and styles of coping with behavioral problems of pupils with special needs. *European Journal of Special Needs Education, 22*(2), 115–129.

American Psychological Association. (2002). *Guidelines on multicultural education, training, research, practice, and organizational change for psychologists.* https://www.apa.org/about/policy/multicultural-guidelines-archived.pdf

Aslan, M., & Kozikoğlu, İ. (2017). Teachers' attitudes toward multicultural education: Sample of Van Dicle University. *Journal of Ziya Gökalp Education Faculty, 31,* 729–737. DOI: http://dx.doi.org/10.14582/DUZGEF.1829

Aslan, S. (2017). An examination of the opinion of the social studies teachers on multicultural education. *Ahi Evran University Journal of Kırşehir Education Faculty, 18*(2), 231-253.

Aydın, H. (2013). *Multicultural education discussion in Turkey and in the world.* Nobel Publishing.

Baloğlu, N., Karadağ, E., Çalışkan, N., & Korkmaz, T. (2006). An evaluation of the vocational self-esteem and satisfaction of primary school teachers. *Ahi Evran University Journal of Kırşehir Education Faculty, 7*(2), 345–358.

Bandura, A. (1997). *Self-efficacy: The exercise of control.* W.H. Freeman.

Banks, C. A. M., & Banks, J. A. (1995). Equity pedagogy: An essential component of multicultural education. *Theory into Practice, 34*(3), 152–158.

Banks, J. A. (1993). Multicultural education: Historical development, dimensions, and practice. *Review of Research in Education, 19,* 3–49.

Banks, J. A. (2004). Multicultural education: Historical development, dimensions, and practice. In J. A. Banks (Ed.), *Handbook of research on multicultural education* (pp. 3–30). Jossey-Bass.

Banks, J. A. (Ed.). (2009). *The Routledge international companion to multicultural education.* Routledge.

Başbay, A., & Kağnıcı, Y. (2011). Perceptions of multicultural competence scale: A scale development study. *Education and Science, 36*(161), 199–212.

Bennett, C. (2001). Genres of research in multicultural education. *Review of Educational Research, 71*(2), 171–217. doi:10.3102/00346543071002171.

Brady, J. S. (2014). *The impact of multicultural education training for preservice teachers* [Unpublished doctoral dissertation]. Walden University, Minnesota.

Buluç, B., & Demir, S. (2015). The relationship between job satisfaction and self-efficacy based on elementary and middle school teacher's perceptions. *Ahi Evran University Journal of Kırşehir Education Faculty, 16*(1), 289–308.

Bulut, C. (2014). *The investigation of teachers' perceptions of multicultural competence* [Unpublished master's thesis]. Ege University, İzmir.

Bulut, C., & Başbay, A. (2014). Determination of teachers' multicultural competence perceptions. *Kastamonu Education Journal, 23*(3), 957–978.

Büyüköztürk, Ş. (2002). *Manual of data analysis for social sciences.* Pegem Academy Publishing.

Büyüköztürk, Ş., Çakmak, E. K., Akgün, Ö. E., Karadeniz, Ş., & Demirel, F. (2009). *Scientific research methods* (3rd ed.). Pegem Academy Publishing.

Büyüköztürk, Ş., Kılıç Çakmak, E., Akgün, Ö. E., Karadeniz, Ş., & Demirel, F. (2016). *Scientific research methods* (20th ed.). Pegem Academy Publishing.

Castles, S. (2004). Migration, citizenship, and education. In J. A. Banks (Ed.), *Diversity and citizenship education: Global perspectives* (pp. 17–48). Jossey-Bass.

Çermik, H. (2013). Pre-service teachers' democratic values and investigation of these values based on some variables. *Education Sciences, 8*(2), 261–274.

Cırık, İ. (2014). Investigation of the relations between objectives of Turkish primary school curriculums and multiculturalism. *Procedia Social and Behavioral Sciences, 116*, 74–76

Colombo, M. W. (2006). Building school partnerships with culturally and linguistically diverse families. *Phi Delta Kappan, 88*(4), 314–318.

Demoulin, D. F., & Kolstad, R. (2000). Assessing the gains of behavioral dynamics essential for success in a democracy for teacher education students. *College Student Journal, 34*(3), 417–417.

Doğanay, A., & Sarı, M. (2004). Elementary school students? Devotion level to democratic values and comparison of the effect of overt and hidden curriculum on gaining democratic values in terms of students and teachers' opinions. *Educational Administration: Theory and Practice, 39*(39), 356–383.

Doytcheva, M. (2009). *Multiculturalism.* İletişim Publishing.

Fackler, S., & Malmberg, L-E. (2016). Teachers' self-efficacy in 14 OECD countries: Teacher, student group, school and leadership effects. *Teaching and Teacher Education, 56*, 185–195.

Gavora, P. (2010). Slovak pre-service teacher self-efficacy: Theoretical and research considerations. *The New Educational Review, 21*(3), 17–30.

Gibson, S., & Dembo, M. H. (1984). Teacher efficacy: a construct validation. *Journal of Educational Psychology, 76*(4), 569–582.

Gollnick, D. M., & Chinn, P. C. (2009). *Multicultural education in a pluralistic society.* Pearson Prentice Hall.

Gordon, A. F., & Newfield, C. (1996). *Mapping multiculturalism.* University of Minnesota Press.

Gorham, R. G. (2001). *Multicultural teaching competence as perceived by elementary school teachers* [Unpublished doctoral dissertation]. Virginia Polytechnic Institute and State University.

Grand National Assembly of Turkey. (2018). *Human Rights Investigation Commission Refugee Rights: Sub-Commission Migration and Integration Report 26th Term 3rd Legislative Year March 2018.* https://www.tbmm.gov.tr/komisyon/insanhaklari/docs/2018/goc_ve_uyum_raporu.pdf

Günay, E., Atılgan, D., & Serin, E. (2017). Migration management in the world and Turkey. *Kahramanmaraş Sütçü İmam University Journal of the Faculty of Economics and Administrative Sciences, 7*(2), 37–60.

Günbayı, İ., & Tokel, A. (2012). A comparative analysis of compulsory school teachers' job satisfaction and job stress levels. *ODU Journal of Social Sciences Research, 3*(5), 77–95.

Heywood, A. (2013). *Politics.* Palgrave Macmillan.

Hidalgo, F., Chávez R., & Ramage, J. (1996). Multicultural education: Landscape for reform in the twenty-first century. In J. Sikula (Ed.), *Handbook of teacher education.* Macmillan.

International Organization for Migration. (2019). *Glossary of migration terms.* https://publications.iom.int/system/files/pdf/iml_34_glossary.pdf

Irvine, J. J., & Armento, B. J. (2001). *Culturally responsive teaching.* Mc Graw Hill.

İsmetoğlu, M. (2017). *Branch teachers' multicultural efficiency levels and their perceptions towards quality of work life* [Unpublished master's thesis]. Abant İzzet Baysal University, Bolu.

Johnson Wells, G. (2011). *Perceptions of change: In-service teachers' reflections on multicultural education, culturally responsive teaching, and transformative learning* [Unpublished doctoral dissertation]. Capella University, Minneapolis, Minnesota.

Kaur, S. (2015). Moral values in education. *IOSR Journal of Humanities and Social Science, 20*(3), 21–26.

Kaya, I., & Aydın, H. (2014). *Pluralism, multicultural and multilingual education.* Anı Publishing.

Kaya, Y., & Söylemez, M. (2014). Determining teachers' perspective about multiculturalism and multicultural education: (Diyarbakır's example). *Dicle University Social Sciences Institute Journal, 6*(11), 128–148.

Kesici, A., Pesen, A., & Oral, B., (2017). Examining teachers' democratizing behaviors in the classroom according to variables. *Electronic Journal of Social Sciences, 16*(60), 34–45. https://doi.org/10.17755/esosder.289649

Kesici, Ş. (2008). Teachers' opinions about building a democratic classroom. *Journal of Instructional Psychology, 35*(2), 192–203.

Kılıç, F., & Kılıç, Ü. (2016). Human rights education and peace. *Abant İzzet Baysal University Journal of Faculty of Education, 16*(Special Issue II), 1513–1521.

Kıncal, R. Y., & Işık, H. (2003). Democratic education and democratic values. *Education Research, 11*, 54–58.

Kıncal, Y. R. (2007). *Citizenship information.* Nobel Publishing.

Kinnier, R., Kernes, J. L., & Dautheribes, T. M. (2000). A short list of universal moral values. *Counseling and Values, 45*(1), 4–17.

Köklü, N., Büyüköztürk, Ş., & Çokluk Bökeoğlu, Ö. (2007). *Statistics for social sciences.* Pegem Academy Publishing.

Midgley, C., Feldlaufer, H., & Eccles, J. S. (1989). Change in teacher efficacy and student self task-related beliefs in mathematics during the transition to junior high school. *Journal of Educational Psychology, 81*(2), 247–258.

Morgül, İ., Seçken, N., & Yücel, A. S. (2016). Based on some investigation of self-efficacy beliefs of preservice chemistry teachers variables. *Journal of Balıkesir University Institute of Science and Technology, 6*(1), 62–72.

Nieto, S. (2017). Re-imagining multicultural education: New visions, new possibilities. *Multicultural Education Review, 9*(1), 1–10.

Nieto, S., & Bode, P. (2008). *Affirming diversity: The sociopolitical context of multicultural education* (5th ed.). Allyn & Bacon.

O'Byrne, W. I., & Smith, S. A. (2015). Multicultural education and multiliteracies: Exploration and exposure of literacy practices with preservice teachers. *Reading & Writing Quarterly, 31*(2), 168–184.

Özdemir, C. E. (2018) *Physical education teachers' multicultural personality of multicultural educational relationship with the attitudes and perceptions of proficiency* [Unpublished master's thesis]. Marmara University, İstanbul.

Pajares, F., & Schunk, D. H. (2001). Self-beliefs and school success: Self-efficacy, self-concept, and school achievement. In R. Riding & S. Rayner (Eds.), *Self-perception* (pp. 239–266). Ablex.

Parekh, B. (2002). *Rethinking multiculturalism: Cultural diversity and political theory* (Trans. Bilge Tanrıseven). Phoenix Press.

Parker, C. W. (2002). Teaching for diversity and unity in a democratic multicultural society. In W. C. Parker (Ed.), *Education for democracy.* Information Age Publishing.

Perkins, R. M. (2012). *The multicultural awareness, knowledge, skills and attitudes of prospective teachers: A quantitative and heuristic phenomenological study* [Unpublished doctoral dissertation]. University of Missouri, Kansas.

Polat, S. (2009). Probationary teachers' level of inclination to multi-cultural education. *International Online Journal of Educational Sciences, 1*(1), 154–164.

Say, Ö. (2013). *Nation, multiculturalism and ethnicity in the 21st century.* Kaknüs.

Schunk, D. H. (1990). Goal setting and self-efficacy during self-regulated learning. *Educational Psychologist, 25*(1), 71–86.

Sheets, R. H., & Chew, L. (2000, April). *Preparing Chinese American teacher: Implications for multicultural education* [Paper presentation]. Annual Meeting of the American Educational Research Association, New Orleans.

Spencer-Oatey, H. (2012). *What is culture? A compilation of quotations.* https://www2.warwick.ac.uk/fac/soc/al/globalpad/openhouse/interculturalsk ills/global_pad_-_what_is_culture.pdf

Strickland, D. L. (2018). *Factor relating to the multicultural efficacy and attitudes of teachers* [Unpublished doctoral dissertation]. Georgia Southern University, Statesboro.

Taştekin, E., Yükçü, Ş. B., İzoğlu, A., Güngör, İ., Uslu, A. E. I., & Demircioğlu, H. (2016). Investigation of pre-school teachers' perceptions and attitudes towards multicultural education. *Hacettepe University The Journal of Educational Research, 2*(1).

Tschannen-Moran, M., & Woolfolk Hoy, A. (2001). Teacher efficacy: Capturing and elusive construct. *Teaching and Teacher Education, 17*, 783–805.

Turnsek, N., & Pekkarinen, A. (2009). Democratisation of early chilhood education in the attidudes of Slovene and Finnish teachers. *European Early Childhood Education Research Journal, 17*(1), 23–42.

Wang, Y. (2004). *The tension between ethnic identity and democratic education* [Paper presentation]. he International Symposium on Democracy Education, Cambridge University, UK.

Washington, E. D. (2003). The multicultural competence of teachers and challenge of academic achievement. In *Handbook of multicultural competencies in counseling and psychology.* SAGE.

Wertheim, C., & Leyser, Y. (2002). Efficacy beliefs, background variables, and differentiated instruction of Israeli prospective teachers. *The Journal of Educational Research, 96*, 54–63.

Yazıcı, F., Pamuk, A., & Yıldırım, T. (2016). The relationship between attitudes of pre-service history teachers toward multiculturalism and patriotism. *Electronic Turkish Studies, 11*(9), 947–964.

Yazıcı, S., Başol, G., & Toprak, G. (2009). Teachers' attitudes toward multicultural education: a study of reliability and validity. *Hacettepe University Journal of Education, 37*(37), 229–242.

Yüksel, A. (2018). *The impact of the teachers' multicultural competence perceptions on the global citizenship perceptions and determination of the mediator effect of cultural intelligence on this relationship* [Unpublished doctoral dissertation]. Gazi University, Ankara.

M. SAİD DOĞRU, PhD, is an Assistant Professor at Vocational School of Vehicle Rafet Araç. His major research interests lie in the area of health, multiculturalism and science education. Email: msaid.dogru@yahoo.com

İBRAHİM DEMİRBAŞ is a doctoral student in the Department of Social Sciences Education at Kastamonu University. His major research interests lie in the area of social science education and multiculturalism. Email: idemirbas28@gmail.com

Peer-Reviewed Article

© *Journal of International Students*
Volume 11, Issue 1 (2021), pp. 41-59
ISSN: 2162-3104 (Print), 2166-3750 (Online)
doi: 10.32674/jis.v11i1.952
ojed.org/jis

OJED
OPEN JOURNALS IN EDUCATION

A Bourdieusian Analysis of the Sociocultural Capital of Chinese International Graduate Students in the United States

Xinxin Wang
Rebekah Freed
University of North Carolina at Chapel Hill, USA

ABSTRACT

For the last decade, Chinese international graduate students (CIGS) have represented the largest portion of international graduate students in the United States. Previous research studies on language barriers and cultural differences have revealed that CIGS experience difficulties in adapting to the American educational system (Zhang-Wu, 2018). Few researchers have critically examined the experiences of CIGS on a more organizational level. In this qualitative study, we analyzed interviews with CIGS utilizing a Bourdieusian (1986a) framework to identify the social and cultural capital (SCC) that CIGS possessed. We argue that SCC concepts can help theoretically and critically examine the experiences of international students as a minority student group in the United States. The results from our in-depth semistructured interviews imply that CIGS are excluded from access to and possession of the SCC necessary to adapt to academic, cultural, and social life in the United States.

Keywords: Chinese international graduate students, cultural capital, social capital, higher education, international education

INTRODUCTION

When international students attend higher education institutions in the United States, it benefits both the international students, as well as the American universities and the broader economy and society. The increase of international student enrollment in U.S. universities has had a significant positive economic impact for the United States. During the 2018–2019 academic year, the 1,095,299 international students studying at U.S. colleges and universities contributed around $45 billion to the U.S. economy. Additionally, international students either created or supported 458,290 jobs in the United States, which benefits the U.S. economy and the job market (National Association of Foreign Student Advisers, 2019). International students also contribute to America's scientific and technical research and bring international and cultural perspectives into U.S. classrooms. International students interact with and influence fellow students at U.S. universities and therefore help prepare American undergraduates for global careers through exposure. International students building friendships and relationships in the United States can lead to long-term business relationships and subsequent economic benefits (Institute of International Education, 2018).

The enrollment of international students has been increasing in American universities, including undergraduate students, graduate students, students with optional practical training, and nondegree students for the past decade. China has been one of the top countries of origin for international students in the United States in recent decades. There are 369,548 Chinese international students currently enrolled in universities in the United States, and more than one third (133,396) are Chinese international graduate students (CIGS; Institute of International Education, 2019). International students benefit from studying abroad because it provides an opportunity to expand their career choices. Many Chinese international students believe that the more merit-based system in the United States is fairer in terms of admission, graduation, and job attainment and will therefore better position graduates to achieve their personal goals. Students' decisions about going abroad are also influenced by their friends or relatives who have already gone abroad (Cao, 1997). Another emerging factor that propels Chinese students to study abroad is social and peer pressure.

Despite Chinese students representing such a large portion of the international student body, they face many obstacles when studying in a foreign country. While they are willing to engage in the difficult journey of leaving their home country and traveling to the United States to pursue higher education, they must also navigate a complex visa process, master a foreign language, adjust to unfamiliar cultural norms, and deal with discrimination, all for the benefit of an education from quality U.S. universities (Gold, 2016; Lee & Rice, 2007). A majority of studies on Chinese international students focus on those individual factors and tend to overblame the international students themselves for adjustment and well-being problems in their host countries (Zhang & Goodson, 2011). Few researchers have explored stressors and inequality from the environmental factors (e.g., American professors, peers, and universities) that critically influence international students' experiences. To fill the literature gap and to provide more insights on practical solutions on how to better support Chinese international students, we use Bourdieu's (1986a) concept of capital as a critical lens through which to study the access to and possession of resources and support for Chinese international graduate students (CIGS) in their academic and social lives in the United States.

LITERATURE REVIEW

International students play an important role in U.S. higher education. However, they may encounter a disparity between their social and educational aspirations and their narrowly defined status as a fee-paying "alien" (Habu, 2000). These challenges often impact international students' lives in complex and intersecting ways. In Kuo's (2011) study of 152 international graduate students' experiences at a Southern university in the United States, the language challenges that international graduate students face in the southern United States were intertwined with cultural challenges due to differences in culture and background. Lin and Scherz (2014) found that Asian international graduate students face similar challenges in the United States. Asian international students, especially Chinese international students, experienced higher levels of stress and discrimination than their European international peers due to larger cultural distance in communication and education between their home and host countries and lower English language proficiency (Alharbi & Smith, 2018). Zhang-Wu (2018) conducted a critical literature review of 21 peer-reviewed articles on Chinese international students since 2000 and found that all publications focused on individual experiences in three aspects: language barriers, acculturation, and intercultural communication. Very few researchers have studied how Chinese international students are supported through organizational, regional, or national efforts. One exception is that Cho and Yu (2015) studied university support for international students at a university in the southeastern United States through surveying 131 international students from 33 countries. They found that university support and students' perceived support is influential in students' wellbeing, including psychological stress and school–life satisfaction. Additionally, Zhang-Wu (2018) noted that few articles employed a critical stance when empirically studying the issues that Chinese international students encounter, typically attributing their negative experiences to cultural differences and failing to highlight issues of race and racism, which are more systemic in institutions.

Distinguishing graduate students from the body of literature on Chinese international students is necessary for our study because CIGS may possess more established Chinese worldviews, values, and habits compared with younger Chinese international undergraduates, so CIGS may experience different challenges or support. Some researchers have begun to study cultural stereotyping and negative labeling experienced by female CIGS in Canada (Ge et al., 2019). In order to deepen the understanding of how CIGS overcome stressors and learn to adapt in U.S. graduate schools, we identified two central research questions:

1. Does the capital that CIGS possess or lack help or hinder their adaptation to the American education system?

2. How does the capital function during the adaptation process of CIGS?

THEORETICAL FRAMEWORK

Pierre Bourdieu's work reveals the contradiction between democratic goals and reforms and how they fail to close achievement gaps and eliminate social inequality (English & Bolton, 2016). Bourdieu (1986b) suggested a relational approach to studying education by introducing three key concepts to explain how this mechanism works: habitus, field, and capital. Habitus can be understood as an individual's life expectations and dispositions shaped by that individual's life space. Habitus is framed by our past and upbringing, but also shapes our future (Bourdieu, 1984). Bourdieu emphasized structure as part of habitus to show that habitus is not random, because it has predictable patterns "inscribed in our bodies, in things, in situations, and everyday lives" (Bourdieu, 1991, p. 51). School systems, for example, are crucial in enhancing existing habitus and in building new habitus. School systems also provide a structure that accepts the dominant social rules. Therefore, it is clear that some groups favor the school's habitus while other groups experience it as confusing, segregating, and contentious (English & Bolton, 2016).

Field is another key concept in Bourdieu's sociology. The term "field" refers to different social "spaces," networks, or configurations imposed by specific values and rules (Bourdieu, 1990). International students are positioned in intersected fields, or different institutional spaces, and are positioned in different policy and regulation fields related to their academic status in the United States (Tran, 2014). Bourdieu also argued that social groups should be classified by people who live in a similar habitus with shared experiences and beliefs. Agents or players within in a field accept the "rules of the game" governing their activities, though the "rules" are often learned unconsciously (Bourdieu, 1986a). For example, social fields exist between Asian students, as well as among Asian students and Americans.

Economic Capital, Social Capital, Cultural Capital

Bourdieu contributed his theoretical applications to the sociological studies to education, including extending the concept of capital. Economic capital refers to a form of capital "which is immediately and directly convertible into money and may be institutionalized in the form of property rights" (Bourdieu, 1986a, p. 15). Research funding, for example, is important economic capital for CIGS. Bourdieu extended the concept of capital beyond its economic realm to include nonmaterial aspects of capital (i.e., social and cultural capital [SCC]; Bourdieu, 1986). These immaterial aspects of capital are considered sources of capital because they can be transferred to economic capital (see Figure 1).

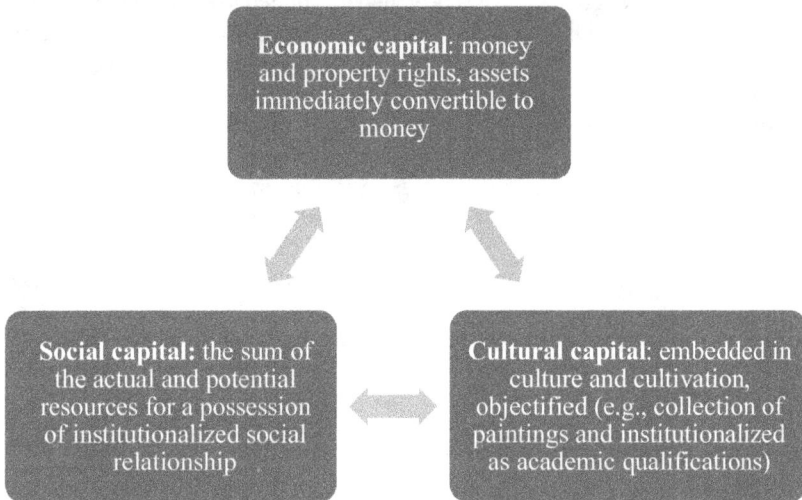

Figure 1: Conversions of Material and Nonmaterial Capitals

Bourdieu (1986a) described social capital as:

> ...the aggregate of the actual or potential resources which are linked to possession of a durable network of more or less institutionalized relationships of mutual acquaintance and recognition—or, in other words, to membership in a group—which provides each of its members with the backing of the collectively owned capital. (p. 21)

Social capital can be considered the ability of the social fields or networks to create or foster capital. Being at the intersection of different fields or networks can mean both unique difficulties, as well as unique possibilities, for CIGS.

Bourdieu (1977) also described cultural capital, which is all of the "instruments for the appropriation of symbolic wealth socially designated as worthy of being sought and possessed" (p. 488). Cultural capital presents itself in three states: an embodied state, an objectified state, and an institutionalized state. Bourdieu (1986a) expressed that an embodied state occurs when one has accumulated cultural capital unconsciously via culture and cultivation (p. 18). Acquiring cultural capital via an embodied state results in "the form of long-lasting dispositions of the mind and body" (Bourdieu, 1986a, p. 17). Material goods and media represent cultural capital in an objectified state (Bourdieu, 1986a, p. 19). For example, a collection of paintings (objectified cultural capital) can be converted to economic capital by sale. Cultural capital in an institutionalized state (Bourdieu, 1986a, p. 20) generally refers to academic qualifications (e.g., a teaching certificate). Cultural capital is invisible and can be overlooked when considering educational investment and gains. As the individual embodies capital, it becomes a type of habitus (i.e., the embodiment of cultural capital; Abbas, 2004, p. 16).

Bourdieu's concept of capital has been widely applied to educational research (Davies & Rizk, 2017; Dika & Singh, 2002), particularly on schooling and the inequalities that students who are racial and ethnic minorities experience (Abbas, 2004; Stanton-Salazar, 1997; Warikoo & Carter, 2009). Research has shown that possessing capital contributes to students' sense of belonging and resilience to schools (Glass & Gesing, 2018). Researchers also frequently show that there is a direct correlation between students' access to and possession of SCC and their educational attainment and achievement outcomes (Bernstein, 2000; Lareau, 2003; Lareau & Horvat, 1999). Stanton-Salazar (1997), in his widely adopted theoretical paper on social capital framework, linked social capital to the racial inequities that minority groups experience, describing how social capital can be leveraged to economic capital through means accessible to those included in a social network or field, and withheld from those who are systemically not included in social fields.

We found Bourdieu's concepts of habitus, field, and capital useful in attempting to understand the CIGS' adaptation into U.S. higher education. International students as a unique ethnic minority group are surprisingly overlooked in racial and educational research. The U.S. educational setting can be considered a social field with its own rules, shared experiences, and beliefs. However, studying CIGS complicates the research, because CIGS are placed in two different social fields: Chinese and American. The concept of habitus is relevant for understanding the structure of dynamic life patterns of CIGS when they move to a new social space (i.e., field) in the United States. In the context of studying Asian international students, Abbas (2004) stated that the social capital concept "elaborates the importance of networks, associations and 'connections'" (p. 27). Abbas (2004) argued that the concept of cultural capital is useful because it "considers the micro-process at work, as pupils engage with parents, teachers and the system itself" (p. 27). The SCC framework has yet to be applied to study CIGS in the United States, though some scholars have utilized the SCC framework to study Chinese students in China (Liu & Brown, 2014; Sheng, 2012). Following the line of research by Abbas (2004), we argue that the SCC framework is more microoriented for categorizing aspects of cultures and social networks, which will then help reveal how CIGS in our study adapt to and navigate U.S. institutions of higher education, as well as if and how these institutions support them during this process.

METHOD

We focused on the interpretation (Lincoln & Guba, 1985) of graduate lives of CIGS and looked for richness in context and narratives to answer the research questions. As such, we decided that a qualitative study was the appropriate research method (Levitt et al., 2018). Furthermore, we applied a multiple-case study (Yin, 2017) analysis on 10 Chinese students. We developed the interview protocol (see Appendix A) guided by the SCC framework and conducted two pilot interviews with two CIGS to revise the interview questions. The first author, as a Chinese graduate student herself, has studied CIGS in the United States from sociological and cultural perspectives for years, so she has a general understanding of the literature and experiences of CIGS. Since she came into the study with ideas about what she wanted to learn, she chose to conduct semistructured interviews, which would provide some flexibility and the possibility of open discussions.

Participants

The sample was chosen according to the convenience of the first author, who is a doctoral student at a southeastern American university and has many personal contacts with CIGS. The targeted research participants in this study were current or recent graduate students (i.e., students who graduated within 5 years) from China who studied in the United States. The first author used snowball sampling (Marshall & Rossman, 2016) and interviewed participants starting with direct contacts and expanding outward to participants with less direct connection to the first author. The first author began interviewing friends who are current or recently graduated CIGS, and then participants recommended others to enlarge the sample size. Participants were purposefully sampled to include meaningful and various perspectives for the study (Marshall & Rossman, 2016). The 10 interviewees attended eight different U.S. higher education institutions located in the northeastern, southeastern, and middle United States.

Data Collection and Analysis

Each interview was designed to last 45 min, although most interviews took longer than expected, because the participants were eager to share their experiences. Overall, the interviews ranged from 36–128 min, with six interviews lasting more than 1 hr each. For participants who lived remotely, the first author scheduled a video chat or phone call to conduct the interview. All names presented in this article are pseudonyms. Running notes and reflection notes were utilized as part of the interview process and for data analysis (Marshall & Grossman, 2016). Appendix B shows interviewee details including gender, major, interview length, location of interviewees, current student status, and mode of interview. All interviews were completed within one month. The first nine participants chose to conduct the interview in Chinese, and the last participant chose English for the interview. All the interviews were audio-recorded for further analysis. The first author translated all Chinese audio interview records to English for constant comparative coding and thematic analysis and to interpret the interview results (Saldaña, 2009). The first author developed codes based on the capital framework and generated new codes if new topics arose from interviews, and then she summarized the codes into themes for future analysis. The second author worked with the first author to provide an impartial view on general methodology and research findings (known as peer debriefing) (Marshall & Rossman, 2016). When the two authors had different interpretations during the coding and data analysis process, we critically examined and communicated our perspectives as researchers and graduate students from different cultures and habitus to reach an agreement.

Positionality

The first author is a Chinese international graduate student in the United States. Her shift from being a member of a majority group in China to a minority group through studying abroad further challenged her life in the United States. She is from the Han ethnicity, which makes up 92% of the population in China. Therefore, she never expected to experience how being a minority complicates everything in life. She experienced extensive stress in adapting to academic and social life in the United States, and she started wondering whether other Chinese students experienced similar problems. The second author is an ethnically Jewish, White female who was raised in Southern California. She lived in areas and attended multicultural schools with a majority of Asian-American students. When she moved to other parts of America to teach, she saw how minority populations were marginalized in predominantly White spaces, and became interested in supporting students from diverse backgrounds. She contributed her knowledge and skills in qualitative methodology and writing, and worked with the first author to validate the coding and themes.

RESULTS

Through the 10 interviews, we found that a combination of language, cultural, social, institutional, and personal factors influenced the academic and social experiences of CIGS. We will discuss factors of adaptation in terms of habitus and cultural capital (particularly embodied cultural capital), sources and benefits of SCC, and disadvantages regarding the lack of access to or possession of capital. We will analyze the stressors and difficulties of CIGS through a Bourdieusian lens, which we will follow with an in-depth discussion of CIGS' experiences in U.S. graduate schools.

Changing Habitus

Unpreparedness emerged as a theme in the interview data in three distinct ways. First, CIGS were not prepared to move to the United States for graduate school when they lived in China before beginning graduate school. Second, CIGS were not prepared for the job market after graduation. Third, American educators seemed unprepared to teach CIGS.

Participants expressed that in China, English learning is focused on writing and reading. The most common class format in China is a lecture format with little student participation due to large class sizes and intensive class agendas. Our participants received minimum language training in school and had minimal contact with native English speakers in China before moving to the United States. Additionally, many participants reflected that they did not have a clear career plan when they came to America, even after they received admission offers from

American schools. Kan reported that he didn't do enough research on his first doctoral program to gain sufficient experience, so he found a big mismatch between his interests and his research teams. Kan reapplied to and enrolled in another doctoral program after 2 years at his first program. The participants reported that such unpreparedness created a lot of confusion and stress.

Coming to the United States from China is a huge change of habitus in educational background, family experiences, and social interactions (English & Bolton, 2014). CIGS are faced with struggles while accumulating new elements of capital in America. Tran (2016) argued that if there is a harmony between international students' habitus and the institutional environment of the host country, students would adapt into the new environment as "fish in water"; if there is a mismatch between the two habitus, students often have difficulty understanding the rules of the game. Our findings corroborate this.

Participants also expressed that American professors seemed underprepared to teach CIGS in their classes. Li and Wu shared that their professors had very little knowledge about Chinese education and did not indicate any willingness to learn more about China's education in order to help their students' transition. Li and Wu felt that the professors' lack of awareness about CIGS made them more academically isolated in class discussions and as they developed their respective research directions. Li felt that knowledge of culturally responsive pedagogical techniques (Gay, 2010) would help American educators to better address CIGS' needs and interests in the classroom. Li said,

> They [professors] listen to me politely and nod occasionally, but I can tell they are not quite interested when I am talking about education in China. I am not angry or disappointed though, it is just like, I feel sorry for them. It is their loss, not mine. Sometimes there are many things worth learning from China's math education.

It is difficult for both CIGS and American educators to discern that their predispositions and unpreparedness are bounded by their respective habitus, which is often unconscious. Introducing the concept of habitus into analysis makes it easier to recognize the educational inequality that CIGS experience in the American system due to the general unpreparedness of the system and individuals to handle them. Brantlinger (2003) commented on the inequality in schooling, saying,

> Given the prevalence of school hierarchies and their resistance to change, it is reasonable to hypothesize that existing structure and practices are durable precisely because they correspond to influential people's desires, hence from their power to create and retain them. (p. 2)

As newcomers to America, CIGS have difficulties in interpreting the existing hierarchies that influence their life, while American educators' resistance to accommodating for the habitus change of their students contributes to an unequal environment for CIGS.

Embodied Cultural Capital Accumulated in China

All participants expressed a huge gap between Eastern and estern cultures. Participants discussed elements of culture relevant to their experiences as being "language and talking patterns," "thinking patterns," "cultural taboos," "common values and beliefs that people share," "food culture," "lifestyle," and "knowing how to reach a certain group of people." The last aspect reflects the idea of social networking. Participants agreed that understanding American culture is the first step for building a useful social network for studying and finding a job in the United States.

Li and Wu emphasized the speaking culture they experienced in and outside of American classrooms. Wu said she learned to speak up in class, and as a result has obtained appreciation from several professors, who in turn helped her secure funding and be more successful in academic learning. Wu's experience shows how CIGS sometimes report accumulating mainstream sociocultural capital (i.e., SCC) and converting it into economic capital (i.e., funding) and social capital (i.e., social networks). Li talked about different speaking cultures between the United States and China:

> Have your voice, speak out. This is what Americans prefer. Chinese prefer to be silent, to be humble, then opportunities are seized by others. Students' requests will be taken up by a higher level of administration [at school], if not solved at a lower level. I think in this case American schools are doing a good job in listening to students and student services. Chinese students have a weaker sense of protecting their rights. Chinese are more complicated. They have different ideas in mind while they don't speak out. It is hard to guess what Chinese think.

Chinese students studying in the United States have moved away from their familiar social settings in which they developed their embodied cultural capital and predispositions (habitus) framed in China to a new social field (Bourdieu, 1990). Language, as an aspect of embodied cultural capital, is influential to their adaptation, but established structures and shared values in the new educational system have more impact. Most participants said that their first year in the United States was the most challenging, but they found that the language barrier diminished after their first year of stay.

One recurring pattern we found was that participants expressed reluctance about talking in class, especially with the extensive class discussions and group work they found in the U.S. classrooms. Some participants expressed that due to the cultural difference regarding expectations for speaking in class, CIGS sometimes feel invisible. According to the literature, two factors can explain CIGS' unwillingness to speak in class. First, students in China are typically taught to be humble in speaking. In Chinese culture, speaking out actively can be seen as wasting the public's time, and time should be allocated to each student evenly in China. The second factor is that Chinese students are taught to make sure their answers are 100% correct before speaking out, since making mistakes is a shameful behavior in Chinese culture (Li, 2012). The ability to remain humble and silent in social settings like classrooms might have been considered a source of cultural capital in the Chinese educational system, but for our participants, this cultural value became a disadvantage when trying to adapt to American classroom culture.

American Academic Advisors as the Only Source of Sociocultural Capital

When asking about social networks, half of the interviewees mentioned their academic advisors as the major (or only) way to reach to a broader social network. Wu said:

> The most satisfying thing in my doctoral study is that I have an excellent academic advisor. She shows genuine care to her advisees. She doesn't only recommend me collaboration opportunities with other scholars for publications, but also tells me the cultural norms, hidden rules, and her life stories. The latter part helps me a lot in adapting to the doctoral program, which is overall not always available to many international students.

Wu's advisor was also her primary source for learning about American culture, including academic culture and school culture. This relationship with her advisor helped Wu accumulate cultural capital so she could adapt into the U.S. education system. Wu's advisor also functioned as her major source of social capital, because she helped Wu build networks with more researchers and professors within and beyond her school. This contributed to Wu's career and scholarship development in terms of publications and job applications. Furthermore, Wu's accumulation of SCC helped her graduate with a PhD degree, a source of institutionalized cultural capital (Bourdieu,1986a). Wu's case demonstrates that social capital (e.g., academic networks) and cultural capital (e.g., academic degrees) can be fluid and interchangeable.

Other participants shared similar sentiments. Cong said that his advisor introduced him to a company manager, which led to his first off-campus internship in the United States. Cong further explained that it was very difficult for international students to find an off-campus internship due to unfamiliarity of the internship search process and noncitizen status. Another participant, Yuan, explained that his major field included only a small circle of people, so almost all researchers in his field know each other. Without an access to the "circle," Yuan couldn't imagine how he would have found a job without his advisor and dissertation committee. Cong and Yuan's cases serve as an example of converting social capital (i.e., social networks) to economic capital (i.e., paid salary; Bourdieu, 1986a).

Hao provided a counterexample, because her advisor was not supportive of her doctoral study. She spoke frankly that there is not much overlap between her advisor's research and her research interests. As a result, she felt that her advisor somewhat overlooked her. She reported that they met less than one time per semester. Hao felt that she received minimum guidance and mentoring from her advisor. Hao's lived experience highlights the importance of CIGS having a supportive academic advisor as the major source of sociocultural capital for adapting into the new habitus without unfairly bearing stress and difficulties at an unnecessary high level due to her limited access to mainstream SCC (Warikoo & Carter, 2009).

The Absence of Institutionalized Sociocultural Capital

Many interviewees expressed that access to international career services provided specifically for international students is critical for CIGS seeking a job in the United States. Surprisingly, four participants mentioned that their programs and universities provided no international career services. Most of the interviewees reported that, due to visa limitations and different language and cultural backgrounds, the current career services provided to mainstream university students are often not useful or applicable to CIGS. One exception is Wang, who experienced some positive examples of institutional effort. Wang said professors in her master's program were responsive and actively came to students to offer references. Wang's master's program organized trips and events for international students to interact with American peers. Chee and Meng also discussed experiencing the "halo effect" of their university having a high reputation, which gave them priority in the competitive job market. However, the "halo effect" disappeared after the first year of graduation.

Participants mentioned the importance of universities having a welcoming and inclusive institutional culture on campus and in programs. Hao felt that her program was not very open in providing individual support and sharing assistantship opportunities. Hao expressed that she was not good at interpreting the competitive institutional culture, and professors and students weren't open about sharing resources and scholarship information during her first year of the PhD program. As a consequence, she said that she felt she often "stepped on people's toes" and caused misunderstandings with other professors or peers, which led to anxiety. It seems like Hao was limited in accumulating helpful SCC to help her understand the "rules of the game" in her program (i.e., an academic field). Bourdieu (1986b) argued that to maintain the membership in a social field and accumulate capital, members of a social field follow the "rules of the game" unconsciously. Moving from one culture to another, CIGS may be following different "rules," which may conflict with their own interests and values. Given the different habitus that CIGS were situated in before their move to another country, the absence of institutionalized SCC for CIGS serves as a clue that many experience injustice and educational inequality.

Isolation and Denied Access to Sociocultural Capital: "I fight for myself all alone"

One unique dimension of SCC that arose during the interviews is that most participants identified themselves as both the major positive force behind learning to adapt to the cultural and social system and the reason for failing to adapt to U.S. higher education. They often blamed themselves for failing to communicate well in English, for not participating actively in American classes, for the mental stress from thinking about and doing things differently, and for American teachers' failure to acknowledge their existence. For example, Cong said, "All of my difficulties are personal. It is due to myself not being perfect enough." Similarly, Hao expressed:

> I don't think my struggles came from others. I deeply blame myself every day. I have visited my doctor for two years for my diagnosed clinical depression. Chinese people like to blame themselves for whatever difficulties they go through. I don't think self-accusation is a bad thing. Self-accusation leads to self-cultivation and growth.

Meng said, "No one and nothing has ever helped me. I am not good at social networking. I fight for myself all alone. I found my job after graduation all on my own." Kan said that personal endeavors and planning are the most important things for doctoral study.

The incredibly high level of self-blame and self-reliance has been interpreted positively by some researchers (Marginson, 2014; Tran, 2014) when studying forms of capital possessed by international students, in that international students are self-performing agents who "have the capability to pursue the course of life that they regard as being worth living" (Tran, 2014, p.2). However, the isolation and required self-reliance that participants expressed is evidence that the U.S. higher education system suffers from a systematic lack of support for CIGS navigating academic and social experiences in the United States. Future studies can provide further inquiry into the reasons CIGS experience so much isolation, because isolation may influence feelings of stress and wellbeing. These feelings may further complicate the relationship between CIGS and their programs, institutions, and educators.

DISCUSSION AND CONCLUSION

Overall, we found that there were more negative than positive comments about CIGS' experiences attending graduate school in the United States. These include differences in capital and habitus that create challenges in teaching, learning, and communicating. Our results indicate that institutional support for CIGS is also minimal. American schools and educators are demonstrably not prepared to teach CIGS, while CIGS are not prepared to enter graduate school in a different language, culture, and education system. Family members and friends seem to be too far away to help supports CIGS' social and cultural adaptation. The SCC framework helped illuminate the difficulties and coping mechanisms of CIGS in U.S. schools. As shown in Figure 2, academic advisors and the students themselves are the major sources of SCC that benefit CIGS in adapting to U.S. education. Portes (1998) recommended that researchers who study SCC should distinguish the three aspects of the social capital concept: "(a) the possessors of social capital (those making claims); (b) the sources of social capital (those agreeing to these demands); (c) the resources themselves" (p. 6). We distinguish between the sources of SCC and resources (benefits) from them in Figure 2.

Cultural Capital	Major Sources of SCC	Resources of Social Captial
Embodied state via culture and self-cultivation; Institutionalized state: mostly refers to academic qualifications		

Mainstream (U.S.) cultural capital
Embedded state:
- Speaking culture
- Shame- and fear- avoid approach
- Success approach
Institutionalized state:
- A master's degree and certification
- A doctoral degree and certification

Non-mainstream cultural capital
Embedded state:
- Communication culture, e.g., unwilling to speak in class;
- A lack of the self-consciousness of safeguarding right by speaking;
- Active teaching and passive learning with no class discussions;
- Culture of shame

Academic adviser
(research committee members)
Major and even only source of SCC
Mentoring American cultural patterns;
providing connections of network;
offering career advice and
recommendations

Self
CIGS rely only on themselves to
overcome barriers and believe self-blame
leads to growth and perfection

Parents
Too far away to be helpful
Little possession of mainstream SCC as
residents in China

Friends
Least helpful to the accumulation of
mainstream SCC
No good friends who are Americans

Institution
A mixed influence on CIGS
Career services for non-citizens are
minimal

Relationship of social network
e.g., scholars in the same field

Conversion to economic capital
- Funding
- Internship
- Jobs

Conversion to cultural capital
- Academic publications;
- Learning American values and culture through expanded social network

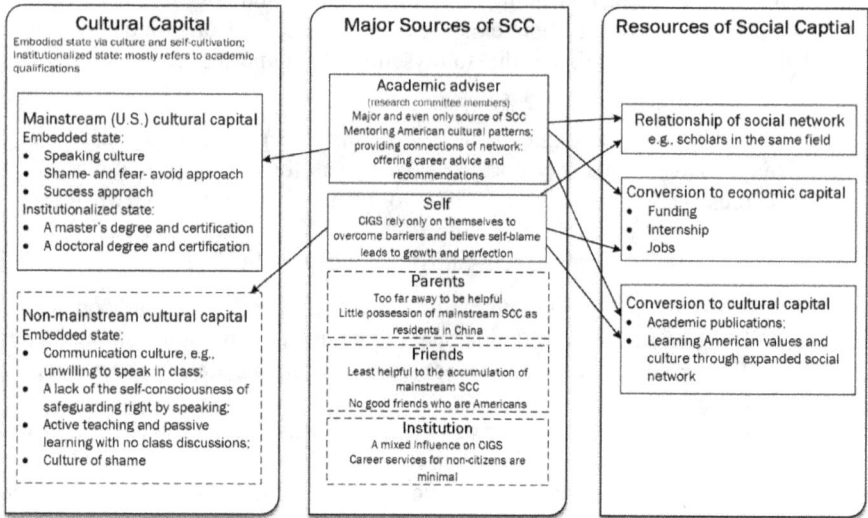

Figure 2: Taxonomy of Sources and Accumulation of SCC of CIGS

Note. The term Sources refers to the subjects that help CIGS to access more benefits; Resources refers to the benefits. Content in solid-lined boxes are positive sources and resources of CIGS in adapting to the U.S. education, while dashed boxed are negative or helpless sources and resources.

CIGS' fear of negative evaluations based on a less-developed foreign language contributed to the participants' fear of leaving a negative social impression, especially for graduate students, who are keenly aware of their social impression (MacIntyre & Gardner, 1989). Being a part of the American speaking culture is a piece of mainstream cultural capital that CIGS do not possess. The Chinese cultural tradition of speaking indirectly and amicably (Li, 2012) rather than speaking to the point and directly explains the difference in SCC. A significant learning tradition in China comes from the value demonstrated in the commonly used phrase, "Actions are better than words." Whether people choose to speak or keep silent carries significant cultural meaning. It would be an interesting avenue of future research to study whether American teachers who demonstrate sensitivity to the cultural values of CIGS find more success of CIGS in assisting their acculturation process in classes.

According to SCC theory as applied to our data, mainstream SCC refers to SCC accumulated in the United States about how to find, locate, or make economic resources. Warikoo and Carter (2009) argued that even though racial minority groups have access to their own forms of capital, their nondominant capital "funds" do not help them succeed in schools in the way that the mainstream capital does for the students who possess it. Mainstream capital prioritizes students who possess this particular kind of capital in negotiating the school environment, which is based on American middle-class culture, values, preferences, and ways of thinking (Lareau, 2003). When the capital that CIGS accumulated in their home country is not helpful in the adaptation process and they have limited access to the mainstream capital, it can be deleterious for CIGS, as having a sense of belonging is key to educational success for all students (Strayhorn, 2012). The huge shift of academic and social habitus, as well as a shift in social spaces (field) can be sensed but is often unconscious or invisible. These invisible challenges provide additional difficulty for CIGS as they struggle to adjust. Culture is an often an invisible, pervasive element of the environment, and it complicates CIGS' already difficult task of navigating their way in the American system and higher educational contexts.

Limitations

This study has limitations in several aspects. First, there is the possibility of response bias among interviewees, because interviewees may not have been willing to share all of their issues, problems, and deep feelings. Second, the SCC framework, though widely adapted in research for social justice and equity issues of marginalized groups, includes some vague definitions. For example, there is no established way to explain the exact content of cultural capital, and researchers may confuse the difference between sources, resources, and benefits of social capital (Portes, 2014). Our study serves as a careful attempt to develop the SCC concept and articulate the difference between sources, resources, and benefits. Third, due to the small sample size and the nature of our study, we cannot generalize the problems and possessions of capital from this sample to the whole population of CIGS. However, we did not intend to extrapolate our findings, because that is not the purpose of qualitative research, which is instead intended to describe in depth answers to research aims (Levitt et al., 2018). Further research can be conducted to establish a more systematic or generalizable interpretation of SCC and CIGS.

Implications

Our study has several implications. Currently, there is no existing research on the SCC of international students in the United States. Further studies in the area of international students' SCC may contribute to a deeper connection between CIGS' experience of support or lack of support and SCC manifestations. International students have diverse backgrounds and identities, and thus are valuable subjects to future research in the field of diversity and social justice. In practice, the themes present in these data provide insights about problems in international education, and our findings reveal how CIGS experience the lack of support for international students. This line of research can enhance mutual understanding between Americans and international students and may also contribute to reforming policies in order to better support education and career services for international students. Our findings suggest that getting to know international students' cultural styles and building connections with them first may be a pedagogical benefit. In the field of teaching and teacher education, this article can also be used as a reference for teachers, as a case for using culturally responsive teaching practices with international students (Gay, 2010). Further research conducted on supporting CIGS at different levels in institutions of higher education would greatly benefit students and universities alike.

Note

Appendices for this article can be found on the JIS website at https://www.ojed.org/index.php/jis

REFERENCES

Abbas, T. (2004). *The education of British South Asians: Ethnicity, capital and class structure*. Palgrave Macmillan.

Alharbi, E. S., & Smith, A. P. (2018). Review of the literature on stress and wellbeing of international students in English-speaking countries. *International Education Studies, 11*(6), 22–44. https://doi.org/10.5539/ies.v11n6p22

Bernstein, B. (2000). *Pedagogy, symbolic control and identity, theory research, critique*. Rowan & Littlefield.

Bourdieu, P. (1977). Cultural reproduction and social reproduction. In J. Karabel & A. H. Halsey (Eds.), *Power and ideology in education* (pp. 487–511). Oxford University Press.

Bourdieu, P. (1984). *Distinction: A social critique of the judgment of taste* (R. Nice, Trans.). Harvard University Press.

Bourdieu, P. (1986a). *The forms of capital.* In J. Richardson (Ed.), *Handbook of theory and research for the sociology of education* (pp. 241–258). Greenwood Press.

Bourdieu, P. (1986b). The production of belief: Contribution to an economy of symbolic goods. In R. Collins, J. Curran, N. Garnham, & P. Scannell (Eds.), *Media, culture and society: A critical reader* (pp. 131–163). SAGE.

Bourdieu, P. (1990). *The logic of practice*. Stanford University Press.

Bourdieu, P. (1991). *Language and symbolic power*. Harvard University Press.

Brantlinger, E. (2003). *Dividing classes: How the middle class negotiates and rationalizes school advantage*. Routledge.

Cao, L. L. (1997). *Dreams and dilemmas: Chinese female students' experiences of overseas education in the United States* [Unpublished doctoral dissertation]. Teachers College, Columbia University.

Cho, J., & Yu, H. (2015). Roles of university support for international students in the United States: Analysis of a systematic model of university identification, university support, and psychological well-being. *Journal of Studies in International Education, 19*(1), 11–27. https://doi.org/10.1177/1028315314533606

Davies, S., & Rizk, J. (2018). The three generations of cultural capital research: A narrative review. *Review of Educational Research, 88*(3), 331–365. https://doi.org/10.3102/0034654317748423

Dika, S. L., & Singh, K. (2002). Applications of social capital in educational literature: A critical synthesis. *Review of Educational Research, 72*(1), 31–60. https://doi.org/10.3102/00346543072001031

English, F. & Bolton, C. (Eds.). (2016). *Bourdieu for educators.* SAGE.

Gay, G. (2010). *Culturally responsive teaching* (2nd ed.). Teachers College Press.

Ge, L., Brown, D., & Durst, D. (2019). Chinese international students' experiences in a Canadian university. *Journal of International Students, 9*(2), 582–612.

Glass, C. R., & Gesing, P. (2018). The development of social capital through international students' involvement in campus organizations. *Journal of International Students, 8*(3), 1274–1292.

Gold, S. J. (2016). International students in the United States. *Society, 53*(5), 523–530.

Habu, T. (2000). The irony of globalization: The experience of Japanese women in British higher education. *Higher Education, 39*(1), 43–46.

Institute of International Education. (2018). International students 2017/18. *Open Doors Report on International Educational Exchange.* Retrieved March 01, 2019 from https://www.iie.org/opendoors

Institute of International Education. (2019). International students by academic level and places of origin 2016/17 - 2018/19. *Open Doors Report on International Educational Exchange.* Retrieved March 01, 2019 from https://www.iie.org/opendoors

Kuo, Y. H. (2011). Language challenges faced by international graduate students in the United States. *Journal of International Students, 1*(2), 38–42.

Lareau, A. (2003). *Unequal childhoods: Class, race, and family life.* University of California Press.

Lareau, A., & Horvat, E. M. (1999). Moments of social inclusion and exclusion: Race, class, and cultural capital in family-school relationships. *Sociology of Education, 72*(1), 37–53.

Lee, J. J., & Rice, C. (2007). Welcome to America? International student perceptions of discrimination. *Higher Education, 53*(3), 381–409. https://doi.org/10.1007/s10734-005-4508-3

Levitt, H. M., Motulsky, S. L., Wertz, F. J., Morrow, S. L., & Ponterotto, J. G. (2017). Recommendations for designing and reviewing qualitative research in psychology: Promoting methodological integrity. *Qualitative Psychology, 4*(1), 2–22.

Li, J. (2012). *Cultural foundations of learning: East and west.* Cambridge University Press.

Lin, S. Y., & Scherz, S. D. (2014). Challenges facing Asian international graduate students in the US: Pedagogical considerations in higher education. *Journal of International Students, 4*(1), 16–33.

Lincoln, Y. S., & Guba, E. (1985). *Naturalistic inquiry.* SAGE.

Liu, D., & Brown, B. B. (2014). Self-disclosure on social networking sites, positive feedback, and social capital among Chinese college students. *Computers in Human Behavior, 38,* 213–219.

MacIntyre, P. D., & Gardner, R. C. (1989). Anxiety and second language learning: Toward a theoretical clarification. *Language Learning, 39*(2), 251–275.

Marginson, S. (2014). Student self-formation in international education. *Journal of Studies in International Education, 18*(1), 6–22.

Marshall, C., & Rossman, G. B. (2016). *Designing qualitative research* (6th ed.). SAGE.

National Association of Foreign Student Advisers. (2019). *Economic value statistics.* https://www.nafsa.org/policy-and-advocacy/policy-resources/nafsa-international-student-economic-value-tool-v2#main-content

Portes, A. (1998). Social capital: Its origins and applications in modern sociology. *Annual Review of Sociology, 24,* 1–24.

Portes, A. (2014). Downsides of social capital. *Proceedings of the National Academy of Sciences of the United States of America, 111*(52), 18407–18408.

Saldaña, J. (2009). *The coding manual for qualitative researchers.* SAGE.

Sheng, X. (2012). Cultural capital and gender differences in parental involvement in children's schooling and higher education choice in China. *Gender and Education, 24*(2), 131–146.

Stanton-Salazar, R. D. (1997). A social capital framework for understanding the socialization of racial minority children and youths. *Harvard Educational Review, 67*(1), 1–40.

Strayhorn, T. L. (2012). *College students' sense of belonging: A key to educational success for all students.* Routledge.

Tran, L. T. (2016). Mobility as 'becoming': A Bourdieuian analysis of the factors shaping international student mobility. *British Journal of Sociology of Education,* 37(8), 1268–1289. https://doi.org/10.1080/01425692.2015.1044070

Warikoo, N., & Carter, P. (2009). Cultural explanations for racial and ethnic stratification in academic achievement: A call for a new and improved theory. *Review of Educational Research, 79*(1), 366–394.

Yin, R. K. (2017). *Case study research and applications: Design and methods.* SAGE.

Zhang-Wu, Q. (2018). Chinese international students' experiences in American higher education institutes: A critical review of the literature. *Journal of International Students, 8*(2), 1173–1197

XINXIN WANG, MPP, is a PhD candidate in the strand of Cultural Studies and Literacies at the School of Education, the University of North Carolina at Chapel Hill. Her research focuses on educational policy analysis, including areas of international and comparative education, higher education, critical multicultural education, and educational policies evaluation. Email: xxcheer@live.unc.edu

REBEKAH FREED, MA, is a PhD student in the Learning Sciences and Psychological Sciences program at UNC-Chapel Hill. Her current research interests include how students self regulate while learning about difficult topics. Email: rfreed@live.unc.edu

Peer-Reviewed Article

© *Journal of International Students*
Volume 11, Issue 1 (2021), pp. 60-80
ISSN: 2162-3104 (Print), 2166-3750 (Online)
doi: 10.32674/jis.v11i1.1670
ojed.org/jis

OJED
OPEN JOURNALS IN EDUCATION

The Touristudent: How International Academic Mobility Can Contribute to Tourism

Mateus José Alves Pinto
Eduardo Henrique Moscardi
Ewerton Lemos Gomes
Marcia Shizue Massukado Nakatani
Federal University of Paraná, Brazil

ABSTRACT

This research aims to analyze how the activities and motivations of international students resemble those of a tourist. The survey-based study of international students enrolled in academic mobility programs in Curitiba (Brazil) demonstrated that the main motivation for students to participate in international mobility relates more to personal motivation (i.e., cultural exchange) than to academic purposes. International students also acknowledged that they enjoyed the city's tourist attractions and overall services. The motivations for choosing Curitiba are mainly the quality of life and the perceived safety of the city. Based on how students visit attractions and utilize tourist services, we propose the idea of the touristudent. Understanding international students' motivations for mobility and their destination choice reinforces the significance that academic mobility programs have for tourism, and the implications of these findings are discussed for the tourism sector in Curitiba.

Keywords: Brazil, international academic mobility, international students, student mobility, touristudent, tourism

The number of international students in mobility doubled to reach 4,056,680 students from 2000 to 2013. One out five (850,000) are regionally mobile international students "who are seeking global education while staying close to their home country" (Choudaha, 2017, p. 830). According to the UNESCO Institute for Statistics (2020), the total outbound internationally mobile tertiary students studying abroad in 2017 was 5,309,240. Between 2012 and 2017, Brazil hosted 94,836 international students. These students accounted for 9.86% of all international mobility in Latin America and the Caribbean. Although not representative on a global scale (only 0.38% of all international students), those numbers are significant to the country, justifying the growing significance of international academic mobility (Krainski et al., 2019; Prolo et al., 2019; Soares et al., 2019; Taschetto & Rosa, 2019).

The largest inbound cohorts who enrolled in Brazilian institutions during 2016 came from Spanish- and Portuguese-speaking countries, and the top 10 source countries were: Colombia (10%); Peru (4%); Argentina, Angola, and Mexico (3% each); and Germany, Spain, Portugal, Bolivia, and Chile (2% each; Robles & Bhandari, 2018). However, little research has examined the factors that draw international students to Brazil's higher education institutions.

The Brazilian Ministry of Tourism (Ministério do Turismo [MTUR], 2010b) uses a wide range of terms synonymously to define travel with educational purposes: educational tourism, exchange tourism, scientific-educational tourism, university tourism, pedagogical tourism, scientific tourism, student tourism, and study tourism. Researchers, on the other hand, use the term academic tourism (Amaro et al., 2019; Bento, 2014; Rodríguez et al., 2012). According to the Brazilian Tourism Thesaurus (Rejowski, 2018), rather than academic tourism, "exchange tourism" relates more to sociocultural impacts and cultural exchange while traveling.

Since 2010, academic tourism has been a priority segment for Brazilian international tourism (MTUR, 2010a). It "consists of tourist movement generated by learning activities and programs and experiences for purposes of qualification, knowledge expansion and personal and professional development" (MTUR, 2010b, p. 15). Academic mobility programs are one of the main modalities for strengthening the internationalization process of universities around the world (de Oliveira & de Freitas, 2016) and are the most visible element of this process (Silva et al., 2013). Studying abroad is also an important element for knowledge transfer from destinations to places of origin, since, upon returning to their home institutions, the students bring with them information, practices, habits, and values that were acquired during their experience abroad (Coelli, 2014; Lombas, 2017; Sheller & Urry, 2006). Above all, leisure activities are not able to define all tourist motivations for travel, as tourism can manifest itself at different levels and for several reasons. Therefore, the present study fills this research gap by describing how the activities and motivations of students in international academic mobility resemble those of a tourist (Amaro et al., 2019; Jamaludin et al., 2018; Roberson, 2018).

Indeed, research on international students takes place from a myriad of academic fields and theoretical perspectives, including education, sociology, economy, migration studies, and other related disciplines. Therefore, one of the contributions of this article is to understand the international student also as a tourist—a touristudent—using a tourism perspective to analyze international academic mobility within a Brazilian destination. Through an empirical setting, we conducted a survey with international students enrolled in academic mobility programs in Curitiba, Brazil. In short, this article offers an understanding of the motivations that led students to participate in academic mobility and to choose Curitiba as their destination, along with the students' demographic information. Finally, we present practical implications of the touristudents' contribution to the tourism sector in Curitiba.

LITERATURE REVIEW

International Academic Mobility and Academic Tourism

The internationalization of higher education has been a subject in educational research (Dolby & Rahman, 2008), emerging as a separate field during recent decades (Bedenlier et al., 2017). Studies on the internationalization of higher education have had three phases. During the early years, studies focused on sociopolitical concerns such as policy analysis. Economic priorities then led studies from the 1990s to the early 2000s. International student migration has been a more in-depth field of migration studies since Lejeune's (2002) research. Finally, the focus changed to academic and sociocultural aspects of international education, such as international students' experiences at their destinations (Dolby & Rahman, 2008).

Understanding the changes in the student profile and needs, Choudaha (2017) analyzed the shifts in international academic mobility through the lens of three waves between 1999 and 2020. Wave I (1999–2006) had its origins in the search for highly qualified professionals (talents) focusing on science, technology, and engineering (or the actual STEM curriculum) to generate cutting edge research in the host institution. Wave II (2006–2013) began during the global financial crisis, which drove institutions' efforts to recruit international students who could afford to pay for their education. This fact also changed the demand for programs, which became concentrated in the business field. In its turn, Wave III (2013–2020) originated from demographic changes and the emergence of new destinations for international students, pointing an increased market share concurrence that drove institutions' innovation and new modes of programs, including transnational and online education (Choudaha, 2017). International students' displacement for academic purposes appears in Wave III including both short stays (meetings and visits at universities and participation in scientific events) and long stays (higher education courses and research training).

Given the scenario of international academic mobility, academic tourism is, in some ways, part of it, since the student or scholar moves from their home country to an international institution motivated by academic purposes (Mota, 2009). Rodríguez et al. (2012, p. 1583) suggested that academic tourism is "a distinct type of tourism that would include any stays in higher education institutions in places outside their [the students'] usual environment," so the student could complete degree-level studies or attend language courses organized by these institutions. Coelli (2014) identified three phases of academic tourism. The first is the pre-exchange phase when the student prepares for the trip. It includes, for example, decisions about which destination and university to go to, the application process, financial planning, visa issues, and still, the emotional mindset about traveling abroad. The second phase, named trans-exchange, is the period when the student enrolls and participates in the mobility program. The post-exchange is the moment of return. In this last phase, the students seek reintegration into their pre-exchange daily life, and the accumulated experience reveals a new role for them in their society of origin (Coelli, 2014).

To this end, the present study focuses on international students enrolled in higher education programs offered by universities located in Curitiba, Brazil. These students remain for a period that normally varies from 5 to 10 months (equivalent to an academic semester or year, respectively), and in other cases can include completing the full undergraduate, master's or doctoral degree in Brazil. Some universities in Curitiba also accept higher education students to attend language courses or internships or to participate in research projects. This research considers both undergraduate and graduate students as well as students coming to other programs as international academic mobility students, as they are in the university milieu.

International Academic Mobility in Brazil

The Brazilian National Education Plan, approved in 2014, has one strategy to consolidate programs, projects, and actions that aim to internationalize Brazilian research and graduate degrees (Nunes & Silva, 2018). Nunes and Silva (2018) stated that Brazilian higher education internationalization is "a goal to be pursued, with legal support, and not just an expectation" (p. 88). Nevertheless, the internationalization of Brazilian universities has proceeded slowly and, in general, has been concentrated in public universities (Silva et al., 2013). Conversely, the country has a strong tradition of domestic mobility due to its geographic dimensions and the lack of substantial investments in internationalization programs (Martinez, 2018).

In the past, Brazil has had significant programs for sending undergraduate students and scholars to renowned universities around the world. One example was Science without Borders (Ciência sem Fronteiras [CSF]), which existed between 2011 and 2014. However, even CSF received some criticism, mostly regarding its aims to qualify only professionals instead of developing research projects. Besides that, CSF reinforced the idea that only countries from the Northern Hemisphere hold knowledge and development, and therefore Brazilian students ought to study abroad (Martinez, 2018). According to Martinez (2018), this notion is common in higher education systems of Latin American countries. The internationalization of peripheral countries ends up fostering European and Anglo-Saxon universities and diminishing the attraction of more international scholars to study and conduct research within Latin America (Martinez, 2018; Silva et al., 2013).

This phenomenon contrasts with the reality of international academic mobility in Europe. The European Union (EU) has developed several programs to stimulate mobility inside the continent, mainly after the Bologna Process. One of the series of ministerial meetings and agreements between European countries was to improve the internationalization of European higher education and, thus, foster educational, professional, personal, and cultural exchange between the community's countries. Erasmus is the most widespread program of the EU. It started in 1987 and has already facilitated mobility experiences for approximately 3 million students among European universities (Lesjak et al., 2015).

The Erasmus program has made considerable contributions to students' individual, academic and professional development. Mizikaci and Arslan (2019) interviewed 12 students from public and private universities in Ankara (Turkey) who attended Erasmus between 2015 and 2017. They asked questions about the students' personal, professional, and academic development. On a personal level, this program supported the students' self-esteem, as well as facilitated the adaptation and development of social and leadership skills. Regarding professional development, the students identified that they had the opportunity to turn theoretical knowledge into practice, to learn new and different techniques, and to observe practice sessions from other disciplines. Lastly, one of the primary development areas of the program was academics, wherein the students mentioned acquiring new knowledge and skills, learning new concepts and research processes, and improving English language skills in their field of study and everyday life.

Hereupon, academic mobility does not exist only for study purposes. It also provides means for the student to know and experience the routine of another country (Tamião, 2010). Sebben (2009) claimed that if someone goes to study, work, and live daily life in another country, then this person is doing an exchange since the cultural exchange is the relationship between different people regardless of the activities performed by the individual. Therefore, exchange depends more on the willingness for intercultural learning than on the mere displacement of the individual (Sebben, 2009).

Motivations for International Academic Mobility

International academic mobility has three main motivations: professional, academic, and personal (Lesjak et al., 2015; de Oliveira & de Freitas, 2016; Silva et al., 2013). In a study with Brazilian and foreign undergraduate and graduate students and Brazilian university scholars, de Oliveira and de Freitas (2016) identified activities related to each of the motivations. The professional motivations include a drive to an international career, an easier transition into the labor market, a search for professional opportunities or professional enhancement, and an alternative to an internship experience. The academic motivations include improving language learning, upgrading curriculum, meeting mandatory requirements, and desiring to study at an internationally renowned university. Personal motivations focus on discovering another culture, achieving personal maturity, facing a personal challenge, getting to know oneself, broadening one's worldview, braving the new and the different, and for leisure, fun and travel purposes.

Lesjak et al. (2015) identified 14 motives for Erasmus students to participate in a mobility program, including professional, academic, and personal motivations. The motives for Erasmus students are: to improve my academic knowledge; make new contacts in the field of studies; receive academic support for my thesis; experience different educational system; meet requirements; have a semester away from home; improve a foreign language; learn about different cultures; enhance employment opportunities; meet new people; grow personally; experience European identity; experience something new; and take advantage of an Erasmus grant. The study also identified 12 motives for Erasmus students to choose the destination. The Erasmus motives for choosing a particular destination are: the popularity; richness in culture, arts, and history; event offerings; low cost; low tourist profile; ease of access; safeness and security; rich natural attractions and sights; interesting nightlife; familiar language and lifestyle; sustainable and ecological living opportunities; and high living standards. According to Lesjak et al. (2015), personal growth and entertainment were the main factors for a student to participate in the academic mobility program and to choose the destination.

In another study, Silva et al. (2013) conducted five in-depth interviews with foreign students from Germany, Austria, Chile, France, and The Netherlands all studying in Brazil. The authors identified that academic aspects, personal aspects, and the destination image are important factors for students to enroll in mobility programs. The cultural characteristics attributed to Brazil—friendliness, people festivities, pleasant weather, fun, and entertainment—all connect with personal motivations. Academic motivations were also intertwined with foreign students' knowledge about Brazilian universities since the interviewees mentioned that they had friends or colleagues who had attended the same university in Brazil. Another factor was the ease of mobility created by the agreements between home and destination universities, which facilitated student decision-making. Moreover, the researchers identified components of Brazil's destination image related to culture, people, and typical elements of the country in the interviewees' discourse. Based on these findings, international academic mobility should be associated with destination image, bearing in mind that "both academic mobility and destination country image also reflect on how each of these themes may be relevant to or influenced by the other" (Silva et al., 2013, p. 249).

The commonality in these studies is the cultural motivation to participate in international mobility programs (Sebben, 2009). In de Oliveira and de Freitas (2016) motivations mentioned included "know another culture" and "brave the new and the different." In Silva et al. (2013) when asked about how culture relates to the destination image, participants responded with reasons such as "friendliness and people festivities," "pleasant weather," and "fun and entertainment." The desire for cultural experiences also showed up in the Erasmus students' motivations such as their desire for "rich natural attractions and sights" and to "meet new people" (Lesjak et al., 2015).

Given these findings, motivations connected to vacation and travel (i.e., tourism) emerge as drivers for many students to pursue these programs. In research about motivation, expectation, and experience conducted by Salyers et al. (2015), "Some students discussed the value of gaining course credits while also having the opportunity to travel as a strong motivator" for global learning experiences (p. 372). This may benefit not only the creation of policies for academic mobility but also for tourism (Lesjak et al., 2015).

Research involving Erasmus students demonstrates the relation between international academic mobility and tourist activity (Amaro et al., 2019; Roberson, 2018). According to Amaro et al. (2019), the behavior of international students is similar to a leisure tourist. This fact is important to national and regional tourism authorities mostly because these Erasmus students usually travel to several tourist attractions within the country. During these trips, students' costs include accommodation, food, transportation, and souvenirs. It is worth noting that in Roberson's (2018) study of travel experiences, Erasmus participants identified themselves as budget travelers. Furthermore, many international students hosted friends and family for visits during their academic year in the host destination, and some also traveled back after the program ended (Amaro et al., 2019). Likewise, Jamaludin et al. (2018, p. 935) counted that "international students share similar characteristics with tourists" because the experiences with the destination will influence their destination loyalty, or the intention to return.

METHOD

This study adopted a descriptive approach to analyze the profile of international students enrolled in academic mobility programs in Curitiba, their motivations for mobility and destination choice. The review of literature on international academic mobility and academic tourism (Choudaha, 2017; Coelli, 2014; Dolby & Rahman, 2008; Rodríguez et al., 2012) and motivations for mobility (Amaro et al., 2019; de Oliveira & de Freitas, 2016; Lesjak et al., 2015; Silva et al., 2013) set up the analytical bases to understand international students' specificities and similarities to leisure tourists. This study is an exploratory effort to consider international students as tourists—therefore called touristudents—since an epistemological perspective of tourism (Panosso Netto, 2005; Triviños, 1987) can also enlighten the dynamics of international students, broadening its research scope.

Sample

The city of Curitiba, in the southern region of Brazil, is the capital of the state of Paraná. The city is considered a national and international reference in urban planning (De Bona et al., 2016), quality of life, innovation, and education (Fryszman et al., 2019). Nowadays, the city's technological park, industries, and start-up environment are the main forces regarding local efforts to develop Curitiba as a smart city (Instituto Municipal de Turismo de Curitiba [IMT], 2013). These elements created a socioeconomic environment that encouraged the IMT to come up with academic tourism as a target market segment, fostering Curitiba to become an "educating city." This visitor segmentation aims to integrate several initiatives related to education occurring independently in the city to make Curitiba a destination choice for international students.

The sample selection was based on accessibility and convenience (Pires et al., 2006; Veal, 2011) since one of the authors is a volunteer at the Exchange Students Network Association of Curitiba (REI Curitiba). REI Curitiba is a nonprofit civil association founded in 2012, whose mission is supporting and promoting cultural and educational integration for international students through projects and events during their stay in Curitiba (REI Curitiba, 2013).

The organization is a partner of the two largest universities in the city: Federal University of Paraná (UFPR) and Pontifical Catholic University of Paraná (PUC-PR). Besides, exchange students from other universities in Curitiba—the Federal Technological University of Paraná (UTFPR), Positivo University (UP), and FAE University Center—also connect with REI. Due to legal reasons, the higher education institutions do not give REI a list of exchange students who are coming to the city. Thus, international students get in touch with REI through suggestions of friends who have previously studied in Curitiba, by recommendations from the universities, or by searching and finding the organization on the internet.

Given this scenario, this sample does not comprehend all international students enrolled in academic mobility in the city, but instead those who were part of REI's social media groups. We published a survey questionnaire created with Google Forms on groups managed by REI Curitiba between 2011 and 2019 (nine groups on Facebook and one on WhatsApp). These groups include international students and local volunteers of the organization, with a total of 2,115 members.

Instrument

The questionnaire had 20 open-ended or multiple-choice questions divided into three sections. The first section collected students' demographic data: the year they came to Curitiba; which educational program they participated in; length of the program; main activities performed during mobility; which university they attended; major studied; if the student received a grant; home university; nationality; birth year; and gender.

The second section focused on motivations for academic mobility and destination choice (in this case the choice of Curitiba). Since international inbound mobility in Brazil proceeds slowly (Silva et al., 2013) and the geographic dimensions of the country allow different educational systems between universities (Martinez, 2018), we did not have a national parameter to measure the motivations. That is why we replicated the motivational statements from Lesjak et al.'s (2015) study (as detailed in the Literature Review), which derived from the Erasmus Student Network Survey 2010, a reference mobility program worldwide. The use of the same statements of the Erasmus (2010) survey for measuring motivation for mobility and destination choice reinforced the internal consistency of the questionnaire since an alternative way to minimize validity problems is to use previously documented measurement scales (Baker et al., 1994). We modified some statements, as the context of inquiry did not include Erasmus students. The motivation "experience European identity" was excluded and "take advantage of Erasmus grant" was replaced with "take advantage of a grant"; "very popular" with "it is a popular destination"; "easy accessible" with "easy access to and from other cities"; and "is sustainable and ecological" with "the city is sustainable and ecological."

The respondents rated the importance of 13 items for motivations for mobility and 12 items for destination choice, using a 5-point Likert scale (1 = *of little importance*; 5 = *very important*). Cronbach's alpha coefficient tested the internal consistency of the scale. The coefficient for motivations for mobility was (.88) for the 13 items and (.87) for the 12 items for destination choice motivations, which evidenced values above acceptable level (Hair et al., 2005). The questionnaire was available to respondents in Portuguese, Spanish, and English, so each participant could choose the language they felt most comfortable with to answer the questionnaire.

The last section inquired about the students' tourist experience in Curitiba. We asked which tourist attractions the students visited; the events they attended; which tourist services they used while they were in the city; and what was the first thing that came to their minds when they thought about Curitiba.

Data Analysis

We used Microsoft Excel and SPSS Statistics (Version 20) to analyze the data obtained with the questionnaires (available from April 26 to May 5, 2019). The tests indicated that the distribution of all the variables was not normal. Therefore, the use of nonparametric data analysis demonstrated the presence or absence of differences between groups.

RESULTS

The first section of the questionnaire shed some light on the characteristics of the international students who came to Curitiba between 2011 and 2019 (see Table 1). The sample comprised of 103 respondents. All of them were born between 1980 and 2000, with 61.17% females ($n = 63$), 38.83% males ($n = 40$), and a mean age of 25 years (range 19–39 years old). Although this gender representativeness does not confirm the Brazilian inbound internationally mobile students (in 2017 comprised of 43.7% females and 56.3% males; UNESCO, 2020), it is similar to the findings of Lesjak et al. (2015).

The main motivations considered to be "very important" to participate in international academic mobility were to grow personally, to learn about different cultures, to experience something new, to meet new people, and to improve a foreign language. The motive "it was compulsory" had the lowest value, which shows that international academic mobility programs are not usually mandatory activities in most universities' curriculum.

The Kruskal-Wallis test for independent samples indicated a statistically significant difference between males and females in two motivations for mobility: to have a semester away from home ($p = .016$) and to improve a foreign language ($p = .022$). The test also confirmed the existence of a statistically significant difference between European and Latin American students in one motivation for mobility: academic support to my thesis ($p = .039$). The mean score for respondents who came from Latin America was 2.51, whereas European respondents' mean score on the scale was 1.95.

Table 1: Participant Demographics

Demographic	n	%
Gender		
Female	63	61.17
Male	40	38.83
Home continent		
Europe	55	53.39
Latin America	42	40.77
North America	5	4.85
Africa	1	0.99
Program duration		
Up to one academic semester	69	67.00
Up to one academic year	17	16.50
More than one academic year	17	16.50
University in Curitiba		
UFPR	53	51.45
PUC-CR	39	37.86
UTFPR	6	5.82
UP	3	2.91
FAE	1	0.99
ILAPEO	1	0.99
Type of degree		
Bachelor's	67	65.04
Master's	25	24.27
PhD	2	1.95
Missing	9	8.73
Study topic (major)		
Business	15	13.51
Architecture and Urbanism	12	10.81
Engineering	12	10.81
Design	6	5.41
Sociology	6	5.41
Medicine	6	5.41
Other	46	41.44
Missing	8	7.20
Grants		
With scholarship	77	74.75
Without scholarship	26	25.55

Note. $N = 103$, except Study topic $N = 111$, due to multiple subjects. UFPR = Federal University of Paraná; PUC-CR = Pontifical Catholic University of Paraná; UTFPR = Federal Technological University of Paraná; UP = Positivo University; FAE = FAE University Center; ILAPEO = Latin American Institute for Dental Research and Teaching

Table 2: The Rankings, Means, and Standard Deviations for Motivations for Mobility ($N = 103$)

Motivation	M	SD
Grow personally	4.49	1.03
To learn about different cultures	4.44	1.00
Experience something new	4.41	1.10
Meet new people	4.31	1.10
Improve a foreign language	4.20	1.21
Experience a different educational system	3.95	1.31
To improve my academic knowledge	3.77	1.27
To have a semester away from home	3.66	1.47
New contacts in the field of studies	3.44	1.29
Enhance employment opportunities	3.37	1.42
Take advantage of a grant	2.79	1.65
Academic support for my thesis	2.33	1.40
Compulsory	1.82	1.16

Considering the type of degree, undergraduate students and master's students represented 89.31% of respondents, and the main purpose for mobility was the same for both groups: to grow personally (undergraduate's mean = 4.57 and for master's mean = 4.16). Opposite to what de Oliveira and de Freitas (2016) showed in their study, this research did not find significant discrepancies between the groups. The other four major motives for mobility were the same for both groups, although in different rankings: to learn about different cultures (second for undergraduates and third for master's students); to experience something new (third and fourth, respectively); to meet new people (fourth and fifth); and to improve a foreign language (fifth and second).

Further analysis between students coming from Europe and Latin America showed that for the Latin Americans, the motivation to improve academic knowledge equals the number of answers to improve a foreign language. Thus, due to cultural familiarity and idiomatic ease, it is possible to imply that Latin American students can focus more on academic studies.

Despite the differences between groups, the major motivations for international students to enroll in mobility and study abroad programs remain nonacademic. This acknowledges the finding of Lesjak et al. (2015) since motives related to personal growth and cultural exchange were also the main factors in the decision-making process for participating in international academic mobility among Erasmus students. It is worth noting that two participants spontaneously listed "party and travel" as their main activity during mobility!

The top five motivations for choosing Curitiba as a destination for mobility were the city's safety and security, high living standard, easy access to and from other cities, rich natural attractions and sights, and familiar language and lifestyle. The least important motivation was the city offering a lot of events.

Table 3: Rankings, Means, and Standard Deviations for the Motivations for Destination (N = 103)

Motivation	M	SD
Safe and secure	3.29	1.26
High living standard	3.23	1.37
Easy access to and from other cities	3.20	1.32
Rich natural attractions and sights	3.13	1.30
Familiar language and lifestyle	3.07	1.37
Not very expensive to live in	3.05	1.22
The city is sustainable and ecological	2.93	1.26
Rich in culture, arts, and history	2.84	1.30
Interesting nightlife	2.73	1.23
It's a popular destination	2.66	1.42
Yet to be discovered by tourists	2.60	1.29
Offers a lot of events	2.58	1.21

For destination choice motivations, the Kruskal-Wallis test for independent samples indicated a statistically significant difference between males and females in two destination choice motivations: safe and secure ($p = 0.042$) and sustainable and ecological ($p = 0.049$). The mean score for male respondents was 2.98 and 2.63, whereas female respondents' mean score on the scale was higher, respectively 3.49 and 3.13.

The test indicated no differences between European and Latin American students, although the ranking of motivations presented relevant divergences. For European students, elements such as security, quality of life, sustainability, and nature appear to be the most important reasons taken into account to select the destination. For Latin Americans, the ease of arriving in the city due to the proximity of the countries, familiar language, lifestyle, and the popularity of Curitiba were the most cited reasons to study in the city. These results show that criteria such as accessibility and adaptation are also essential for students. The main destination choice motivations are align with Curitiba's national and international reputation for the quality of life and urban planning (IMT, 2013).

The tourist attractions most visited by students were iconic landmarks of the city, with the botanical garden being the most visited attraction, followed by the city's municipal market, railway, Barigui Park, Oscar Niemeyer Museum, and Tiradentes Square. Even so, it was noticeable from the answers that the students still visited other parks, monuments, museums, and theaters, actively participating as tourists in Curitiba.

Unlike, the students did not attend city events frequently. Carnival was the most relevant event cited, in which 54 students participated, followed by Curitiba's birthday and the theater festival (with 37 students attending each), and the biennial of Curitiba and the cinema festival (22 students each). The low participation in the city's events agrees with the fact that the motivation "offers a lot of events" was the least important for the students when choosing the destination for international mobility.

International students may receive information about events when they are already in the city or they do not have any knowledge about the local calendar of events, therefore ending up not interested in enjoying these events. Entertainment and transportation services were the most used tourist services, while few students booked accommodation or hired a travel agency. Even the tourism bus line—one of the lead tourist products of Curitiba, which in 2018 had over 500,000 boardings (IMT, 2018)—had little demand. These may be the main differences found in the results between students and leisure tourists, showing that even though international students contribute to tourist activity in the destination, they also may require targeted promotional actions to influence their pretravel decision-making and satisfy their in-destination needs.

The results show similarities between leisure visitors and students, strengthening the argument that the international student is, in fact, a tourist (Amaro et al., 2019; Jamaludin et al., 2018; Roberson Jr., 2018). For Tamião (2010) the student "must firstly live as a resident of that country" (p. 5). However, the Brazilian Ministry of Tourism (MTUR, 2010b) states that incoming tourism operators, accommodation, food services, transportation services, and local entrepreneurs are responsible for complementing the offer of tourist services for international students.

Furthermore, the overall definition of tourist excludes certain travelers. This definition considers elements (such as the type of establishment or overnight spent) that answer mainly to economic needs and disregard the social and cultural characteristics of tourism. This ends up misrepresenting and reducing tourism to economic activity, creating a phenomenon distinct from what tourism truly is.

Seeking an understanding of what qualifies international students as tourists, the student enjoys the attractions and tourist services as well as the leisure tourist. Additionally, the motivations for the international student to undertake a mobility program have a strong relation to cultural exchange, also observed in the tourist definition. Although the students interact more often with locals and have more time to enjoy the city and try different experiences, they remain tourists. Therefore, they can be called touristudents, mainly because they do not have to stop being one to become another.

Practical Implications for the Tourism Sector in Curitiba

The student is a tourist who does not fit into tourist activity seasonality, as they live in the city during the academic year and return to their home country or continue traveling around the host country or region during vacations. For this reason, international students generate economic income in low tourist seasons, which may become a reason to draw them to the city. Curitiba's Tourism Institute indicates the possibility of "the creation of tourism products in the academic tourism segment" (IMT, 2013, p. 353). However, data shows that those actions are expendable and not profitable since the touristudent can enjoy the same products of other visitors' segments.

Touristudents are a business opportunity for travel agencies and tour operators, who can organize trips and sell products that suit students' specific needs (Amaro et al., 2019). Consequently, the city should improve some attractions, events, and services given singularities of the touristudents' behavior for them to better enjoy their experiences in the destination. One example found in this study was that the Cultural Foundation's events calendar, which is not widespread in the international students' community, does not have promotional actions in the pre-exchange period (Coelli, 2014) and is available only in Portuguese. Incoming travel agencies can prepare itineraries and specific trips so the students can get to know the regions around Curitiba. Tour operators can put together flight tickets, hotels, and tours to other Brazilian cities that might interest touristudents looking to make the most out of their experience in Brazil. Accommodation providers can coordinate with universities to give discounts and payment plans for the students when they arrive in the city and do not have a place to stay, or even when they host their family and friends who come to visit them. The tourism bus line may extend the 24-hour restriction of its boarding pass since the touristudent stays at least one academic semester in the city and can visit fewer known attractions in a broad range of time.

Additionally, Curitiba's Tourism Institute should know the motivations that lead students to participate in international mobility programs and to choose Curitiba, as tourist activity connects with motivations related to cultural exchange, to the abundance of natural resources, landscape, quality of life, and the accessible city location. Thus, and in partnership with universities, the institute has a substantial role in creating policies that foster academic mobility alongside tourism (Lesjak et al., 2015). However, the municipality does not have any demographic data about foreign students and does not conduct continuous surveys to identify these tourists. The lack of information about touristudents creates difficulties for improving actions to retain them and to help the internationalization of local universities.

Considering that one of the roles of a destination management organization is to collaborate with universities to better promote the destination (Amaro et al., 2019), IMT, together with other organizations that work with these students (i.e. REI Curitiba), may join forces with higher education institutions to increase the promotion of Curitiba as a destination for academic tourism. To outline this relationship and considering that international academic mobility and destination image cannot be dissociated (Silva et al., 2013), the questionnaire asked the respondents to write the first word that came to their minds when they thought about Curitiba. The word cloud (Figure 1) presents the results.

Figure 1: The Word Cloud of Curitiba's Image for International Students

The results show words related to tourist activity—parks, culture, nature, green, Botanical Garden, *Araucária* (type of tree endemic to the region of Curitiba), and XV Street. "Quality of life" and "safe" were motivations cited for destination choice, reinforcing the concept of Curitiba as a planned and developed city. The weather image of the city, the coldest capital of Brazil, appeared in the words rain, cold, and cloud. Some cultural aspects related also with the major motivations for mobility appear in words like exchange, friends, *curitibanos* (person born in Curitiba), family, life, and, mainly, *saudade* (feeling of missing someone or something).

CONCLUSION

This study aimed to examine international academic mobility in the city of Curitiba, Brazil, to understand international students' specificities and similarities to leisure tourists. The main contribution of the research is the idea of the touristudent, for the sake that being one (a student) does not exclude the other (a tourist) and showing that international academic mobility students have similar motivations and experience similar activities to leisure tourists. We found the major motivations for students to participate in international mobility programs were personal rather than academic. Personal motivations and cultural exchange have an important role in the students' decision-making process and the leisure activities experienced at the host destination. The results also point out that international students acknowledged that they enjoyed the city's tourist attractions and overall services.

Touristudents create a bond with their destination. They build relationships with the locals. They visit the attractions. They engage in the destination cultural scene. They carry the city with them when it is time to return home (Sheller & Urry, 2006). Even though learning is intrinsic to the very concept of academic mobility, both the literature and the results show that cultural, personal, and touristic motivations complement its definition. The students' motivations to participate in international academic mobility demonstrate that leisure activities can enrich their experience abroad beyond academic knowledge

The practical implications of how international mobility contributes to academic tourism in Curitiba were outlined. As some countries are concerned with mobility as a form of academic, cultural, and economic growth (Yu & Moskal, 2018), public administrations should gather data on inbound and outbound international students.

The touristudent is a real tourist and visitor segment for Curitiba, since it exists and renews itself semiannually following universities' calendars. However, Curitiba's Tourism Institute does not have enough information about the international student, impairing the improvement of actions that might satisfy this type of tourist. For this reason, the students' demographic profiles and motivations are important findings of this study, as they have the potential to point out the benefits of hosting international students and to show why the municipality should reinforce its efforts to promote and develop academic tourism in Curitiba.

Ultimately, we acknowledge the limitations of this research. Though the results may not be generalizable to all international students enrolled in academic mobility programs in Curitiba, they are likely to provide direction and insights for future researchers to build upon the impact of mobility programs in tourism. Moreover, further studies could focus on tourism organizations' perspectives on the impact of international students on local tourism, developing a stronger base for practitioners to improve tourism in destinations. In terms of theoretical foundations, new research on touristudents can also be conducted within the new mobilities paradigm (Hannam, 2009; Sheller & Urry, 2006) if taken into account that what characterizes academic tourism is the mobility itself—that is, the displacement of students and scholars to another country to gain further educational, professional, and personal deepening (Lombas, 2017). In sum, the understanding of international students' motivations for mobility and destination choice reinforces the significance that academic mobility programs have for tourism.

REFERENCES

Amaro, S., Barroco, C., Martins, C., & Antunes, J. (2019). Erasmus students in Portugal: From students to tourists and advocates. *European Journal of Tourism Research, 22,* 94–106.

Baker, K. G., Hozier, G. C., Jr., & Rogers, R. D. (1994). Marketing research theory and methodology and the tourism industry: A nontechnical discussion.

Journal of Travel Research, *32*(3), 3–7. https://doi.org/10.1177/004728759403200302

Bedenlier, S., Kondakci, Y., & Zawacki-Richter, O. (2017). Two decades of research into the internationalization of higher education: Major themes in the Journal of Studies in International Education (1997–2016). *Journal of Studies in International Education,* *22*(2), 108–135. https://doi.org/10.1177/1028315317710093

Bento, J. P. C. (2014). The determinants of international academic tourism demand in Europe. *Tourism Economics,* *20*(3), 611–628. https://doi.org/10.5367/te.2013.0293

Choudaha, R. (2017). Three waves of international student mobility (1999–2020). *Studies in Higher Education,* *42*(5), 825–832. https://doi.org/10.1080/03075079.2017.1293872

Coelli, T. (2014). Turismo de Estudos e Intercâmbio: Antes, Durante e Depois – Uma análise sobre ex-intercambistas da Universidade Federal de Juiz de Fora (Minas Gerais, Brasil) [Tourism Studies and Exchanges: Before, During and After – An analysis on former exchange students from Federal University of Juiz de Fora (Minas Gerais, Brazil)]. *Turismo & Sociedade, 7*(4), 733–754. http://dx.doi.org/10.5380/tes.v7i4.36677

De Bona, A. A., Fonseca, K. V. O., Rosa, M. O., Lüders, R., & Delgado, M. R. B. S. (2016). Analysis of public bus transportation of a Brazilian city based on the theory of complex networks using the p-space. *Mathematical Problems in Engineering, 2016,* 1–12. https://doi.org/10.1155/2016/3898762

de Oliveira, A. L., & de Freitas, M. E.. (2016). Motivações para mobilidade acadêmica internacional: A visão de alunos e professores universitários [Motivations for international academic mobility: The perspective of university students and professors]. *Educação em Revista, 32*(3), 217–246. http://dx.doi.org/10.1590/0102-4698148237

Dolby, N., & Rahman, A. (2008). Research in international education. *Review of Educational Research,* *78*(3), 676–726. https://doi.org/10.3102/0034654308320291

Erasmus Student Network. (2010). *ESNSurvey 2010: E-value-ate your exchange.* https://esn.org/ESNSurvey/2010

Fryszman, F., Carstens, D. D. S., & Da Cunha, S. K. (2019). Smart mobility transition: a socio-technical analysis in the city of Curitiba. *International Journal of Urban Sustainable Development, 11*(2), 141–153. https://doi.org/10.1080/19463138.2019.1630414

Hair, J. F., Black, W. C., Babin, B. J., Anderson, R. E., & Tatham, R. L. (2005). *Análise multivariada de dados [Multivariate data analysis].* Bookman.

Hannam, K. (2009). *The end of tourism? Nomadology and the mobilities paradigm.* In J. Tribe (Ed.), *Philosophical issues in tourism* (pp. 101–113). Channel View Publications.

Instituto Municipal de Turismo de Curitiba. (2013). *Plano de desenvolvimento integrado do turismo sustentável [Integrated development plan for sustainable tourism].* http://multimidia.turismo.curitiba.pr.gov.br/2015/3/pdf/00000485.pdf

Instituto Municipal de Turismo de Curitiba. (2018). *Perfil do turista da Linha Turismo* [*Tourism line tourists' pofile*]. http://multimidia.turismo.curitiba.pr.gov.br/2019/3/pdf/00003118.pdf

Jamaludin, N. L., Sam, D. L., Sandal, G. M., & Adam, A. A. (2018). The influence of perceived discrimination, orientation to mainstream culture and life satisfaction on destination loyalty intentions: The case of international students. *Current Issues in Tourism, 21*(8), 934–949. https://doi.org/10.1080/13683500.2015.1119102

Krainski, L. B., Schimanski, É. & Schimaleski, A. B. C. (2019). Internacionalização da educação superior: Estratégias institucionais na valorização da mobilidade acadêmica [Internationalization of higher education: Institutional strategies in the valuation of academic mobility]. *Proceedings of Encontro Internacional de Política Social, Vitória-ES, 7*, 1–14. http://periodicos.ufes.br/einps/article/view/25351

Lejeune, M. (2002). *Student mobility and narrative in Europe.* Routledge.

Lesjak, M., Juvan, E., Ineson, E. M., Yap, M. H. T., & Axelsson, E. P. (2015). Erasmus student motivation: Why and where to go? *Higher Education, 70*(5), 845–865. https://doi.org/10.1007/s10734-015-9871-0

Lombas, M. L. de S. (2017). A mobilidade internacional acadêmica: características dos percursos de pesquisadores brasileiros [The international academic mobility: Characteristics of Brazilian researchers' paths]. *Sociologias, 19*(44), 308–333. http://dx.doi.org/10.1590/15174522-019004413

Martinez, C. A. F. (2018). Geografias da mobilidade acadêmica internacional brasileira (ou por que a internacionalização da educação superior é um problema geográfico?) [Geographies of Brazilian international academic mobility (or why is the internationalization of higher education a geographic problem?)]. *Terra livre, 1*(50), 13–33. https://www.agb.org.br/publicacoes/index.php/terralivre/article/view/1433/1385

Ministério do Turismo. (2010a). *Segmentação do turismo e o mercado* [*Tourism segmentation and the market*]. Ministério do Turismo. http://www.turismo.gov.br/sites/default/turismo/o_ministerio/publicacoes/downloads_publicacoes/Segmentaxo_do_Mercado_Versxo_Final_IMPRESSxO_.pdf

Ministério do Turismo. (2010b). *Turismo de estudos e intercâmbio: Orientações básicas* [*Study and exchange tourism: Basic guidelines*]. Ministério do Turismo. http://www.turismo.gov.br/sites/default/turismo/o_ministerio/publicacoes/downloads_publicacoes/Turismo_de_Estudos_e_Intercxmbio_Versxo_Final_IMPRESSxO_.pdf

Mizikaci, F., & Arslan, Z. U. (2019). A European perspective in academic mobility. *Journal of International Students, 9*(2), 705–726. https://doi.org/10.32674/jis.v9i2.1138

Mota, K. C. N. (2009). Turismo de intercâmbio [Exchange tourism]. In A. Panosso Netto & M. G. dos R. Ansarah (Eds.), *Segmentação do mercado* turístico: Estudos, produtos e perspectivas [*Tourism market segmentation: Studies, products and perspectives*] (pp. 389–406). Manole.

Nunes, F. W. B., & Silva, I. S. R. (2018). Ações de treinamento e desenvolvimento de pessoal com foco na internacionalização: Um estudo nas universidades públicas federais brasileiras [Training and personnel development actions with a focus on internationalization: A study in the Brazilian federal public universities]. *Gestão Universitária na América Latina, 11*(4), 82–99. https://doi.org/10.5007/1983-4535.2018v11n4p82

Panosso Netto, A. (2005). *Filosofia do turismo: Teoria e epistemologia* [*Tourism philosophy: Theory and epistemology*]. Aleph.

Pires, N. C. M., Arantes, E. C., Silva, W. V., & Kato, H. T. (2006). Diferenças e semelhanças nos métodos de amostragem de pesquisas Top of Mind: Um estudo comparativo [Differences and similarities among sampling methods in Top of Mind research: A comparative study]. *RBGN, 8*(22), 37–45. https://rbgn.fecap.br/RBGN/article/view/67/61

Prolo, I., Vieira, R. C., Lima, M. C. & Leal, F. G. (2019). Internacionalização das Universidades Brasileiras - Contribuições do Programa Ciência sem Fronteiras [The internationalisation of Brazilian universities: Contributions of the 'Science Without Borders' programme]. *Administração: Ensino e Pesquisa* (*RAEP*), *20*(2), 1–27. https://doi.org/10.13058/raep.2019.v20n2.1330

REI Curitiba. (2013). *Estatuto Social* [*Social Statute*].

Rejowski, M. (2018). *Tesauro brasileiro de turismo* [*Brazilian tourism thesaurus*]. ECA-USP. http://www.livrosabertos.sibi.usp.br/portaldelivrosUSP/catalog/view/208/187/876-1

Roberson, D. N., Jr. (2018). Learning while traveling: The school of travel. *Journal of Hospitality, Leisure, Sport & Tourism Education, 22,* 14–18. https://doi.org/10.1016/j.jhlste.2017.11.001

Robles, C., & Bhandari, R. (2018). *Expanding vistas - International academic mobility in Brazil.* IEE Center for Academic Mobility Research and Impact. https://www.iie.org/Research-and-Insights/Publications/Expanding-Vistas

Rodríguez, X. A., Martínez-Roget, F., & Pawlowska, E. (2012). Academic tourism demand in Galicia, Spain. *Tourism Management, 33*(6), 1583–1590. https://doi.org/10.1016/j.tourman.2012.01.010

Salyers, V., Carston, C. S., Dean, Y., & London, C. (2015). Exploring the motivations, expectations, and experiences of students who study in global settings. *Journal of International Students, 5*(4), 368–382.

Sebben, A. S. (2009). *Intercâmbio cultural: Para entender e se apaixonar* [*Cultural exchange: To understand and fall in love*]. Artes e Ofícios.

Sheller, M., & Urry, J. (2006). The new mobilities paradigm. *Environment and Planning A, 38,* 207–226. https://doi.org/10.1068/a37268

Silva, C. C. dos S., Lima, M. C., & Riegel, V. (2013). Os fatores de motivação na definição de estudantes estrangeiros em mobilidade acadêmica internacional no Brasil [Motivation factors of the definition of foreign students in international academic mobility in Brazil]. *Gestão Universitária na América Latina, 6*(3), 232–251. http://dx.doi.org/10.5007/1983-4535.2013v6n3p232

Soares, C. C., de Lucena-Neto, C. S., & Onofre, E. G. (2019). O processo de internacionalização de instituição superior: Universidade Estadual da Paraíba em foco [The internationalization process of the higher education institution: Paraíba State University in focus]. *Research, Society and Development, 9*(2), 1–22. http://dx.doi.org/10.33448/rsd-v9i2.1887

Tamião, T. S. (2010). *Revisão da literatura sobre intercâmbio cultural estudantil: renovação das práticas turísticas* [Literature review on student cultural exchange: Renewal of tourist practices]. *Proceedings of Seminário de Pesquisa em Turismo do Mercosul, Caxias do Sul, 6*, 1806-0447. Retrieved from https://www.ucs.br/ucs/eventos/seminarios_semintur/semin_tur_6/arquivos/02/Revisao%20da%20literatura%20sobre%20intercambio%20cultural%20estudantil%20renovacao%20das%20praticas%20turisticas.pdf

Taschetto, L. R., & Rosa, G. C. (2019). Mobilidade acadêmica internacional: Caminhos para vínculos transculturais [International academic mobility: Pathways for transcultural connections]. *Textura, 21*(47), 300–319. https://doi.org/10.17648/textura-2358-0801-21-47-4783

Triviños, A. (1987). *Introdução à pesquisa em ciências sociais: A pesquisa qualitativa em educação* [*Introduction to social science research: Qualitative research in education*]. Atlas.

UNESCO. (2020). *UIS Statistics.* Retrieved January 20, 2020, from http://data.uis.unesco.org/

Veal, A. J. (2011). *Metodologia da pesquisa em lazer e turismo* [*Research methods for leisure and tourism*]. Aleph.

Yu, Y., & Moskal, M. (2018). Missing intercultural engagements in the university experiences of Chinese international students in the UK. *Compare: A Journal of Comparative and International Education, 49*(4), 654–671. https://doi.org/10.1080/03057925.2018.1448259

MATEUS JOSÉ ALVES PINTO, BA, is a master's student and researcher in the Department of Tourism at the Federal University of Paraná. His major research interests lie in the areas of higher education in tourism, information and communication technologies, tourist information, smart tourism destinations, and tourism communication. Email: mateusjose.trilhas@gmail.com

EDUARDO HENRIQUE MOSCARDI, BA, is a master's student and researcher in the Department of Tourism at the Federal University of Paraná. His major research interests lie in the areas of tourist information, research methods, tourism communication, destination marketing, and information and communication technologies. Email: moscardi.eduardo@gmail.com

EWERTON LEMOS GOMES, MSc, is a researcher in the Department of Tourism at the Federal University of Paraná. His major research interests lie in the areas of tourism communication, tourism semiotics, smart tourism destinations, tourism marketing, and destination image. Email: ewertonlegomes@gmail.com

MARCIA SHIZUE MASSUKADO NAKATANI, PhD, is a professor and researcher in the Department of Tourism at the Federal University of Paraná. Her major research interests lie in the areas of methodologies and knowledge construction in tourism, tourism communication and information, and higher education in tourism. Email: marcia.nakatani@ufpr.br

Peer-Reviewed Article

© *Journal of International Students*
Volume 11, Issue 1 (2021), pp. 81-102
ISSN: 2162-3104 (Print), 2166-3750 (Online)
doi: 10.32674/jis.v11i1.1618
ojed.org/jis

OJED
OPEN JOURNALS IN EDUCATION

American Undergraduate Students' Experiences in Conversational Partnerships with Chinese International Students

Takahiro Sato
University of Tsukuba, Japan

Ryan Miller
Kent State University, USA

ABSTRACT

The purpose of the current study was to describe American domestic students' experiences interacting with international students in a conversation partner program at an American university. This study used in-depth, semi-structured interviews grounded in positioning theory. Seven American students (three men and four women) participated. They served as conversation partners of Chinese international exchange students every fall semester. Four major interrelated themes emerged from the data. They were (a) seeking strategies for overcoming intercultural communication challenges, (b) addressing challenges for explaining sarcasm concepts, (c) finding mutual hobbies and interests, and (d) integrating field trips into the conversational program. This study encourages academic departments and faculty to develop a study group of conversational partnerships associated with value, origins, languages, and cultures of international students. This will contribute to a greater appreciation of the richness of diversity and to meaningful academic and social experiences at American universities for all students.

Keywords: conversational partnerships, international students, positioning, sarcasm language

81

INTRODUCTION

International students increasingly play an important role in the vibrant diversity of college and university campuses in the United States (Sato & Hodge, 2015a). According to the *Open Doors Report on International Exchange* (Institute of International Education, 2019), over 1 million international students are enrolled in American colleges and universities, and international students contribute over $44 billion to the U.S. economy through tuition, room and board, and other expenses. More specifically, students from China are the largest group of international students, with nearly 370,000 Chinese undergraduate and graduate students studying in U.S. higher education during the 2018–2019 academic year, representing over a third of all international students in the United States (Institute of International Education, 2019).

Although there are many social and academic benefits of campus internationalization that are facilitated by interaction between international and domestic students (Welikala & Watkins, 2008), several researchers have reported a number of challenges in facilitating this interaction. American students may harbor negative stereotypes, which may result in social avoidance (Arkoudis et al., 2012; Spencer-Rodgers, 2001). American domestic students have been found to perceive international students as maladjusted, naive, and confused about American customs, social practices, and the U.S. educational system (Leong & Chou, 1996). Language and cultural barriers can lead to interaction challenges and to the perception by domestic students that international students are socially inhibited, withdrawn, or insular (Pedersen, 1991). Moreover, international students' friendship patterns may contribute to American students' perceptions of international students as cold, distant, and clannish (Pedersen, 1991).

Wilson (1993) suggested that students benefit from conversational partnership programs that help both American and international students gain substantive knowledge and perceptual understanding of a global perspective and develop interpersonal relationships. Through such programs, American students can also expand their cultural knowledge and development of intercultural relationships. The purpose of conversational partnership programs is to pair students and ask them to meet weekly within the academic year to discuss communication concepts and other topics of mutual interest (Wilson, 1993). Much of the previous research on conversation partner programs has focused on the experiences of international students or language learners (e.g., Abe et al., 1998; Nishioka, 2014; Ursell, 2014), rather than the experiences of domestic students. However, the experiences of international and domestic students in conversation partner programs can be quite different. For example, E. J. Lee (2016) found that international students benefitted from a conversation partner program in terms of linguistic development, while domestic students benefitted in terms of cultural exchange. Other research on conversation partner programs has focused on ways to help international students understand American universities (e.g., Chang, 2011) or to structure and facilitate conversation partner programs (e.g., Aaron et al., 2018; Geary, 2016; Spitzman & Waugh, 2018; Thomas et al., 2018). Little research has focused specifically on describing and explaining

American domestic students' experiences in conversation partner programs with Chinese international students. Examining the experiences of American domestic students is an important endeavor in a time of increasing international student diversity at U.S. educational institutions to better understand and improve their experiences as academic supporters. The purpose of the current study was to describe and explain American domestic students' experiences interacting with nonnative English-speaking international students as part of a conversational partnership at an American university. Two research questions guided this study: (a) How interested are American students in learning and understanding the ways international students think, behave, and speak? (b) How do American students overcome challenges in communication with international students during conversation?

LITERATURE REVIEW

Research on American students' stereotypes of Chinese international students specifically has shown that American students may perceive Chinese international students as having poor English-speaking skills, only being friends with Chinese students, not being interested in American culture, being socially awkward, and being either quiet and shy or loud and annoying (Ruble & Zhang, 2013). While these are stereotypes (rather than factual truth), they may nonetheless create challenges in communication between American domestic students and Chinese international students. These challenges exist despite the fact that international students generally, and Chinese students specifically, are highly talented individuals who are hardworking, intelligent, determined, and eager to learn from their experiences in the United States (Leong & Chou, 1996; Spencer-Rodgers, 2001).

Several studies have focused on social interaction between international and domestic students as an important arena for developing students' cognitive abilities (Ryan & Hellmundt, 2005; Sheets, 2005) and creating opportunities for learning (Ryan & Viete, 2009). Through interactions with people from different linguistic and cultural backgrounds, people realize how their own perceptions, assumptions, values, and general understanding of the world differ from those of others (Arkoudis et al., 2012). Luo and Jamieson-Drake (2013) conducted a survey of 5,676 alumni of four American universities to investigate the influence of interaction with international students on college outcomes among domestic students. They found that American students who engaged with international students, in any format, were more likely to question their own beliefs and values, and that such questioning was related to greater skill development, intellectual development, and leadership skills. In a study of a peer-mentoring program, Geelhoed et al. (2003) found domestic students who interacted with international students showed increased cross-cultural awareness and sensitivity.

A number of studies have made recommendations about how to best facilitate interaction between international and domestic students. Thomas et al. (2018) found leveraging common ground (e.g., cultural celebrations, faith, common experiences, challenges) can lead to positive outcomes when it comes to mutual interaction and cross-cultural learning. Aaron et al. (2018) presented recommendations for student-coordinated conversation partner programs. They suggested recruiting domestic students from student leadership organizations, developing a partner-matching program, and offering certificates of ambassadorship to domestic and international students (who attended at least four sessions). Through these experiences, their conversation partnership program promoted student-centered learning that encouraged positive changes in domestic and international students' communication skills, cultural knowledge, and relationship development (Aaron et al., 2018).

In the past decade, there has been an increase in studies that explored Chinese international students' acculturative patterns (e.g., Cheng & Erben, 2012), cross-cultural experiences of Chinese international students who studied in the United S (e.g., Batterton & Horner, 2016; J. J. Lee & Rice, 2007), and media and internet usage and habits in the United States (Li & Chen, 2014). These studies have explained various types of academic and social challenges, culture shock, and adjustments during study abroad. In a synthesis of research on Chinese international students' experiences in American institutions of higher education, Zhang-Wu (2018) found that the experiences of Chinese international students may be different from those of other students.

Particularly relevant to the present study are culturally based communication patterns that may affect communication between American and Chinese students. The United States has been described as a "low-context" culture, while China is considered a "high-context" culture (D. Kim et al., 1998). In a low-context culture, communication between people is made more explicit and nonpersonal, new information is more easily introduced, and confrontation and open disagreement is more acceptable. In a high-context culture, on the other hand, communication depends more on the physical or social context, and less information is conveyed in the verbalized portion of the message. In high context cultures, such as China, direct confrontation is avoided in order to maintain social harmony and to save face, leading to more indirect communication (D. Kim et al., 1998).

CONCEPTUAL FRAMEWORK

The current study was grounded in positioning theory (Harré & van Langenhove, 1999). This is a theory of social behavior that explains the fluid patterns of dynamic and changing rights and duties among groups of social actors (Varela & Harré, 1996). The term "positioning" means to analyze interpersonal encounters from a discursive viewpoint (Hollway, 1984). This framework allows researchers to explore the capacity of American conversation partners to position themselves and, in this case, to describe how they negotiate and implement English-speaking practices with international university students who use English as a second language. Relationships with international university students are operationalized in the current study as getting along well with and being liked by their peers. High quality interactions with peers are associated with both academic and nonacademic outcomes among college students (Hamm & Zhang, 2010; Ladd et al., 2009), including engagement (Buhs, 2005), perceived communication competence (Buhs, 2005), and social support. Positioning theory helps us better understand and explain what American conversation partners might or might not do based on their experiences, which influences their thoughts, feelings, and perceptions about interacting with international students.

One perspective of positioning theory is intentional self-positioning, which incorporates both a conceptual repertoire and a location for persons within the structure of rights and duties (Yoon, 2008). Hermans (2001) identified two factors that affect an individual's position to manage the environment and time—that is, internal and external factors of self-positioning. An internal factor refers to a position within the inner group that the individual feels is part of themselves (e.g., I as a native speaker, I as an American). An external factor refers to a position within the outer group (e.g., my group of international students). Both internal and external factors are considered self-positions, because they are part of a self that is intrinsically or extrinsically extended to the group environment and culture that responds to individual experiences in the environment that is perceived as 'mine' (Hermans, 2001). Self-positions identify the complex shifts between internal and external factors that help to describe an individual's professionalism, social behaviors, and challenges in a variety of meanings in interaction (Hermans, 2001).

Davies and Harré (1990) used the term "reflective positioning," which is useful in explaining how American conversation partners position their own roles as conversational mentors. The term "reflexivity" refers to how conversation partners critically monitor and understand the role of the self in interactions. Reflective positioning is closely related to the personal interpretative framework (in particular, conversational task perception) or the normative assumptions about good communication that are the basis on which individuals ground their decisions for actions in particular situations (Vanassche & Kelchtermans, 2014). Conversation partners' reflective positions shape how they perform their roles, responsibilities, and duties (Yoon, 2008). For example, the conversation partners might use patterns of reflection that negotiate themselves and international students in their conversation sessions (Jones, 1997). Because conversation partners participate in diverse discourses, they must combine different positions (e.g., roles as friends, facilitators, mentors, or helpers; Jones, 1997). Although they might consciously understand that they play various roles when working with international students, the domestic students might unintentionally position such students as powerless learners in isolated spaces, which can lead to negative consequences such as marginalizing (Yoon, 2008). Jones (1997) explained that it is important that conversation partners analyze and reflect on their own disposition as opposed to or aligned with other positioning in conversation sessions.

Conversation partners' reflexivity is determined by "indexing one's statements with the point of view one has on its relevant world" (Harré & van Langenhove, 1999, p. 62). This means that conversation partners' experiences and backgrounds influence their positioning (beliefs, thoughts, judgments), and in turn, their actions (Yoon, 2008). According to Davies and Harré (1990), interactive positioning is "how one person positions another" (p. 48).

Conversation partners' positioning limits or extends what they can inhibit or provide in terms of speaking forms and actions (Harré & van Langenhove, 1999). Interactive positioning helps to identify conversation partners' self- and other-discourse based on interaction among the partners themselves and international students of diverse backgrounds. Andreouli (2010) asserted that an interactive position emphasizes the other as an integral part of the positioning process. Individuals jointly (re)produce relational meanings so that they may see the world from one position, such as using metaphors, storylines, and concepts that may or may not be relevant to others within the self–other discourse. It explains conversation partners' decision-making about social support, communication styles, and conversation content that positively or negatively influence interactive positions for international students. Interactive positioning helps to identify hierarchical interactions among conflicting values or norms on the part of the college student(s) with and without language barriers. In fact, a conversation partner might reject or accept international students as a function of their positioning (Harré & Moghaddam, 2003). Some conversation partners are not aware of how to support international students of diverse backgrounds. Rose-Redwood and Rose-Redwood (2018) and Thomas et al. (2018) discussed that if domestic students (non conversation partners) only interact with local peers, this isolation must have the effect of limiting cultural literacy as well as diminishing their ability to socially interact with peers from diverse cultural backgrounds in different geographical contexts. Positioning theory is, therefore, a powerful lens to examine how conversation partners position themselves and are positioned in cross-cultural interaction contexts.

METHOD

Research Design

The research method involved a descriptive qualitative approach using in-depth, semi-structured interviews (Seidman, 1998). The aim of the interviewing method was to solicit students' perspectives about their conversation experiences and to unpack the meaning they ascribed to those experiences. Interviewing is a powerful way to gain insight into the educational and social phenomena experienced by individuals in higher education contexts (Seidman, 1998). Interviews are unique as they allow the researcher "to acquire data not obtainable in any other way" (Gay, 1996, p. 223). In line with that logic, the interviewing method is appropriate for exploring American students' conversational partnership experiences with Chinese international students.

Research Site

One flagship university, Midwestern University (pseudonym), was the site for this study. We chose this site because there is a large international student population in both year- and semester-long academic exchange programs within undergraduate programs. The rationale was to include participants from Midwestern University in the accessible geographical region.

Participants and Sampling

We used a nomination process (Yin, 2003) to identify participants. It consisted of collecting relevant information about the American conversation partners of international students. The selection of participants involved contacting the university's international education office for nomination of American students matching the selection protocol criteria. The first selection criterion was that all American students must serve as an English-speaking conversation partner of international students, and the second was that they must meet international students and exchange conversations on a weekly basis. In this study, participants were recruited by the lead researcher during the spring semester of 2019. The study was approved by the lead researcher's university's Institutional Review Board. We contact American undergraduate students via email to ask for participants. In this study, we sought prospective participants who agreed to participate and complete two interview sessions during the spring 2019 semester. Seven participants provided permission to use interview data from this study.

Table 1: Participant Demographics

Student	Age	Gender	Years in the conversation program	Academic major
Chuck	22	Male	2	Mathematics
Heather	22	Female	3	Journalism
Izzy	22	Female	2	Art
Kyle	22	Male	2	Accounting
Lisa	20	Female	1	International Studies
Mary Beth	20	Female	2	English
Ronnie	21	Male	1	Computer Science

Note. All participants were Caucasian and native English speakers.

The participants were seven American undergraduate students (three men and four women) at Midwestern University. All seven participants were born and raised in the Midwest region of the United States. We used pseudonyms to protect the identities of participants. The participants served as conversation partners of Chinese international exchange students every fall semester. Approximately 30 to 40 Chinese international exchange students participated in English as a second language programs and registered for a few academic major courses each fall semester. Each conversation partner was assigned to meet a few Chinese students as one group on a weekly basis. Two participants (Kyle and Chuck) subsequently traveled and participated in a summer program at the Chinese university where their Chinese international exchange student partners attended.

We purposefully sampled participants using maximum variation sampling (Patton, 2002). All participants were undergraduate students with varying academic status (sophomore through senior), age, gender, location, and types of high schools they had attended, and academic majors (see Table 1).

Data Collection

Face-to-Face Open-Ended Interviews

According to Yin (2003), researchers have two jobs in conducting interviews: (a) to follow the interview protocol, and (b) to ask the researcher's actual (conversational) questions. The interviewing researcher asked participants open-ended questions about factual information as well as their opinions about people, places, and events related to the conversation partnership program. Interviews were face-to-face and lasted approximately 60–90 min. Interviews remained open-ended and assumed a conversational tone. We adapted the interview questions from those in Lewis et al. (2004) and by Sato and Hodge (2009), as their interview questions were well designed to include theoretical framework and research questions. Examples of interview questions included: (a) How have your experiences in communicating with Chinese international students in conversational sessions changed over time? (b) What are the challenges of speaking with Chinese international students in your conversation sessions? Did you use any techniques or strategies for overcoming these challenges? (c) In what ways could your friends or professors (e.g., language faculty) serve your needs and help solve issues and concerns you are facing in communicating Chinese international students in conversational sessions? For this study, we modified specific questions and carefully worded them so as to be relevant to the current investigation of undergraduate students in conversation partnership programs.

Trustworthiness

Member checking and peer debriefing established trustworthiness. We used member checking to reduce the impact of subjective bias (Patton, 2002). We mailed participants copies of the interview transcripts and themes. Their acknowledgment of the accuracy of the transcripts and of our interpretations of the data ensured that trustworthiness was established (Merriam, 1998). Peer debriefing is a process of exposing oneself to a knowledgeable peer in a manner paralleling an analytic session, with the purpose of exploring aspects of inquiry that might remain only implicit in the inquirer's mind (Patton, 2002). For this study, two professional colleagues who have expertise in qualitative research agreed to serve as peer debriefers. They deemed the interpretations of the data to be accurate and representative of the participants' statements.

Data Analysis

We used a constant comparative method (Boeije, 2010) to interpret the data. The basic strategy of this analytical process is to constantly compare pieces of data while inductively deriving meaning or themes. More specifically, we independently coded the transcripts for themes and then discussed differences until we reached agreement. In addition, two peer debriefers reviewed the codes to avoid potential researcher bias. We compared further coded data from the sets of transcripts from each participant to identify similarities and differences. For example, after peer debriefing, we conducted a second round of coding key terms (e.g., practices, culture, speaking) in the transcripts of data sources (i.e., recoded the original ones). We combined some codes during this process, whereas we split others into subcategories (subthemes). Finally, we examined the final codes to organize them into a hierarchical structure using individual and group coding percentage (how many times key terms appear in the data source). Then we sent back all data and definition of key terms to participants for a second round of member checking. We received final confirmation from all participants and then grouped the codes into thematic categories, which we then refined into recurring themes (Boeije, 2010).

RESULTS

Four major interrelated and complex themes emerged from the data. They were (a) seeking strategies for overcoming intercultural communication challenges, (b) addressing challenges for explaining sarcasm concepts, (c) finding mutual hobbies and interests, and (d) integrating field trips into the conversation program.

Theme I: Seeking Strategies for Overcoming Intercultural Communication Challenges

This theme captures that the participants felt that there were differences in communication styles that created challenging situations. The participants perceived that Chinese international students were shy and that participants believed that indirect communication styles were important for implicit understanding of their conversation partners (Banks, 2016). Learning indirect communication styles was an eye-opener for them because they often used direct styles and provided straight messages in order to clarify their intentions. For example, when Kyle (one of the participants) had conversations with Chinese international students in a group setting, he had a hard time understanding what Chinese international students said. He said in the interview that:

> When I had a hard time to understand their spoken English, I clearly told them "I do not understand what you said." Then, I realized that the Chinese international students became quiet and were shy and hesitant to talk to me, so I learned it is not about what to say. It is about how to say it. When we were silent, I was not comfortable, because there is an absence of communication during the conversation. I think this is a challenge of intercultural communication.

Kyle believed that it was important that he should be knowledgeable about the cultural differences and find a way to solve intercultural communication issues and concerns (Shaules, 2007). Izzy explained that when she found Chinese international students were quiet during the conversation time, she began to think of alternative communication strategies to make the conversation feel more private (e.g., one-on-one communication). For example, she said:

> In order to prevent silence and overcome students' shyness, I believe that one-on-one conversation is extremely important, because I would hope that each Chinese international student makes him or herself feel that the conversations are private and they need to practice and improve their spoken English. I scheduled to meet them individually. I am a psychology major and would like to go to an art therapy graduate program in future, so I took each Chinese international student at a different timeframe. One Chinese international student who was very quiet in the group setting, her facial expression changed when I took her to an art museum. We became so close to each other.

Izzy believed that her contact should occur in a variety of contexts with various in-group and out-group members, because she viewed each Chinese international student as an intercultural communication partner rather than a conversation partner.

> One of the strategies of overcoming internal cultural communication challenges is that I need to improve my skills in questioning during the conversation. I hoped that I could have flowing conversations, but sometimes it is not happening with Chinese international students. I need to change my mind that it is ok that conversations are not consistent. A conversation partner should support Chinese students to speak English more and help their speaking in English. I strongly believe that developing skills in questioning are important.

She believed that skills in questioning are important, because her questions ask Chinese students to extend and deepen their understanding of the knowledge beyond information. She also mentioned that she used a textbook of teaching English as second language to begin the conversation. She hoped to become a teacher and would like to teach English as second language at public schools. She hoped to see significant changes, improvement, and outcomes during the conversations. Therefore, she began to use various strategies of prompting, clarification, seeking critical awareness, and refocusing questions.

Theme II: Addressing Challenges for Explaining Sarcasm Concepts

The participants used various verbal and nonverbal ways to express sarcasm during the conversations with Chinese international students, including vowel lengthening, increased articulation, slurred speech, raised eyebrows, and eye-rolling. However, Chinese international students had difficulty extracting the meaning of the participants' sarcastic expressions, because the participants' sarcasm employed contradictions between literal and intended meaning. The Chinese international students were positioned in uncomfortable and confused situations during the conversation. For example, Chuck often used sarcastic expressions when he talked to Chinese international students. However, they had a hard time understanding the true meaning of his sarcastic expressions. He said:

> Chinese international students and I went to one event, to bowling together. All Chinese students knew that I am not good at bowling, but I said that "I am ready to have a perfect score today!!" All the Chinese students looked confused. I am not sure if they understood my sarcastic expressions or not. I realized that I should test whether my sarcastic expressions are working or not.

He found that he needed to be careful about how to use sarcastic expressions, because he learned that the sarcastic expressions might position international students in uncomfortable situations. Izzy also shared and explained another case, saying, "[I told my conversation partner] when the [English as second language] classes make you bored, you don't need to go to school, just call me and I will be your instructor.....it was a joke, but the Chinese international student believed it." Izzy used sarcasm, but the Chinese international students did not catch that it was a joke.

Ronnie explained that there are multiple indicatory cues (e.g., gestures, facial expressions, body movements, personal space) of sarcasm that Chinese international students had difficulty detecting. He said:

> I used different types of humor using facial expressions and gestures. Some students gave me weird looks and it seemed that they looked at me as if I am a strange person. I used sarcasm to build friendships, but I thought...I should understand their cultural backgrounds rather than checking their English competency. I also found that I used sarcasm expressions that have multiple meanings, but many Chinese international students had difficulty to analyze the concept.

Lisa explained that the Chinese international students sensed that sarcasm is closely related to irony. Lisa believed that she had to be cautious about when and how to use sarcastic expressions, or else it would turn to unethical behaviors and ruin social relationships with the international students during the conversations.

> I have a fear that sarcasm may ruin our relationships because of cultural differences. I learned that sarcasm turned to ironic expressions that are not acceptable in certain cultures. All conversation partners must understand each international student's background and culture before using sarcastic expressions including showing emotions and expressing surprise. I learned one thing from the conversational partnership, that Chinese international students must develop friendships with others before they accept others' sarcastic expressions. This was very interesting.

Lisa found that there are significant influences of cultural and language proficiency on the Chinese international students' ability to appropriately analyze the sarcastic concepts that increase positive social interactions.

Theme III: Finding Common Hobbies and Interests

This theme exposed that the participants felt it was important to seek international students' common hobbies and interests to develop their friendships. They thought that their roles and responsibilities were to help the Chinese international students improve their English-speaking competency. However, they began to think that the conversational practice should not only be based on doing specific tasks, but also on international students' social needs. Therefore, they began to seek common hobbies and interests for developing better social relationships. Through their conversations with the international students, they began to seek interactive relationships rather than task-oriented relationships. For example, Heather explained:

> When I began conversation practice with international students. I thought that I needed to help their English-speaking proficiency. I was more interested in learning about their personal backgrounds, so I began to seek common hobbies and interests. One student told me that she was a big fan of one musician I liked, so we began to talk about songs and lyrics. I learned about the student more and more. I missed her when she left.

Heather determined the conversational topics in the beginning and initiated the conversation. However, she searched for topics of conversation and mutual interests, so that the Chinese international students could engage in the conversations more. Therefore, she believed that establishing common ground with the Chinese international students was an important feature of great conversations, similar to the findings of Arkoudis et al. (2012), Clark et al. (2019), and Thomas et al. (2018). Ronnie explained:

> Three male students and I found a mutual hobby of basketball. I think playing sports was an excellent way to develop mutual understanding, trusting relationships, and social care. When we played basketball together, we tried to find a way to avoid miscommunication during the game. Our motivation was to win the game, so we had common goals of how to play better. After the games, we hanged out and practiced a lot. I am not sure that I was a helpful mentor for them, but for me, they allowed me to become a part of their friends.

Ronnie believed that if social aspects of conversational interaction were absent, he would not be able to find natural conversation or help the Chinese international students to improve their speaking competency (Clark et al., 2019).

Theme IV: Integrating Field Trips into the Conversational Partnership Program

The participants believed that field trips helped them to think and try various instructional skills and techniques during the conversations with the Chinese international students. During a trip to Washington D.C., the participants were assigned to serve as the tour guides for the Chinese international students at various tourist and historical sites. Therefore, the participants not only improved their interpersonal relationships, but also served as cultural mediators who helped translate the culture and history of the United States in order to share information and develop learning relationships (Wilson, 1993). Kyle indicated that the conversation partnership during the field trip was a challenge, but he learned about how to explain the cultural and historical concepts of this country to the Chinese international students. He felt that the field trip was important for the conversation partnership program.

> I think the field trip of the conversation partnerships was so important for both American and international students. It is not only about cross-cultural understanding, but especially for American students, they learned how to explain and make the international students understand about cultural and historical concepts. We visited many monuments I did not know how to explain...This is very difficult to explain... I think this type of challenge is so important for me.

Kyle believed that the field trip not only increased his knowledge and skills of cultural mediation, but also helped him self-reflect on his own perspectives. Izzy also shared her experiences:

> I felt that the field trip was the only way to learn international students' habits. For example, I am Christian, so I pray before having meals, but some of Chinese international students were Buddhists. I learned different religious habits and practices. I have a holy cross pendant. They had Buddhist rosaries and amulets. I felt that the field trip broadened my world views, beliefs, and faith. I felt that there were some topics I was hesitant to ask...but the field trip helped me to gain multicultural understanding toward religions and habits.

Izzy explained that she increased her understanding of global perspectives including open-mindedness and non-prejudiced. She felt that it is important to individualize and respect the Chinese international students, not criticize them based on their beliefs or faith.

DISCUSSION

Our findings indicate that these American conversation partners gave meaning to four different themes (seeking strategies for overcoming intercultural communication challenges, addressing challenges for explaining sarcasm concepts, finding mutual hobbies and interests, and integrating field trips into the conversational program) in interacting with Chinese international students during their conversations. Their struggles were related to communication barriers, sarcasm concepts, and cultural differences associated with the experiences of international students.

All seven American conversation partners found that when they had English language conversations with Chinese international students, they unintentionally positioned some international students outside or in a powerless learning environment, based on the communication barriers. Crawford (2000) explained that international students' accent or use of different expressions could interfere with communication, and American conversation partners were uncomfortable, frustrated, and fearful of international students' shyness during the conversations. Banks (2016) described that American conversation partners explicitly expressed their ideas and clarified their intentions by using direct messages (low-context culture). However, like many other Asian countries, Chinese international students are considered to be collectivists who value interpersonal relationships and close relationships and use indirect messages (high-context culture). American conversation partners must understand that Chinese international students may have situation-specific anxiety (e.g., being shy and quiet) that directly and negatively affects an individual in specific situations (e.g., speaking to conversation partners; Sato & Hodge, 2015b; Woodrow, 2006).

American conversation partners scheduled individual meetings with their Chinese international student partners and avoided group meetings because they hoped to develop a true cross-cultural friendship. Using positioning theory (Harré & Moghaddam, 2003), we can explain this as the American conversation partners making choices for improving the conversational quality and finding rationale for their choices. Finally, they began to reflect, assess, and evaluate the consequences of choices for self and others. Therefore, it is important that American conversation partners and Chinese international students experience cross-cultural friendships and accept cultural pluralism through the interactions (Wilson, 1993).

These American conversation partners learned that language patterns such as use of sarcasm are understood differently in another language (van Nes et al., 2010). It seems that the conversation partners felt that Chinese international students failed to detect a native speakers' sarcastic cues, because they struggled to capture linguistic accuracy and nuance from conversation partners' sarcastic expressions (J. Kim & Lantolf, 2018). Polkinghorne (2005) explained that the relation between individuals' experiences and language is a two-way process. Language is used to express meaning. However, language influences how meaning is constructed. Giving words to experience is a complicated process as the meaning of experiences may not be accessible for individuals and may be difficult to express in language. In positioning theory, the conversation partners' social and academic positions were governed by Chinese international students' expectations, definitions, and norms (Hermans, 2001). Therefore, their positions significantly impacted how Chinese international students organized their own learning and oral communication. The conversation partners should focus on intercultural language and communicative practices that emphasize culturally relevant communication (Sato, 2016) so that the Chinese international students find their own style of learning, and possibly gain the ability to understand sarcastic expressions in English.

The current study found that the American conversation partners thought that the conversation experiences with Chinese international students were new, exciting, and fascinating. However, they had difficulties in assimilating to new cross-cultural environments. They felt that their language barriers and cultural differences may become prolonged communication obstacles throughout their interactions. That is to say, communication patterns were very different from the American conversation partners (see also Sato & Hodge, 2015a). These American conversation partners investigated hobbies (e.g., sports) and common interests (e.g., music) from their host country of China to offer social support or mutual understanding with Chinese international students on the university campus. They self-reflected and positioned themselves to seek and support the emotional and academic needs of the Chinese international students (Davies & Harré, 1990; Tung, 2011). This reflects Thomas et al.'s (2018) suggestion of leveraging common ground to facilitate communication. Nilsson et al. (2008) suggested that student group activities (e.g., playing weekly sports) may offer social bonding opportunities that help Chinese international students feel welcomed, and through participation in conversation sessions they can share information such as the transition into new academic courses and common issues of acculturation stress on an American university campus. The way American conversation partners position themselves and others during conversational practices was important, because their positioning affected the nature of Chinese international students' interactions and their access to learning opportunities. Interactive positioning occurs in the moment of academic and social interaction (Harré & van Langenhove, 1999), but it is also contextually tied across interaction or scale of conversational activities (Kayi-Aydar, 2013, 2014).

The American conversation partners believed that field trips with the Chinese international students helped them to generate positive perceptions, increase friendships, and improve their conversational speaking skills (Behrendt & Franklin, 2014). Kolb (1983) explained that field trips are a type of authentic, first-hand, and sensory-based experiential learning. Experiential learning activities involve exploring, touching, listening, watching, moving things, disassembling and reassembling, and learning, and consist of grasping an experience and then transforming it into a result (Kolb, 1983). The American conversation partners sought and partook in field trip opportunities outside the conversation sessions and began to engage in self-directed learning to improve their own conversational skills and techniques (e.g., explaining American history & culture) at the historical sites such as monuments and museums. They were positioned and motivated to initiate their own self-directed learning, which helped them to make decisions and become responsible for their own learning process. Behrent and Franklin (2014) suggested that field trips play a significant beneficial role in cross-cultural learning. For example, college and university students who have hands-on, authentic experiences develop curiosity and interest about history and culture and are then motivated to learn more. In positioning theory, through these field trip experiences, social skills develop as the students share perceptions and knowledge with others. Students may begin to look forward to classes and connect previous knowledge and experiences with the new concepts.

Study Limitations

This study has several limitations. First, the participants were deliberately selected from just one public research university in the Midwest of the United States. Statistically speaking, therefore, the findings are not generalizable. From a qualitative perspective, however, the reader may assume transferability to contexts of colleges or universities elsewhere where there are contextual similarities with conversation partners (Leininger, 1994). Second, the number of participants was small, and this study only focused on American conversation partners of Chinese international students with relatively similar backgrounds and experiences. However, qualitative inquiries typically use small samples, and in the logic of variation sampling, the intent is to capture and describe the central themes that cut across a vast array of participant variation (Patton, 2002). Our intent in using this sampling approach was to uncover common themes reflecting American conversation partners who interacted with Chinese international students. Future studies should investigate conversation partner programs with international students from different national and cultural backgrounds in order to more fully understand the effects of these variables on conversation partner program outcomes. Future research should also include perspectives of both domestic and international students in order to better understand the similarities and differences in their experiences. Future research could also investigate longitudinal changes in experiences over time.

CONCLUSION

Based on their conversational experiences with Chinese international students, the American conversation partners experienced intercultural communication challenges such as understanding sarcastic expressions. These findings are consistent with previous findings involving conversation partners at U.S. colleges and universities (e.g., J. Kim & Lantolf, 2018; Wilson, 1993). American colleges and universities still need to do more to promote cultural learning and positive relationship outcomes between conversation partners and international students.

First, offices of international education should include an orientation session on strategies for communicating with international students in conversation partnerships. This echoes a suggestion also made by E. J. Lee (2016). Such an orientation session could address potential interactional and linguistic challenges and dichotomies on campus (e.g., language of ideas and language of display; Bunch, 2009). When American conversation partners communicate with international students, they need to choose either the language of ideas (any language necessary to complete an academic task, regardless of whether it follows academic norms) or the language of display (language for presenting ideas to particular academic audiences in academic contexts) during the conversations. Such an orientation session would be helpful for American conversation partners in developing linguistic and communication resources, seeking opportunities for peer support, and facilitating equal opportunity for international students' participation in group discussions.

Second, an email partnership program is another possible strategy to support a mood of transnationalism so that American conversation partners and international students may begin to understand each other's cultural, linguistic, and behavioral norms (Guidry Lacina, 2002). This approach allows both international and American students to better understand each other's preferences regarding group versus individual meetings, format, setting, and duration of the conversation so that the conversation partners help answer questions, reduce each other's concerns, and avoid cultural misunderstandings (Yakunina et al., 2011).

Lastly, international sport events and/or movie nights can help promote friendships between the conversation partners and international students (Guidry Lacina, 2002). Such events could be seen as a type of common ground, which Arkoudis et al. (2012) and Thomas et al. (2018) suggested would facilitate interaction between international and domestic students. For example, the conversation partner program could promote awareness of foreign films from around the world and offer inexpensive opportunities for other potential conversation partners as well as the local community. This opportunity may allow the international students to practice English in the local community.

To better support conversation partner programs, we encourage academic departments and faculty to develop a study group for those participating in conversational partnerships to better understand the variety of values, origins, languages, and cultures of participants. This may contribute to a greater appreciation for the richness of diversity and to meaningful academic and social experiences available at American universities for all students.

REFERENCES

Aaron, R., Cedeno, C., Garies, E., Kumar, L., & Swaminathan, A. (2018). Peer to peers: Developing a student-coordinated conversation partner program. *Journal of International Students, 8*(3), 1316–1327.

Abe, J., Talbot, D. M., & Geelhoed, R. J. (1998). Effects of a peer program on international student adjustment. *Journal of College Student Development, 39*, 539–547.

Andreouli, E. (2010). Identity, positioning and self-other relations. *Papers on Social Representations, 19*(1), 14.1–14.13.

Arkoudis, S., Watty, K., Baik, C., Yu, X., Borland, H., Chang, S., Lang, I., Lang, J., & Pearce, A. (2012). Finding common ground: Enhancing interaction between domestic and international students in higher education. *Teaching in Higher Education, 18*, 222–235.

Banks, S. (2016). Behind Japanese students' silence in English classroom. *Accents Asia, 8*(2), 54–75.

Batterton, J., & Horner, S. L. (2016). Contextual identities: Ethnic and national identities of international and American students. *Journal of Studies in International Education, 20*(5), 472–487.

Behrendt, M., & Franklin, T. (2014). A review of research on school field trips and their value in education. *International Journal of Environmental and Science Education, 9*, 235–245.

Boeije, H. R. (2010). *Analysis in qualitative research.* SAGE.

Buhs, E. S. (2005). Peer rejection, negative peer treatment, and school adjustment: Self-concept and classroom engagement as mediating process. *Journal of School Psychology, 43*(5), 407–424.

Bunch, G. C. (2009). "Going up there": Challenges and opportunities for language minority students during a mainstream classroom speech event. *Linguistics & Education, 20*(2), 81–108.

Chang, M. (2011). Helping the international student understand the American university. *New Directions for Higher Education, 153,* 21–24.

Cheng, R., & Erben, A. (2011). Language anxiety: Experiences of Chinese graduate students at US higher institutions. *Journal of Studies in International Education, 16*(5), 477–497.

Clark, L., Pantidi, N., Cooney, O., Doyle, P., Garaialde, D., Edwards, J., Spillane, B., Murad, C., Munteanu, C., Wade, V., & Cowan, B. R. (2019). *What makes a good conversation? Challenges in designing truly conversational agents.* The 2019 ACM CHI Conference on Human Factors in Computing Systems. doi:10.1145/3290605.3300705

Crawford, J. (2000). *At war with diversity: US language policy in an age of anxiety.* Multilingual Matters.

Davies, B., & Harré, R. (1990). Positioning: The discursive production of selves. *Journal for the Theory of Social Behaviour, 20,* 43–63.

Gay, L. R. (1996). *Educational research: Competencies for analysis and application* (5th ed.). Prentice-Hall.

Geary, D. (2016). How do we get people to interact? International students and the American experience. *Journal of International Students, 6,* 527–541.

Geelhoed, R. J., Abe, J., & Talbot, D. M. (2003). A qualitative investigation of U.S. students' experiences in an international peer program. *Journal of College Student Development, 44,* 5–17.

Guidry Lacina, J. (2002). Preparing international students for successful social experience in higher education. *New Directions for Higher Education, 117,* 21–28.

Hamm, J. V., & Zhang, L. (2010). The schooling context of adolescents' peer relations. In J. Meece & J. Eccles (Eds.), *The handbook of schools and schooling effects on development* (pp. 518–554). Erlbaum.

Harré, R., & Moghaddam, F. M. (Eds.). (2003). *The self and others: Positioning individuals and groups in personal, political and cultural contexts.* Praeger.

Harré, R., & van Langenhove, L. (1999). The dynamics of social episodes. In R. Harré & L. van Langenhove (Eds.), *Positioning theory: Moral contexts of intentional action* (pp. 1–13). Blackwell.

Hermans, H. J. M. (2001). The dialogical self: Toward a theory of personal and cultural positioning. *Culture & Psychology, 7*(3), 243–281.

Hollway, W. (1984). Gender difference and the production of subjectivity. In J. Henriques, W. Hollway, C. Urwin, C. Venn, & V. Walkerdine (Eds.), *Changing the subject: Psychology, social regulation and subjectivity* (pp. 227–263). Methuen.

Institute of International Education. (2019). *Open Doors: Report on international educational exchange.* Retrieved December 11, 2019 from http://www.iie.org/opendoors.

Jones, R. A. (1997). Direct perception and symbol forming in positioning. *Journal for the Theory of Social Behaviour, 29,* 37–58.

Kayi-Aydar, H. (2013). Scaffolding language learning in an academic ESL classroom. *ELT Journal, 67*(3), 324–335.

Kayi-Aydar, H. (2014). Social positioning, participation, and second language learning: Talkative students in academic ESL classroom. *TESOL Quarterly, 48,* 686–714.

Kim, D., Pan, Y., & Park, H. S. (1998). High- versus low-context culture: a comparison of Chinese, Korean, and American cultures. *Psychology & Marketing, 15,* 507–521.

Kim, J., & Lantolf, J. P. (2018). Developing conceptual understanding of sarcasm in L2 English through explicit instruction. *Language Teaching Research, 22,* 208–229.

Kolb, D. (1983). *Experiential learning, experiences as the source of learning and development.* Prentice Hall.

Ladd, G. W., Herald-Brown, S. L., & Kochel, K. P. (2009). Peers and motivation. In K. R. Wentzel & A. Wigfield (Eds.), *Handbook of motivation at school* (pp. 323–348). Routledge.

Lee, E. J. (2016). International and American students' perceptions of informal English conversations. *Journal of International Students, 6,* 14–34.

Lee, J. J., & Rice, C. (2007). Welcome to America? International student perceptions of discrimination. *Higher Education, 53*(3), 381–409.

Leininger, M. (1994). Evaluation criteria and critique of qualitative research studies. In J. M. Morse (Ed.), *Critical issues in qualitative research methods* (pp. 95–115). SAGE.

Leong, F. T. L., & Chou, E. L. (1996). Counseling international students. In P. B. Pedersen, J. G. Draguns, W. J. Lonner, & J. E. Trimble (Eds.), *Counseling across cultures* (pp. 210–242). SAGE.

Lewis, C., Ginsberg, R., Davis, T., & Smith, K. (2004). The experiences of African American PhD students at a predominantly White Carnegie I-research institution. *College Student Journal, 38*(2), 231–245.

Li, X., & Chen, W. (2014). Facebook or Renren? A comparative study of social networking sit use and social capital among Chinese international students in the United States. *Computers in Human Behavior, 35,* 116–123.

Luo, J., & Jamieson-Drake, D. (2013). Examining the educational benefits of interacting with international students. *Journal of International Students, 3,* 85–101.

Merriam, S. B. (1998). *Qualitative research and case study applications in education.* Jossey-Bass.

Nilsson, J. E., Butler, J. Shouse, S., & Joshi, C. (2008). The relationship among perfectionism, acculturation, and stress in Asian international students. *Journal of College Counseling, 11,* 147–158.

Nishioka, H. (2014). Activating the Zone of Proximal Development of Japanese language learners: Language-exchange partnerships (LEPs) at an Australian university. *New Voices, 6*, 145–171.

Patton, M. Q. (2002). *Qualitative research and evaluation methods* (3rd ed.). SAGE.

Pedersen, P. B. (1991). Counseling international students. *The Counseling Psychologist, 19*, 10–58.

Polkinghorne, D. (2005). Language and meaning: Data collection in qualitative research. *Journal of Counseling Psychology, 52*, 137–145.

Rose-Redwood, C., & Rose-Redwood, R. (2018). Building bridges across the international divide: Fostering meaningful cross-cultural interactions between domestic and international students. *Journal of International Students, 8*(3), 1328–1336.

Ruble, R. A., & Zhang, Y. B. (2013). Stereotypes of Chinese international students held by Americans. *International Journal of Intercultural Relations, 37*, 202–211.

Ryan, J., & Hellmundt, S. (2005). Maximizing international students' cultural capital. In J. Carroll & J. Ryan (Eds.), *Teaching international students: Improving learning for all.* Routledge.

Ryan, J., & Viete, R. (2009). Respectful interactions: Learning with international students in the English-speaking academy. *Teaching in Higher Education, 14*(3), 303–314.

Sato, T. (2016). Doctoral sojourn experiences of adapted physical education students from Asian countries. *Journal of International Students, 6*(2), 339–366.

Sato, T., & Hodge, S. R. (2009). Asian international doctoral students' experiences at two American university: Assimilation, accommodation, and resistance. *Journal of Diversity in Higher Education, 2*(3), 136–148.

Sato, T., & Hodge. S. R. (2015a). Academic and social experiences of exchange students from Japan attending an American university. *College Student Journal, 49*(1), 78–92.

Sato, T., & Hodge, S. R. (2015b). Japanese exchange students' academic and social struggles at an American university. *Journal of International Students, 5*(3), 208–227.

Seidman, I. (1998). *Interviewing as qualitative research: A guide for researchers in education and the social sciences* (2nd ed.). Teacher College Press.

Shaules, J. (2007). *Deep culture: The hidden challenges of global living.* Multilingual Matters.

Sheets, R. H. (2005). *Diversity pedagogy: Examining the role of culture in the teaching-learning process.* Pearson Education.

Spencer-Rodgers, J. (2001). Consensual and individual stereotypic beliefs about international students among American host nationals. *International Journal of Intercultural Relations, 25*(6), 639–657.

Spitzman, E., & Waugh, M. (2018). Structured and critical intercultural programming: Faculty and staff collaborate to put research into action. *Journal of International Students, 8*, 1337–1345.

Thomas, V. F., Ssendikaddiwa, J. M., Mroz, M., Lockyer, K., Kosarzova, K., & Hanna, C. (2018). Leveraging common ground: Improving international and domestic students' interaction through mutual engagement. *Journal of International Students, 8*(3), 1386–1397.

Tung, W.-C. (2011). Cultural barriers to mental health services among Asian Americans. *Home Health Care Management & Practices, 23*(4), 303–305.

Ursell, E. F. (2014). Conversation partners in the writing center. *Praxis: A Writing Center Journal, 11*, 1–6.

van Nes, F., Abma, T., Jonsson, H., & Deeg, D. (2010). Language differences in qualitative research: Is meaning lost in translation? *European Journal of Ageing, 7,* 313–316.

Vanassche, E., & Kelchtermans, G. (2014). Teacher educators' professionalism in practice: Positioning theory and personal interpretative framework. *Teaching and Teacher Education, 44,* 117–127.

Varela, C., & Harré, R. (1996). Conflicting varieties of realism: Causal powers and the problems of social structure. *Journal for the Theory of Social Behaviour, 26,* 313–325.

Welikala, T., & Watkins, C. (2008). *Improving intercultural learning experiences in higher education: Responding to cultural scripts for learning.* Institute of Education, University of London.

Wilson, A. H. (1993). Conversation partners: Helping students gain a global perspective through cross-cultural experiences. *Theory into Practice, 32*(1), 21–26.

Woodrow, L. (2006). Anxiety and speaking English as a second language. *Regional Language Center Journal, 37*(3), 308–332.

Yakunina, E. S., Weigold, I. K., & McCarthy, A. S. (2011). Group counseling with international students: Practical, ethical, and cultural considerations. *Journal of College Student Psychotherapy, 25,* 67–78.

Yin, R. K. (2003). *Case study research design and methods* (3rd ed.). SAGE.

Yoon, B. (2008). Uninvited guests: The influence of teachers' roles and pedagogies on the positioning of English language learners in the regular classroom. *American Educational Research Journal, 45,* 495–522.

Zhang-Wu, Q. (2018). Chinese international students' experiences in American higher education institutes: A critical review of the literature. *Journal of International Students, 8,* 1173–1197.

TAKAHIRO SATO, PhD, CAPE, is a professor and chair of the joint master's program in International Development and Peace through Sport at the University of Tsukuba, Ibaraki, Japan. His scholarship and research focus is on Japanese education, multicultural physical education, disability studies, adapted physical education professional development, and diversity in higher education. Email: sato.takahiro.gf@u.tsukuba.ac.jp

RYAN MILLER, PhD, is an associate professor in the TESL program at Kent State University, Ohio, USA. His research focuses on second language (L2) reading and writing. Within L2 reading, he investigates how reading and reading subskills (e.g., morphological awareness, phonological awareness, lexical inferencing ability) developed in a first language can support reading in a second language. Within L2 writing, he researches development of disciplinary genre knowledge using the tools of systemic functional linguistics. Email: rmill129@kent.edu

Peer-Reviewed Article

© *Journal of International Students*
Volume 11, Issue 1 (2021), pp. 103-121
ISSN: 2162-3104 (Print), 2166-3750 (Online)
doi: 10.32674/jis.v11i1.1200
ojed.org/jis

OJED
OPEN JOURNALS IN EDUCATION

Supporting Nonnative English Speakers at the University: A Survey of Faculty and Staff

Bethany D. Peters
Greenville University, USA

Michael E. Anderson
University of Minnesota, USA

ABSTRACT

This study reports on a survey designed to understand the experiences of faculty and staff who work with nonnative speakers of English (NNESs) at a U.S. public research university. Over 1,500 faculty and staff responded to the survey, and the findings highlight their perspectives on the benefits of having NNESs on campus, as well as the challenges that they experience in teaching and advising this population of students. We conclude with a discussion about possible resources and strategies that may provide enhanced support for NNESs and the faculty and staff who work with them.

Keywords: faculty development, internationalization, multilingual learners, nonnative English speakers

INTRODUCTION

In the past several decades, the internationalization of higher education has become an increasingly important priority for U.S. institutions. Many colleges and universities have expended greater efforts to not only send more students abroad, but also to internationalize their campuses by recruiting international students, facilitating intercultural interactions through co-curricular activities, and infusing the curriculum with global learning outcomes (Urban & Palmer, 2014). Recent studies have highlighted important benefits that intercultural contact can afford all students, such as growth in cultural awareness, an increase in critical thinking abilities, and improved interpersonal communication skills (Loes et al., 2012; Soria & Triosi, 2014; Yefanova et al., 2015).

When actualized in a classroom environment, internationalization is intended to enhance students' learning experiences and prepare them to be successful in a global society (Galinova, 2015). However, one critique of internationalization is that faculty and staff have not been adequately prepared to support the growing numbers of diverse learners (Andrade et al., 2014; Crose, 2011; Peterson & Helms, 2013). Because of their diverse cultural and linguistic backgrounds, international and multilingual students have unique learning needs and may benefit from enhanced staff support and instructional adjustments (Anderson et al., 2012; Andrade, 2006; Kingston & Forland, 2008). Many scholars have placed responsibility on faculty and staff to make adaptations that will enhance the learning experience for international and multilingual students (Carroll & Ryan, 2007; Crose, 2011; Kingston & Forland, 2008), yet only a handful of studies address the perspectives of faculty and staff, what barriers they perceive students to face, what challenges they experience, and what strategies they use to help provide support to students. Addressing this gap in the relevant literature provides the rationale for our current study.

LITERATURE REVIEW

Background

Andrade (2009) made the important point that institutions seeking to expand international student enrollments need to be accountable to providing effective support services for those students. As an integral part of the higher education system, faculty and staff play specific roles in providing both curricular and co-curricular support (Leask, 2009). According to Yefanova et al. (2015), faculty assume a vital role in orienting students to a new academic culture and structuring a classroom experience that helps to facilitate meaningful engagement between students of diverse backgrounds. Staff also play an important role in providing international students with various support services, such as academic advising, resource awareness, and emotional and psychological support (Harryba et al., 2012). Although there is extensive research about the experiences of international students and their academic, cultural, social, and personal struggles within the U.S. higher education system (Anderson et al., 2012; Andrade, 2006; Kingston & Forland, 2008), there are fewer studies that contribute to our understanding of the needs of faculty and staff who support these students. Furthermore, very little research exists to highlight strategies that faculty and staff can use to more effectively support the linguistic and cultural needs of nonnative English speakers (NNESs).

Research on Faculty and Staff Perceptions

A handful of studies provide some insight on how faculty in various institutions perceive the growing presence of NNESs and international students on campuses across the United States and Europe. In a few studies, faculty reported to hold relatively positive regard for the goals of internationalization and the enhanced diversity on college campuses contributed by international students (Andrade, 2010; Haan et al., 2017; Jin & Schneider, 2019; Mantzourani et al., 2015; Trice, 2003). In addition to these positive perceptions, faculty have also described key challenges they experience in interactions with international and multilingual students, often primarily referencing language and communication challenges as prominent barriers (Kingston & Forland, 2008; Trice, 2003). Faculty in Robertson et al.'s (2000) study explained that in addition to language challenges, students struggled to adapt to a new academic environment, and to demonstrate critical thinking in the ways that were normalized in an Australian university.

Another point of interest in relevant studies is the degree to which faculty members adapt their teaching methods to be more inclusive of NNES students. Andrade (2010) found that faculty respondents in a private U.S. institution reported adapting their instructional methods with some degree of frequency to better support NNESs. However, the faculty indicated little interest in learning how to further accommodate their teaching methods to the needs of NNESs. Mantzourani et al. (2015) demonstrated that although faculty integrated some inclusive teaching practices, they also experienced some level of disconnect with the university's internationalization goals, and felt somewhat underprepared to support the linguistic and cultural needs of international students. Similarly, faculty in Haan et al.'s (2017) study voiced concerns regarding the complications internationalization posed for their teaching and indicated gaps in their understanding and their ability to implement best practices for instructing NNESs. Jin and Schneider (2019) also reported that faculty described some level of uncertainty regarding how to develop an inclusive pedagogy that effectively supports linguistically and culturally diverse learners.

Although inquiry about staff perceptions is less common in the literature, Harryba et al. (2012) investigated and differentiated between the challenges experienced by academic staff (faculty) and general staff when supporting international students at an Australian university. General support staff discussed communication barriers, concern with English proficiency standards, and extra time needed to support international students as some of the primary areas of challenge they experienced.

The current study contributes to the field by contributing to the knowledge base on how faculty perceive both benefits and challenges of working with NNESs. Staff were also included in our study since their perspectives are underrepresented in the current literature and they also have significant interactions with NNESs. Furthermore, since faculty in previous studies have indicated a need for understanding more inclusive strategies to better support NNESs, this study explores what strategies faculty and staff currently use in their support of NNESs, and what additional training or support they perceive to be valuable.

Research Questions

In this study, we sought to answer the following research questions:

1. What benefits do staff and faculty perceive NNESs to contribute?
2. What challenges do faculty and staff report when supporting NNES students?
3. What strategies do faculty and staff perceive to be helpful in supporting NNES students?
4. What further support resources would faculty and staff perceive to be helpful in their support of NNESs?

Definition of Terms

When conducting our survey, we chose to inquire specifically about the views that faculty and staff held toward supporting NNESs. We used "nonnative English speaker" as a term to provide a clear reference to students whose first language is not English, recognizing that this population may include domestic students whose first language is not English, as well as international students. In choosing to use the term, we were concerned that it could reinforce the possible perception that these students bring more challenges than opportunities to campus, which was not our intent. We also did not want to just focus on the language deficits of students (by using a term that highlights what they are not) because these are students who already have a high proficiency in at least two languages. However, while we did not want to overlook the strengths of multilingual students, the term "multilingual student" can be ambiguous and we wanted to ensure that everyone responding to the survey clearly understood the population about which we were inquiring. After discussion and consultation, we decided to use nonnative English speaker (NNES) in this survey because it clearly describes the group we were asking about, but we highlighted the possible implications of using different terms in our reporting of the results. We included an explanation in the first section of the survey so terminology would be clear to respondents and we could also raise awareness about different terminology.

METHOD

Context

The context for our study was a large public research university in the United States. During the spring semester 2016, when our survey was administered, the student population was comprised of over 28,000 undergraduate students. NNES domestic students accounted for around 9% of the undergraduate student population, and international students, most of whom are NNESs, accounted for another 9% of the undergraduate student population.

Survey Design

We developed and administered an online survey to learn more about how faculty and staff perceive the benefits and challenges they experience when supporting students who are NNESs. The survey instrument was adapted, with permission, from the questionnaire utilized in Andrade's (2010) study "Increasing Accountability: Faculty Perspectives on the English Language Competence of Nonnative English Speakers." We also sought input from representatives of various campus offices, piloted the survey with instructors and staff who represented the target population, and incorporated revisions based on this feedback. Once all feedback was incorporated, approval for the study was granted from the university's Institutional Review Board.

The survey was categorized into four broad sections according to our research questions. Faculty and staff answered questions to explain their perceptions of the following: (a) ways in which NNES students benefit the classroom and campus; (b) difficulties faculty and staff experience when supporting NNES students; (c) strategies perceived to be most useful when working with NNESs; and (d) interest in further faculty/staff training or resources. Within each section, respondents were asked to complete multi-option, Likert scale, and open-ended questions. The survey branched to different sets of questions depending on whether the respondent's primary role at the university was faculty or staff.

Data Collection

We collaborated with the university's institutional research office to design a sample for this study. We chose faculty and staff participants randomly from colleges and units on campus that work with undergraduate students. We then narrowed the pool to job titles within those units most likely to interact with students. We also invited survey respondents to recommend others who should take the survey, and the sent the survey to all those referred who were not already part of the sample. Because of this, the final sample is not a completely random sample.

Out of 6,727 people invited to take the survey, 1,502 faculty and staff completed the survey, resulting in a 22% response rate. Forty-eight percent of survey respondents identified as staff and 52% identified as a faculty member, instructor, or teaching assistant. From the staff respondents, 11% identified as advisors, 11% represented administrative staff, 9% reported from student services, and 21% did not specify their staff role.

When asked which population of students they primarily worked with, 44% of respondents reported working with undergraduate students, 22% indicated they worked with graduate students, and 35% responded that they served both undergraduate and graduate student populations. The majority of survey respondents, approximately 51%, indicated that they work with some NNESs, 24% reported that they work with many NNESs, 19% reported they work with very few, only 4% indicated that they did not work with any NNESs, and just 1%

reported working with all NNESs. Appendix Table A1 demonstrates the various campus units represented by faculty and staff survey respondents.

Data Analysis

To analyze the quantitative data, we reported the descriptive statistics. For the qualitative portion of the data, we utilized NVivo software to conduct textual analysis, which included identifying and categorizing themes for responses to seven open-ended questions. We also facilitated an intercoder reliability check on a portion of the qualitative data. The intercoder reliability check was conducted as follows: the Principal Investigator (PI) of the study prepared a segment of survey responses for three collaborators from two different campus units to review and code. Each collaborator provided their coded responses to the PI, and the PI reviewed all coded responses for areas of discrepancy. The collaborators and PI met to discuss the text segments where different codes were applied, and after discussion and reconciliation, intercoder agreement of 93% was achieved on the data sample.

RESULTS

Faculty and Staff Perceptions Regarding Benefits

Our first research question was to identify the benefits that faculty and staff perceived of having NNESs on campus, specifically how the presence of NNESs enhances the learning environment for all students. A majority of faculty and staff respondents, 85%, expressed agreement or strong agreement that all students learn about diverse perspectives, whereas only 4% of respondents expressed that they either somewhat or strongly disagreed. Similarly, when asked if they agreed that all students develop intercultural communication skills, a majority of survey respondents, 82%, also indicated agreement or strong agreement, and only 3% of respondents indicated some level of disagreement in response to this item. Appendix Table A2 illustrates respondents' views about the various ways in which NNESs enhance the learning environment for all students.

In response to open-ended questions about the benefits of having NNESs on campus, staff and faculty respondents shared many comments, including that NNESs helped to bring diverse perspectives, provided opportunities for cross-cultural communication and networking, and often modelled hard work and academic excellence for their native-speaking peers. Table 1 provides an illustrative comment for each of the themes described in this section, representing both faculty and staff responses.

Table 1: Faculty and Staff Perceptions of How Nonnative English Speakers Enhance the Learning Environment

Benefits	Representative comment
Cultural diversity (*n* = 178)	*They [NNESs] are incredibly helpful in my field where international practice differs in many ways from practice in the USA.*
Communication skills (*n* = 21)	*Cross-cultural interaction/collaboration encourages students to build effective active-listening skills and the ability to explain complex information in multiple ways ...*
Learning languages (*n* = 19)	*It may encourage domestic students to learn another language and see the benefit of being bilingual.*
Building relationships (*n* = 18)	*I think students' lives are richer for having formed bonds with people from other cultures; they also learn that close relationships can form from underlying core values, despite any language or cultural barriers.*
Modeling excellence (*n* = 18)	*Non-native speakers who come to study at the [University] are often at the top of their class in their home country, smart and hard-working. They enrich the learning environment due to their intellectual capabilities, not just by bringing in a different perspective.*
Teaching (*n* = 15)	*Non-native English speakers push instructors to reflect more carefully on their course materials ... to write more careful exam questions, to avoid potentially confusing errors or telegraphic writing in power points and assignment descriptions. To include examples that are meaningful and useful to a wider range of students.*
Future preparation (*n* = 11)	*It prepares them to live in a multicultural world where opinions and means of expressing one's self varies.*

Although respondents' comments were primarily positive, it is important to note some faculty and staff respondents (*n* = 59) wrote about various factors that they felt could jeopardize the benefits of having NNESs in class. Specifically, faculty and staff respondents discussed how the benefits may not be realized when students (domestic or international) choose not to interact, when NNESs do not participate in class, and when the course format does not foster interactions. For example, one respondent noted,

> In my experience, the presence of NNESs has the potential to aid in the goals outlined above, but their presence does not automatically create these benefits. The course must be structured in a way that creates opportunities for cross-cultural interaction to occur and the students must be willing to interact. The potential positive impacts, therefore, are highly dependent on the course and the specific students and instructor.

Faculty and Staff Perceptions of Student Challenges

We asked our second research question to better understand the challenges faculty and staff experienced in supporting NNES students. In response to a question about factors that may limit students' abilities to meet course requirements, the majority of faculty respondents, 59%, indicated either strong agreement or agreement that language proficiency posed the greatest difficulties for students, when compared to other possible factors such as cultural differences, prior academic preparation, and study skills. Appendix Table A3 summarizes faculty responses to this question.

When asked a similar question, approximately 50% of staff respondents either agreed or strongly agreed that NNESs experience communication challenges primarily due to low English proficiency. However, an almost equal percentage of staff respondents (48%) expressed agreement or strong agreement that students' communication challenges were related to confusion about university processes. Appendix Table A4 summarizes staff responses to this question.

In response to various open-ended questions, staff and faculty respondents shared more nuanced insights about a range of complex factors that may contribute to NNESs' learning barriers, including previous academic background, cultural difference, reticence to seek help, confidence levels, and difficulties interacting with peers and faculty. Some faculty respondents commented that students' language-related challenges seemed to overlap with academic tasks such as acquiring discipline-specific vocabulary and coping with heavy reading loads. Both faculty and staff respondents described how various types of cultural differences created barriers for students, particularly related to applying cultural norms in communication, understanding cultural references embedded in the curriculum, and meeting expectations in the U.S. education system. Some faculty respondents expressed how difficult it often was to discern whether a student was struggling with a cultural or a language challenge; for example, participation was often discussed as an area of concern, but some faculty were unsure if students did not participate due to differences in cultural norms or because they lacked the language proficiency necessary to do so. Table 2 provides a representative comment for each of the themes described in this section, illustrating both faculty and staff comments.

Table 2: Faculty and Staff Perceptions of Challenges for Nonnative English Speakers

Challenges	Representative comments
English proficiency ($n = 347$)	*I feel it is primarily English proficiency that can negatively impact their performance in class.*
Academic skills ($n = 187$)	*... many students come to the classroom without the preparation in critical thinking skills ... that is necessary for success in this work; they are used to a model based more on memorization and recitation than interpretation and analysis.*
Cultural differences ($n = 121$)	*Cultural, political, and legal references may be unfamiliar to them.*
Campus resources ($n = 91$)	*Many seem reluctant to use the resources on campus and instead push themselves harder in studying to make up any deficits.*
Asking for help ($n = 76$)	*I have noticed that many students that struggle with fluency in English are hesitant to ask for assistance or clarification.*
Peer interactions ($n = 58$)	*When given the choice, students prefer to stick with partners or group members from their own cultures (both U.S. and international students).*
Confidence ($n = 43$)	*Their confidence level in their English-speaking abilities and the cultural differences in communication style.*
Attitudes & expectations ($n = 22$)	*Fear of making mistakes, shame/stigma about what they're dealing with, uncertainty about what information is needed and why it's important.*
Faculty interactions ($n = 20$)	*However, another very, very big barrier is the fundamental MOTIVATION for NN students to approach instructors. They are afraid!*

Faculty and Staff Challenges

Some of the most commonly cited concerns faculty and staff respondents voiced about the barriers they experienced when working with NNESs included insufficient resources and training, communication barriers, concerns about proficiency standards, grading difficulties, role limitations, uncertainty about how to offer help, and anxiety about offending students. Table 3 provides an illustrative comment representing both faculty and staff views for each of the themes that emerged from our data analysis in this section. Although these themes emerged based on combined feedback from faculty and staff, faculty tended to be more likely to articulate concerns about making sure students met proficiency standards upon admissions, finding effective grading strategies, and not having time to address the unique learning needs of NNESs. Staff were more likely to express concerns about how to respond to specific communication challenges they experienced with NNESs, such as communicating policy information and confirming that students understood them. Respondents from both faculty and staff groups described concerns with resources and training, and difficulties they have knowing how to best approach students with their concerns without causing insult.

Table 3: Faculty and Staff Challenges in Supporting Nonnative English Speakers

Challenges	Representative comments
Challenges with resources & training ($n = 109$)	*I think instructors often feeling [sic] burdened by nonnative English speakers in their courses because they don't feel they have adequate resources to support them.*
Communication difficulties ($n = 42$)	*I think the hardest part is to comfortably figure out a way to communicate when I receive blank stares or lack of understanding body language. How do I respectfully communicate when their [sic] is a pause in understanding...visual, written, or verbal? What are we both trying to understand?*
Concerns about proficiency standards ($n = 41$)	*Increasing international presence on campus is a very important goal, but we are not serving anyone (students, faculty, staff) well by accepting students who are at the lowest end of language proficiency.*
Grading challenges ($n = 29$)	*It can be overwhelming to grade when the written English is so poor.*
Role limitations ($n = 20$)	*It is not my job to teach people how to speak English. I am prepared, willing, and always available to help my students with my course, but this is the university's responsibility.*
Uncertainty about how to help ($n = 18$)	*I can often identify a problem, but am utterly unable to give them the right sort of advice for addressing it or to direct them to the appropriate tutor or center on campus.*
Fear of offending students ($n = 18$)	*Feeling stigmatized or singled out when asked to get help can lead to further frustration and inhibit a student from taking advantage of existing resources.*

Table 4: Faculty and Staff Supportive Strategies for Nonnative English Speakers

Strategy	Representative comments
Communication strategies ($n = 94$)	*I check for clarification to make sure they understand me, restate what I think they are saying to me if I have difficulty understanding them, and follow up via email if it seems clear that they didn't get verbal instructions.*
Accommodations ($n = 92$)	*I always give nonnative speakers (along with anyone who has an accommodation) extra time to turn in written assignments.*
One-on-one support ($n = 61$)	*Working one on one in office hours, for me, is the only way to really successfully address nonnative speakers' individual needs.*
Visuals ($n = 37$)	*I provide handouts and PowerPoint slides to students before class so that they can follow along. I make all handouts and PowerPoint slides available on Moodle for follow up work.*
Campus resource promotion ($n = 33$)	*Offering them to talk with someone who works primarily with nonnative English speakers and suggest programs that help polish their English skills.*
Encouragement ($n = 30$)	*I recognize that there might be cultural barriers that would cause international students to feel intimidated by faculty, and I do my best to be as friendly and approachable as possible.*
Peer support ($n = 25$)	*Learning assistants who are well versed in biology but also speak Chinese or Korean (the most frequent languages of our international students).*
Linguistic resources ($n = 8$)	*I add a tab in Moodle available to all students that lists grammar and style worksheets and quizzes.*

Faculty and Staff Strategies

We also asked questions to learn specific strategies faculty and staff were already putting to use when working with NNES students. When asked about how frequently they used various strategies to support NNESs, 63% of faculty respondents reported that they adjust their communication style to be clearer, and 55% indicated that they encourage NNES students to use campus resources, with higher degrees of frequency (combining responses for often, most of the time, and always). Appendix Table A5 provides an overview of these responses, including other strategies that faculty indicated using with lower degrees of frequency. When asked a similar question about how often they used various strategies, 79% of staff respondents reported that they adapt their communication style to be more comprehensible with higher degrees of frequency (combining responses for often, most of the time, and always).

Appendix Table A6 demonstrates a summary of staff responses. Through response to open-ended survey questions, staff and faculty respondents offered additional insights about supports they offer when working with NNESs on campus, including specific communication strategies, accommodations, one-on-one assistance, visual materials, and promoting campus resources. Table 4 provides representative comments illustrating various methods faculty and staff respondents provide to NNES students.

Support for Faculty and Staff

Faculty and staff respondents were also asked a series of questions to determine what kinds of support would position them to be more effective in their teaching and support of NNESs. Overall, a majority of respondents (72% or higher) reported either "interested" of "very interested" in learning about all of the topics and strategies we listed as options to support NNESs. Of these, faculty and staff expressed the strongest degree of interest (combining "interested" and "very interested" responses) in strategies to help NNESs improve comprehension (81%), strategies to encourage participation from NNESs (78%), and awareness about campus resources (76%). Appendix Table A7 illustrates a summary of this data. Regarding the format of how they would prefer to receive training or resources, over half of faculty and staff respondents indicated they preferred to receive support through online resources, such as a resource website (59%) or an online training course (52%). Other faculty and staff respondents expressed interest in attending an in-person workshop (49%) and receiving an e-newsletter (42%). A smaller number of respondents reported interest in participating in an individual consultation (20%). Appendix Table A8 summarizes this data.

Faculty and staff also provided further explanation of additional types of support they would perceive to be valuable in their responses to relevant open-ended questions. Several respondents expressed interest in specific support options being developed for NNES students (such as enhanced transition support, language workshops, and one-on-one tutoring) and in learning more information about which campus resources were most helpful for NNESs. Some respondents also reported an interest in receiving culture and language training, communication support, and strategies for grading/giving feedback. Table 5 demonstrates the qualitative themes by providing an illustrative response from a faculty or staff respondent.

Table 5: Potential Resources for Faculty and Staff Who Support Nonnative English Speakers

Resources	Representative comments
Student support suggestions ($n = 76$)	*I think a range of support is needed, from intensive English language courses, to workshops on study skills / writing for American-style courses, to one-on-one tutoring around assignments.*
Information about campus resources ($n = 37$)	*... I wish I knew what university resources are available to help them [nonnative English speakers]. As far as I'm aware, none of the faculty in my department know where to direct these students, so this is a problem that goes beyond my individual class or experience.*
Culture & language training ($n = 18$)	*I would like to receive some training in at least the basics of a one or two of the languages that many of my nonnative English-speaking students speak. I also think we at the university should do a better job of gaining cultural competency ...*
Communication style ($n = 11$)	*I would love some tips on how to best adapt my communication style if I am noticing a language barrier. I want to make sure I am understood and the students know what is going on, but I also don't want to be condescending or "speak down" to anyone.*
Feedback & grading strategies ($n = 9$)	*General strategies for providing feedback on written work that is helpful to students but allows them to take ownership of making improvements in their English language skills.*
Student needs assessment ($n = 7$)	*Information / feedback about nonnative English speaker graduate students' background and experiences that would allow me to help with their transition and during their program of study in the department.*
Guidance on accommodations ($n = 5$)	*I always consider different backgrounds, but have no formal training in what changes to make to better accommodate such backgrounds.*

DISCUSSION

In this study, we sought to address a gap in the literature by better understanding the perspectives of university faculty and staff who support NNES learners, and by identifying instructional and support strategies that faculty and staff perceive as valuable when interacting with NNESs. One key finding is that faculty and staff report primarily positive views regarding various benefits of the diversity that NNES students contribute on campus, a finding which has been demonstrated in relevant literature (Andrade, 2010; Haan et al., 2017; Jin & Schneider, 2019; Mantzourani et al., 2015; Trice, 2003). However, as Haan et al. (2017) indicated, despite their apparent positive regard for diversifying the student population, faculty (and staff) in our study also demonstrated varying degrees of concern and bewilderment regarding the challenges NNES students experience, and how they can provide support to help students navigate the challenges they may encounter.

Understanding the Complexity of NNES Student Challenges

Our survey results confirm previous findings that even NNES students who have high levels of language proficiency are likely to experience challenges with language and cultural barriers in U.S. higher education (Andrade, 2006, 2010). We build on this previous understanding by illuminating a more nuanced complexity of the challenges that NNES students often encounter in their academic experience. Our survey findings indicate that challenges NNES students experience not only relate to language but also cultural differences, both of which often overlap with their abilities to adapt to new academic processes, policies, and expectations, and to interact with peers and faculty from a place of confidence. Further complicating these challenges is the finding that many students may be reticent to seek help for the complex pressures they face; as one survey respondent stated, "I have noticed that many students that struggle with fluency in English are hesitant to ask for assistance or clarification." Another respondent commented, "Despite my attempts to be open and welcoming of conversation about challenges, students still appear reluctant to ask for my help or consideration on their assignments." Students who see challenges with language as a deficit, may try to hide the challenges they are experiencing in an attempt to not lose credibility with their instructors instead of seeking out support resources. In previous studies, scholars have demonstrated that international students may resist seeking mental or emotional help due to cultural stigma (Becker et al., 2018; Tung, 2011). Our study demonstrates that some faculty and staff perceive NNES students are hesitant to seek help for academic or language related challenges. Further research is warranted to understand how NNES students seek support when navigating cultural difficulties and facing language barriers.

Gaining Insight on Faculty and Staff Challenges

Similar to recent studies illuminating the needs of faculty and staff who are working to support increasingly diverse student populations (Haan et al., 2017; Harryba et al., 2012), the findings in the present study confirm that faculty and staff encounter complicated barriers in providing support to NNES students. As in the findings reported by Harrbya et al. (2012), staff and faculty in our study indicated concern about navigating language concerns, proficiency standards, and clarifying communication with NNESs. Highlighting a more nuanced complication, our respondents indicated that it may be difficult to discern if an NNES is primarily experiencing language or cultural difficulty, when in actuality, it is possible that a combination of various factors may be influencing a student's experience. As noted by one respondent,

> It is hard because culture confounds the relationship with a lot of these variables. A lot of my nonnative English-speaking students come from Eastern cultures where it may not be as culturally appropriate to ask questions, speak up in groups, etc. so I cannot tell you whether it is language or culture that impacts participation; thus, I answered not sure.

In fact, Sawir (2005) demonstrated how academic behaviors may be influenced not just by cultural values and norms, but by a student's previous learning experience and their beliefs about learning.

Additionally, some faculty and staff indicated they are simply unsure of how to help a student who is experiencing a language challenge. For those faculty and staff who try to intervene, they may face difficulties in talking to students about support resources, either because they are unaware of the correct resource to refer students to, or they are concerned that they may offend students by making a referral. Some faculty may even see English language support as a form of othering, or marginalizing students. This is an important phenomenon that is not addressed by current literature. Although our findings help to illuminate some of the complexities, we recommend that further research highlighting student perspectives would help to clarify how faculty and staff can offer support in ways that are perceived to be helpful and not insulting or marginalizing to students.

Offering Enhanced Resources for Faculty and Staff

Although a few recent studies document faculty perceptions on instructing multilingual student populations (Andrade, 2010; Haan et al., 2017), our study expands on these studies by demonstrating the types of additional support that would be helpful for faculty and staff who work with NNES students. Our respondents demonstrated high levels of interest in receiving support in various formats for working with NNES students. To effectively develop this support, it would be helpful if campus experts who specialize in language, culture, and faculty development could collaborate to provide more accessible resources for those who work with NNESs. Strategic collaboration across the curriculum is essential to support faculty and staff in determining what student support will be most useful in each situation (Zamel & Spack, 2004). Faculty and staff need training on the language acquisition process and how to differentiate a grammatical mistake from a more important language issue (Carroll & Ryan, 2007). Further, faculty and staff need to be informed about relevant campus resources and promote the use of these resources in ways that normalizes seeking support for NNESs.

Reframing Language Development

As mentioned previously, some of our survey respondents expressed confusion over how to normalize support seeking for NNESs. Our survey data also revealed that there is a range of perspectives from faculty on what their role should be in supporting NNESs. Some instructors felt it was not their job to support students in respect to language issues. Some people have a lower tolerance for language errors, while others recognize that language development is a natural process that should be supported for all students as we prepare them to succeed in the global marketplace. As one respondent described,

> Instead of creating an environment where students expect native fluency (a maximum of communication), why not promote tolerance of diversity by creating an expectation that speakers and audiences, writers and readers, must SHARE responsibility for making meaning? What if their non-native speaker status was an asset, rather than an inconvenience?

Although no one would argue that students need a high level of English in order to access the curriculum and thrive at a university, we need to also recognize that all students come to study at the university in order to acquire the language of their discipline (Swales, 1990). For students for whom English is not their first language, we must strike a balance between maintaining rigorous standards of academic excellence which include language use, and teaching NNESs the skills they need to meet those standards. As an institution, we have an opportunity to recognize the strengths that NNESs bring to our classes and community and help them further develop their language abilities. This may be more easily accomplished if we openly recognize multilingualism as a strength and also recognize that second language development is an ongoing process for students who study in a second language.

We must move away from seeing English language development as remedial, and instead encourage students to continue to develop their English skills throughout their time at the university. Supporting and encouraging language development through a variety of means benefits everyone and can help all students prepare to communicate cross-culturally and cross-linguistically.

LIMITATIONS

While this study built on previous work with student perspectives (Anderson et al., 2012), it only includes the views of faculty and staff from one institution. Although there are clearly some parallel themes that emerged between the previous data collected from students and this current data from faculty and staff, there are also some key gaps. For example, some of the questions that were asked of faculty and staff were not addressed with students, or vice versa. Furthermore, some of the data reported here by faculty and staff necessitate a clearer understanding of student perceptions on certain topics. Therefore, future research should incorporate the viewpoints of students and faculty using an intentional study design to gain a more comprehensive understanding of the key issues from both groups.

When inviting participant feedback on the survey, we clearly specified that our goal was to learn about faculty and staff perceptions of NNESs. We clarified in the opening text of the survey that "this population may include international students, as well as domestic students whose first language is not English." It may be, therefore, beneficial for future research to explore the different challenges that domestic and international NNES students face.

This study was conducted at a university in the United States where English is the language of instruction. Future studies could also include nonnative speakers of other languages studying in an environment where the instruction is not in their native language.

Note

Appendices for this article can be found on the JIS website at https://www.ojed.org/index.php/jis

REFERENCES

Anderson, M., Isensee, B., Martin, K., Godfrey, L. A., & O'Brien, M. K. (2012). *Student voices: A survey of international undergraduate students' first-year challenges*. Global Programs and Strategy Alliance, University of Minnesota. https://global.umn.edu/icc/resources/umntc-ugis-data/student-voices-summary.html

Andrade, M. S. (2006). International students in English-speaking universities. *Journal of Research in International Education, 5*(2), 131–154.

Andrade, M. S. (2009). The effects of English language proficiency on adjustment to university life. *International Multilingual Research Journal, 3*(1), 16–34.

Andrade, M. S. (2010). Increasing accountability: Faculty perspectives on the English language competence of nonnative English speakers. *Journal of Studies in International Education, 14*(3), 221–239.

Andrade, M. S., Evans, N. W., & Hartshorn, K. J. (2014). Linguistic support for NNES: Higher education practices in the United States. *Journal of Student Affairs Research and Practice, 51*(2), 207–221.

Becker, M. A. S., Dong, S., Kronholz, J., & Brownson, C. (2018). Relationships between stress and psychosocial factors with sources of help-seeking among international students. *Journal of International Students, 8*(4), 1636–1661.

Carroll, J., & Ryan, J. (Eds.). (2007). *Teaching international students: Improving learning for all*. Routledge.

Crose, B. (2011). Internationalization of the higher education classroom: Strategies to facilitate intercultural learning and academic success. *International Journal of Teaching and Learning in Higher Education, 23*(3), 388–395.

Galinova, E. (2015). Promoting holistic global citizenship in college. In R. D. Williams & A. Lee (Eds.), *Internationalizing higher education: Critical collaborations across the curriculum* (pp. 17–34). SensePublishers.

Haan, J. E., Gallagher, C. E., & Varandani, L. (2017). Working with linguistically diverse classes across the disciplines: Faculty beliefs. *Journal of the Scholarship of Teaching and Learning, 17*(1), 37–51.

Harryba, S., Guilfoyle, A., & Knight, S. A. (2012). Challenges faced by university staff members when providing services to international students: An Australian perspective. *The International Journal of Learning, 18*(6), 15–36.

Jin, L., & Schneider, J. (2019). Faculty views on international students: A survey study. *Journal of International Students, 9*(1), 84–96.

Kingston, E., & Forland, H. (2008). Bridging the gap in expectations between international students and academic staff. *Journal of Studies in International Education, 12*(2), 204–221.

Leask, B. (2009). Using formal and informal curricula to improve interactions between home and international students. *Journal of Studies in International Education, 13*(2), 205–221.

Loes, C., Pascarella, E., & Umbach, P. (2012). Effects of diversity experiences on critical thinking skills: Who benefits? *The Journal of Higher Education, 83*(1), 1–25.

Mantzourani, E. E., Courtier, N., Davies, S., & Bean, G. (2015). Perceptions of faculty in health care and social sciences on teaching international students. *Currents in Pharmacy Teaching and Learning, 7*(5), 635–644.

Peterson, P. M., & Helms, R. M. (2013). Internationalization revisited. *Change: The Magazine of Higher Learning, 45*(2), 28–34.

Robertson, M., Line, M., Jones, S., & Thomas, S. (2000). International students, learning environments and perceptions: A case study using the Delphi technique. *Higher Education Research and Development, 19*(1), 89–102.

Sawir, E. (2005). Language difficulties of international students in Australia: The effects of prior learning experience. *International Education Journal, 6*(5), 567–580.

Soria, K. M., & Troisi, J. (2014). Internationalization at home alternatives to study abroad: Implications for students' development of global, international, and intercultural competencies. *Journal of Studies in International Education, 18*(3) 261–280.

Swales, J. M. (1990). *Genre analysis: English in academic and research settings.* Cambridge University Press.

Trice, A. G. (2003). Faculty perceptions of graduate international students: The benefits and challenges. *Journal of Studies in International Education, 7*(4), 379–403.

Tung, W. C. (2011). Acculturative stress and help-seeking behaviors among international students. *Home Health Care Management & Practice, 23*(5), 383–385.

Urban, E. L., & Palmer, L. B. (2014). International students as a resource for internationalization of higher education. *Journal of Studies in International Education, 18*(4), 305–324.

Yefanova, D., Baird, L., Montgomery, M. L., Woodruff, G., Kappler, B., & Johnstone, C. (2015). *Study of the educational impact of international students in campus internationalization at the University of Minnesota.* Global Programs and Strategy Alliance, University of Minnesota. http://global.umn.edu/icc/documents/15_EducationalImpact-IntlStudents.pdf

Zamel, V., & Spack, R. (2004). Strangers in academia: The experiences of faculty and ESOL students across the curriculum. In *Crossing the Curriculum* (pp. 17–32). Routledge.

BETHANY D. PETERS is a faculty member at Greenville University, where she teaches multiple MA courses in the Teaching English as a Second Language (TESL) track. Her research interests include intercultural communication, group dynamics, and intercultural development strategies.
Email: bethany.peters@greenville.edu

MICHAEL E. ANDERSON is the Director of English Language Programs at the University of Minnesota - Twin Cities. His research interests include advanced study in a second language environment, second language assessment, and language teacher education.
Email: ande1819@umn.edu

Peer-Reviewed Article

© *Journal of International Students*
Volume 11, Issue 1 (2021), pp. 122-143
ISSN: 2162-3104 (Print), 2166-3750 (Online)
doi: 10.32674/jis.v11i1.2063
ojed.org/jis

Who Spends Too Much Time Online? Associated Factors of Internet Addiction Among International College Students in the United States

Katie K. Koo
Texas A&M University-Commerce, USA

Gudrun Nyunt
Northern Illinois University, USA

Boshi Whang
Northern Arizona University, USA

ABSTRACT

This study investigated the relation between Internet addiction and several associated factors (mental health, academic performance, socioeconomic status, self-esteem, demographic characteristics) for international students in the United States. One hundred and fifty-seven international students at a U.S. university completed five questionnaires: an Internet usage behavior questionnaire, an Internet addiction scale, a self-esteem inventory, a mental health inventory, and a demographic questionnaire. Data were analyzed using SPSS to examine the relation between Internet addiction and associated factors. The results indicated that male students who speak English as a second language and who are not religious are more likely to develop Internet addiction. Academic performance and socioeconomic status were found to be positive predictors of Internet addiction, and mental health and self-esteem were found to be negative predictors of Internet addiction. The relations between other associated factors were also examined.

Keywords: academic performance, English proficiency, international students, Internet addiction, mental health

INTRODUCTION

College students in the United States spend a significant amount of their day online (Jones et al., 2009). They use the Internet more frequently than the general population and are often the first to adopt new Internet tools and applications (Jones et al., 2009). The Pew Research Center (2019) reported that in 2019, 100% of U.S. 18- to 29-year-olds used the Internet. But while the Internet has become woven into the fabric of college students' lives, excessive use can negatively influence physical and mental health (Derbyshire et al., 2013).

International students in the United States may be particularly at risk for problematic Internet use (Park et al., 2014). They often rely on the Internet to seek information needed for daily life, to stay connected to friends and family at home, to make new friends in the host country, and for entertainment and relaxation (Lee et al., 2011; Sin & Kim, 2013; Yoon & Kim, 2014). Spending a lot of time online, coupled with feeling isolated and struggling to make friends, particularly with domestic students (Girmay & Singh, 2019; Liu, 2009), could lead to problematic reliance on the Internet.

Problematic use of the Internet has been referred to as Internet addiction (Cash et al., 2012). Internet addiction is defined as "non-chemical dependency on the use of the Internet" (Tikhonov & Bogoslovskii, 2015, p. 97). Individuals suffering from Internet addiction experience excessive or poorly controlled preoccupations, desires, or behaviors regarding Internet access that lead to impairment or distress (Shaw & Black, 2008).

While research on international students' Internet use is growing (e.g., Lee et al., 2011; Mikal et al., 2015; Sin & Kim, 2013; Yoon & Kim, 2013), many studies focus on how students use the Internet to help adjust to a new environment, failing to explore potential negative effects on students' mental health. The few studies that have looked at Internet use and mental health indicate that there may be a connection between mental health issues and frequent Internet use among international students (Han et al., 2013; S. E. Kim et al., 2015; Park et al., 2014). However, there is still the paucity of studies exploring Internet addiction and its associated factors among international students in the United States.

Purpose of the Study and Research Questions

The purpose of this quantitative study is to examine factors associated with international students' Internet addiction. Specifically, the study strives to answer the following three research questions: (a) How does the rate of Internet addiction among international college students vary based upon demographic factors?; (b) What are predictors of Internet addiction among international college students?; and (c) To what extent are academic performance, parents' education, socioeconomic status (SES), self-esteem, mental health, and Internet addiction associated with one another among international college students? To answer these questions, we explored the rate of Internet addiction associated with students' demographic factors and other factors to provide an in-depth understanding of Internet addiction among international college students.

LITERATURE REVIEW

International Students in the United States

In 2018–2019, over 1 million international students attended a higher education institution in the United States (Institute of International Education [IIE], 2019). International students, defined as anyone studying at a U.S. higher education institution on a temporary visa that allows for academic coursework, now make up 5.5% of the U.S. higher education student population (IIE, 2019). International students contribute billions to the U.S. economy each year (IIE, 2019), enhance intellectual capital, contribute to innovations, and promote diverse campus climates (National Association of International Educators, 2019).

Past research has documented the challenges international students face (e.g., Bastien et al., 2018; Koo & Nyunt, 2020; Liu, 2009; Li et al., 2018; Wu et al., 2015). International students, particularly those from non-English speaking countries with cultures that differ greatly from the United States, often experience language and academic barriers, homesickness, and social isolation (Liu, 2009; Koo et al., 2021; Mori, 2000; Wu et al., 2015). Individuals' struggle to adjust to a new cultural environment, referred to as "acculturative stress" (Berry, 2006), has been linked to mental health issues (Girmay & Singh, 2019; Liu, 2009; Mori, 2000; Zhang & Goodson, 2011a). For example, Zhang and Goodson (2011a) found that international students who experienced higher levels of acculturative stress and had less social support experienced more negative psychological symptoms.

Mental health issues, in general, seem to be on the rise among the college-age population (American College Health Association, 2008, 2017). International students seem to be particularly at risk of developing anxiety and other mental health issues (Forbes-Mewett & Sawyer, 2016). Researchers estimate that 15%–20% of international students in the United States experience poor mental health (Zhang & Goodson, 2011b). Such statistics are particularly concerning as much literature documents international students' hesitance to seek professional help (Forbes-Mewett & Sawyer, 2016).

Internet Usage and Acculturation

Internet use has been expanding rapidly. In 2001, 513 million users existed worldwide (Cohen-Almagor, 2011). By 2016, there were over 3.4 billion users worldwide, with China and India reporting the most, despite only 50% and 26% of their population being online, respectively (Roser et al., 2019). The amount of time individuals spend online has also increased. In 2019, about eight in 10 U.S. adults indicated that they accessed the Internet daily (Perrin & Kumar, 2019). About three in 10 (28%) indicated that they were online almost constantly; among those aged 18–29, almost half (48%) were online almost constantly (Perrin & Kumar, 2019).

To our knowledge, specific statistics on the Internet usage of international students in the United States are not available. However, as international students fall in the 18–29 age range, they are likely to be among those using the Internet frequently. In addition, previous research indicates that the unique acculturation challenges international students face may make them turn to the Internet, which has been found to, at times, be helpful in the acculturation process (Mikal et al., 2015). Using English-language Internet sites can positively impact English proficiency, which reduces acculturative stress (Ye, 2005). International students may use the Internet to look up everyday life information such as health information (Yoon & Kim, 2014) or to build emotional and social support networks with individuals in their home or the host country (Mikal et al., 2015). This can be positive or negative as, when such networks consist primarily of co-nationals, the Internet may allow international students to limit their cultural learning and integration into the new environment (Mikal et al., 2015; Park et al., 2014).

Individual differences and approaches to acculturation may shape how international students use the Internet (Wang & Sun, 2009). Chinese students in the United States who felt lonely have been found to be more likely to use the Internet for companionship and to pass time, while students who were not lonely used it for acculturation purposes (Wang & Sun, 2009). How Chinese international students in the United States approached acculturation (whether they focused on assimilating to U.S. culture, maintaining their own culture, etc.) has been found to influence whether they accessed U.S. or Chinese Websites (J. Li et al., 2018).

Internet Addiction and its Associated Factors

While the Internet presents many opportunities, the use of the Internet can become problematic, and turn into Internet addiction (Cash et al., 2012). Clinicians and scholars have disagreed on what exactly Internet addiction is and how to diagnose it (Yellowlees & Marks, 2007). Some argue that it should be classified as its own disease; others see the Internet as a tool used for addictive behaviors such as gambling, gaming, or pornography (Yellowlees & Marks, 2007). The American Psychiatric Association (2013) listed "Internet gaming disorder" as a mental illness but does not highlight Internet addiction as a separate disorder in the fifth edition of the *Diagnostic and Statistical Manual of Mental Disorders*.

Many scholars, however, have suggested definitions and diagnostic criteria for Internet addiction, sometimes referred to as "problematic Internet use," "computer addiction," "Internetomania," or "pathological Internet use" (e.g., Griffith, 2000; Shapira et al., 2003; M. C. Shaw & Black, 2008; Tikhonov & Bogoslovskii, 2015). Shapira et al. (2003) classified Internet addiction as an impulse control disorder. Diagnostic criteria include use for longer periods than planned, preoccupation with the Internet, and/or Internet use becoming one's most important activity (Griffith, 2000; Shapira et al., 2003). In addition, for addicted individuals, Internet use leads to significant distress or impairment in social, occupational, or other important areas of functioning (Shapira et al., 2003).

Much research has linked problematic Internet use to other mental illnesses (e.g., J. Kim et al., 2009; Şenormancı et al., 2014; Shang-Yu et al., 2019). For example, several studies indicate that problematic Internet usage such as excessive online shopping, gambling, gaming, and aimless surfing lead to higher levels of depression (Morgan & Cotton, 2003; Şenormancı et al., 2014; Shang-Yu et al., 2019; Yau et al., 2013). Others found that loneliness and/or depression can be the cause as well as the effect of problematic use (Ceyhan & Ceyhan, 2008; J. Kim et al., 2009). Connections seem to exist between low mental well-being, low self-esteem, and problematic Internet use (Akin & Isekender, 2011; H. K. Kim & Davis, 2009; Nie et al., 2017; Niemz et al., 2005; Younes et al., 2016). While most studies highlight negative impacts on mental health, some indicate that Internet use can also have positive impacts. For example, L. H. Shaw and Gant (2002) found that it can decrease loneliness and depression and increase self-esteem and social support. These studies indicate a need to further explore the connections between mental health, Internet use, and other factors.

While much literature exists on associations between Internet addiction, mental well-being, and self-esteem, fewer studies address additional factors associated with Internet addiction. A study on Korean youth (Heo et al., 2004) revealed that a higher SES has an indirect, inverse association with Internet addiction, as children with higher SESs were found to have higher self-esteem, which was considered as a negative factor associated with Internet addiction in that study. In another study on Korean youth, Hur (2006) found an association between academic performance and Internet addiction with students who received poor grades in school being more likely to be addicted to the Internet.

Several studies have examined the association between Internet addiction and demographic factors, though none of the studies focused on international students. Several studies found that men are at greater risk than women (Anderson, 2001; Lee et al., 2001; Şenormancı et al., 2014). Studies on Malaysian youth (Charlton et al., 2013) and Muslim university students (Nadeem et al., 2019) found that religious affiliation was associated with lower Internet usage.

A study on the association between parents' education and Internet addiction found that parental education was inversely associated with Internet addiction among boys but found no association among girls (Heo et al., 2014). Heo et al. (2014) argued that parents with a higher educational status are more likely to guide their children toward healthy and desirable Internet use, and the different results among genders might indicate Korean parents (where this study was conducted) had more concern and supervision on boys' Internet use as they were perceived as more vulnerable to video games and sexual and violent images.

Very few studies have focused on the topics of Internet addiction among international students in the United States. A few studies, however, have explored this topic among international students in other countries. For example, a study on Chinese international students in Korea by S. E. Kim et al. (2015) found that international students' smartphone addiction, a particular form of Internet addiction, could lead to poorer physical health. This could be caused by international students spending less time on physical activities when excessively using their smartphone (S. E. Kim et al., 2015). A study on international students in Singapore by Dutta and Chye (2017) found that international students who felt depressed, lonely, and socially isolated reported higher levels of problematic Internet use. The authors suggested that international students may use the Internet to escape from psychological distress, which could lead to overuse and addiction. They also noted that depression may interfere with one's ability to self-regulate.

One of the few studies on international students in the United States indicated that little use of Internet could also be an indicator of poorer mental health (Han et al., 2013). Based on a mental health survey from Yale University, the study revealed that international students at Yale who spent a moderate amount of time on the Internet had better mental health than students who spent too little time using the Internet (Han et al., 2013). Spending too little time using the Internet could indicate that the students' work or academic schedules are too rigorous, which could negatively impact students' mental health (Han et al., 2013).

In conclusion, although a wide range of studies have examined the association between various demographic factors, mental health, and Internet addiction, study participants were typically domestic residents of the country where the studies were conducted. As discussed earlier, international students' experience of living in a foreign country is quite unique and could affect their mental health and relationship with the Internet. To our knowledge, no study has systematically explored the relation between problematic Internet use (or Internet addiction), mental health, and other associated (demographic) factors for international students in the United States. Building on previous research, this study will examine these relations among international students in the United States.

METHOD

Data and Procedure

Data was collected through self-reported Internet surveys in Fall 2010. Upon receiving Institutional Review Board approval, the first author and three international student advisors from the Office for International Students and Scholars recruited participants via flyers, online advertisements, international student orientations, seminars and workshops for international students, and word of mouth. Only international undergraduate students enrolled in a degree program under an F-1 student visa were recruited. We gave interested participants detailed information about the purpose of the study and directed them to an online informed consent form and online survey. Out of the 200 students we initially targeted, 166 responded. Nine students did not fully complete the questionnaire; thus their data were excluded, resulting in a final sample of 157 participants.

Table 1: Characteristics of Participants (*N* = 157)

Category	%
Gender	
Male	46.0
Female	54.0
Year in college	
First	17.6
Second	25.5
Third	19.6
Fourth	25.5
Fifth+	15.2
Major	
Pre-med	35.0
Biology	27.0
Nursing	15.0
Business	11.0
Engineering	5.0
Education	4.0
Grade point average	
3.5–4.0	7.1
3.0–3.5	39.8
2.5–3.0	26.9
2.0–2.5	18.2
1.5–2.0	6.7
Length of stay in the US	
<6 mo	3.0
6 mo–1 yr	12.1
1–2 yr	24.2
2–3 yr	13.5
3–4 yr	33.8
4–5 yr	12.5
>5 yr	7.3
Socioeconomic Status	
High	36.0
Middle-high	54.3
Middle	8.3
Middle-low	1.1
Religion	
Protestant	32.3
Buddhist	28.6
Catholic	18.0
Muslim	16.9
Other	0.9
Father's highest education	
High school	18.9

Category	%
College	46.2
Graduate	35.9
Mother's highest education	
High school	16.2
College	36.1
Graduate	47.1
Parents' marital status	
Together	67
Divorced	25.7
Separated	7.0
Deceased	2.6

Participants

Participants in this study were 157 international undergraduate students from 14 different countries who were enrolled in a large private research institution located in the Mid-Atlantic region of the United States. Fifty-four percent were female. Over 80% were Asian, 9% Hispanic, 7% White, and 5% African American. Regarding country of origin, 35% were from China, 31% from India, 17% from Korea, 10% from Saudi Arabia, 7% from Taiwan, 2% Turkey, and 2% from Mexico. More than half were in pre-med or biology majors. Approximately 40% had lived in the United States for less than 2 years. Thirty-six percent indicated that they came from a high SES family, while 54% reported coming from a middle-upper class and 8% from a middle SES family. Lastly, 81% spoke English as a second language. See Table 1 for demographics of participants.

Instruments

Based on previous studies on Internet addiction and associated factors (Şenormancı et al., 2014; Shang-Yu et al., 2019), we examined how demographic factors (gender, primary language, and religion), family factors (parents' marital status, SES, birth order, and parents' education), and personal characteristics (grade point average [GPA], self-esteem and mental health) were associated with Internet addiction. Instruments used to measure the various factors are described below.

Internet Addiction Scale

The Internet Addiction Scale (I-Scale) developed by C. T. Kim et al. (2002) was employed to measure the presence and severity of Internet addiction. The Internet Addiction Scale is a self-reported questionnaire composed of 40 questions using 4-point Likert scales (1 = *never* to 4 = *always*). Sample questions include: "Do you stay online longer than originally intended?" and "Have you jeopardized or risked the loss of a significant relationship, job, educational or career opportunity because of the Internet?" Cronbach's alpha for the current study was .95. We treated Internet addiction as a continuous variable for all statistical performance in the study.

Self-Esteem Inventory

The Self-Esteem Inventory (SEI; Coopersmith, 1981) was applied to measure self-esteem in this study. The SEI is a self-reported questionnaire composed of 25 questions using 4-point Likert scales (1 = *never* to 4 = *frequently*) with the following sample questions: "There are lots of things about myself I'd change if I could" and "I can make up my mind without too much trouble." Cronbach's alpha was .85.

Mental Health Inventory

Mental health was measured by a brief version of the Mental Health Inventory-5 (MHI-5) by Berwick et al. (1991), which is based on the MHI developed by Veit and Ware (1983). The brief version of the MHI-5 is a self-reported questionnaire composed of five questions using 6-point Likert scales (1 = *never* to 6 = *always*). Five questions asked participants about their mental health status in the past month. Sample questions include: "How much of the time, during the last month, have you been very nervous?" and "How much of the time, during the last month, have you felt downhearted and blue?" A high score represents good mental health, and a low score indicates poor mental health. Cronbach's alpha was .91.

The aforementioned instruments were selected for the study after confirmatory factor analysis for validity testing (Johnson, 1983; C. T. Kim et al., 2002; Rivera-Riquelme et al., 2019).

Demographic Questionnaire

In the demographic questionnaire, participants reported information about gender, age, type of school, GPA, family background, religion, SES, religiosity, parents' highest degree, and parents' marital status.

Data Analysis

After we completed coding and data-cleaning procedures, we analyzed the data from our 157 participants using SPSS Version 22. We first analyzed our data through descriptive statistics to get a sense of who our participants were. We then conducted t tests to compare Internet addiction, which we treated as a continuous variable, by demographic factors (gender, native English speakers, religiosity—comparing religious vs. nonreligious, and parents' marital status—comparing together vs. not together). Next, we conducted correlation analysis with Pearson Product-Moment and hierarchical multiple regression analysis to gain insights into relations between Internet addiction and other associated factors.

RESULTS

We performed a preliminary analysis to examine whether relations existed among dependent variables, independent variables, and demographic variables. With the presence of relations, we performed advanced analysis on all variables. Prior to performing regression analysis, statistics for multicollinearity were conducted. For all variables, the variance inflation factor was between 1.14 and 2.77, and the collinearity tolerance was above .9, indicating that the variables were not multicollinear. In addition, we evaluated the normality of all variables for skewness, kurtosis, and quantile-quantile plots. Because skewness and kurtosis for all of the independent variables in this study were within normal ranges (Boylan & Cho, 2012), further transformation of variables was not necessary. Lastly, for missing data, we employed pairwise deletion for data cleaning.

Internet Addiction by Demographic Factors

Independent t tests were conducted to examine distributions of Internet addiction by demographic factors (gender, native English speaker, religiosity, and parents' marital status) for international students (see Table 2). Men ($M = 68.22$, $SD = 20.296$) reported significantly higher scores for Internet addiction than women ($M = 60.31$, $SD = 16.99$), $t = 11.697$, $p < .01$, and international students who spoke English as their second language showed significantly higher scores ($M = 63.22$, $SD = 18.90$) than native English speakers ($M = 61.49$, $SD = 18.90$), $t = 2.62$, $p < .01$. The Internet addiction scores of religious international students were significantly lower ($M = 58.33$, $SD = 17.71$) than those of nonreligious international students ($M = 61.84$, $SD = 19.26$), $t = 3.51$, $p < .05$. There was no significant difference by parents' marital status.

Table 2: Means, Standard Deviations, and Results of the t Test Comparisons for Internet Addiction by Demographic Factors

Categories	n	M	SD	t
Gender				
Male	71	68.22	20.30	11.69**
Female	86	60.31	16.99	
Native English speaker				
Native	32	61.49	18.90	2.62**
Nonnative	125	63.22	18.08	
Religiosity				
Religious	110	58.33	17.71	3.51*
Non-religious	47	61.84	19.26	
Parents' marital status				
Together	95	62.72	19.29	0.82
Not together	66	62.18	17.74	

Note. N = 157. *p < .05, **p < .01, **p < .001

Correlations Among Internet Addiction and Associated Factors

We conduced correlation analyses to examine how each associated factor related to Internet addiction (see Table 3). International students' Internet addiction was positively associated with academic performance ($r = .09, p < .01$) and SES ($r = .09, p < .01$) and negatively associated with self-esteem ($r = -.38, p < .01$), and mental health ($r = -.24, p < .01$). Internet addiction tended to be positively associated with parents' education ($r = .02$) and birth order ($r = .03$), but these results were not statistically significant.

We further analyzed how other factors were correlated with one another (see Table 3). Students' academic performance was positively associated not only with Internet addiction but also with SES ($r = .16, p < .01$) and birth order ($r = .07, p < .01$), while it was negatively associated with self-esteem ($r = -.17, p < .01$) and mental health ($r = -.07, p < .01$). SES was positively associated with Internet addiction ($r = .09, p < .01$), academic performance ($r = .16, p < .01$), and parents' education ($r = .14, p < .01$), and negatively associated with self-esteem ($r = -.28, p < .01$). Self-esteem was positively associated with mental health ($r = .56, p < .01$) and negatively associated with Internet addiction ($r = -.38, p < .01$), academic performance ($r = -.17, p < .01$), and SES ($r = -.28, p < .01$). The last factor, mental health, was positively associated with self-esteem ($r = .56, p < .01$) and negatively associated with Internet addiction ($r = -.24, p = <.01$), academic performance ($r = -.07, p < .01$), and SESs ($r = -.18, p < .01$).

Predictors of Internet Addiction

Lastly, we performed a hierarchical multiple regression analysis to examine predictors of international students' Internet addiction guided by conceptualizations of Internet addiction and associated factors (Şenormancı et al., 2014; Shang-Yu et al., 2019). As presented in Table 3, the regression model accounted for 20.5% of the variance in international students' Internet addiction ($R^2 = .205$).

Table 3: Correlations Among Variables

Variable	M	SD	1	2	3	4	5	6	7
1 Internet addiction	62.45	18.54	1						
2 Academic performance	3.08	1.01	.106**	1					
3 Parents' education	4.58	1.13	.02	.10	1				
4 Socioeconomic status	2.87	.85	.09**	.16**	.14**	1			
5 Self-esteem	83.12	12.58	−.38**	−.17**	−.01	−.28**	1		
6 Birth order	2.04	1.06	.03	.07**	−.01	.02	−.01	1	
7 Mental health	19.73	4.80	−.24**	−.07**	.02	−.18**	.56**	.03	1

Note. N = 157. *p < .05, **p < .01, ***p < .001

Table 4 illustrates a summary of the hierarchical multiple regression analysis. Each column contains the final beta (standardized regression coefficient) of each independent variable after all variables were entered into the regression model. Among six independent variables, four were significant predictors. SES and academic performance were positive predictors ($\beta = .09$, $p < .01$ and $\beta = -.103$, $p < .01$, respectively), meaning that affluent students and students with high GPAs were more likely to be addicted to the Internet. Self-esteem and mental health were negative predictors ($\beta = -.120$, $p < .001$ and $\beta = -.130$, $p < .001$, respectively), indicating that students with high self-esteem and those who were psychologically well were less likely to be addicted.

Table 4: Predictors of Internet Addiction

Variable	R^2	r	Step 1	Step 2	Final β Step 3	Step 4	Step 5	Step 6
Birth order	.008	.032	.04	.04	.05	.05	.05.	.05
Parents' education	.010	.026		.03	.03	.03	.04	.04
SES	.101	.098			.09**	.11**	.11**	.11**
Self-esteem	.150	−.380				−.120***	−.122***	−.122***
Academic performance	.177	.106					.103**	.107**
Psychological well-being	.205	−.240						−.130***

Note. $N = 157$. $*p < .05$, $**p < .01$, $***p < .001$

DISCUSSION

While international students in the United States often benefit from using the Internet to find information, stay connected to family and friends back home, and have access to entertainment (Lee et al., 2011; Sin & Kim, 2013; Yoon & Kim, 2014), problematic use, or Internet addiction, can lead to negative outcomes (Derbyshire et al., 2013). This study explored factors associated with Internet addiction to get a better sense of who, among international students in the United States, may be particularly at risk.

Our first research question asked how the rate of Internet addiction varies based on demographic factors among international students in the United States. We found that men and international students who spoke English as a second language showed significantly higher scores of Internet addiction than women and native-English speaking international students, respectively, while students who were religious had significantly lower scores in Internet addiction than nonreligious peers.

Our findings support previous studies that found gender differences in Internet addiction (Anderson, 2001; Lee et al., 2011; Senormanic et al., 2014). Gender dynamics among international students in the United Sates appear to be similar to those among U.S. college students (Anderson, 2001), with men being at greater risk of Internet addiction. Research on U.S. college student men indicates that they spend more time videogaming and other leisure activities online, while women spend more time on communication and educational activities (Weiser, 2000). These differing activities may explain the higher risk for men of developing an addiction, as online gaming has been found to have a strong association with problematic Internet use (Van Rooij et al., 2010).

Our findings further support previous studies that found that religious students are less likely to be addicted to the Internet than their nonreligious peers (Charlton et al., 2013; Nadeem et al., 2019). This difference, previously explored for Malaysian youth (Charleton et al., 2013) and Hong Kong university students (Nadeem, 2019) appears to hold true for our participants as well. This finding could be explained by the current literature (Charlton et al., 2013; Laurin et al., 2012; Rounding et al., 2012) indicating that religiosity is associated with better self-control and ability to delay gratification, which may weaken dependence on addictive behaviors such as Internet use.

Our study adds to the literature by finding that international students who speak English as a second language are at a greater risk than their native English-speaking peers. Much research indicates that those who speak English as a second language face unique challenges related to adjusting to U.S. culture and academics (Liu, 2009; Mori, 2000; Wolf & Phung, 2019). Being socially isolated and struggling academically may lead those for whom English is a second language to turn to the Internet to get support from family and friends at home, find information about the host country, or access entertainment and leisure activities in their native language. Such reliance may lead to overuse, which may result in addiction.

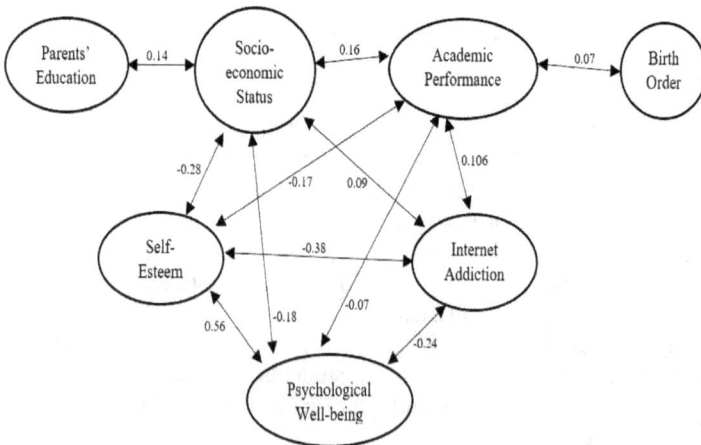

Figure 1: Relations of Internet Addiction and Associated Factors

Our second research question asked to what extent academic performance, parents' education, SES, self-esteem, mental health, and Internet addiction are associated with one another among international college students in the United States. Our findings indicate that SES, academic performance, self-esteem, and mental health are associated with Internet addiction as well as with each other. Our model (see Figure 1) supports and expands on existing research. Previous research on various populations has found associations between Internet addiction and academic performance (Hur, 2006), SES (Heo et al., 2014), self-esteem (Akin & Isekender, 2011; H. K. Kim & Davis, 2009; Nie et al., 2017; Niemz et al., 2005; Younes et al., 2016), and mental health (Ceyhan & Ceyhan, 2008; J. Kim et al., 2009; Morgan & Cotton, 2003; Şenormancı et al., 2014; Shang-Yu et al., 2019; Yau et al., 2013). Our study indicates that the same associations exist for international students.

Our final research question explored predictors of Internet addiction among international college students in the United States. Our regression analysis found that affluent students, students with high GPAs, students with low self-esteem, and those with poor mental well-being are more likely to be addicted. Our study supports findings from previous studies and indicates that these apply to international students in the United States as well; our study also contradicts some findings from previous studies.

First, unlike Heo et al. (2004) found, participants in our study who were from a higher SES were more likely to be addicted to the Internet. The difference in findings may be due to the different populations. Heo et al.'s (2004) participants were Korean youth. For our participants, international students in the United States, being more affluent may mean having access to more devices that provide Internet access, and thus more opportunities to spend time online. Previous studies indicate that the amount of time spent online is a significant predictor of addiction (Hur, 2006).

Second, our study contradicted previous research that found a relation between low grades and Internet addiction (Akhter, 2003; Hur, 2006; Kubey et al., 2001) by indicating that international students with higher GPAs were more likely to be addicted to the Internet. Previous studies focused on different populations: domestic college students (Akhter, 2003; Kubey et al., 2009) and Korean youth (Hur, 2006). More research is needed to understand why this dynamic may be different for international students in the United States.

Finally, our findings support previous research indicating that low levels of well-being and self-esteem are predictors of Internet addiction (Akin & Iskender, 2011; Ceyhan & Ceyhan, 2008; J. Kim et al., 2009; Nie et al., 2017). Individuals who experience high levels of stress or anxiety and those experiencing low self-esteem, loneliness, depression, or other mental health issues may turn to the Internet for distraction, comfort, and to find connections, which may increase their likelihood of becoming addicted. Considering that many international students experience loneliness, homesickness, and other mental health issues while adjusting to studying in the United States (Girmay & Singh, 2019; Koo & Nyunt, 2020; Liu, 2009; Mori, 2000; Zhang & Goodson, 2011b), the connection between these symptoms and Internet addiction is concerning and indicates a need to provide information and support related to healthy Internet use to international students.

Limitations

While this study's results provide meaningful insights regarding Internet addiction and international students' experiences, several limitations must be acknowledged. First, generalizability of our findings is limited since data were collected only in one institution and from only 157 students. Since international students at this institution may differ in important ways from those at other institutions, these findings cannot be generalized to the entire population of international students at U.S. higher education institutions. Our study, however, is one of the first exploring associated factors of Internet addiction for international students in the United States. As such, our study can be seen as an exploratory study indicating factors that may be associated with Internet addiction for international students in the United States. Future research should replicate this study with different international student populations in the United States.

Another limitation is that all measures elicited self-reported data and thus were vulnerable to common method bias and inflated correlations because of halo rating effects. Because participants were young adults, ranging in age from 19 to 27, and researchers could not closely supervise all 157 participants, the reliability of the survey results is limited. In addition, although correlation and regression analyses provide a snapshot of predictors of a dependent variable and the predictive value of independent variables, they do not prove cause and effect relations or directional relations between dependent and independent variables. Thus, the methodology is limited in its ability to show causal relations.

Finally, our data was collected in Fall 2010. Access to Internet and thus Internet usage has drastically increased in the past 10 years; new technologies have also altered the ways we access the Internet. This may raise concerns that our study results no longer hold. We, however, do not regard this as likely. Our study was not concerned with specific ways individuals access the Internet nor how much time individuals spend on the Internet; rather we were exploring the relations between various factors such as student demographics and Internet addiction. These relations are likely to stay constant over time. For example, research has consistently shown that men are more likely to be addicted to the Internet than women, a gender dynamic that was found about 20 years ago by Anderson (2001) but held true for our data, which was collected 10 years later.

Implications

Our study suggests several important implications for future research and practice. First, considering the vulnerability of international students in the United States to Internet addiction and the limitations of this study, future research should explore factors associated with addiction with a larger sample from multiple institutions. In addition, research should explore how unique aspects of international students' experiences and acculturation shape their Internet use and thus impact addiction, such as looking at links between acculturation strategies and addiction. Other research may strive to identify types of Internet use that lead to addiction for international students in hopes of providing practitioners with insights into types (e.g., social media use, entertainment, academic use) that should be encouraged or discouraged.

Our study also provides important insights for practitioners working with international students in the United States. While the Internet can provide international students with helpful information and opportunities to connect (Lee et al., 2011; Sin & Kim, 2013; Yoon & Kim, 2014), practitioners should proactively address the differences between healthy and unhealthy use. Advisors and counselors may also ask questions about international students' Internet use, particularly for those at higher risk of becoming addicted, in hopes of recognizing problematic use and being able to intervene early on.

Proactive interventions should also address various factors associated with Internet addiction, particularly those to which international students may be most vulnerable. Proactive measures may include fostering friendships between domestic and international students to reduce loneliness and homesickness and thus improve international students' well-being. Proactive measures could also focus on providing academic support specifically geared toward international students to reduce the risk of academic stress.

Finally, when working with international students who struggle with problematic Internet use, practitioners should not only address the addiction but also consider factors associated with it. Adequate support may require identifying underlying factors that may have led to problematic use, which could include academic stress, low self-esteem, or poor mental well-being, and providing assistance to address these.

CONCLUSION

Most importantly, practitioners and educators need to recognize that while the Internet provides many opportunities and beneficial resources to international students in the United States, excessive use may place international students at risk of addiction (Park et al., 2014). This study highlighted who, among international students in the United States, may be particularly at risk of developing an addiction and the factors associated with addiction. We hope that researchers, educators, and higher education administrators can use this information to develop proactive educational interventions to better support international students who are struggling with problematic Internet use.

REFERENCES

Akhter, N. (2013). Relationship between internet addiction and academic performance among university undergraduates. *Educational Research and Reviews*, 8(19), 1793–1796. https://doi.org/10.5897/ERR2013.1539
Akin, A., & Iskender, M. (2011). Internet addiction and depression, anxiety and stress. *International Online Journal of Educational Sciences*, 3(1), 138–148.

American College Health Association. (2008). *American College Health Association National College Health Assessment Fall 2008 Reference Group Data Report.* http://www.acha-ncha.org/docs/ACHANCHA_Reference_Group_Report_Fall2008.pdf

American College Health Association. (2017). *American College Health Association National College Health Assessment Fall 2008 Reference Group Data Report.* http://www.acha-ncha.org/docs/ACHANCHA_Reference_Group_Report_Fall2017.pdf

American Psychological Association. (2013). *Diagnostic and statistical manual of mental disorders* (5th ed.).

Anderson, K. J. (2001). Internet use among college students: An exploratory study. *Journal of American College Health, 50*(1), 21–26. https://doi.org/10.1080/07448480109595707

Bastien, G., Seifen-Adkins, T., & Johnson, L. R. (2018). Striving for success: Academic adjustment of international students in the U.S. *Journal of International Students, 8*(2), 1198–1219. https://doi.org/10.32674/jis.v8i2.143

Berry, J. W. (2006). Acculturative stress. In P. T. P. Wong &. L. C. J. Wong (Eds.), *Handbook of multicultural perspectives on stress and coping* (pp. 287–298). Springer.

Berwick, D., Murphy, J., Goldman, P., Ware, J., Barsky, A., & Weinstein, M. (1991). Performance of a five-item mental health screening test. *Medical Care, 29*(2), 169–176. https://doi.org/10.1097/00005650-199102000-00008

Boylan, G. L., & Cho, B. R. (2012). The normal probability plot as a tool for understanding data: A shape analysis from the perspective of skewness, kurtosis, and variability. *Quality and Reliability Engineering International, 28*(3), 249–264. https://doi.org/10.1002/qre.1241

Cash, H., Rae, C. D., Steel, A. H., & Winkler, A. (2012). Internet addiction: A brief summary of research and practice. *Current Psychiatry Review, 8*(4), 292–298. https://doi.org/10.2174/157340012803520513

Ceyhan, A. A., & Ceyhan, E. (2008). Loneliness, depression, and computer self-efficacy as predictors of problematic internet use. *Cyberpsychology & Behavior, 11*(6), 699–701. https://doi.org/10.1089/cpb.2007.0255

Charlton, J. P., Soh, P. C., Ang, P. H., & Chew, K. W. (2013). Religiosity, adolescent internet usage motives and addiction: An exploratory study. *Information, Communication & Society, 16*(10), 1619–1638. https://doi.org/10.1080/1369118X.2012.735251

Cohen-Almagor, R. (2011). Internet history. *International Journal of Technoethics, 2*(2), 45–64.

Coopersmith, S. (1981). *SEI: Self-esteem Inventory.* Consulting Psychologist Press.

Derbyshire, K. L., Lust, K. A., Schreiber, L. R., Odlaug, B. L., Christenson, G. A., Golden, D. J., & Grant, J. E. (2013). Problematic Internet use and associated risks in a college sample. *Comprehensive Psychiatry, 54*(5), 415–422. https://doi.org/10.1016/j.comppsych.2012.11.003

Dutta, O., & Chye, S. Y. L. (2017). Internet use and psychological wellbeing: A study of international students in Singapore. *Journal of International Students, 7*(3), 825. https://doi.org/10.5281/zenodo.570036

Forbes-Mewett, H., & Sawyer, A. (2016). International students and mental health. *Journal of International Students, 6*(3), 661–677.

Girmay, M., & Singh, G. K. (2019). Social isolation, loneliness, and mental and emotional well-being among international students in the United States. *International Journal of Translational Medical Research and Public Health, 3*(2), 75–82. https://doi.org/10.21106/ijtmrph.82

Griffith, M. D. (2000). Does Internet and computer "addiction" exist? Some case studies. *Cyberpsychology & Behavior, 3*, 211–218.

Han, X., Han, X., Luo, Q., Jacobs, S., & Jean-Baptiste, M. (2013). Report of a mental health survey among Chinese international students at Yale University. *Journal of American College Health, 61*(1), 1–8. https://doi.org/10.1080/07448481.2012.738267

Heo, J., Oh, J., Subramanian, S.V., Kim, Y., & Kawachi, I. (2014). Addictive Internet use among Korean adolescents: A national survey. *PLoS ONE, 9*(2), e87819. https://doi.org/10.1371/journal.pone.0087819

Hur, M. H. (2006). Demographic, habitual, and socioeconomic determinants of internet addiction disorder: An empirical study of Korean teenagers. *Cyberpsychology & Behavior, 9*(5), 514–526. https://doi.org/10.1089/cpb.2006.9.514

Institute of International Education. (2019). *Open Doors 2019 report on international students in the United States.* https://opendoorsdata.org/fast_facts/fast-facts-2019/

Johnson, B. (1983). The Coopersmith self-esteem Inventory: A construct validity study. *Educational and Psychological Measurement, 43*(3), 907–913. https://doi.org/10.1177/001316448304300332

Jones, S., Johnson-Yale, C., Millermaier, S., & Perez, F. S. (2009, October 5). Everyday life, online: U.S. college students' use of the internet. *First Monday: Peer-reviewed Journal on the Internet, 14*(10). https://doi.org/10.5210/fm.v14i10.2649

Kim, C. T., Kim, D. I., Park, J. K., & Lee, S. J. (2002). *A study on Internet addiction counseling and the development of prevention programs.* National IT Industrial Promotion Agency.

Kim, H. K., & Davis, K. E. (2009). Toward a comprehensive theory of problematic Internet use: Evaluating the role of self-esteem, anxiety, flow, and the self-rated importance of Internet activities. *Computers in Human Behavior, 25*(2), 490–500. https://doi.org/10.1016/j.chb.2008.11.001

Kim, J., LaRose, R., & Peng, W. (2009). Loneliness as the cause and the effect of problematic Internet use: The relationship between Internet use and psychological well-being. *Cyberpsychology & Behavior, 12*(4), 451–455. https://doi.org/10.1089/cpb.2008.0327

Kim, S. E., Kim, J. W., & Jee, Y. S. (2015). Relationship between smartphone addiction and physical activity in Chinese international students in Korea.

Journal of Behavioral Addictions, 4(3), 200–205. https://doi.org/10.1556/2006.4.2015.028

Koo, K., & Nyunt, G. (2020). Culturally sensitive assessment of mental health for international students. *New Directions for Student Services, 2020*(169), 43–52. https://doi.org/10.1002/ss.20343

Koo, K., Baker, I., & Yoon, J. (2021). The first year acculturation: A longitudinal study on acculturative stress and adjustment among the first year international college students. *Journal of International Students, 11*(2). https://doi.org/10.32674/jis.v11i2.1726

Kubey, R. W., Lavin, M. J., & Barrows, J. R. (2001). Internet use and collegiate academic performance decrements: Early findings. *Journal of Communication, 51*(2), 366–382. https://doi.org/10.1111/j.1460-2466.2001.tb02885.x

Laurin, K., Kay, A. C., & Fitzsimons, G. M. (2012). Divergent effects of activating thoughts of God on self-regulation. *Journal of Personality and Social Psychology, 102*, 4–21. https://doi.org/10.1037/a0025971

Lee, E. J., Lee, L., & Jang, J. (2011). Internet for the internationals: Effects of internet use motivations on international students' college adjustment. *Cyberpsychology, Behavior, and Social Networking, 14*(7–8), 433–437. https://doi.org/10.1089/cyber.2010.0406

Li, J., Wang, Y., Liu, X., Xu, Y., & Cui, T. (2018). Academic adaptation among international students from East Asian countries: A consensual qualitative research. *Journal of International Students, 8*(1), 194–214. https://doi.org/10.32674/jis.v8i1.160

Liu, M. (2009). Addressing the mental health problems of Chinese international college students in the United States. *Advances in Social Work, 10*(1), 69–86. https://doi.org/10.18060/164

Mikal, J. P., Yang, J., & Lewis, A. (2015). Surfing USA: How Internet use prior to and during study abroad affects Chinese students' stress, integration, and cultural learning while in the United States. *Journal of Studies in International Education, 19*(3), 203–224. https://doi.org/10.1177/1028315314536990

Morgan, C., & Cotton, S. R. (2003). The relationship between Internet activities and depressive symptoms in a sample of college freshmen. *Cyberpsychology & Behavior, 6*(2), 133–142. https://doi.org/10.1089/109493103321640329

Mori, S. C. (2000). Addressing the mental health concerns of international students. *Journal of Counseling and Development, 78*(2), 137–144. https://doi.org/10.1002/j.1556-6676.2000.tb02571.x

National Association of International Educators. (2019). *International students contribute to our economy and American innovation.* https://www.nafsa.org/Policy_and_Advocacy/Policy_Resources/Policy_Tre nds_and_Data/International_Students_Contribute_to_Our_Economy_and_ American_Innovation/

Nadeem, N., Buzdar, M. A., Shakir, M., & Naseer, S. (2019). The association between Muslim religiosity and Internet addiction among young adult college students. *Journal of Religion and Health*, *58*(6), 1953–1960. https://doi.org/10.1007/s10943-018-0697-9

Nie, J., Zhang, W., & Liu, Y. (2017). Exploring depression, self-esteem and verbal fluency with different degrees of internet addiction among Chinese college students. *Comprehensive Psychiatry*, *72*, 114–120. https://doi.org/10.1016/j.comppsych.2016.10.006

Niemz, K., Griffiths, M., & Banyard, P. (2005). Prevalence of pathological Internet use among university students and correlations with self-esteem, the General Health Questionnaire (GHQ), and disinhibition. *Cyberpsychology & Behavior*, *8*(6), 562–570. https://doi.org/10.1089/cpb.2005.8.562

Park, N., Song, H., & Lee, K. M. (2014). Social networking sites and other media use, acculturation stress, and psychological well-being among East Asian college students in the United States. *Computers in Human Behavior*, *36*, 138–146. https://doi.org/10.1016/j.chb.2014.03.037

Perrin, A., & Kumar, M. (2019). *About three-in-ten U.S. adults say they are "almost constantly" online*. Pew Research Center. https://www.pewresearch.org/fact-tank/2019/07/25/americans-going-online-almost-constantly/

Pew Research Center. (2019). *Internet/broadband fact sheet*. https://www.pewresearch.org/internet/fact-sheet/internet-broadband/#internet-use-over-time

Rivera-Riquelme, M., Piqueras, J. A., & Cuijpers, P. (2019). The Revised Mental Health Inventory-5 (MHI-5) as an ultra-brief screening measure of bidimensional mental health in children and adolescents. *Psychiatry Research*, *274*, 247–253. https://doi.org/10.1016/j.psychres.2019.02.045

Roser, M., Ritchie, H., & Ortiz-Ospina, E. (2019). *Internet*. Our World in Data. https://ourworldindata.org/internet

Rounding, K., Lee, A., Jacobson, J. A., & Ji, L. J. (2012). Religion replenishes self-control. *Psychological Science*, *23*, 635–642. https://doi.org/10.1177/0956797611431987

Şenormancı, Ö., Saraçlı, Ö., Atasoy, N., Şenormancı, G., Koktürk, F., & Atik, L. (2014). Relationship of internet addiction with cognitive style, personality, and depression in university students. *Comprehensive Psychiatry, 55*(6), 1385–1390. https://doi.org/10.1016/j.comppsych.2014.04.025

Shang-Yu, Y., Shih-Hau, F., Kai-Li, C., Pei-Lun Hsieh, & Lin, P. (2019). Relationships between depression, health-related behaviors, and Internet addiction in female junior college students. *PLoS One, 14*(8). https://doi.org/10.1371/journal.pone.0220784

Shapira, N. A., Lessig, M. C., Goldsmith, T. D., Szabo, S. T., Lazoritz, M., Gold, M. S., & Stein, D. J. (2003). Problematic Internet use: Proposed classification and diagnostic criteria. *Depression and Anxiety*, *17*(4), 207–216. https://doi.org/10.1002/da.10094

Shaw, L. H., & Gant, L. M. (2002). In defense of the Internet: The relationship between Internet communication and depression, loneliness, self-esteem, and perceived social support. *Cyberpsychology & Behavior*, *5*(2), 157–171. https://doi.org/10.1089/109493102753770552

Shaw, M. C., & Black, D. (2008). Internet addiction: Definition, assessment, epidemiology and clinical management. *CNS Drugs, 22*(5), 353–365. https://doi.org/10.2165/00023210-200822050-00001

Sin, S. C. J., & Kim, K. S. (2013). International students' everyday life information seeking: The informational value of social networking sites. *Library & Information Science Research, 35*(2), 107–116. https://doi.org/10.1016/j.lisr.2012.11.006

Tikhonov, M. N., & Bogoslovskii, M. M. (2015). Internet addiction factors. *Automatic Documentation and Mathematical Linguistics, 49*(3), 96–102. https://doi.org/10.3103/S0005105515030073

Van Rooij, A. J., Schoenmakers, T. M., Van de Eijnden, R. J., & Van de Mheen, D. (2010). Compulsive internet use: The role of online gaming and other internet applications. *Journal of Adolescent Health, 47*(1), 51–57. https://doi.org/10.1016/j.jadohealth.2009.12.021

Veit, C. T., & Ware, J. E. (1983). The structure of psychological distress and well-being in general populations. *Journal of Consulting and Clinical Psychology, 51*(5), 730-742. https://doi.org/10.1037/0022-006X.51.5.730

Wang, Y., & Sun, S. (2009). Examining Chinese students' internet use and cross-cultural adaptation: Does loneliness speak much? *Asian Journal of Communication, 19*(1), 80–96. https:// doi.org/10.1080/01292980802618494

Weiser, E. B. (2000). Gender differences in Internet use patterns and Internet application preferences: A two-sample comparison. *Cyberpsychology & Behavior, 3*(2), 167–178. https://doi.org/10.1089/109493100316012

Wolf, D. M., & Phung, L. (2019). Studying in the United States: Language learning challenges, strategies and support services. *Journal of International Students, 9*(1), 211–224. https://doi.org/10.32674/jis.v9i1.273

Wu, H. P., Garza, E., & Guzman, N. (2015). International student's challenge and adjustment to college. *Education Research International, 2015.* https://doi.org/10.1155/2015/202753

Yau, Y. H., Potenza, M. N., & White, M. A. (2013). Problematic Internet use, mental health and impulse control in an online survey of adults. *Journal of Behavioral Addictions, 2*(2), 72–81. https://doi.org/10.1556/jba.1.2012.015

Ye, J. (2005). Acculturative stress and use of the internet among East Asian international students in the United States. *Cyberpsychology & Behavior, 8*(2), 154–161. https://doi.org/10.1089/cpb.2005.8.154

Yellowlees, P. M., & Marks, S. (2007). Problematic Internet use or Internet addiction? *Computers in Human Behavior, 23*(3), 1447–1453. https://doi.org/10.1016/j.chb.2005.05.004

Yoon, J., & Kim, S. (2014). Internet use by international graduate students in the USA seeking health information. *Aslib Journal of Information Management, 66*(2), 117–133. https://doi.org/10.1108/AJIM-01-2013-0005

Younes, F., Halawi, G., Jabbour, H., Osta, N. E., Karam, L., Hajj, A., & Khabbaz, L. R. (2016). Internet addiction and relationships with insomnia, anxiety, depression, stress and self-esteem in university students: A cross-sectional designed study. *PLoS ONE, 11*(9), e0161126. https://doi.org/10.1371/journal.pone.0161126

Zhang, J., & Goodson, P. (2011a). Acculturation and psychosocial adjustment of Chinese international students: Examining mediation and moderation effects. *International Journal of Intercultural Relations, 35*(5), 614–627. https://doi.org/10.1016/j.ijintrel.2010.11.004

Zhang, J., & Goodson, P. (2011b). Predictors of international students' psychosocial adjustment to life in the United States: A systematic review. *International Journal of Intercultural Relations, 35*, 139–162. https://doi.org/10.1016/j.ijintrel.2010.11.011

KATIE KOO, PhD, is an Assistant Professor in Higher Education at Texas A&M University-Commerce. Her research focuses on diversity issues in higher education and underrepresented students' mental health and psychological well-being. She is interested in marginalized students' collegiate experiences and mental health issues, and international students' adjustment and well-being. Email: katie.koo@tamuc.edu

GUDRUN NYUNT, PhD, is a Clinical Assistant Professor in Higher Education at Northern Illinois University. Her research interests revolves around educational practices that foster the development of intercultural maturity and prepare students for active engagement in a global society. In addition, she engages in research that strives to better understand the experiences of international, underrepresented minority, and women graduate students, faculty, and student affairs staff at U.S. higher education institutions. Email: gnyunt@niu.edu

BOSHI WANG, MA, is a Senior Academic Advisor at Northern Arizona University, where he advises first year and major-exploratory students. Prior to this position, he worked at Center for International Education at NAU. His research interests include the mental health of international students, quantitative studies, and student development theories. Email: boshi.wang@nau.edu

Peer-Reviewed Article

© *Journal of International Students*
Volume 11, Issue 1 (2021), pp. 144-155
ISSN: 2162-3104 (Print), 2166-3750 (Online)
doi: 10.32674/jis.v11i1.1096
ojed.org/jis

OJED
OPEN JOURNALS IN EDUCATION

Reflexive Account of an Indonesian International Student's Challenges and Opportunities in a U.K. University's Doctoral Education Program

Udi Samanhudi
Sultan Ageng Tirtayasa University, Indonesia

ABSTRACT

This study is an autoethnography focused on providing an in-depth understanding of my personal experiences as an international doctoral student from Indonesia in a university in the United Kingdom. In this article, I share and discuss some challenging situations during my doctoral study particularly in writing a 5,000-word-essay for nine modules, which required me to explicitly perform critical thinking in my writing. I found that expressing my critical voice in writing was not easy, especially at the outset of my doctoral study period. I believe my previous education experiences neglected critical thinking pedagogy in the classroom, which is one of the most important factors causing this kind of difficulty of demonstrating critical thinking especially in writing.

Keywords: autoethnography, critical thinking, international students

INTRODUCTION

Born and raised in a small town in Indonesia, I never thought that I could get an opportunity to pursue my doctoral degree in a British university; yet in September 2016, I got the chance to start my doctoral study in the United Kingdom after winning a scholarship from the Indonesian government through the Directory General of Higher Education. Many international students coming from different countries and sociocultural environments often find it difficult when entering a new system of education, such as British universities that emphasize self-directed and critical thinking learning traditions (Arkoudis & Tran, 2010; Quality Assurance Agency for Higher Education, 2008; Richmond, 2007; Yeoh & Terry,

2013). International students, particularly from Asian countries, such as myself from Indonesia, often find it difficult to adapt to these expectations, especially in the beginning of study (Ai, 2015a, 2015b, 2015c). At the outset of my study period, I found I had to adjust from a model of learning that emphasized memorization to one that focused on critical thinking.

Today, critical thinking has been one of the main agenda items for education in Indonesia (Indah, 2017). However, during my schooling period in Indonesia from primary to university level, I experienced a pedagogical system that was still based more on a teacher-centered, textbook-focused approach (Gu & Maley, 2008). According to this pedagogical system, explanation is a dominant instructional practice with an emphasis on rote learning to be reproduced in examinations (Kameo, 2007). As a student, I was expected to be a passive recipient by simply listening to my teachers' explanations and a reproducer of knowledge in which critical thinking was rarely practiced. I grew up in this educational culture and learning atmosphere that emphasized utmost respect for teachers. This background shaped me to be someone who is always reluctant to express contradictory ideas, especially ideas opposed with those of my teachers. At that time, I was afraid that critiquing them would be considered rude and impolite. A similar situation has been well described by Wu (2002) who critically highlighted the difference in approach between East Asian and Western pedagogy as that of "filling the pot or lighting the fire" (p. 7).

In this article, I intend to provide insight and guidance from the experiences of an international doctoral student in the United Kingdom. In addition, my experiences may provide educational services and relevant government agencies a greater understanding on how to support international doctoral students more effectively in the future.

LITERATURE REVIEW

The Educational System in Indonesia

In order to fulfill the demand of globalization, the Indonesian government, as manifested in the 2003 National Education System Act of Indonesia, focused on critical thinking as an important issue in national education at both school and university levels (Indah, 2017). Despite the Indonesian government's placement of critical thinking as a main agenda item, implementation is difficult due to teachers' lack of understanding of critical thinking and their reluctance to apply these concepts and skills in their classroom (Emilia, 2010; Indah, 2017). This hesitancy might be because critical thinking is still considered as a Western approach of learning that places more concern on individuals than groups (Novera, 2004; Shaheen, 2012).

Kameo (2007) wrote that no matter how good critical thinking sounds in theory, it cannot be automatically transplanted into a culture that holds different values. Kameo (2007) further argued that critical thinking cannot be easily transplanted to the educational culture in Indonesia. This statement is supported by current findings of critical thinking–related studies conducted by other

Indonesian scholars such as Gustine (2014) and Indah (2017). Gustine (2014) reported that Indonesian students' critical thinking, especially in the context of writing, lags behind their counterparts from Western countries due to the previous "spoon-feeding" model of teaching and learning.

This educational background influenced me when entering a British university for my doctoral study. Dealing with critical thinking, especially in academic writing, is challenging not only because of my low understanding of the critical thinking concept but also because of my lack of proficiency in English in general and academic English in particular. This has been the hardest part I have experienced as a doctoral student, particularly at the outset of my study abroad.

Education in the United Kingdom

Higher education in the United Kingdom has attracted many international students. The United Kingdom has been reported the second most popular destination for international students to continue their studies, following the United States (Lillyman & Bennett, 2014). For example, in 2019, the total number of international students enrolled in U.S. colleges was 1, 095, 299 (IIE, 2019) followed by U.K. universities with 485, 645 international students (HESA, 2019). The motivation to study in British universities for international students is not only to gain a degree, but also to improve their maturity as a person, to improve their English proficiency, to build an international network, and to enhance their cultural understanding (Huang & Turner, 2018; Yamazaki, 2005). Studying abroad also helps international students enhance their job options and uplifts their social recognition in their own community (Mazzarol & Soutar, 2002). In other words, studying in U.K. universities opens opportunities for international students to grow personally, academically, and professionally (Furnham, 2004).

Critical thinking forms the heart and soul of every subject in the higher education system in the United Kingdom (Fell & Lukianova, 2015; Vyncke, 2012). It is an important component of students' learning assessments (Swatridge, 2014). This commitment is evidenced, for example, in the National Committee of Inquiry in the UK Higher Education, which clearly indicates that international students studying in the British universities are encouraged to be self-directed learners, who possess both disciplined thinking and high curiosity (Shaheen, 2012).

Studies Concerning International Doctoral Students

Many studies have focused on international doctoral students' experiences in British universities (e.g., Brown & Holloway, 2008; Cadman, 2000; Evan, 2007; Shaheen, 2012). Some of these studies have reported that international doctoral students in the United Kingdom suffer from some disadvantages. Robinson (2008) found that international students in the United Kingdom struggled with feeling lost and anxious on their arrival. Ingleton and Cadman (2002) found that instead of feeling successful, newly arrived international doctoral students felt isolated and uncertain. Studies have contended that a lack of familiarity with the language and the target culture often leads to international students' confusion, misunderstandings, anxiety, and stress (Gu & Maley, 2008; Karuppan & Barari, 2011). Proficiency in English, especially academic English, is significantly related to academic and psychological success in the program (Poyrazili & Grahame, 2007).

Other researchers have focused their studies on critical thinking issues among international students from Asian countries in the United Kingdom (e.g., Shaheen, 2012). Shaheen (2012) noted that most Asian students found it hard to make a comparison, evaluation, argumentation, and presentation of ideas in their writing. Shaheen (2012) wrote that the inability of most Asian students to express their critical thinking in their writing is due to differences of culture and low abilities in English. Bruce and Brameld (1999) further mentioned that the low ability of most Asian students to express their critical thinking in writing is due to their previous educational cultures that are more didactic, structured, and hierarchical than the Western education cultures. Forming a new learning strategy is not easy for most international students (Wierstra et al., 2003). Finally, in terms of English, Lea and Street (1998) emphasized that doctoral students might think clearly in their home language, but find it difficult to express their thoughts in English easily and find it hard to understand lessons during lectures and group discussions.

However, international students have still expressed their happiness with their study in the United Kingdom given they have more opportunities to meet with other international students (Brown & Holloway, 2008). These opportunities make it possible for them to build a professional network in the future (Cadman, 2000) and to increase their self-confidence levels and maximize their learning (Wong & Warring, 2010). Gu and Male (2008) reported that the educational environment in U.K. universities support international students in the exploration of their personal interests in learning independently (Gu & Maley, 2008). Thus, research of international students in the United Kingdom has identified common issues but also shared success, which my experiences attest to, as well.

METHOD

Autoethnography

This study is an autoethnography, which is interpretive in nature (Butz & Besio, 2009). It is a formal, structured approach to the study of the self (Austin & Hickey 2007). An autoethnography is often used in research and writing that seeks to understand cultural experience through a systematic narration, evocative thick descriptions, and analysis of personal experiences (Ai, 2015c; Sparkes, 2000). In Pelias' words, autoethnography is a study that "lets you use yourself to get to culture" (Pelias, 2003, p. 372). In other words, an autoethnography is a study that shows a link between a person with his/her culture (Wall, 2006). In this autoethnography I show the connection between my previous educational culture, which is teacher- and textbook-focused (Gu & Maley, 2008, p. 230) in Indonesia, and my experience in my first year as a doctoral student in a U.K. university, which puts emphasis on creativity and independent learning (Vyncke, 2012). I concentrate on ways of producing meaningful, accessible, and evocative research that is grounded from my personal experience.

As a qualitative method, autoethnography is "both process and product" (Hughes & Pennington, 2016). In this study, I use personal narration as a method to explore my experiences as a doctoral student in a British university, examining opportunities this doctoral program offers and challenges I have encountered. By using an autoethnography, this research bears the signature and voice of my own personal interpretation of my experiences (Schon, 1987); therefore, subjectivity, emotionality, and my influence as the researcher on the study is inextricable (Ellis et al., 2011). As both researcher and subject of this study, I have the opportunity to speak as a participant in the research. Integrating my voice, thoughts, and reflections into the text made the study more than "a mere summary and interpretation of the works of others, with nothing new added" (Clandinin & Connelly, 1994, p. 3).

Rationale and Justification

To follow Ai (2016), in this research I only focus on myself as the participant and use my experiences as a doctoral student in a university in the United Kingdom. I examine my own experiences because I want to provide an in-depth understanding of my personal experiences as an international doctoral student coming from a different tradition of learning in Indonesia. This self-study illuminates the educational "cultural experience" (Wall, 2006, p. 146) of my doctoral experiences to make this research more purposeful and powerful. Believing that "writing is a way of knowing, a method of inquiry" (Richardson, 2000, p. 13), in this autoethnography study, I did a free writing activity and jotted down all my experiences related to opportunities I gained from my doctoral program and challenges I encountered as suggested by Farrell et al. (2017). I relate events and actions to one another and "explore the cultural theme at play in the context of working in a setting with educational structures that differed vastly from those experienced by the author as a learner" (Farrell et al., 2017, p. 979).

Finally, to enhance the trustworthiness of my research, I used two validation strategies including detailed descriptions of my data and triangulation of my primary data with another source through returning to the literature in my discussion as another way to add rigor to the study (Wall, 2006).

FINDINGS

Challenges

One of the hardest challenges for me as an international doctoral student in a U.K. university has been learning critical thinking, especially in the context of writing for both module assignments and my dissertation. Expression of critical thinking is in conjunction with an individualist Western pedagogical tradition. My doctoral program demands the development of high levels of intellectual skills in which existing knowledge is mastered, synthesized, evaluated, critiqued, and communicated, and an original contribution to new knowledge is made (Chalungsoth & Schneller, 2011). The emphasis on critical thinking in my doctoral program is in line with what is expected of a doctoral degree—the highest level of academic award that demands every doctoral candidate is able "to conceptualize, design and implement projects for the generation of significant new knowledge and understanding" (Quality Assurance Agency for Higher Education, 2001, p. 2).

As an international student, however, I come from a pedagogical system that expected me to be a passive recipient and reproducer of knowledge. This system of education did not allow for practice of critical thinking, as assignments given emphasized rote learning. I also grew up in a culture in which teachers and intellectuals should be highly respected. Critiquing them is considered rude and impolite. These cultural expectations strongly affected me when entering a doctoral program at a U.K. university, where I am encouraged to be an independent learner and thinker. For some time, I was not able to adjust to the practice of critical thinking, especially in the context of writing at the beginning of my study period. I was confused when every module tutor said that my essay writing should be presented critically. I was nervous at that time that this inability to write critically would stop my journey in this doctoral program and I would return back home with no doctoral certificate in hand. It was such a terrible moment! I was so fearful every time the results of every module assessment were issued.

What I felt is similar to what was reported by Evans and Stevenson (2010), who cited a Chinese student participating in their study saying, "At home they want to know what you know from a text, not so much from your own critical thinking – here they encourage critical thinking which is very hard for me" (p. 9). My teachers in Indonesia wanted me to show my understanding of what I read through repeating phrases I gained from the textbooks.

As writing critically is not easy for me, often tutors commented on the clarity of ideas in my essay assignments. This occurred due to my English barriers and lack of understanding and skills in terms of academic writing in English. This situation coincides with the views of Facione (1990), who emphasized that clarifying meanings, purposes, ideas, and information is the most difficult part in writing an essay. This has also been a main problem many international students from Asian countries encounter (Campbell, 2008). Another main problem in dealing with writing is performing a critical analysis of the existing theories. Facione (1990) stated that in order to analyze critically, students will need to be able to organize ideas in their writing in a systematic and logical way.

In addition to demonstrating critical thinking, I also found expressing my thoughts in English during lecturing sessions challenging because of my lack of confidence in my English language skills. For example, it was not easy for me to understand or to explain a certain concept during a class session because I lacked familiarity with certain terms in English. This has led to confusion, misunderstandings, anxiety, and stress. I felt insecure as it took longer for me to be more proficient in academic English in order to fully participate in my module meeting sessions. The difficulty was doubled because a strong local accent (Irish) of several tutors was not easy to understand. Almost two decades ago, Takahashi (1989) reported a study concerned international students in universities in the United States. He wrote that acquiring academic English may take a longer time for international students due to its complexity and strong linguistic abilities the students must have. This finding is still relevant to the situation that I experienced during my first year of doctoral study.

A similar thing occurred during interactions with my local friends. Their strong local accent was a barrier to fully grasp what they said and meant during conversations with them both in and outside the classroom. For me, an interaction with my local colleagues was actually an opportunity to better understand local culture and values. However, it was very difficult to mingle with them due to my lack of familiarity with their English and accent. This situation was so irritating to me at that time and was a daunting barrier in my adjustment process in the early stage of my study. I am aware that this lack of English proficiency happened due to my lack of exposure with English in my previous education and my environment in general in Indonesia. When I was at primary and secondary school levels, for example, my teacher of English, spoke in Bahasa Indonesia more than English. A similar situation occurred even when I was studying at the English education department for both my bachelor and master's degrees; only a few of my professors applied an English-only policy in the classroom. The rest of them explained mostly in Bahasa Indonesia during lessons in the classrooms.

All in all, my experiences coincide with findings of studies focused on international students' experiences of study. For example, Mahmud et al. (2010) said that language is one of the basic aspects for adjustment process for international students. According to their study, students' poor English proficiency and understanding local dialect may hinder their adjustment process, especially in the early stage of their study abroad. Other researchers have found that instead of feeling successful, many international doctoral students start their study feeling isolated and uncertain due to their low proficiency in English (Ingleton & Cadman, 2002), which is significantly relating with their academic and psychological success in the program (Poyrazili & Grahame, 2007).

Opportunities

Apart from those challenges above, as an international student studying in one of the outstanding universities in the United Kingdom, today I realize that those challenges were a part of my journey as a doctoral student. I have realized that this university and the doctoral program have provided me opportunities to grow personally and professionally. For example, studying at the professional doctoral program in this university has allowed me to to engage in interprofessional communities of learning and practice through module class sessions, which has shaped my new self-identity as someone who is more confident with his current knowledge and experience as an academician in my home country in general and as a doctoral student in particular. The discourse of professional doctorates which emphasises the connection between theory and practice (Neumann, 2005) has also provided me with a new perspective of the importance of linking what I learn in my doctoral program with my professional context in Indonesia.

The process of learning in my doctoral program, which emphasizes critical thinking, has provided me with more opportunities for my personal and academic development, especially in the context of critical writing abilities and skills. Tutor feedback has helped me to learn about critical thinking in the context of writing. In addition, essay writing itself has been a real exercise to improve my critical thinking because through writing essays, I have learned directly how to analyze, synthesize, and evaluate theories. In addition, I have also learned to provide arguments that are supported by evidence to make them persuasive and convincing. All these are essential aspects of critical thinking, which I must show in any piece of writing (Chaffee, 2014). By having a better idea of critical thinking, as well as knowing how to apply this concept in my daily life as a student and as an academician in my home country, I hope I can be an independent thinker and an agent of change in the future.

Moreover, I also find myself at the moment, through this doctoral program, feeling more confident with my own learning and my way of expressing my ideas to others especially through writing. This is evidenced by, for example, my new role as an article writer for a local newspaper in my home country that I do regularly. This doctoral program has also transformed my ideas and mindset in relation to engagement with the world (Intolubbe-Chmil et al., 2012) and to intercultural learning and competence (Ippolito, 2007). I have also learned to challenge my sense of self, as well as improve my language skills, especially in academic English, which is useful in the completion of both writing and oral presentation assignments.

Finally, I also feel that my sense of independence in learning is stronger than before. I am aware that here, in this university, I am given freedom as a doctoral student to decide my way of learning. I have a lot of space to develop myself as a doctoral student, as well as an academician. Now, I can write research proposals, which allow me to learn a lot about a research topic of my interest. My potential supervisor encourages me to be more independent and choose any topic that fits in my interest. She gives me more and more freedom with my research. This surely challenges my creativity and my critical thinking. All these experiences as an international doctoral student, I am sure, will be enormously beneficial for me in the future and will also "shape my new outlook for the rest of my lives" (Furnham, 2004, p. 23).

CONCLUSION

In this autoethnography study, I have shared and discussed my personal experiences as a doctoral student in a university in the United Kingdom. For example, I shared some challenging situations during the first year of my study, particularly in writing a 5,000-word-essay for seven modules in which critical thinking should clearly be performed. I found that expressing my critical voice in writing was not easy, especially at the outset of my doctoral study period. I have emphasized in this study that my previous education experiences provided no emphasis in giving personal opinion in writing assignments, which was one of the most important factors that caused my failure in expressing critical thinking in writing. Apart from those challenges, in this writing I have also explained that today I feel more confident with my own learning and with my way of expressing ideas to others especially through writing as realized, for example, in my new role as an article writer for a local newspaper in my home country. What I learned most from my experience is the fact that this doctoral journey has helped me transform my ideas and mindset in relation to engagement with the world. I hope that this story of my first-year doctoral journey provides insights especially, on the importance of a clear guidance in terms of the expected standards for critical thinking in my doctoral program and in other contexts in which similar situations may be found.

Acknowledgments

I would like to thank Professor Ruth Leitch (Senior Lecturer, School of Social Sciences, Education and Social Works, Queens University Belfast, UK) for her expert advice and comments on this paper and the Indonesian Endowment Fund for Education Scholarship (LPDP) for its funding support.

REFERENCES

Ai, B. (2015a). Crossing the border: The sense of belonging and identity work of Chinese students in Australia. *International Journal of Interdisciplinary Educational Studies, 10*(1), 13–26.

Ai, B. (2015b). Living in-between: A narrative inquiry into the identity work of a Chinese student in Australia. *Life Writing, 12*(3), 353–368.

Ai, B. (2015c). A study of the EFL writing of Chinese learners: A critical narrative. *Changing English, 22*(3), 294–306.

Arkoudis, S., & Tran, L. (2010). Writing blah, blah, blah: Lecturers' approaches and challenges in supporting international students. *International Journal of Teaching and Learning in Higher Education, 22*(2), 169–178.

Austin, J., & Hickey, A. (2007). Autoethnography and teacher development. *International Journal of Interdisciplinary Social Sciences, 2*(1), 3–11.

Brown, L., & Holloway, I. (2008). The adjustment journey of international postgraduate students at an English university: An ethnographic study. *Journal of Research in International Education, 7*(2), 232–249.

Bruce, C. S., & Brameld, G. (1999). Encouraging student-directed research and critical thinking in NESB students. In Y. Ryan & O. Zuber-Skerrit (Eds.), *Supervising postgraduates from non-English speaking backgrounds*. SRHE and Open University Press.

Butz, D., & Besio, K. (2009). Autoethnography. *Geography Compass, 3*(5), 1660–1674.

Cadman, K. (2000). 'Voices in the air': Evaluations of the learning experiences of international postgraduates and their supervisors. *Teaching in Higher Education, 5*(2), 475–491.

Chaffee, J. (2014). *Critical thinking, thoughtful writing.* Cengage Learning.

Chalungsoth, P. & Schneller, G.R. (2011). Development of translation materials to assess international students' mental health concerns. *Journal of Multicultural Counselling and Development, 39*(4), 180–189.

Clandinin, D. J., & Connelly, F. M. (1994). Personal experience methods. In N. K. Denzin & Y. S. Lincoln (Eds.), *Handbook of qualitative research* (pp. 413–427). SAGE.

Ellis, C., Adams, T., & Bochner, A. P. (2011). Autoethnography: An overview. *Forum: Qualitative Social Research, 12*(1), 1–18.

Emilia, E. (2010). *Teaching writing: Developing critical learners.* Rizqi Press.

Evans, C. (2007). The experience of international doctoral education in nursing: An exploratory survey of staff and international nursing students in a British university. *Nurse Education Today, 27*(1), 499–505.

Evans, C., & Stevenson, K. (2010). The learning experiences of international doctoral students with particular reference to nursing students: A literature review. *International Journal of Nursing Studies, 47*(2), 239–250.

Facione, P. A. (1990). *The California critical thinking skills test-college level: Factors predictive of CT skills* (Technical Report #2). California Academic Press.

Farrell, L., Bourgeois-Law, G., Ajjawi, R., & Regehr, G. (2017). An autoethnographic exploration of the use of goal oriented feedback to enhance brief clinical teaching encounters. *Advances in Health Sciences Education, 22*(1), 91–104.

Fell, E. V., & Lukianova, N. A. (2015). British universities: International students' alleged lack of critical thinking. *Procedia-Social and Behavioral Sciences. 7*(5)*, 215,* 2–8.

Furnham, A. (2004). Education and culture shock. *Psychologist, 17*(1), 16–27.

Gu, Q., & Maley, A. (2008). Changing places: A study of Chinese students in the UK. *Language and Intercultural Communication, 8*(4), 224–245.

Gustine, G. (2014). *Critical literacy in an Indonesian EFL setting: Sustaining professional learning* [Unpublished doctoral dissertation]. Deakin University.

Higher Education Statistics Agency. (2019). *Higher education student statistics in the UK: 2019 to 2020.* https://www.gov.uk/government/statistics/announcements/higher-education-student-statistics-uk-2019-to-2020

Huang, R., & Turner, R. (2018). International experience, universities support and graduate employability–perceptions of Chinese international students studying in UK universities. *Journal of Education and Work, 31*(2), 175–189.

Hughes, S. A., & Pennington, J. L. (2016). *Autoethnography: Process, product, and possibility for critical social research.* SAGE.

Indah, R. N. (2017). Critical thinking, writing performance and topic familiarity of Indonesian EFL learners. *Journal of Language Teaching and Research, 8*(2), 229–236.

Institute of International Education. (2019). *Open doors 2019 data.* https://www.iie.org/Why-IIE/Announcements/2019/11/Number-of-International-Students-in-the-United-States-Hits-All-Time-High

Intolubbe-Chmil, L., Spreen, C. A., & Swap, R. J. (2012). Transformative learning: Participant perspectives on international experiential education. *Journal of Research in International Education, 11*(2), 165–180.

Ippolito, K. (2007). Promoting intercultural learning in a multicultural university: Ideals and realities. *Teaching in Higher Education, 12*(5–6), 749–763.

Kameo, R. M. (2007). Critical thinking in the classroom: Some cultural constraints. *English Education Journal of Language Teaching and Research, 7*(1), 1–13.

Karuppan, C., & Barari, M. (2011). Perceived discrimination and international students' learning: An empirical investigation. *Journal of Higher Education Policy and Management, 33*(1), 67–83.

Lea, M. R., & Street, B. V. (1998). Student writing in higher education: An academic literacies approach. *Studies in Higher Education, 23*(2), 157–172.

Lillyman, S., & Bennett, C. (2014). Providing a positive learning experience for international students studying at UK universities: A literature review. *Journal of Research in International Education, 13*(1), 63–75.

Mahmud, Z., Amat, S., Rahman, S., & Ishak, N. M. (2010). Challenges for international students in Malaysia: Culture, climate and care. *Procedia-Social and Behavioral Sciences, 7*, 289–293.

Mazzarol, T., & Soutar, G. N. (2002). "Push-pull" factors influencing international student destination choice. *International Journal of Educational Management. 16*(2), 18–28.

Neumann, R. (2005). Doctoral differences: Professional doctorates and PhDs compared. *Journal of Higher Education Policy and Management, 27*(2), 173–188.

Novera, I. A. (2004). Indonesian postgraduate students studying in Australia: An examination of their academic, social and cultural experiences. *International Education Journal, 5*(4), 475–487.

Pelias, R. J. (2003). The academic tourist: An autoethnography. *Qualitative Inquiry, 9*(3), 369–373.

Poyrazili, S., & Grahame, K. M. (2007). Barriers to adjustment: Needs of international students within a semi-urban campus community. *Journal of Instructional Psychology, 34*(1), 28–45.

The Quality Assurance Agency for Higher Education. (2008). *The framework for higher education qualification in England, Wales and Northern Ireland.* https://www.qaa.ac.uk/docs/qaa/quality-code/qualifications-frameworks.pdf

Richardson, L. (2000). Writing as a method of inquiry. In N. Denzin & Y. Lincoln (Eds.), *Handbook of qualitative research* (2nd ed., pp. 923–948). SAGE.

Richmond, J. E. (2007). Bringing critical thinking to the education of developing country professionals. *International Education Journal, 8*(1), 1–29.

Scriven, M., & Paul, R. (1987). *Critical thinking as defined by the National Council for Excellence in Critical Thinking.* 8th Annual International Conference on Critical Thinking and Education Reform, Rohnert Park, CA.

Schön, D. (1987). *Educating the reflective practitioner.* Jossey-Bass.

Shaheen, N. (2012). *International students at UK universities: Critical thinking-related challenges to academic writing* [Unpublished doctoral dissertation]. University of Huddersfield.

Sparkes, A. C. (2000). Autoethnography and narratives of self: Reflections on criteria in action. *Sociology of Sport Journal, 17*(1), 21–43.

Swatridge, C. (2014). *Oxford guide to effective argument and critical thinking.* OUP Oxford.

Takahashi, Y. (1989). Suicidal Asian patients: Recommendations for treatment. *Suicide and Life-Threatening Behavior, 19*(4), 305–313.

Vyncke, M. (2012). *The concept and practice of critical thinking in academic writing: An investigation of international students' perceptions and writing experiences* [Unpublished doctoral dissertation]. King's College London.

Wall, S. (2006). An autoethnography on learning about autoethnography. *International journal of qualitative methods, 5*(2), 146-160.

Wierstra, R. F. A., Kanselaar, G., & Van der Linden, J. L. (2003). The impact of the university context on European students' learning approaches and learning environment preferences. *Higher Education, 45*(1), 503–523.

Wong, J., & Waring, Z. (2010). *Conversation analysis and second language pedagogy: A guide for ESL/EFL teachers.* Routledge.

Wu, S. (2002). Filling the pot or lighting the fire? Cultural variations in conceptions of pedagogy. *Teaching in Higher Education, 7*(4), 387–395.

Yamazaki, Y. (2005). Learning styles and typologies of cultural differences: A theoretical and empirical comparison. *International Journal of Intercultural Relations, 29*(2), 521–548.

Yeoh, J. S. W., & Terry, D. R. (2013). International Research Students' Experiences in Academic Success. *Universal Journal of Educational Research, 1*(3), 275-280.

UDI SAMANHUDI is a senior lecturer in the Department of English Education at Sultan Ageng Tirtayasa University, Indonesia. His major research interests lie in the area of genre analysis, discourse analysis, academic literacies, academic writing, critical pedagogy, and identity construction in ELT. Email: udisamanhudi@untirta.ac.id

Peer-Reviewed Article

© *Journal of International Students*
Volume 11, Issue 1 (2021), pp. 156-175
ISSN: 2162-3104 (Print), 2166-3750 (Online)
doi: 10.32674/jis.v11i1.1377
ojed.org/jis

OJED
OPEN JOURNALS IN EDUCATION

Helping International Students Identify Themselves: Social Media Usage and Organizational Attachment

Gustavo Valdez Paez
Ning Hou
James A. Tan
Zhan Wang
St. Cloud State University

Jing Hua
Troy University

ABSTRACT

The relationship between social media usage and personality has received increased scrutiny recently. The current study studies international students' organizational attachment through the exploration of their personality and usage of university social media. Participants were 51 international students from a Midwest State University and 49 domestic (U.S.) students for comparison purposes. Results showed some differences in the structure of personality, level of social media usage, and level of organizational attachment comparing international students and domestic students. Results also supported the complementary purpose of using social media for international students, where agreeableness and openness to experience are negatively associated with social media usage. Moreover, the relationship was stronger when students' English proficiency is lower. An overall model demonstrated the relationship among international students' personalities, university social media usage, and organizational attachment.

Keywords: Big Five Personality, organizational attachment, social media usage

INTRODUCTION

Global academic mobility is progressively more documented and researched; however, not much research has been conducted from the perspective of fundamental personality traits to understand the difference between international and domestic students. By applying a scientific lens on this phenomenon, the present study aims to discover similarities and differences in university social media usage between international and domestic students from the perspective of personality profiles, and investigate the association with university organizational attachment.

Using the Big Five Personality Traits to Understand Current Students

Personality is the result of life experiences, forged on observation, trial and error, and environmental factors; every decision we make contributes to its development (McCrae & Costa, 2003). In recent years, people have increasingly relied on digital technology for commonplace tasks; everything we do online creates a quantifiable digital footprint that can be analyzed and tracked to give us an insight on our habits and personality traits (Ai et al., 2019; Youyou et al., 2015).

International students face the challenge of adapting to a new language, new culture, and a substantially different environment. The whole process of adaptation is different for every individual, but learning about students' personalities through this digital footprint will allow us to understand the way people are reacting to different situations relative to their perception and potentially improve communication by building data-based bridges between academic institutions and students.

For this first study, we used the Big Five model to find trends in international students' opinions regarding social media usage and university communications. The Big Five factors include extraversion (e.g., sociability, assertiveness), emotional stability (e.g., anxiousness, insecurity), agreeableness (e.g., courteousness, cooperative), conscientiousness (e.g., dependability, perseverance), and openness to experience (e.g., imaginative, curious; Barrick & Mount, 1991; Gosling et al., 2003).

Understanding the Younger Generations

The majority of traditional-aged students in universities are now considered "Generation Z (Gen Z)" or students born from the mid- to late-1990s and early 2000s (Mintz, 2019). Gen Z has lived in a world without a barrier to technology; they have been bombarded with information and have different filtering habits from other generations. In addition, their preferred method of communication is through social media and apps (Andserson & Jiang, 2018; Twenge, 2017). Gen Z is also characterized as being more ethnically diverse, likely to be enrolled in college, and living with a college-educated parent (Wang, 2018).

Some of the top social media networks for U.S. teens are YouTube, Instagram, and Snapchat, with lower percentages reporting Facebook use

(Anderson & Jiang, 2018; Green, 2019). Among international users, WeChat is a popular messaging app, with about 1 billion users (Lee, 2019). Facebook and Twitter are also popular internationally (Poushter et al., 2018). These platforms, with their unique emphases, attract this younger generation by allowing them to create and share multimedia content with the public or private audiences (Binsahl et al., 2015).

Even though there have been studies on domestic students' social media usage from the personality perspective, the results have not been consistent (Huang, 2019). In the current study, we explore the issue of retention of international millennial and Gen Z students using the lens of university social media use and interaction from a personality perspective.

International Student Profile

Research has shown the support for the Big Five structure, but most research focuses on personality patterns in different countries (cf. Schmitt et al., 2007), different cultures (Hofstede & McCrae, 2004), different economic prosperities (Lynn & Martin, 1995), and various geographic factors (Allik & McCrae, 2004). Our current study contributes to the existing literature by using a unique sample from a specific geographic location with a diverse international student community. Similar to expatriates, international students move to a different country and a majority of them are using a different (nonnative) language to communicate and study. As such, we believe these students who self-select to study abroad are likely to have different levels of Big Five traits compared with domestic students (Caligiuri, 2000) under an etic perspective (Allik & Allik, 2002). For instance, individuals who choose to go abroad for their education are more likely to have higher openness to experience and are more curious and broad-minded (Barrick & Mount, 1991). Moreover, individuals who come from a culture with the ideology of obedience (e.g., Young, 2017) and decide to study abroad might tend to have different levels of sociability and emotionality. Thus, we would like to propose that international students have a different Big Five profile compared to domestic students:

H1: International students show a different pattern of personality portraits comparing to domestic students.

Social Media Usage Difference

Social media platforms such as Facebook, Instagram, and Snapchat serve multiple purposes, and college students use them to share information and manage previously acquired and new social connections (Ellison et al., 2007). International students face challenges and opportunities adapting to the new culture and new environment and may not have the typical local or face-to-face social support system that domestic students may have. As such, international students may rely more on online social support systems, using one or more social media apps to address communication challenges. International students may also be selective in the information they share with new acquaintances, and they have to do it in a second or third language.

Compared with face-to-face interactions, online social networking has certain advantages, including reducing obstacles (e.g., language barrier, culture differences), increasing communications, and finding communities through shared interests. With these features, we believe international students might be more likely to use social media websites than their domestic peers. Specifically, international students might be more likely to connect to their institution through Facebook, even though members of the Gen Z cohort might not use this as their primary social network site (Anderson & Jiang, 2018; Hodak, 2019). While Instagram and Snapchat are more popular with Gen Z, universities face far more hurdles in using these compared to individuals (e.g., need to post from a smartphone on Snapchat).

International students might be more likely to obtain information from social media sites since it allows them to avoid potentially awkward in-person interactions. Therefore, social media sites may be used by international students to establish communications with locals to gain social capital (Lin et al., 2012) and social support (Ye, 2006). In addition, students from Eastern cultures might perceive themselves as guests—observing, absorbing, and learning in the new culture—and, therefore, consider themselves to be less extraverted in expressing themselves (Hou et al., 2018). Culture shock is also a common experience induced by the different behavioral expectations in the host culture, and misunderstandings often occur (Hua et al., 2019; Zhou et al., 2008). Therefore, these cultural norms and customs could be the reason that international students are more likely to follow the sites than American students: For instance, in Eastern cultures, obedience to authority (i.e., university social media sites) is an important value of Confucian Dynamism (Young, 2017). Therefore, we propose:

> H2: The frequency of social media using for international students is higher compared to domestic students.

Big Five and Social Media Usage

Are personality traits the reason for different usage frequency of social media? With the increase and obsessive use of social media for young generations, researchers have been trying to examine the relationship of personality (e.g., Big Five) with social media uses (e.g., Correa et al., 2010; McCrae & Costa, 1997). Such research using U.S. samples have shown the relationships between Big Five dimensions and Internet activities, but interestingly, the relationships are moderated by the anonymity of the activities (e.g., Amichai-Hamburger, 2002). For nonanonymous social networking sites, studies found the usage related to extraversion (Quan-Haase, 2007; Zywica & Danowski, 2008), neuroticism (Ehrenberg et al., 2008), and openness to experience (Ross et al., 2009). In the current study, we are interested in seeing if similar relationships exist in international students.

Using social media provides additional connections for people (Correa et al., 2010). We argue individuals who interact with more people (i.e., extraverted) are more likely to have more friends on social networking sites, therefore using these resources more often; people who are less emotionally stable (i.e., high in neuroticism) are more likely to use messaging functions for additional communications in addition to face-to-face conversations; and people who are more open to new experiences (high in openness) are more likely to accept new method (i.e., online) to connect with other people. Therefore, the presentation of these traits might be related to the usage of social media sites.

However, we believe the purposes and psychological needs of international students are different from those of domestic students. Instead of using social media sites to extend their social network, international students are more likely to use it as a tool to fulfill their psychological needs. For individuals higher in extraversion, agreeableness, and openness to experience are more likely to immerse in the new culture—making more friends and being able to absorb further information from friends; while their counterparts would rely more on social media/internet to seek information. Therefore, we propose a complementary purpose of using social media for international students.

H3: International students with lower extraversion, agreeableness, and openness are more likely to visit the university social media sites, while international students with lower consciousness and neuroticism are less likely to visit the university social media sites.

However, this complementary model may be moderated by how hard it is for international students to adapt to the host culture. English proficiency might make social media profiles and usage display higher similarities to those presented by their domestic counterparts, lowering the difference in social media habits. Therefore, we propose:

H4: The relationship between personality and social media usage will be stronger for students with lower English proficiency.

Big Five, Social Media Usage, and Organizational Attachment

There is often a difference in identification levels between international and domestic students. International students choose to attend an institution outside of their home country based on limited contextual information; this decision demands the use of financial and human capital resources and requires a substantially different level of commitment (Mazzarol & Soutar, 2002). Rooted on sunk cost and the avoidance of cognitive dissonance, international students are more likely to express higher commitment and identification with their chosen institution (Ashforth & Mael, 1989; Meyer et al., 2002). Social media thus represents an opportunity to manage their image, and escalation of commitment can prompt these students to show higher levels of identification with the university to mark a difference from peers in their own home countries. Overall, we propose international students are more likely to show higher organizational attachment, which is conceptualized by higher organizational identification and higher affective organizational commitment.

H5: International students show higher organizational attachment.

Besides the differences between international students and domestic students in their organizational attachment, personality also plays a role. Different personality characteristics of the students affect their perceived identification and commitment to the university in different ways. Therefore, we propose,

H6: Big Five personality dimensions are associated with organizational attachment.

Finally, the use of social media is related to organizational attachment (Gonzalez et al., 2013). Therefore, we propose an overall model that social media usage mediates the relationship between the Big Five personality and organizational attachment (Figure 1).

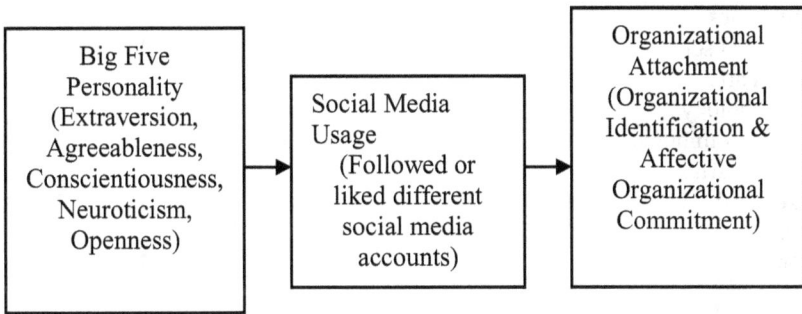

Figure 1: Interaction Effect of English Ability and Openness on University Social Media Usage

METHOD

Sample

Participants were 51 first-year international students enrolled at a public Midwestern state university. Data were collected during the university's international student orientation period. The University's Center for International Studies (CIS) incorporated the survey in the new student check-in orientation, and the staff from CIS facilitated the implementation and collection of the surveys during orientation. The average age of the sample was 20.1 and 53% were women. Students were pursuing multiple majors (e.g., business 41%; see Table 1) and from different countries (e.g., China 45.1%; see Table 1). The majority of the students (56.8%) have been in the United States for less than one month (and

78.4% had been in the United States less than three months) before this visit. To compare with the international students, we also collected similar data from 46 domestic students. The average age of the domestic students was 20.6 and 59% were women.

Table 1: Majors and Nationalities (N=51)

Variable	*n*	%
Major		
Business		
Finance	18	35.3
Management	1	2.0
Accounting	1	2.0
General business	1	3.0
Science and engineering		
Biomedical science	5	9.8
Computer science	4	7.8
Engineering	4	7.8
Statistics	1	2.0
General science	1	2.0
Liberal arts		
Psychology	2	3.9
Mass communication	1	2.0
Public affairs	1	2.0
Political science	1	2.0
Health		
Nurse	1	2.0
Art		
Music	1	2.0
Unspecified	8	15.7
Nationality		
Asia		
China	23	45.1
Nepal	4	7.8
Malaysia	4	7.8
Pakistan	4	7.8
Republic of Korea	3	5.9
India	3	5.9
Japan	1	2.0
Africa		
Nigeria	4	7.8
Ethiopia	2	3.9
Malawi	1	2.0
Rwanda	1	2.0
Kenya	1	2.0

Measures

Demographic Variables

The demographic survey of the international students included the following questions: country of origin, age, gender, on- or off-campus living situation, and self-report of English fluency. Age and gender information were collected for domestic students.

Big Five Personality

The mini-International Personality Item Pool scale was used to assess participants' Big Five personalities (Donnellan et al., 2006) and reliability estimates are as follows: extraversion (α = .77), agreeableness (α = .70), conscientiousness (α = .69), emotional stability (α = .68), and openness (α =.65). The measure contains 20 items with four items for each dimension. Reversed items are included in the measure. One sample item was: "In general, I am the life of the party" for the extraversion dimension. Items were rated on a scale ranging from 1 (*strongly disagree*) to 5 (*strongly agree*).

Social Media Usage

We measured the self-reported social media usage including a general question "Have you visited any of University A's social media accounts?" and specific questions for different sites including, "Have you followed or liked: University A's official account; university mascot's social media account; University A's admission office; University A athletics, and University A International Studies Center?" Students checked the boxes in the metrics and results were coded by subject matter experts.

Organizational Identification

Organizational identification was measured using Mael and Ashforth's (1992) six-item measure (α = .88). A sample item is "When someone criticizes (Name of School), it feels like a personal insult. Items were rated on a scale ranging from 1 (*very weak*) to 5 (*very strong*).

Affective Organizational Commitment

Affective organizational commitment was measured using Meyer et al.'s (1993) eight-item measure (α = .78) with a sample item "I feel as if this organization's problems are my own." Items were rated on a scale ranging from 1 (*very weak*) to 5 (*very strong*).

RESULTS

Big Five Profile

Descriptive information, including means, standard deviations, correlations, and coefficient alphas, are listed in Table 2. We conducted independent samples *t* tests to test our hypotheses of differences between international and domestic students on various personality traits. Results showed that international students showed different patterns comparing with domestic students: higher neuroticism, $t(95) = 2.6, p < .05$, and higher openness to experience, $t(95) = 2.5, p < .05$ (see Table 3).

Table 2: Means, Standard Deviations, and Correlations for Study Variables

	M (SD)	1	2	3	4	5	6	7	8	9	10	11	12	13	14	15
Ext	3.04 (0.87)	.65														
Agr	3.48 (0.86)	.17	.64													
Con	3.44 (0.86)	.26**	.35**	.60												
Neu	2.89 (0.74)	-.04	.14	-.04	.43											
Ope	3.43 (0.87)	-.07	.33**	.24*	-.30	.60										
OI	3.20 (1.04)	.07	.04	-.12	.38**	.06	.88									
AOC	3.11 (0.83)	.02	.31**	0.03	.38**	.21*	.69**	.53								
Any	0.42 (0.50)	-.08	.03	.04	.00	-.03	.16	.09	—							
Off	0.47 (0.50)	.13	-.01	-.14	.14	-.23*	.02*	.17	.15	—						
Bli	0.16 (0.40)	.09	-.17	-.18	.09	-.17	.26*	.08	.01	.23*	—					
Adm	0.26 (0.44)	-.01	-.20*	-.20*	.21*	-.07	.20*	.09	.07	.34**	.29**	—				
Ath	0.33 (0.47)	.22*	-.11	-.05	.04	-.29**	.13	.04	.11	.52**	.37**	.34**	—			
CIS	0.26 (0.44)	.09	-.18	-.09	.10	-.10	.34**	.18	.07	.38**	.35**	.57**	.39**	—		
EA	0.20 (0.40)	-.03	-.29**	-.18	.16	-.12	.15	-.05	.05	.31**	.45**	.66**	.43**	.54**	—	
Lib	0.22 (0.41)	.03	-.25*	-.08	.08	-.15	.12	-.07	.16	.50**	.35**	.66**	.48**	.55**	.69**	—

Note. Numbers on the diagonal are coefficient alphas for various scales. Ext = extraversion; Agr = agreeableness; Con = conscientiousness; Neu = neuroticism; Ope = openness to experience; OI = organizational identification; AOC = affective organizational commitment; Any = visited any university social media sites; Off = followed or liked university official account; Bli = university branding website; Adm = university admissions; Ath = university athletics; CIS = Center for International Studies; EA = education abroad; Lib = library. $*p < .05$, $**p < .01$.

Social Media Usage Difference

We proposed that international students are more likely to use university social media sites than domestic students. We conducted multiple analyses of variance and independent samples *t* tests to determine differences in usage between the two groups. The multiple analyses of variance was conducted first to test if the overall effect was significant. If the overall effect is significant, individual *t* tests would be conducted to determine individual effects. Results showed significant difference in international and domestic students' social media sites usage, $F(7, 89) = 2.19, p < .05$; Wilk's $\Lambda = 0.853$, $\eta_p^2 = .147$. Results for independent samples *t* test showed international students were more likely to visit university social media sites compared with domestic students in general (.53 vs.

.30, $t[95] = -2.28, p < .05$). We further examined whether the two groups differed on the frequency of following or liking specific university websites using a series of independent samples t tests. Results indicate international students were more likely to follow or like the University's International Studies Center account (.35 vs. .15, $t[95] = -2.30, p < .05$; see Table 4).

Table 3: Big Five Profile of International Student and Domestic Students

Trait	International ($n = 51$)	Domestic ($n = 46$)	t (df)	p
Extraversion	2.93	3.17	-1.37 (95)	.17
Agreeableness	3.50	3.45	0.31 (95)	.76
Conscientiousness	3.34	3.56	-1.26 (95)	.21
Neuroticism	3.07	2.69	2.60* (95)	<.05
Openness to experience	3.63	3.20	2.51* (95)	<.05
Organizational identification	3.62	2.74	4.58** (95)	<.01
Affective organizational commitment	3.43	2.76	4.35** (95)	<.01

Note. *$p < .05$, **$p < .01$.

Table 4: Means, Standard Deviations, Standardized Differences for Social Media Usage

Variable	International students ($n = 51$)	Domestic students ($n = 46$)	t	p
Visited any university social media sites	0.53 (0.50)	0.30 (0.47)	-2.28*	.03
University official account	0.49 (0.51)	0.46 (0.50)	-0.33	.74
University mascot	0.22 (0.46)	0.11 (0.32)	-1.30	.19
University admission offices	0.33 (0.48)	0.17 (0.38)	-1.80	.07
University athletics	0.27 (0.45)	0.39 (0.49)	1.22	.23
Center for International Studies	0.35 (0.48)	0.15 (0.36)	-2.30*	.02
Education abroad	0.25 (0.44)	0.13 (0.34)	-1.55	.13
Library	0.24 (0.43)	0.20 (0.40)	-0.47	.64

Note. For t, negative values indicate the international students' higher frequency of using the site. *$p < .05$.

Big Five and Social Media Usage

Results showed consistent associations between certain Big Five traits with social media usage. Specifically, we proposed agreeableness and openness to experience were more likely to show a negative relation with using multiple university social media sites (see Table 5). Therefore, Hypothesis 3 was partially supported.

Table 5: Social Media Usage and International Student Profile Correlation

Have you followed or liked	Ext	Agr	Con	Neu	Ope	OI	AOC
Off	.11	−.41**	−.17	.03	−.37**	.37**	.13
	(.16)	(.30*)	(−.11)	(.22)	(−.18)	(−.14)	(.20)
Bli	.10	−.27	−.26	−.01	−.43**	.29*	−.06
	(.15)	(−.09)	(−.09)	(.12)	(−.04)	(.17)	(.13)
Adm	.08	−.37**	−.19	.02	−.34*	.16	−.17
	(-.05)	(−.07)	(−.19)	(.33*)	(.04)	(.13)	(.20)
Ath	.14	−.59**	−.20	.04	−.38**	.18	−.28*
	(.26)	(.24)	(.02)	(.10)	(−.21)	(.23)	(.35*)
CIS	.23	−.44**	−.10	−.10	−.34*	.30*	−.14
	(.06)	(.05)	(−.02)	(.20)	(−.04)	(.27)	(.33*)
EA	.05	−.62**	−.22	.00	−.47**	.18	−.35*
	(−.06)	(.00)	(−.13)	(.25)	(.07)	(.00)	(.07)
Lib	.03	−.60**	−.20	.05	−.42**	.18	−.36**
	(.05)	(.04)	(.01)	(.10)	(.00)	(.05)	(.11)

Note. Numbers on the diagonal are coefficient alphas for various scales. Ext = extraversion; Agr = agreeableness; Con = conscientiousness; Neu = neuroticism; Ope = openness to experience; OI = organizational identification; AOC = affective organizational commitment; Off = followed or liked university official account; Bli = university branding website; Adm = university admissions; Ath = university athletics; CIS = Center for International Studies; EA = education abroad; Lib = library. *$p < .05$, **$p < .01$.

We used the Hayes Process (Hayes, 2012) to test whether international students' English ability moderates the relationship between the Big Five personality traits and social media usage (Hypothesis 4). We found English ability interacted with several Big Five traits in predicting social media usage (see Table 6). To demonstrate these interactions, we plotted the impact of English Ability * Openness on the usage (i.e., followed or liked) of the International Studies Center website (see Figure 2). We used a median split to categorize international students as having high English ability (median of 4.25 or higher; Category 1 in Figure 2) or low English ability (Category 0 in Figure 2). Results show that the negative relation between openness and social media usage is higher for those low in English ability. Hypothesis 4 is therefore partially supported.

Table 6: Behavior of Followed or Liked Social Media Sites Predicted from Personality and English Ability

SMS	Ext*EnA	Agr*EnA	Con*EnA	Neu*EnA	Ope*EnA
Off		−0.24*			0.25*
		(−1.21, 0.74)			(−0.62, 1.12)
Bli	−0.23*	2.02**	−0.52*	2.85**	2.30**
	(−2.05, 1.58)	(0.28, 3.75)	(−2.62, 1.57)	(0.35, 5.36)	(−0.03, 4.63)
Adm	0.92*	0.70*			1.41**
	(−0.39, 2.23)	(−0.46, 1.86)			(0.31, 2.51)
Ath	−0.24*	2.87**		1.67*	1.10**
	(−1.66, 1.18)	(0.32, 5.41)		(−0.27, 3.62)	(−0.06, 2.27)
CIS	0.49*	0.54**			1.30**
	(−0.78, 1.75)	(−0.64, 1.73)			(0.24, 2.37)
EA	−0.75**	−0.28**	0.02*	2.08**	0.99**
	(-2.01, 0.52)	(−7.04, 6.46)	(−1.47, 1.51)	(−0.22, 4.37)	(−0.57, 2.55)
Lib	−0.66*	−0.55**	0.03*	1.86**	0.80**
	(−1.91, 0.59)	(−7.24, 6.13)	(−1.46, 1.51)	(−0.37, 4.08)	(−0.64, 2.24)

Note. β and 95% CI are reported only for significant interactions ($p < .05$ for the model significance) in the table. SMS = social media sites; EnA = English ability; Ext = extraversion; Agr = agreeableness; Con = conscientiousness; Neu = neuroticism; Ope = openness to experience; Off = followed or liked university official account; Bli = university branding website; Adm = university admission; Ath = university athletics; CIS = University Center for International Studies; EA = education abroad; Lib = library.

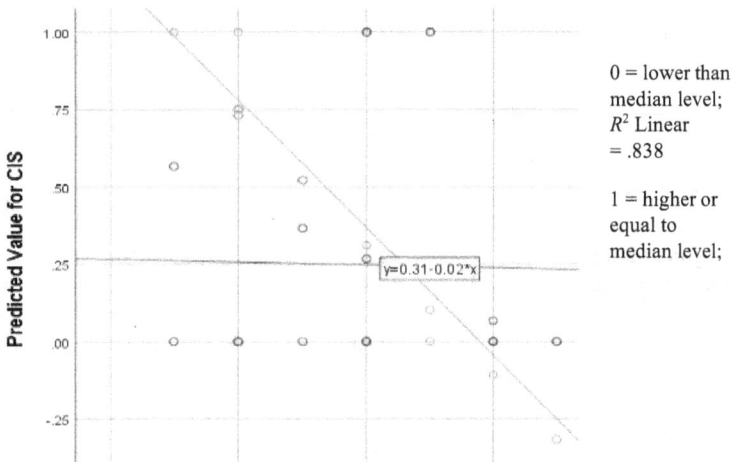

Figure 2: Interaction Effect of English Ability and Openness on CIS usage (followed or liked)

Big Five, Social Media Usage, and Organizational Attachment

Table 7: Multiple Regression Analyses for Big Five Personality Predicting Organizational Identification and Affective Organizational Commitment

Variable	Organizational identification			Affective organizational commitment		
	B	$SE\ B$	β	B	$SE\ B$	β
Extraversion	0.04	0.12	0.03	−0.06	0.10	−0.06
Agreeableness	−0.06	0.13	−0.05	0.20	0.10	0.20*
Conscientiousness	−0.28	0.13	0.22*	−0.13	0.10	−0.13
Neuroticism	0.34	0.15	0.24	0.25	0.11	0.23*
Openness	−0.01	0.13	−0.01	0.04	0.10	0.04
R^2		0.14			0.13	
F		2.86*			2.89*	

Note. $N = 51$. *$p < .05$.

Table 8: Behavior of Followed or Liked Social Media Sites Predicted from Personality and Group (International vs. Domestic Students)

SMS	Ext*Group	Agr*Group	Con*Group	Neu*Group	Ope*Group
Off		−2.06**			−0.87**
		(−3.33, −0.79)			(−2.11, 0.37)
Bli					−0.28*
					(−0.48, −0.09)
Adm		−0.94*	0.05*	−1.25*	−1.48**
		(−2.29, 0.40)	(−1.24, 1.36)	(−2.90, 0.39)	(−2.89, −0.07)
Ath		−4.52**			−2.16**
		(−7.41, −1.64)			(−4.03, −0.29)
CIS	0.72*	−1.69**			−1.18**
	(−0.64, 2.07)	(−3.19, −0.19)			(−2.64, 0.28)
EA		−6.39**			−3.52**
		(−11.7, −1.02)			(−5.88, −1.16)
Lib		−6.22**			−4.70**
		(−11.49, −0.97)			(−7.91, −1.50)

Note. β and 95% CI are reported only for significant interactions ($p < .05$ for the model significance) in the table. SMS = social media sites; Ext = extraversion; Agr = agreeableness; Con = conscientiousness; Neu = neuroticism; Ope = openness to experience; Off = followed or liked university official account; Bli = university branding website; Adm = university admissions; Ath = university athletics; CIS = Center for International Studies; EA = education abroad; Lib = library.

Our analysis also showed international students are more likely to identify with the university and have a higher affective organizational commitment (see Table 3), supporting Hypothesis 5.

Correlations showed that neuroticism is positively related to organizational identification and affective organizational commitment, while conscientiousness is related to affective organizational commitment. To test whether international students' Big Five personality traits predict organizational attachment (i.e., organizational identification and affective organizational commitment), we conducted multiple linear regression analyses. A significant regression equation was found, $F(5, 90) = 2.86$, $p < .05$, predicting organizational identification, with an R^2 of .14 and specifically, conscientiousness and neuroticism were significant predictors of organizational identification (see Table 8). We also found a significant regression equation for affective organizational commitment, $F(5, 90) = 2.59$, $p < .05$, with an R^2 of .13. Among five factors, agreeableness and neuroticism were significant predictors of affective organizational commitment (see Table 7). Therefore, hypothesis 6 is partially supported.

There are multiple factors to indicate social media usage while there are five dimensions in the personality measure. Therefore, an overall structural equation model was used to test the relationships among Big Five personality, social media usage, and organizational attachment; and is tested in Mplus. SEM results showed moderate fit: $\chi^2(df = 15) = 26.82$ ($\chi^2/2 < 2$), CFI = .81, RMSEA = .12, SRMR = .07.

DISCUSSION

For Gen Z, social media communication is a part of their daily life. Businesses have adapted and are using social media to reach out, and it is time for universities to adapt similar methods for recruitment and retention. Our study provides the first attempt to learn more about how international students' personalities interact with a university's social media presence. Our results provide several insights on the associations of the personality and the social media usage, which universities could use in their recruitment and retention process of international students (Redden, 2019).

First, this study highlighted the need for universities to use social media sites to interact with international students before and after they are admitted. In line with previous studies (e.g., Huang, 2019), our results indicate international students have a different profile compared with domestic students: Students who travel to study at a university in the United States generally are more sensitive and open to new experiences than domestic students who attend the same institution. They are also more likely to use the internet to gather information and follow the university's social media profiles (Esfahani & Chang, 2012; Kim et al., 2011; Saw et al., 2013). Therefore, universities can better utilize their social media pages to improve organizational attachment of international students by providing more information and better interactions with international students.

We also found an interesting variation: Domestic students are more likely to follow or like university athletic social media sites. Athletics are an important part of the college culture and they even impact domestic students' choice of universities, which leads us to think that they could be an excellent integration tool. In addition, domestic students are typically more familiar with university sports teams and would more likely identify with them (Cialdini et al., 1976).

Second, the findings confirmed that Big Five traits are crucial to international students' social media usage, and English proficiency further strengthens the ties.

Our study found that agreeableness and openness to experience showed negative associations with the use of multiple university social media sites. International students with a higher level of agreeableness and openness are usually more cooperative and eager to enjoy new experiences; thus, they are more comfortable and confident with interpersonal communications. Traditional and less prosocial students tend to prefer social media or websites to avoid human interactions. High English proficiency could boost their confidence while poor English skills push them to interact less. Social media becomes a safer platform to acquire information and interact with others. Previous research indicates that international students who socialize with domestic students generally adapt better than those who only make friends from their own countries (Gomes et al., 2015). Universities can design their social media pages as a useful social tool to help international students make friends extend their social network, to build a social media home away from home (Gomes et al., 2014).

Moreover, the findings also indicated the moderating role of social media on the relationship between personality and organizational attachment: The level of organizational identification and affective commitment with the university are associated with students' personality, and social media surveying is one of the mechanisms that can help us visualize this trend. The influx of a new generation is forcing universities to change their social media strategies to integrate and meet Gen Z's needs (Bizirgianni & Dionysopoulou, 2013). As suggested by previous studies (see Chang & Gomes 2017; Sleeman et al., 2016), universities become more humanized by interacting on social media with students to improve their "digital journey," which refers to "the transition that an individual makes online from relying on one digital bundle of sources to the other new bundle, perhaps based on the new host country or internationally" (Chang & Gomes, 2017, p. 355). Higher education institutions need to improve their efforts to become a part of this generations' activity.

CONCLUSION

The restrictions of our study can provide guidelines for future research. First, our sample is relatively small and only from one university, which makes the moderation effect less reliable. We conducted further analyses to verify our hypotheses of the differences in usage between international and domestic students and the direction of the results aligned with our expectations. Future research may further explore with a larger sample size from more universities. Another potential limitation was the reliance on self-report data, which posed an internal validity threat. Before collecting the data, we did a presentation to explain the purpose of this study, answered questions, and helped translate some questions to those students with relatively lower English proficiency.

Moreover, the scope of this study was limited to show that university social media pages give rise to student's emotional attachment. Some international students rely heavily on their peers and senior colleagues other than academic advisors (Chen & Ross, 2015). They also use other social media (such as Weibo, WeChat for Chinese students, Cyworld for Korean) other than University social media pages (Hjorth, 2007; Martin & Rizvi, 2014). It would be interesting to explore how interactions among international students on university social media pages drive their behaviors.

REFERENCES

Ai, P., Liu, Y., & Zhao, X. (2019). Big five personality traits predict daily spatial behavior: Evidence from smartphone data. *Personality and Individual Differences, 147,* 285–291.

Allik, I., & Allik, I. U. (2002). *The five-factor model of personality across cultures.* Springer Science & Business Media.

Allik, J., & McCrae, R. R. (2004). Toward a geography of personality traits: Patterns of profiles across 36 cultures. *Journal of Cross-Cultural Psychology, 35,* 13–28.

Amichai-Hamburger, Y. (2002). Internet and personality. *Computers in Human Behavior, 18,* 1–10. doi:10.1016/S0747-5632(01)00034-6

Anderson, M., & Jiang, J. (2018, May 31). *Teens, social media, & technology 2018.* Pew Research Center. https://www.pewresearch.org/internet/2018/05/31/teens-social-media-technology-2018/

Ashforth, B. E., & Mael, F. (1989). Social identity theory and the organization. *Academy of Management Review, 14,* 20–39.

Barrick, M. R., & Mount, M. K. (1991). The big five personality dimensions and job performance: A meta-analysis. *Personnel Psychology, 44,* 1–26.

Binsahl, H., Chang, S., & Bosua, R. (2015). Identity and belonging: Saudi female international students and their use of social networking sites. *Crossings: Journal of Migration & Culture, 6,* 81–102.

Bizirgianni, I., & Dionysopoulou, P. (2013). The influence of tourist trends of youth tourism through social media (SM) & information and communication technologies (ICTs). *Procedia-Social and Behavioral Sciences, 73,* 652–660.

Caligiuri, P. M. (2000). The Big Five personality characteristics as predictors of expatriate's desire to terminate the assignment and supervisor-rated performance. *Personnel Psychology, 53,* 67–88.

Chang, S., & Gomes, C. (2017). Digital journeys: A perspective on understanding the digital experiences of international students. *Journal of International Students, 7,* 347–466.

Chen, Y., & Ross, H. (2015). "Creating a home away from home": Chinese undergraduate student enclaves in US higher education. *Journal of Current Chinese Affairs, 44,* 155–181.

Cialdini, R. B., Borden, R. J., Thorne, A., Walker, M. R., Freeman, S., & Sloan, L. R. (1976). Basking in reflected glory: Three (football) field studies. *Journal of Personality and Social Psychology, 34,* 366–375.

Correa, T., Hinsley, A. W., & De Zuniga, H. G. (2010). Who interacts on the Web? The intersection of users' personality and social media use. *Computers in Human Behavior, 26,* 247–253.

Donnellan, M. B., Oswald, F. L., Baird, B. M., & Lucas, R. E. (2006). The Mini-IPIP scales: Tiny-yet-effective measures of the Big Five factors of personality. *Psychological Assessment, 18*, 192–203.

Ehrenberg, A., Juckes, S., White, K. M., & Walsh, S. P. (2008). Personality and self- esteem as predictors of young people's technology use. *Cyber Psychology and Behavior, 11*, 739–741. doi:10.1089/cpb.2008.0030

Ellison, N. B., Steinfield, C., & Lampe, C. (2007). The benefits of Facebook "friends:" Social capital and college students' use of online social network sites. *Journal of Computer-Mediated Communication, 12*, 1143–1168.

Esfahani, L., & Chang, S. (2012, December). Factors impacting information seeking behaviour of international students: Towards a conceptual model. In *Proceedings of the 2012 ISANA International Education Association Conference.* http://isana.proceedings.com.au/docs/2012/isana2012Final00044.pdf

Gomes, C., Berry, M., Alzougool, B., & Chang, S. (2014). Home away from home: International students and their identity-based social networks in Australia. *Journal of International Students, 4*, 2–15.

Gomes, C., Chang, S., Jacka, L., Coulter, D., Alzougool, B., & Constantinidis, D. (2015, December). Myth busting stereotypes: The connections, disconnections and benefits of international student social networks. In *26th ISANA International Education Association Conference.* http://isana.proceedings.com.au/docs/2015/Abstract-Catherine_Gomes.pdf

Gonzalez, E., Leidner, D., Riemenschneider, C., & Koch, H. (2013). The impact of Internal social media usage on organizational socialization and commitment. In *Proceedings of the 34th International Conference on Information Systems.*

Gosling, S. D., Rentfrow, P. J., & Swann Jr, W. B. (2003). A very brief measure of the Big-Five personality domains. *Journal of Research in Personality, 37*, 504–528.

Green, D. (2019, July 2). *The most popular social media platforms with Gen Z.* Business Insider Malaysia. https://www.businessinsider.my/gen-z-loves-snapchat-instagram-and-youtube-social-media-2019-6/

Hayes, A. F. (2012). *PROCESS: A versatile computational tool for observed variable mediation, moderation, and conditional process modeling [White paper].* http://www.afhayes.com/ public/process2012.pdf

Hjorth, L. (2007). Home and away: A case study of the use of Cyworld mini-hompy by Korean students studying in Australia. *Asian Studies Review, 31*, 397–407.

Hodak, B. (2019, November 29). *As Gen Z reshapes the social media landscape, marketers need to be open to change.* AdWeek. https://www.adweek.com/brand-marketing/as-gen-z-reshapes-the-social-media-landscape-marketers-need-to-be-open-to-change/

Hofstede, G., & McCrae, R. R. (2004). Personality and culture revisited: Linking traits and dimensions of culture. *Cross-Cultural Research, 38*, 52–88.

Hou, N., Fan, J., Tan, J. A., Hua, J., & Valdez, G. (2018). Cross-cultural training effectiveness: Does when the training is delivered matter? *International Journal of Intercultural Relations, 65,* 17–29.

Hua, J., Fan, J., Walker, A., Hou, N., Zheng, L., & Debode, J. (2019). Examinations of the role of individual adaptability in cross-cultural adjustment. *Journal of Career Assessment, 27*(3), 490–509.

Huang, C. (2019). Social network site use and Big Five personality traits: A meta-analysis. *Computers in Human Behavior, 97,* 280–290.

Kim, K. S., Yoo-Lee, E., & Joanna Sin, S. C. (2011). Social media as information source: Undergraduates' use and evaluation behavior. *Proceedings of the American Society for Information Science and Technology, 48,* 1–3.

Lee, C. (2019, January 9). *Daily active users for WeChat exceed 1 billion.* ZDNet.com. https://www.zdnet.com/article/daily-active-user-of-messaging-app-wechat-exceeds-1-billion/)

Lin, J. H., Peng, W., Kim, M., Kim, S. Y., & LaRose, R. (2012). Social networking and adjustments among international students. *New Media & Society, 14,* 421–440.

Lynn, R., & Martin, T. (1995). National differences for thirty-seven nations in extraversion, neuroticism, psychoticism and economic, demographic and other correlates. *Personality and Individual Differences, 19,* 403–406.

Mael, F., & Ashforth, B. E. (1992). Alumni and their alma mater: A partial test of the reformulated model of organizational identification. *Journal of Organizational Behavior, 13,* 103–123.

Martin, F., & Rizvi, F. (2014). Making Melbourne: Digital connectivity and international students' experience of locality. *Media, Culture & Society, 36,* 1016–1031.

Mazzarol, T., & Soutar, G. N. (2002). "Push-pull" factors influencing international student destination choice. *International Journal of Educational Management, 16,* 82–90.

McCrae, R. R., & Costa, P. T. (1997). Personality trait structure as a human universal. *American Psychologist, 52,* 509–516.

McCrae, R. R., & Costa, P. T. (2003). *Personality in adulthood: A five-factor theory perspective.* Guilford.

Meyer, J. P., Allen, N. J., & Smith, C. A. (1993). Commitment to organizations and occupations: Extension and test of a three-component conceptualization. *Journal of Applied Psychology, 78,* 538–551.

Meyer, J. P., Stanley, D. J., Herscovitch, L., & Topolnytsky, L. (2002). Affective, continuance, and normative commitment to the organization: A meta-analysis of antecedents, correlates, and consequences. *Journal of Vocational Behavior, 61*(1), 20–52.

Mintz, S. (2019, March 18). *Are colleges ready for Generation Z?* Inside HigherEd. https://www.insidehighered.com/blogs/higher-ed-gamma/are-colleges-ready-generation-z.

Poushter, J., Bishop, C., & Chwe, H. (2018, June). *Social media use continues to rise in developing countries but plateaus across developed ones.* Pew Research Center. https://www.pewresearch.org/global/2018/06/19/social-media-use-continues-to-rise-in-developing-countries-but-plateaus-across-developed-ones/.

Quan-Haase, A. (2007). University students' local and distant social ties: Using and integrating modes of communication on campus. *Information, Communication & Society, 10*, 671–693.

Redden, E. (2019, November 18). *Number of enrolled international students drops.* Inside Higher Education. https://www.insidehighered.com/admissions/article/2019/11/18/internationa l-enrollments-declined-undergraduate-graduate-and

Ross, C., Orr, E. S., Sisic, M., Arseneault, J. M., Simmering, M. G., & Orr, R. R. (2009). Personality and motivations associated with Facebook use. *Computers in Human Behavior, 25*, 578–586. doi:10.1016/j.chb.2008.12.024

Saw, G., Abbott, W., Donaghey, J., & McDonald, C. (2013). Social media for international students—It's not all about Facebook. *Library Management, 34*, 156–174.

Schmitt, D. P., Allik, J., McCrae, R. R., & Benet-Martínez, V. (2007). The geographic distribution of Big Five personality traits: Patterns and profiles of human self-description across 56 nations. *Journal of Cross-Cultural Psychology, 38*, 173–212.

Sleeman, J., Lang, C., & Lemon, N. (2016). Social media challenges and affordances for international students: Bridges, boundaries, and hybrid spaces. *Journal of Studies in International Education, 20*, 391–415.

Twenge, J. (2017, September). *Has the smartphone destroyed a generation?* The Atlantic. https://www.theatlantic.com/magazine/archive/2017/09/has-the-smartphone-destroyed-a-generation/534198/

Wang, H. (2018, November 15). *Generation Z is the most racially and ethnically diverse yet.* National Public Radio. https://www.npr.org/2018/11/15/668106376/generation-z-is-the-most-racially-and-ethnically-diverse-yet.

Ye, J. (2006). Traditional and online support networks in the cross-cultural adaptation of Chinese international students in the United States. *Journal of Computer-Mediated Communication, 11*, 863–876.

Young, J. T. (2017). Confucianism and accents: Understanding the plight of the Asian international student in the US. *Journal of International Students, 7*(3), 433–448.

Youyou, W., Kosinski, M., & Stillwell, D. (2015). Computer-based personality judgments are more accurate than those made by humans. *Proceedings of the National Academies of Science, 112*, 1036–1040.

Zhou, Y., Jindal-Snape, D., Topping, K., & Todman, J. (2008). Theoretical models of culture shock and adaptation in international students in higher education. *Studies in Higher Education, 33*, 63–75.

Zywica, J., & Danowski, J. (2008). The faces of Facebookers: Investigating social enhancement and social compensation hypotheses; predicting Facebook™ and offline popularity from sociability and self-esteem, and mapping the meanings of popularity with semantic networks. *Journal of Computer-Mediated Communication, 14*, 1–34.

GUSTAVO VALDEZ PAEZ is an artist and researcher at St. Cloud State University. His major research interests are personality, self-expression and team building. Email: gvaldez@stcloudstate.edu

NING HOU, PhD, is an assistant professor in the Department of Management and Entrepreneurship at St. Cloud State University. Her major research interests include cross cultural issues in organizations, leadership, and individual differences. Email: nhou@stcloudstate.edu

JAMES A. TAN, PhD, is a professor in the Department of Management and Entrepreneurship at St. Cloud State University. His major research interests lie in the area of staffing, employee development, and individual differences. Email: jatan@stcloudstate.edu

ZHAN (MYRA) WANG, PhD, is an assistant professor in the Department of Marketing at St. Cloud State University. Her major research interests focus on social media and digital marketing, marketing strategy, sales management, and the in-depth exploration of cause-effect-relationships in different fields of international marketing. Email: zwang3@stcloudstate.edu

JING HUA, PhD, is an assistant professor in the Department of Management and HR, Sorrell College of Business, Troy University. Her major research interests lie in the area of cross-cultural adjustment, positive psychology. Email: jhua@troy.edu

Peer-Reviewed Article

© *Journal of International Students*
Volume 11, Issue 1 (2021), pp. 176-194
ISSN: 2162-3104 (Print), 2166-3750 (Online)
doi: 10.32674/jis.v11i1.1454
ojed.org/jis

An Exploration on the Attachment, Acculturation, and Psychosocial Adjustment of Chinese International Students in Japan

Mengxi Yin
Cleveland State University, USA

Kikuyo Aoki
Ochanomizu University, Japan

Kelly Yu-Hsin Liao
Cleveland State University, USA

Hui Xu
Loyola University Chicago, USA

ABSTRACT

In this study, we selected Chinese students ($N = 277$) studying in Japan as research participants to examine the relation among their attachment, acculturation, and psychosocial adjustment. The study's first finding revealed that Chinese students studying in Japan had a better adjustment outcome than those in America in terms of sociocultural adjustment but not psychological adjustment. The second set of findings from the results of hierarchical multiple regression analyses showed that psychological distress and sociocultural adjustment could be predicted by attachment anxiety and avoidance. Third, we found a positive correlation between acculturation to the host culture and sociocultural adjustment difficulties. Fourth, we did not find a correlation between acculturation to the host culture and attachment anxiety and avoidance. We offer a discussion on the findings and limitations in light of the unique Japanese sociocultural context.

Keywords: acculturation, attachment, Chinese international students, Japan, psychosocial adjustment

176

Introduction

Higher education has seen a rapid rise in Chinese students enrolling in institutions in many countries like America and Japan (Organisation for Economic Cooperation and Development, 2017). This population is becoming the biggest group of international students, which causes the psychological well-being and cultural adaptation of Chinese international students to receive extensive attention. Research has been carried out to examine the joint issue of mental health and cultural adaptation in the context of Western individualism, but little research has been conducted to investigate the similar phenomenon in the collectivistic context of eastern countries (Ward & Lin, 2010). That is, the majority of the research studies to date on Chinese international students have been conducted in the United States, which values individualism and is the top destination for Chinese international students (Hofstede, 1980). The relationships between the cultural adaptation and mental health of Chinese international students may not be the same in individualistic and collectivistic contexts, which have different expectations and norms for the acculturation of Chinese international students. We chose Japan as the country to represent the collectivist context because it is the top destination in Asia for Chinese international students and has been intensively studied as an example of collectivist culture (Bond, 2002). Moreover, not enough is yet known about international students' adjustment issues in Japan from empirical journals (Lee, 2017).

The acculturation issues of Chinese international students are cross-culturally universal and special in collectivistic contexts (Ge, 2007; Ma, 2007), which is an important issue not only for an expanded theoretical understanding of acculturation in cross-cultural settings, but also teachers, helping professionals, and policy makers in collectivistic contexts. Among the studies on the acculturation of Chinese international students, modes of acculturation based on Berry's acculturation framework (Berry et al., 1987) and attachment based on attachment theory (Bowlby, 1988) appeared to be two important theoretical frameworks that were conducive to predicting the psychological outcomes of the acculturation process (e.g., Chen et al., 2002; Hayashi, 1997; Sun, 2013; Wang & Mallinckrodt, 2006). Therefore, our primary research question is: How do acculturation modes and attachment affect the acculturation process of Chinese students studying in Japan? Additionally, what is the difference in psychosocial adjustment between Chinese international students in Japan and Chinese/Taiwanese international students in the United States? Built on these research questions, we developed the following hypotheses:

Hypothesis 1: Chinese students studying in Japan would have a better adjustment outcome than those in the United States in both sociocultural and psychological domains.

Hypothesis 2: Greater identification with the home culture and adaptation to the host culture would exert a positive influence on the acculturation outcomes of Chinese students studying in Japan.

Hypothesis 3: High attachment avoidance and anxiety would predict more psychological distress and difficulties in sociocultural adjustment.

Hypothesis 4: There would be a negative correlation between attachment anxiety and avoidance and acculturation to the host culture.

Chinese International Students in Japan

For a number of western countries, China was the largest source of international students, accounting for over 30% of the total in America, Canada, Australia, and New Zealand (Center for China and Globalization [CCG], 2018). The number of overseas Chinese students has been expected to grow continuously in terms of its population size and academic diversity (CCG, 2018). However, Chinese international students are often faced with a variety of challenges, including academic stress, academic uncertainties, general life difficulties, and cultural adaptation problems (Yeh & Inose, 2003; Chen & Zhou, 2019). The researchers also found that they were often vulnerable to psychological issues such as depression and anxiety, and underutilized counselling services. Therefore, understanding the academic and personal challenges of Chinese international students is of great importance to their academic performance and mental health, which has been extensively studied in individualistic contexts (e.g., the United States).

As noted previously, remarkably little research has examined the acculturation of Chinese international students in collectivistic contexts like Japan. Studying the acculturation of Chinese international students in the Japanese context has practical implications. Due to globalization and falling birth rate in Japan, the Japanese government has been striving to take positive measures to accept highly skilled foreign human resources and promising foreign students continuing higher education. The "300,000 Foreign Students Plan" was proposed by the Japanese government in 2008 with a view of increasing international students to 300,000 as of 2020. Since then, the international student population has begun to increase rapidly and reached up to 267,042 by 2017, giving Japan the biggest share in Asia (Japan Student Services Organization, 2018). The aforementioned policy not only increased the number of international students, but also encouraged universities to offer more courses taught in English and create opportunities like exchange student programs that place an emphasis on motivation, language abilities, and academic preparedness. A priority for colleges and universities in Japan is to think about how to provide the best support for international students' adaptation to a new environment and the demands of higher education. In order to help overseas students to adapt in Japan, researchers have focused on the acculturation of overseas students from a variety of aspects since 1989. However, fewer studies have been conducted in Japan that focus on the acculturation of international students in its cultural context compared with western countries that have a longer history of accepting international students (Ge, 2007).

Chinese students, totaling 107,260 as of 20xx, constitute the largest subgroup of international students in Japan and have covered around or above half of the population since 1999 (JASSO, 2018). Individuals originating from a culture close to the host culture are likely to adapt well in the sociocultural domain (Ward et al., 2001), which may be associated with better psychological adjustment (Berry et al., 2006). China and Japan have been classified as collectivistic societies (Hofstede, 1993), and the cultural distance between China and Japan is considered to be close (Muthukrishna et al., 2018), thus the adaptation of Chinese students in Japan tends to be considered easier than that of students from English-speaking countries (Inoue & Merino, 2007). Indeed, research on Chinese international students revealed that students report less difficulties in learning Japanese (Tanaka et al., 1994), and the similarities shared in daily life routines between China and Japan contribute to students' adaptation to some degree (Yin & Aoki, 2017). However, when compared to their peers from other countries, cross-sectional research indicated that Chinese international students were faced with more sociocultural difficulties during the process of cultural adaptation and tended to suffer from more psychological distress than domestic students and international students from western countries (Ge, 2007; Ma, 2007). Research also highlighted that compared with domestic students, Chinese international students are less likely to initiate professional help-seeking behavior than domestic students (An & Nagai, 2019). In particular, research suggested that in addition to gender, duration of stay, language proficiency, and other demographic characteristics, international students from China were challenged by the insufficient emotional support and friends from the host country, and limited support systems that are tailored to their needs (An & Nagai, 2019; Wu, 2017). Jou and Fukada (2011) emphasized that despite the increase in the degree of total support for Chinese international students, the degree of stress perceived by the student group has increased. Following this, there is a critical need to develop interventions tailored to this student group.

In sum, overseas Chinese students are more likely to have difficulties in adapting to a new cultural environment, which thus highlights the need for targeted research attention and facilitation to this particular student group. So far, few studies have investigated the acculturation-related influence factors for the psychological well-being of this student group in Japan.

Theoretical Framework

Many experiences of Chinese international students can be understood within the framework of acculturation. Acculturation refers to both the process of adaptation and changes in psychology resulting from first-hand contact between individuals and/or groups from different cultural backgrounds (Berry et al., 1987). Berry and his colleagues (Berry et al., 1987) proposed a holistic model for acculturation, which has been widely used in contemporary studies on cultural adaptation. According to this model, the relation between acculturation and adjustment depends on five groups of moderating factors, including social nature, acculturating group type, individuals' social and demographic characteristics, and acculturation modes, as well as individuals' psychological characteristics.

When Berry et al.'s (1987) acculturation model was applied to Chinese international students, research predominantly focused on the modes of acculturation composed of integration, assimilation, separation, and marginalization. These modes were based on an orthogonal framework containing two cultural dimensions, namely attitudes toward the host and home cultures (Berry et al., 1987), each of which reflects a position on these two dimensions. Integration refers to highly identifying with host and home cultures; assimilation refers to highly identifying with the host culture, but weakly identifying with the home culture; marginalization refers to the opposite of integration on both dimensions; and separation refers to the opposite of both dimensions.

Conceptually, people who highly identify with both cultural dimensions (i.e., integration) were expected to show better psychosocial adjustment due to their ability to integrate two potentially conflicting cultures. Conversely, people who weakly identify with both cultural dimensions (i.e., marginalization) were expected to encounter psychosocial adjustment problems due to suffering from alienation with both host and home cultures (Berry et al., 1987; Bourhis et al., 1997). Research generally supported these theoretical predictions in individualistic cultural contexts. For example, Ward and Kennedy (1994) found that lower acculturation to the host culture predicted more difficulties in sociocultural adjustment, while strongly identifying with the home culture played a role in protecting mental health for a group of sojourners in New Zealand. Additionally, international students who highly identified with both cultural dimensions (i.e., integration) in America were found to experience less acculturative stress (Sullivan & Kashubeck-West, 2015). Since extant research predominantly focused on individuals from collectivistic cultural backgrounds (e.g., China and Korea) in individualistic contexts (e.g., Canada and the United States), Berry et al.'s (1987) theoretical proposition and related research on the benefits of identifying with both host and home cultures were heavily contextualized in individualistic contexts, whose cross-cultural validity remains to be explored in collectivistic contexts. The cultural specificity of acculturation is important for the expanded understanding of acculturation in a global context and the practice of mental health counseling in specific contexts (e.g., Japan). Thus, this study also aimed to explore the effects of acculturation modes on the adjustment outcomes of Chinese students studying in Japan.

The acculturation of Chinese international students in Japan is not only an increasingly important issue, but also possibly exhibits a different acculturation process from that in an individualistic context. The difference is attributable to the fact that collectivist cultures have different expectations and provide different hosting environments for the acculturation of Chinese international students compared with individualistic cultures. For example, collectivistic contexts might emphasize identifying with the host culture (for instance, a Chinese saying "ruxiangsuisu" and a Japanese proverb "gou ni itte wa gou ni shitagae" in collectivistic contexts could be translated into "When in Rome, do as the Romans do") because within-group homogeneity is a valued norm in collectivistic contexts

(Yasuda, 2011). Although Japan's government has made efforts in policy to represent a shift from a homogeneous-centered society toward a more pluralistic and diverse society, its effectiveness remains limited in the sociocultural level (Nagy, 2012). The pressure of identification with Japanese culture and the feeling of rejection from the host culture in its process have been highlighted in acculturation literature in Japan (e.g., Suzuki, 2007) especially among Chinese international students (Han, 2004; Yin & Aoki, 2017). Relatedly, identification with host cultures in collectivistic contexts may overlap with identification with Chinese culture due to the cultural similarities between collectivistic contexts and Chinese culture, reducing the additive prediction of the two identification factors for the adjustment outcomes of Chinese international students in collectivistic contexts. Thus, these culturally specific factors suggested different relationships between acculturation modes and outcomes of Chinese students studying in Japan, as demonstrated in previous studies. According to a study conducted by Sun (2013) on Chinese students studying in Japan, integration was not associated with psychological adjustment in spite of being seen as the most preferred mode. Han (2004) discussed that for some international students from China, ethnocentrism might have led to rejection of acculturation to the host country and therefore interfered with their adaption. When examining the modes of acculturation from two underlying cultural dimensions, Hayashi (1997) revealed that only acculturation to the host culture could directly predict acculturation outcomes for East Asian international students in Japan. Exploring the acculturation of Chinese international students in collectivistic contexts may provide the cross-cultural validity for Berry et al.'s (1987) acculturation framework.

Attachment and Acculturation

The other major topic of this study pertained to the effects of attachment styles on the cultural adaptation of overseas Chinese students. According to attachment theory (Bowlby, 1988), children or adults with secure attachment to caregivers are most capable of exploring the physical or social environment. Anxiety and avoidance are conceptualized as two dimensions underlying insecure attachment (Brennan et al., 1998). Individuals with high attachment anxiety or avoidance are likely to be afraid of being rejected and abandoned or being intimate and dependent (Brennan et al., 1998). Attachment exerts an influence on many facets of an individual's various life transitions, like the adjustment process of college students in western countries (e.g., Wei et al., 2005). Freshmen with a high level of attachment anxiety reported feelings of loneliness and depressive symptoms (Wei et al., 2005). Previous research findings also showed greater self-confidence in college students with secure attachment (low attachment avoidance and anxiety), which was associated with better learning and social and emotional adaptation (Lopez & Gormley, 2002; Mattanah et al., 2004).

Recently, researchers have argued that an individual's adult attachment style, a psychological characteristic, acted as a moderator in Berry et al.'s (1987) model and could account for the adjustment outcomes of overseas students (e.g., Chen et al., 2002; Wang & Mallinckrodt, 2006). Attachment researchers have indicated that international students studying abroad have to physically leave their loved ones in home nations, a journey that is similar to the process in which infants attempt to explore the physical environments around them (Wang & Mallinckrodt, 2006). Thus, to promote successful adaptation, students could benefit from immersing themselves in the new surroundings in host countries. Empirical research has shown that international students who come from East Asia and study in the United States with secure attachment are able to regulate anxiety and develop a network of new supportive friendships (Chen et al., 2002). For Asian international students in the United States, parental and professor attachment buffer against acculturative stress (Han et al., 2017). Gouin and MacNeil (2019) revealed that attachment anxiety led to increased health risk through weakened immune system in the acculturation process. Wang and Mallinckrodt (2006) also found that attachment anxiety and avoidance were the significant positive predictors of the mental and sociocultural adaptation of international students from a Chinese cultural background who were studying in the United States. This study puts forward the hypothesis that students from China who are high in attachment avoidance and anxiety would encounter more adjustment difficulties while studying in Japan.

Studies have investigated the relationship between the styles of attachment and two cultural dimensions (e.g., Wang & Mallinckrodt, 2006). For example, one study showed a negative correlation between attachment anxiety and acculturation of students to the host culture among international students from Chinese cultural backgrounds in America (Wang & Mallinckrodt, 2006). While previous research indicated that low levels of anxiety and avoidance were beneficial for individuals to explore and adapt to host individualistic contexts, it is unclear whether or to what extent such a relation holds in collectivistic contexts.

Current Study

Given the theoretical and practical needs of research on the acculturation of Chinese students studying in Japan, this study selected Chinese students studying in Japan as research participants to examine how acculturation modes and attachment styles would predict their adjustment outcomes. However, it should be first noted that this study focused on two distinct outcomes of acculturation, namely psychological and sociocultural adjustment (Ward & Kennedy, 1994). The former referred to mental and emotional health while the latter referred to the capability of acquiring and performing culturally proper behavioral competence and social skills to integrate into the host culture (Ward & Kennedy, 1994). This study argued that both outcomes were of importance to the mental health and academic success of Chinese international students, and thus included them as adjustment outcomes.

Four hypotheses on the processes and outcomes of acculturation of Chinese students studying in Japan were proposed in this study. First, Chinese students studying in Japan would have better adjustment outcomes than their counterparts in the United States in both the sociocultural and psychological domains (Hypothesis 1). The cultural adaptation of an individual is affected by the cultural differences between host and home cultures (Berry, 2003; Ward et al., 2001). According to the studies conducted in western societies, students from Asia found it more challenging to adapt to the host culture compared with other groups due to larger cultural differences. Supporting this, Yeh and Inose (2002) indicated that Chinese, Korean, and Japanese international students studying in western societies were especially challenged by the differences between collectivism and individualism. Since China shares similarities with Japan in culture and both are collectivist societies, students from China would encounter fewer difficulties during the acculturation process in Japan (Inoue & Merino, 2007). In addition, with the progress of multicultural coexistence policy (e.g., increased multilingual information and advisory services) promoted by Japan's government, more and more international students are reporting Japan as convenient and safe with regard to daily life (Han, 2004).

The second hypothesis proposed that identifying with the home culture and adapting to the host culture would be positively associated with the adjustment outcomes of Chinese students studying in Japan. As Japanese culture has the expectation of within-group homogeneity (e.g., Nagy, 2012), we hypothesized that cultural adaptation to the host country would be associated with less psychological distress and difficulties in sociocultural adjustment. On the other hand, identifying with the home culture would negatively predict adjustment outcomes (Hypothesis 2).

As for the third hypothesis, previous research highlighted the influence of attachment styles on the acculturation process of overseas students in western societies (e.g., Chen et al., 2002). A previous study indicated that securely attached overseas students showed greater perception of social support from others in the home and host countries, felt less psychologically distressed, and reported fewer difficulties in sociocultural adjustment (Chen et al., 2002). Therefore, the current study proposed that high attachment avoidance and anxiety would predict more psychological distress and difficulties in sociocultural adjustment (Hypothesis 3).

The last hypothesis proposed a negative correlation between attachment anxiety and avoidance and acculturation to the host culture (Hypothesis 4). Because securely attached individuals would tend to fully explore a new cultural environment and report higher cultural adaptation to the host country (Wang & Mallinckrodt, 2006), those with insecure attachment were expected to encounter more difficulties in adjusting to the host culture.

METHOD

Participants and Procedures

With the help of the international student support organizations, we sent an email invitation to Chinese international students in various universities in the Kanto region as well as to Chinese international student associations in Kanto Region. The email described the research purpose and contained the link of the online survey. When participants clicked the survey link, they were first directed to the informed consent form prior to the study's questionnaire. Anonymity was assured. Respondents were given the option to quit the survey at any time. The entire survey took approximately 20 min.

A total of 316 individuals participated. Among these, we excluded 39 individuals from the final analysis who responded only to the demographic questions. One response was removed because the respondent was under age 18. Thus, we used a total of 277 responses to test the hypotheses, and none of them included missing data. About 67% participants identified as female and 33% of the participants identified as male. The mean age of the participants was 24.18 years ($SD=3.1$, range 18–38 years). All participants reported their country of origin as Mainland China. This sample consisted of 117 graduate students (42%) and 160 undergraduates (58%). The majority of the students reported that their length of time in Japan was longer than 4 years (27.4%), followed by 2–3 years (19.9%), 1–2 years (18.8%), less than 6 months (14.1), 3–4 years (11.2%), and 6 months to 1 year (8.7%). Almost 70.8% of the participants reported their Japanese proficiency as good, 29.2% of the participants reported their Japanese proficiency as fair, and none of participants reported their Japanese as low or excellent.

Measures

Participants completed an online survey in both Mandarin Chinese and traditional Chinese in 2015. It contained the following measures.

Experiences in Close Relationships Scale

In this study, the adult attachment was assessed by the Experienced in Close Relationships Scale (ECRS; Brennan et al., 1998) using the Chinese version (Mallinckrodt & Wang, 2004). This scale consists of two attachment subscales—attachment anxiety and avoidance—each of which comprises a total of 18 items with responses given on a 7-point Likert scale (ranging from 1 = *strongly disagree* to 7 = *strongly agree*). The scales were reliable and valid, which was repeatedly verified in both English and Chinese (e.g., Brennan et al., 1998; Mallinckrodt & Wang, 2004). The internal reliability of the scale of the Chinese version was reported as .91 and .88 for attachment avoidance and anxiety, respectively (Mallinckrodt & Wang, 2004). In this study, Cronbach's alpha was .91 and .92 for attachment avoidance and anxiety, respectively.

Acculturation Index

With two independent subscales of cultural identification with the native (Chinese) culture and cultural adaptation to the host (Japanese) culture, the Acculturation Index (AI; Ward & Kennedy, 1994) consisted of 21 items that measured three aspects, including values, cognition, and behavior. The respondents indicated how similar their various experiences of daily life were compared with Chinese and Japanese cultures by means of a 6-point response scale (ranging from 1 = *not at all similar* to 6 = *very similar*). The scales were reliable and valid, which was demonstrated in previous research on Chinese international students in western countries (e.g., Wang & Mallinckrodt, 2006). We adopted translation and back-translation methods to translate theAI into Chinese. In this study, Cronbach's alpha was .96 and .93 for the two subscales including the native (Chinese) culture and the host (Japanese) culture, respectively.

Socio-Cultural Adaptation Scale

We used the Socio-Cultural Adaptation Scale (SCAS; Ward & Kennedy, 1999) to assess the level of sociocultural adjustment. The SCAS measured the degree of difficulties caused by cultural differences and experienced by individuals in behavior and cognition. Ward and Kennedy (1999) indicated that the SCAS was flexible as an instrument and could be modified based on the characteristics of sojourners as samples. This scale has been shown to be highly reliable in numerous cultural contexts. In a previous study, 25 cultural-general items that represent three subscales (survival, academic adaptation, and interpersonal adaptation) most relevant for the international students in Japan were selected (Simic-Yamashita & Tanaka, 2010). The respondents evaluated each item by indicating the degree of difficulties they experienced in a variety of sociocultural situations using a 5-point scale varying from 1 (*not difficult*) to 5 (*extremely difficult*). We completed the English–Chinese translation of items by adopting the back-translation method of bilingual researchers. In this study, coefficient alphas were .91, .71, .80, and .67 for the total scale, survival, academic adaptation, and interpersonal adaptation, respectively.

Brief Symptom Inventory 18

This study used the Brief Symptom Inventory (BSI-18; Derogatis & Savitz, 2000) to measure psychological distress. This scale has 18 items for measuring three dimensions of psychiatric disorders, including anxiety, depression, and somatization (six items for each). The participants reported the level of their different symptoms in the past week by means of a 4-point scale (ranging from 1 = *not at all* to 4 = *quite a bit*). Previous studies used this scale with a sample of Chinese students studying in the United States and reported .88 for internal reliability (Wang & Mallinckrodt, 2006). The validity of the BSI-18's Chinese version was demonstrated in drug abusers in Mainland China (Wang et al., 2013). In this study, internal reliability was .93 and varied from .78 to .86 for the total scale and three subscales, respectively.

International Comparison Data

In addition to exploring the relationship between attachment, acculturation, and psychosocial adjustment of Chinese international students in Japan, the current research also compared Chinese international students in Japan to their counterparts in the United States. While a considerable body of measurement has been developed to capture international students' adaptation, especially in the sociocultural domain (e.g., Sun, 2013), researchers have argued for the importance of consistency in measurements in understanding international students' acculturation holistically (Takai, 1989; Tan et al., 2011). The validation of the SCAS (Ward & Kennedy, 1999) and BSI-18 (Derogatis & Savitz, 2000) in international students has been established in the United States and Japan (Wang & Mallinckrodt, 2006; Simic-Yamashita & Tanaka, 2010). Thus, in the current research we compared our results with those of Chinese international students in the United States using data from Wang and Mallinckrodt (2006). Their study was chosen as a reference because it was the only one to our knowledge that used the same measures as the current study and offered a fair comparison point.

RESULTS

Preliminary Analysis

We computed descriptive statistics for all variables. Table 1 summarizes the means, standard deviations, and bivariate correlations between the variables under study. We conducted normality tests and found normal skewness (ranged from .07 to .95) and kurtosis (ranged from .53 to .70). Correlations for the primary measures indicated that length of time in Japan ($r = -.2$, $p < .001$) and students' self-reported Japanese ability ($r = -.42$, $p < .001$) were both significantly negatively associated with sociocultural adjustment, but they were not significantly correlated with psychological distress. Additionally, sociocultural adjustment was found to be significantly positively correlated with psychological distress ($r = .49$, $p < .001$).

Testing of Research Hypotheses

Hypothesis 1 stated that Chinese international students in Japan would have a better adjustment outcome than those in the United States in sociocultural and psychological domains. To test this hypothesis, we made a comparison of psychological distress and sociocultural adjustment difficulties between the two student groups in Japan and the United States by conducting an independent samples t test. According to the results, Chinese students studying in Japan had fewer social adjustment difficulties, $t(379) = 2.99$, $p < .01$, yet higher psychological distress, $t(379) = 4.68$, $p < .001$, compared with their counterparts in the United States.

Hypothesis 2 posited that psychological distress and sociocultural adjustment difficulties would be negatively related to acculturation to the host culture and positively related to identification to the home culture. Hypothesis 3 stated that individuals with a high level of attachment avoidance and anxiety would have more psychological distress and sociocultural adjustment difficulties. In order to test Hypotheses 2 and 3, we used psychological distress and sociocultural adjustment difficulties as dependent variables to perform two groups of two-step hierarchical multiple regression separately (Table 2).

Table 1: Correlations of Demographic, Attachment, Acculturation, and Psychosocial Adjustment Variables

Variable	*M*	*SD*	1	2	3	4	5	6	7	8
Length of stay	4.02	1.84	—	0.30**	0.05	0.19	0.14	0.11	0.10	0.11
Japanese proficiency	1.30	0.46		—	0.17	0.04	0.10	0.16	0.10	0.36**
Attachment avoidance	3.43	1.03			—	0.21*	0.19	0.08	0.29**	0.27**
Attachment anxiety	3.86	1.22				—	0.11	0.10	0.40***	0.38***
Identification with Chinese culture	3.78	1.09					—	0.18	0.20	0.01
Acculturation to Japanese culture	3.14	0.89						—	0.02	0.21***
Psychological distress	1.86	0.66							—	0.49**
Sociocultural adjustment difficulties	1.70	0.52								—

Note. $* p < .05$; $** p < .01$; $*** p < .001$.

Table 2: Hierarchical Regression Analyses of Psychological Adjustment

	Psychosocial adjustment (N = 277)			
	Psychological distress (β)		Sociocultural adjustment difficulties (β)	
Variable				
Gender	−.06	.00	−.13*	−.09
Japanese abilities	−.14*	−.11*	−.26***	−.09
Length of residence	.13*	.19	−.14*	−.18
Attachment avoidance		.20***		.15**
Attachment anxiety		.45***		.35***
Acculturation to host culture		.01		−.19***
Identification with host culture		−.03		.05
R^2	.03	.29	.12	.32
ΔR^2	.03	.26***	.12***	.2***

Note. $* p < .05$; $** p < .01$; $*** p < .001$.

As revealed by the hierarchical multiple regression, gender, Japanese proficiency, and duration of stay in Japan had no significant effects on the regression model of sociocultural adaptation in the first step and accounted for

3% of the variation. However, Japanese proficiency and duration of stay in Japan produced significant effects on the regression model of psychological distress.

The introduction of attachment and acculturation variables in step two additionally explained 20% of the variance in sociocultural adjustment and 26% in psychological distress, which partly supported Hypothesis 2—that is, only acculturation to Japanese culture significantly predicted sociocultural adjustment difficulties, while acculturation variables were not significant predictors of psychological distress. These results supported Hypothesis 3 in that attachment anxiety and avoidance significantly predicted psychological distress and sociocultural adjustment difficulties.

Hypothesis 4 proposed a negative correlation between attachment anxiety and avoidance and acculturation to the host culture, which was tested by conducting a Pearson product-moment correlation. As shown in Table 1, no significant correlations were found between attachment anxiety ($r = -.10, p = .33$) and avoidance ($r = -.08, p = .48$) and acculturation to the host culture.

DISCUSSION

This study had two objectives. The first was to capture the adjustment outcomes of Chinese international students in Japan by comparing them with those in the United States. The second one aimed to examine whether identification to home versus host culture and attachment predicted the psychosocial adjustment of Chinese international students. Four significant findings were revealed. First, Chinese international students in Japan had better outcome than those in America in sociocultural adjustment rather than psychological adjustment. Second, both attachment avoidance and anxiety significantly predicted psychological and sociocultural adjustment difficulties. Third, a positive correlation was found only between acculturation to the host culture and sociocultural adjustment difficulties. Fourth, no relationships were found between acculturation to the host culture and attachment anxiety and avoidance.

A comparison of Chinese students studying in Japan and the United States showed significant differences in both domains of psychosocial adjustment. As predicted, the findings indicated that Chinese students studying in Japan encountered fewer sociocultural adjustment difficulties than those in the United States. The sociocultural adjustment could be promoted by many factors such as the supportive environment including physical and informative support in the host country. Chinese international students in Japan reported that "Public transportation is very convenient and safe," "Daily life is very convenient," and "Information about a variety of services is well provided" in Japan (Han, 2004). Thus, it might be said that Japan generally provided a good supportive environment for this specific group of international students in terms of food, clothing, and living, which could also be facilitated by the similarities shared between China and Japan. However, it was found that Chinese students studying in Japan encountered more difficulties than those in the United States with regard to psychological distress. The psychological and sociocultural adjustment were conceptually distinct but empirically related to some extent (Berry, 2003).

Specifically, previous research suggested that the sociocultural adjustment of individuals originating from cultures similar to the host culture was likely to influence their psychological adjustment due to the strong correlation between the two domains of adjustment (Berry et al., 2006). Furthermore, this study suggested that Chinese international students still experienced more psychological distress than those in the United States while encountering fewer difficulties in sociocultural adjustment, indicating that additional factors might influence the mental health of Chinese international students.

We hypothesized that more acculturation to Japanese culture and less identification with Chinese culture would both lead to better acculturation outcomes. However, the current findings suggested that only acculturation to Japanese culture significantly predicted the sociocultural adjustment of Chinese students; furthermore, two domains of the acculturation mode were not predictors of the psychological adjustment of this student group after controlling for the influence of Japanese proficiency and duration of stay. We offer several speculations on the results. Han (2004) posited ambivalent attitudes toward Japan as one characteristic of international students from China and proposed that such attitudes led to their maladjustment. Previous qualitative research on Chinese students in Japan has also suggested that their expectations for and ambivalent emotions toward acculturation to Japanese culture were one of the important factors affecting their adjustment (Yin & Aoki, 2018). Based on the results, the current study highlighted the important interaction between host and home cultures and provided a culture-specific (rather than universal) acculturation map for Chinese international students in Japan. That is to say, while understanding Japanese culture could improve their sociocultural adjustment, efforts directly made toward facilitating their identification with both home culture and host culture might not always lead to the desired psychological adjustment outcome. For clinician or faculty who work with Chinese students struggling with acculturation, clarifying their attitude toward both cultures and acknowledging their potential ambivalent feelings might encourage them to fully take steps toward resolving acculturation difficulties.

This study showed that the attachment of Chinese international students plays a role in their acculturation process in Japan's collectivistic society. After controlling for the effects of gender, Japanese proficiency, and duration of stay, attachment avoidance and anxiety remained significant predictors of psychological and sociocultural adjustment difficulties. Consistent with findings of international students in individualistic cultures, these findings suggested that attachment was critical to Chinese students' adjustment in Japan. We also note that attachment was the only factor influencing students' psychological adjustment among all the factors involved in the current study. Based on these findings, institutions or organizations should take attachment into consideration when supporting this student group. Outreach/psychoeducational programs and individual interventions focusing on attachment can be recommended to Chinese international students in Japan. Clinicians who work with international students can initiate outreach activities to provide students with on-campus resources of psychotherapy. In addition, psychoeducation on the benefits of psychotherapy as well as the acculturation process can promote students' self-awareness and help-seeking behavior. Furthermore, research needs to explore other factors contributing to the psychological adaptation of Chinese students.

Limitations and Suggestions for Future Research

The current study has several limitations. First, the cross-sectional design made it impossible to strictly infer the causality among the variables. Additional studies are needed that employ a longitudinal design to cross-validate the effects of attachment and acculturation over time. Second, existing factors predicting the psychological adjustment of Chinese international students in Japan remain limited. More studies need to be carried out to explore and explain factors influencing the psychological adjustment of the student group in Sino-Japan relationship and Japanese contexts. Third, online questionnaires were distributed by student organizations and completed by voluntary participants in Kanto Region. Thus, participants in this study might not represent the general population.

CONCLUSION

The present study revealed an important relationship among the attachment, acculturation, and adjustment outcomes of international students from China in a collectivistic cultural background, which significantly contributes to the literature by showing a culturally universal role of attachment and a culturally specific role of acculturation in Chinese international students' adjustment in Japan.

REFERENCES

An, Y., & Nagai, S. (2019). Factors related to help-seeking process of Chinese international students in depressed situation: Comparing Chinese international students studying at language school to Japanese university students. *Japanese Journal of Community Psychology, 23*(1), 34–51.

Berry, J. W. (2003). Conceptual approaches to acculturation. In K. M. Chun, P. B. Organista, & G. Marin (Eds.), *Acculturation: Advances in theory, measurement, and applied research* (pp. 17–38). American Psychological Association.

Berry, J. W., Kim, U., Minde, T., & Mok, D. (1987). Comparative studies of acculturative stress. *International Migration Review, 21*(3), 491–511.

Berry, J. W., Phinney, J. S., Sam, D. L., & Vedder, P. (2006). Immigrant youth: Acculturation, identity, and adaptation. *Applied Psychology: An International Review, 55*(3), 303–332. https://doi.org/10.1111/j.1464-0597.2006.00256.x

Bond, M. H. (2002). Reclaiming the individual from Hofstede's ecological analysis—A 20-year odyssey: Comment on Oyserman et al. (2002). *Psychological Bulletin, 128*(1), 73–77. https://doi.org/10.1037/0033-2909.128.1.73

Bourhis, R. Y., Moïse, L. C., Perreault, S., & Senécal, S. (1997). Towards an interactive acculturation model: A social psychological approach. *International Journal of Psychology, 32*(6), 369–386. https://doi.org/10.1080/002075997400629

Bowlby, J. (1988). *A secure base: Parent–child attachment and healthy human development.* Basic Books.

Brennan, K. A., Clark, C. L., & Shaver, P. R. (1998). Self-report measurement of adult attachment: An integrative overview. In J. A. Simpson & W. S. Rholes (Eds.), *Attachment theory and close relationships* (pp. 46–76). Guilford Press.

Center for China and Globalization. (2018). *Annual report on the development of Chinese studying abroad 2017.* Social Science Academic Press.

Chen, H.-J., Mallinckrodt, B., & Mobley, M. (2002). Attachment patterns of East Asian international students and sources of perceived social support as moderators of the impact of U.S. racism and cultural distress. *Asian Journal of Counselling, 9*(1–2), 27–48.

Chen, J., & Zhou, G. (2019). Chinese international students' sense of belonging in North American postsecondary institutions: A critical literature review. *Brock Education: A Journal of Educational Research and Practice, 28*(2), 48–63. https://doi.org/10.26522/brocked.v28i2.642

Derogatis, L. R., & Savitz, K. L. (2000). The SCL–90–R and Brief Symptom Inventory (BSI) in primary care. In M. E. Maruish (Ed.), *Handbook of psychological assessment in primary care settings* (pp. 297–334). Lawrence Erlbaum Associates.

Ge, W. (2007). *Cross-cultural adaptation of Chinese students and technical trainees in Japan.* Keisuisha.

Gouin, J.-P., & MacNeil, S. (2019). Attachment style and changes in systemic inflammation following migration to a new country among international students. *Attachment & Human Development, 21*(1), 38–56. https://doi.org/10.1080/14616734.2018.1541515

Han, I. (2004). Psychological study about the maladjustment and inferiority complex of Chinese students in Japan. *The Sanyo Review, 11,* 105–125. https://doi.org/10.24598/sanyor.11.0_105

Han, S., Pistole, M. C., & Caldwell, J. M. (2017). Acculturative stress, parental and professor attachment, and college adjustment in Asian international students. *Journal of Multicultural Counseling and Development, 45*(2), 111–126. https://doi.org/10.1002/jmcd.12068

Hayashi, S. (1997). The effects of self-perception and attitudes to cultures on international students' feeling of adjustment. *The Japanese Journal of Psychology, 68*(5), 346–354.

Hofstede, G. (1980). *Culture's consequences: International differences in work-related values.* SAGE.

Hofstede, G. (1993). Cultural constraints in management theories. *Academy of Management Executive, 7*(1), 81–94. http://dx.doi.org/10.5465/ame.1993.9409142061

Inoue, N., & Merino, A. C. (2007). Intercultural academic adjustment of Japanese government scholarship students: A multiple case study at Kyushu University. *Kyushu Communication Studies, 5,* 61–74.

Japan Student Services Organization. (2018). *International students in Japan 2017.* Retrieved from http://www.jasso.go.jp

Jou, Y-H., & Fukada, H. (2011). The influence of stress and social support on the mental and physical health of Chinese students in Japan: Was there change in seventeen years? *International Students Education, 16,* 1–12.

Lee, J. S. (2017). Challenges of International students in a Japanese university: Ethnographic perspectives. *Journal of International Students, 7*(1), 73–93. https://doi.org/10.32674/jis.v7i1.246

Lopez, F. G., & Gormley, B. (2002). Stability and change in adult attachment style over the first-year college transition: Relations to self-confidence, coping, and distress patterns. *Journal of Counseling Psychology, 49*(3), 355–364. https://doi.org/10.1037/0022-0167.49.3.355

Ma, B. (2007). The relationship between mental health status and psychosociological factors among Chinese postgraduate students in Japan. *Juntendo University Medicine, 53,* 200–210.

Mallinckrodt, B., & Wang, C.-C. (2004). Quantitative methods for verifying semantic equivalence of translated research instruments: A Chinese version of the experiences in close relationships scale. *Journal of Counseling Psychology, 51*(3), 368–379. https://doi.org/10.1037/0022-0167.51.3.368

Mattanah, J. F., Hancock, G. R., & Brand, B. L. (2004). Parental attachment, separation-individuation, and college student adjustment: A structural equation analysis of mediational effects. *Journal of Counseling Psychology, 51*(2), 213–225. https://doi.org/10.1037/0022-0167.51.2.213

Muthukrishna, M., Bell, A., Henrich, J., Curtin, C., Gedranovich, A., McInerney, J., & Thue, B. (2018). Beyond WEIRD psychology: Measuring and mapping scales of cultural and psychological distance. *SSRN.* http://dx.doi.org/10.2139/ssrn.3259613

Nagy, S. R. (2012). Japanese-style multiculturalism? A comparative examination of Japanese multicultural coexistence. *Japan Journal of Multilingualism and Multiculturalism, 18*(1), 1–18.

Organisation for Economic Cooperation and Development. (2017). *Education at a glance 2017: Indicators.* https://doi.org/10.1787/eag-2017-en

Simic-Yamashita, M., & Tanaka, T. (2010). Exploratory factor analysis of the Sociocultural Adaptation Scale (SCAS) among international students in Japan. *Journal of Humanities and Social Sciences, 29,* 206–195

Sullivan, C., & Kashubeck-West, S. (2015). The interplay of international students' acculturative stress, social support, and acculturation modes. *Journal of International Students, 5*(1), 1–11.

Sun, Y. (2013). Chinese students in Japan: The mediator and the moderator between their personality and mental health. *International Journal of Psychology, 48*(3), 215–223. https://doi.org/10.1080/00207594.2011.648942

Suzuki, E. (2007). The present of multicultural in Japan. in T. Menju & E. Suzuki (Eds.), *Introductory course 4 for cooperative activities exchange:*

Multicultural power—overcoming multicultural coexistence (pp. 14–39). Akashi Shoten.

Takai, J. (1989). An overview of international student adjustment studies in Japan. *Bulletin of the School of Education Psychology*, *36*, 139–147. https://doi.org/10.18999/bulfep.36.139

Tan, H., Watanabe, T., & Konno, H. (2011). A review of psychological studies on the cross-cultural adaptation of international students in Japan. *Mejiro University Psychology Studies*, *7*, 95–114.

Tanaka, T., Tkai, J., Kohyama, T., & Fujhihara, T. (1994) Adjustment patterns of international students in Japan. *International Journal of Intercultural Relations*, *18*(1), 55–75. https://doi.org/10.1016/0147-1767(94)90004-3

Wang, C.-C. D., & Mallinckrodt, B. (2006). Acculturation, attachment, and psychosocial adjustment of Chinese/Taiwanese international students. *Journal of Counseling Psychology*, *53*(4), 422–433. https://doi.org/10.1037/0022-0167.53.4.422

Wang, J., Kelly, B. C., Liu, T., Zhang, G., & Hao, W. (2013). Factorial structure of the brief symptom inventory (BSI)-18 among Chinese drug users. *Drug and Alcohol Dependence*, *133*(2), 368–375. https://doi.org/10.1016/j.drugalcdep.2013.06.017

Ward, C., Bochner, S., & Furnham, A. (2001). *The psychology of culture shock* (2nd ed.). Routledge.

Ward, C., & Kennedy, A. (1994). Acculturation strategies, psychological adjustment, and sociocultural competence during cross-cultural transitions. *International Journal of Intercultural Relations*, *18*(3), 329–343. https://doi.org/10.1016/0147-1767(94)90036-1

Ward, C., & Kennedy, A. (1999). The measurement of sociocultural adaptation. *International Journal of Intercultural Relations*, *23*(4), 659–677. https://doi.org/10.1016/S0147-1767(99)00014-0

Ward, C., & Lin, E.-Y. (2010). There are homes at four corners of the seas: Acculturation and adaptation of overseas Chinese. In M. H. Bond (Ed.), *The Oxford handbook of Chinese psychology* (pp. 657–677). Oxford University Press.

Wei, M., Russell, D. W., & Zakalik, R. A. (2005). Adult attachment, social self-efficacy, self-disclosure, loneliness, and subsequent depression for freshman college students: A longitudinal study. *Journal of Counseling Psychology*, *52*(4), 602–614. https://doi.org/10.1037/0022-0167.52.4.602

Wu, X. (2017). A review of social network studies for international students in Japan. *Integrated Sciences for Global Society Studies*, *6*, 29–39.

Yasuda, T. (2011). *The fantasy of multilingual society: Reconsidering the history of modern Japanese language*. Sangensha.

Yeh, C., & Inose, M. (2002). Difficulties and coping strategies of Chinese, Japanese, and Korean immigrant students. *Adolescence*, *37*(145), 69–82.

Yeh, C. J., & Inose, M. (2003). International students' reported English fluency, social support satisfaction, and social connectedness as predictors of acculturative stress. *Counselling Psychology Quarterly*, *16*(1), 15–28. https://doi.org/10.1080/0951507031000114058

Yin, M., & Aoki, K. (2018). A qualitative study about the cross-cultural adaptation of Chinese international students in Japan. *Bulletin of Center of Clinical Psychology & Counseling at Ochanomizu University, 19*, 49–59.

MENGXI YIN is a doctoral student in the Department of Counseling Psychology at Cleveland State University. Her major research interests lie in the area of cross-cultural adjustment. Email: m.yin@vikes.csuohio.edu

KIKUYO AOKI, PhD, is an associate professor in clinical and developmental psychology at Ochanomizu University. She studies attachment, mother–infant emotional interactions and school mental health. Email: aokiku@jcom.home.ne.jp

KELLY YU-HSIN LIAO, PhD, is an assistant professor in the doctoral specialization in Counseling Psychology at Cleveland State University. She studies minority-related stress, positive psychology, and health psychology in ethnic minorities. Email: y.liao54@csuohio.edu

HUI XU, PhD, is an assistant professor in counseling psychology at Loyola University Chicago. His scholarship focuses on vocational, counseling science, assessment, and cross-cultural issues. Email: hxu2@luc.edu

Peer-Reviewed Article

© *Journal of International Students*
Volume 11, Issue 1 (2021), pp. 195-214
ISSN: 2162-3104 (Print), 2166-3750 (Online)
doi: 10.32674/jis.v1i1.1901
ojed.org/jis

OJED
OPEN JOURNALS IN EDUCATION

Self-Directed Learning for Nonnative English-Speaking Graduate Students Across Disciplines: Translanguaging Practices and Perspectives

Hong Shi
China University of Petroleum-Beijing

ABSTRACT

The influx of international students in U.S. colleges has resulted in linguistically diverse classrooms, raising attention to translanguaging practices. The purpose of this study is to examine the self-directed translanguaging practices and perspectives of nonnative English-speaking (NNES) graduate students in the U.S. university setting by using narrative stories, individual interviews, and focus group discussion. Twelve NNES graduate students from Asian countries participated in this research. These students demonstrated their self-management, motivation and persistence, and self-monitoring in their academic learning. Although they reported the difficulties from academic English language, they identified the value of translanguaging practices, and they developed some characteristics of autonomous learning due to "teacher-directed translanguaging" and "student-directed translanguaging." Scaffolding and collaborative learning benefited and effectively engaged NNES graduate students in self-directed learning.

Keywords: higher education, nonnative English-speaking graduate student, self-directed learning, translanguaging

INTRODUCTION

Self-directed learning is "a process in which individuals take initiative, with or without the help of others, to diagnose their learning needs, formulate learning goals, identify resources for learning, select and implement learning strategies, and evaluate learning outcomes" (Knowles, 1975, p. 18). Self-directed learning enables learners to become more independent and autonomous in how they think, learn, and behave even after they complete formal studies. Studies about self-directed learning have shown an increase in the consideration of cultural factors (e.g., Collier, 2011; Overzat, 2011), with some aspects of collectivist cultures appearing to be impediments to autonomous learning. In particular, Asian learners have often been associated with passive learning, rote learning, and being teacher-dependent and unable to engage in independent learning (Z. Fang, 2014; Kember, 2000). However, some research (e.g., Biggs & Watkins, 2001; Littlewood, 2001) has questioned the previous research and claimed that when these students were no longer told what to do but had to manage resources and time, make decisions, deal with problems, and communicate with people from other cultures, they could develop characteristics of autonomous learning. There is no agreement about nonnative English-speaking (NNES) learners' self-directedness. This study examined self-directed learning of NNES learners in the U.S. university setting.

With the increasing number of NNES students crossing the globe to gain international experience, the United States has been a popular place for NNES students to pursue college education. Students from Asian countries now represent approximately 69% of the total enrollment of NNES students in the United States (Institute of International Education, 2019). Many universities in the United States have had to face questions about how to provide successful educational experiences for these students, given apparent differences between American and Asian cultures of learning (Ade-ojo, 2005; Jingnan, 2011). In the present study, the term "NNES student" refers to any student who self-reported that their first language was not English. They all learned English as a second or foreign language. Most NNES students are still developing their academic language proficiency (Biancarosa & Snow, 2004).

As for NNES students, they have the potential for translanguaging in the classroom with high linguistic diversity. Translanguaging is defined as the ability of multilingual speakers to shuttle between languages, treating the diverse languages that form their repertoire as an integrated system (Canagarajah, 2011). Translanguaging gives students agency in negotiating their linguistic repertoires (García et al., 2011). Jiménez et al. (2015) stated that translanguaging made learners strengthen important components of their reading comprehension tool kits, such as summarizing and understanding vocabulary. Translanguaging provides support for their self-esteem and thus for their motivation and persistence for learning (Middelborg, 2005; World Bank, 2005). In the present study, we frame students' strategic use of multiple languages or the practices associated with moving across languages and registers of speech to make meaning as translanguaging (García, 2009).

The purpose of this study is to identify NNES graduate students' self-directed learning in the U.S university setting from the translanguaging perspective. The research on these students' self-directed learning not only contributes to their learning behaviors but also predicts their chances of continuing learning after completing their academic program requirements. It is paramount to help NNES graduate students address their self-directed learning and increase their feelings of self-direction. According to Pintrich (2004) and Zimmerman (2002), learners should apply strategies proactively in a self-directive style in which they plan, monitor, and regulate their learning throughout academic activities. But can all NNES graduate students plan, monitor, and regulate their learning appropriately? Fewer studies in international student literature explore the Asian NNES graduate students' self-directed learning. Moreover, up to now, not much has been heard of students' views of their actual language choices and effective instructional practices. This study thus intends to bridge the gap. The research question is as follows: What instructional strategies support NNES graduate students' self-directed learning from the perspective of translanguaging? In order to explore this question, 12 NNES graduate students from Asian countries participated in the study. This article presents the situation of self-directed learning of these Asian NNES graduate students and how these students perceive translanguaging practices.

LITERATURE REVIEW

A large body of research focuses on the issues that NNES students confront at the postsecondary level (e.g., Casanave, 2005; Erichsen & Bolliger, 2011). NNES graduate students have to learn advanced literacy in specific academic disciplines (Casanave & Li, 2008). NNES graduate students need to perform in-depth reading of course materials; complete understanding of content knowledge, classroom culture, and norms; and interact with peers and professors in order to participate competently (Kim, 2012). They have to become competent or qualified to prepare to enter the profession in a related academic field after graduation. However, in the process of becoming academically competent, it has been found that these NNES students have confronted lack of autonomy, limited mentoring, and insufficient familiarity with English academic vocabulary (Ariza, 2010; Braine, 2010; Cheung, 2010; Lim, 2017). Ade-ojo (2005) found that English speakers of other languages (ESOL) college students preferred an instructor-driven curriculum, and because of sociocultural and psychological factors, students were hesitant to work independently. Issues Asian NNES students confront include classroom participation patterns (reluctance to participate or nonparticipation, lack of questioning, no indications of understanding), lack of initiative or critical thinking, dependency in student–teacher relations, and lack of autonomy in study practices (Z. Fang, 2014; Kember, 2000).

However, Jingnan (2011) found that NNES students were conscious that learning was their own responsibility, but few learners had the necessary knowledge and skills to undertake classwork totally independently. Learners either lack information and resources or the ability to use available resources effectively in their self-directed learning (McKinney et al., 2004). These barriers have brought challenges for learners' autonomy and caused difficulties for these students in participating in group work or discussion activities (Hailu & Ku, 2014; Mukminin & McMahon, 2013; Xue, 2013). Most NNES students identified that it was difficult for them to become independent learners without guidance from teachers, and they expected teachers to help them in using learning strategies, selecting resources, and establishing class environment for autonomous learning

(F. M. Fang & Zhang, 2012; Z. Fang, 2014). Did NNES students in this study also confront these problems in their academic learning? If yes, how did they deal with these issues?

Braine (2010) stressed that it was essential for teachers or faculty advisors to aid NNES graduate students with advanced academic literacy to socialize into a new academic community. Effective instruction strategies for college NNES students have been reported in previous studies (e.g., Bista, 2015; Samimy et al., 2011). Hornberger and Link (2012) argued that translanguaging and transnational literacies in classrooms were necessary and desirable educational practices. Marshall and Moore (2018) and Martínez-Álvarez and Ghiso (2017) referred to translanguaging as a means of enacting bilinguals' agency. According to García's (2009) concept of translanguaging, linguistic resources (i.e., knowledge of multiple languages and dialects) are part of a single language system that an NNES student uses to create meaning and accomplish goals. Students' linguistic resources have tremendous pedagogical, psychological, and cognitive functions in classrooms (Lee & Macaro, 2013; Lin, 2015; Moore, 2013). Translanguaging enables self-directed and small group learning, which at least in the early years of a strictly second language (L2)-medium education, is almost impossible to accomplish (Clegg & Simpson, 2016). Cummins (2000) stated that knowledge and abilities acquired in one language were potentially available for the development of another because of a common underlying proficiency. Translanguaging can enhance cognitive, language, and literacy abilities (W. G. Lewis, 2008; W. Li, 2009). A translanguaging perspective has been regarded as meaningful linguistic innovation for NNES students (Wei, 2020). Students valued translanguaging strategies while developing their proficiency through a dialogical pedagogy (Canagarajah, 2011). Lin (2015) discussed benefits of translanguaging in content- and language-integrated learning and claimed that translanguaging helped to distinguish instructional practices from monolingual L2 immersion education models by becoming more flexible and balanced about the role of the primary language. Translanguaging facilitates academic meaning making, and it is student-centered and helps to acknowledge students' input and the importance of rapport among all classroom participants.

Additionally, studies have found that postsecondary NNES students' perceived autonomous support predicts emotional well-being and achievement (Hall & Webb, 2014; Sawtelle et al., 2012). The autonomous support can be scaffolding that helps to move students progressively toward stronger understanding and, ultimately, greater independence in the learning process. NNES students' English language was relatively limited, and therefore they were more likely to resort to other languages for scaffolding. Effective scaffolding strategies also include peer group discussion or interactions, clear directions and explanations, peer revision, and timely feedback (Davis & Miyake, 2004; Rojas-Drummond & Mercer, 2003). To sum up, the previous classroom-based research has explored translanguaging practices and analyzed how teachers and students behave with multiple languages in different contexts (e.g., Clegg & Simpson, 2016; Gu, 2014; Palfreyman & Al-Bataineh, 2018; Wang, 2019). However, there are few studies on NNES students in graduate-level settings directly linking effective instruction practices to self-directed learning in U.S. colleges from the perspective of translanguaging, and this study contributes to this field.

THEORETICAL FRAMEWORK

Translanguaging can be extended as a conceptual framework to interpret hybridity and creativity of language use in classrooms, where the high degree of diversity of students' linguistic and cultural backgrounds means that they can draw on huge linguistic resources (Wang, 2019). As García (2011) pointed out, translingualism encourages flexible concurrent language use rather than continuing to keep students' linguistic knowledge separate or treating prior languages as nonexistent or purely negative influences. According to G. Lewis et al. (2012) and García and Li (2014), there are two types of translanguaging strategies: (a) teacher-directed translanguaging to give voice and clarity, manage the classroom, and ask questions, and (b) student-directed translanguaging to participate, elaborate ideas, and raise questions. Both types of strategies complement each other. These strategies are vital especially for NNES graduate students since they have to autonomously participate in academic work, perform in-depth understanding of content, and interact with peers and professors in professional field competently. The current study examined both teacher-directed and student-directed translanguaging from NNES graduate students' perspectives.

Different scholars have proposed various models to understand self-directed learning (e.g., Brockett & Hiemstra, 1991; Candy, 1991; Garrison, 1997). Apart from translanguaging, Candy's and Garrison's models were selected for further analysis, as they seem to be appropriate and comprehensive representations of self-directed learning in this context.

Candy (1991) considered self-directed learning as a goal as well as a process. He proposed a four-dimensional model, that is:

> "Self-direction" as a personal attribute (personal autonomy); "self-direction" as the willingness and capacity to conduct one's own education (self-management); "self-direction" as a mode of organizing instruction in formal settings (learner-control); and "self-direction" as the individual, non-institutional pursuit of learning opportunities in the "natural societal setting" (autodidaxy). (p. 23)

Personal autonomy is a series of attributes that include students' independence and freedom of choice. Self-management refers to a learner's willingness and ability or competence to manage their own learning, with competence including research skills, time management, goal setting, and critical thinking. With competence, one is able to exercise control effectively in a certain situation. Learner control of instruction is vital for effective learning strategies (Entwistle & Peterson, 2004). Garrison (1997) had a similar discussion about self-directed learning from three interacting dimensions: self-management, which involves learners' use of resources to achieve objectives in a given context; self-monitoring; and motivation. Self-directed learning recognizes the significance of motivation in initiating and maintaining NNES graduate students' efforts.

Students need to collaborate and interact with others in the process of self-management, assessment, and self-reflection. This model is appropriate to support the analysis of NNES students' self-directed learning in this study.

METHOD

This study used a qualitative research methodology to explore instructional strategies that support NNES graduate students' self-directed learning from the perspective of translanguaging. It also described the self-directed learning and perceptions of translanguaging experienced by NNES graduate students across disciplines.

Participants

The participants in this study were 12 NNES graduate students who were enrolled at a major university in the Southeastern United States. The interviews were administered to a convenience sampling, which is recommended by Cohen et al. (2013) as a suitable recruitment strategy for a study that does not aim to study a representative sample. These 12 participants were selected because their native language was not English, and they majored in different fields. Participants also had passed the Test of English as a Foreign Language and matriculated to university graduate level courses. Furthermore, these participants did not receive any support services, nor were they enrolled in remediation courses or courses designed to improve their English skills. Data were collected confidentially. Student responses are presented using pseudonyms. Four of the students, Xi, Ziaul, Seong, and Jang, were pursuing master's degrees, while the other eight students were pursuing doctoral degrees. Participants majored in different academic areas: agricultural economics, applied economics, business, chemistry, consumer science, electric engineering, English for speakers of other languages, geology, higher education, mechanical engineering, and statistics. Seven of them were from the STEM field and five of them were in non-STEM disciplines. They were all NNES students whose primary languages were not English and who were acquiring English and were not proficient in the language. There were six male and six female students. The length of time they were in the United States ranged from 1 to 3.5 years, and all of them had never lived in an English-speaking country besides the United States. All of them, except participants Xi, Juan, and Jang who rated their English level as "fair", rated their overall English proficiency as "good." This rating is self-reported, and participants chose from "excellent", "good" "fair", or "poor" to rate their English proficiency. The following table provides more detailed background information about all the participants in this study.

Table 1: Demographic Information of Participants

Participant	Age	Gender	Country of origin	Major	Length of time in US (yrs)	Self-perceptions of English proficiency
Bala	26	M	India	Mechanical Engineering	3	Good
Xi	24	F	China	Statistics	1	Fair
Asuka	28	F	Japan	Geology	3.5	Good
Ziaul	27	M	Bangladesh	Applied Economics	1.5	Good
Ashraff	32	M	Malaysia	Higher Education	3.5	Good
Seong	24	F	Korea	Consumer Science	1	Good
Juan	29	F	China	Chemistry	2.5	Fair
Sanuwar	33	M	Bangladesh	Geology	2	Good
Wei	29	F	China	Agricultural Economics	3.5	Good
Pei	32	F	China	English for Speakers of Other Languages	1	Good
Trivedi	27	M	India	Electrical Engineering	2	Good
Jang	25	M	Korea	Business	2	Fair

Procedures

Data were collected from three sources: (a) narrative stories, (b) transcriptions of audiotaped interviews with each student, and (c) transcriptions of audiotaped focus group discussions. The data collection methods are based on methodologic triangulation. Triangulation is the combination of two or more data sources, methodologic approaches, or theoretical perspectives (Kimchi et al., 1991) in the same study. By using multiple methods, the researcher aims to create innovative ways of understanding a phenomenon, reveal unique findings, increase confidence in research data, decrease the "deficiencies and biases that stem from any single method" (Mitchell, 1986, p. 19), and provide a clearer understanding of the problem (Jick, 1979). In order to have a more comprehensive and in-depth understanding of NNES graduate students' self-directed learning from the perspective of translanguaging, the three data collection methods were used in this study.

I collected narrative stories from all the participants. I asked participants to write narrative stories or reflections about their self-directed learning. I also gave rubrics for the reflections to all the participants. The rubrics included describing self-directed learning experience in the home country as well as in the United States; discussing English learning processes and experiences; discussing problems encountered, strategies used, and supports received in self-directed learning; and, if possible, providing reflections about the whole self-directed learning process. I performed a content analysis of the narrative stories, and major themes of comments emerged from repeated data analysis of two researchers from the field of adult education. The analysis provided further information for individual interviews and focus group discussion.

I interviewed participants individually with open-ended questions related to their self-directed learning in U.S. university classrooms and translanguaging experience, such as use of knowledge of multiple languages and dialects, code-switching, or concurrent language use. I developed the questions based on the literature in the area. Each interview lasted about 40 minutes. I asked the interview questions in English, and participants answered in English. I recorded and transcribed the interviews. The participants read the transcriptions to verify their own words and comments. I then analyzed the transcriptions of interviews and two researchers in the field of adult education coded the interviews using a qualitative analysis software package, Atlasti, with a specific focus on the research questions of the present study. After coding the data, the two researchers reviewed, compared, and analyzed the major themes to establish the reliability of interpretations. I used the emerging themes from interviews to develop the focus group discussion topics and then facilitated the interview. The focus group generated in-depth discussions among participants and created a more elaborate picture of the perspectives of NNES graduate students. Quotations are drawn from narrative stories, the audiotaped interviews, and focus group discussions.

RESULTS

After coding and analysis, four major themes emerged: (a) self-management and translanguaging, (b) motivation and persistence, (c) self-monitoring and translanguaging, and (d) effective instructional strategies.

Self-Management and Translanguaging

Self-management involves learners' willingness and capacity to conduct their own education and their use of resources to achieve objectives in a given context. Participants stated that they tried to "transfer knowledge across languages," "plan class work," and "seek more resources" to facilitate their academic courses learning and English learning. For example,

> I always try to seek opportunities to ask questions and communicate with peers. When I have paper work, I always try to search books in library, and seek information online, information in English and in my own language. I try to use all resources to help me to finish the work successfully. —*Ashraff*

> I know I have some language problems, so I always preview the class content with the help of the related materials in my language (Korean) before the class. Then, I can transfer the knowledge, and it really make my academic course learning easier, then I can have more confidence. —*Jang*

This shows that these participants had attributes as well as willingness to conduct and manage their own learning. They showed their behavior of shuttling between languages. In their narrative stories, participants further reported that they used strategies in their academic course learning, such as searching reference literature in their home languages, previewing/reviewing lecture materials by translating, and asking native peers for clarity. This reveals the translanguaging strategy "student-directed translanguaging"—to participate, to elaborate ideas, and to raise questions. Participants identified the value of group work and participation in classroom discourse in the United States, which is one of the characteristics of self-directed learning. Students can use groups to develop their own learning processes and achieve learning goals. For instance, they noted in the focus group discussion:

> In group work you have to convey yourself and make yourself understood and you learn how to communicate with others and how to finish class work. —*Ashraff*

> Group presentation is the most exciting activity. I feel less stressful. We can work in a group, communicate with natives and make friends with others. —*Pei*

Peer-support was initiated by teachers and students. Participants reported that they often interacted with each other using multiple languages to translate questions raised by teachers. Some also mentioned that they often confirmed with each other the homework requirements through their individual primary languages.

Additionally, students were willing to conduct their own learning and also tended to take responsibility for their own learning in a translanguaging-friendly environment. For instance, one participant wrote in his narrative story:

> The most important role for the teacher is a facilitator for me. To teach a person to fish is better than to give the person a fish. If the professor can teach us how to learn, and create a context where I have freedom to interact and resources, materials or dialects to use to improve my comprehension, it is better than he just give us some knowledge. —*Jang*

It seemed that participants valued and developed the awareness of self-directed learning with the help of translanguging strategies. When they encountered difficulties, they were more likely to use strategies and seek assistance and resources to solve problems and achieve learning goals. Meanwhile, participants reported in interviews that teachers in the U.S. classrooms encouraged self-directed learning in ways such as:

> Professors give much freedom…they give the basic introduction and support you to find the answer. I can ask peers to help me. In the class, teachers don't force us to speak English and encourage us to interact and use all resources or background knowledge. —*Pei*

It showed that "teacher-directed translanguaging" strategy was used to give voice, clarity, and reinforcement, and to manage the classroom. Participants valued teacher support for their self-directed learning development with translanguaging practices. Furthermore, two participants from STEM fields stated in the focus group discussion as well as their narrative stories that there were not many various activities in their classrooms, such as class discussion or group projects. For these graduate students, most of their time was spent in labs. Professors from STEM fields may choose to focus on students' research abilities and the curriculum instead of classroom activities. The two participants added that, "we try to improve our research ability by using all resources."

Motivation and Persistence

Self-directed learners are reflective and self-aware, demonstrate motivation, and are persistent and responsible (Candy, 1991). Self-directed learning recognizes the significance of agency in maintaining learners' efforts. NNES students in this study were found to be persistent in their academic courses as well as in English language learning. One participant showed high persistence in the academic learning in the focus group discussion by stating:

> I want to be a college teacher when I return to my home country. I have enough freedom to use all resources to overcome the difficulties. I use my background knowledge to comprehend class content and communicate with my natives. Because of these possible ways I can learn more advanced knowledge and skills to be qualified as a college teacher in the future. —*Ashraff*

When students have more agencies in their academic learning, they are more likely to persist in their learning. One participant continued to note:

> As a graduate student if I want to make success in the research I have to keep on studying, doing research and writing papers and make a lot of efforts. As an international student, I have more language difficulties, but luckily I can use my prior knowledge to make meaning and have an open mind to communicate to make up for my shortcomings compared with native speakers. —*Xi*

Self-Monitoring and Translanguaging

Participants developed the attribute and ability of self-monitoring. They were willing to adjust their behavior and readily and easily modified their behavior in response to the demands of the situation. Participants commented, "The situation is totally different for me, and I tried to seek resources and assistance from natives"; "I like classmates' comments and it is useful for me, and I would like to change my behavior in classes"; and "If my classmates cannot understand me, I try to make change and modify my speech or words to make me understood."

Participants also reported they faced difficulties and challenges from academic languages in making adjustment in their self-monitoring. All participants except for Bala reported challenges from academic English language. These students were simultaneously learning the language of instruction as well as the vocabulary and content of different subjects. They made statements such as:

> Professors try to explain very well in class, but the problem is I don't know the exactly English meaning. It makes me feel difficult to learn by myself in the class and after class. —*Juan*

> I don't know technically what the words mean when I study the reference literature after class. —*Ziaul*

> Final exam is very stressful. Although I know the answer of the question, I could not remember the correct English academic vocabulary. If I want to continue my study, I have to make more efforts to learn outside of classroom, and I have to overcome this problem. —*Jang*

These statements show that the participants faced challenges from English academic language, especially its vocabulary in their self-directed learning. English academic language can be a barrier for these students to engage in interactions with others and make adjustments in their self-monitoring. Since they were all graduate students, their study and classwork was filled with professional terms and formal language of study. These students had to learn not only interpersonal communication language and skills but also the content of different subjects and all of the associated complex and abstract vocabulary and technical terms.

Juan further stated in the interview:

> Sometimes, when teachers give us tasks or assignments, I cannot understand, I write it down with my [native] language. When I do the work, I go back and read what I write down and I understand what the teacher want me to do.

Additionally, in the face of challenges from academic language, Asuka showed her learning autonomy by saying:

> I go search each [academic English] word online and make a translated database of the course for myself.

But one participant (Bala) expressed or referred to conflicting attitudes toward this code-switching in the focus group. He reported code-switching as a result of linguistic deficit or compensation strategy used and related to the inability to remember English vocabulary.

Furthermore, participants reported the differences of classroom practices between their home country and the United States in their narrative stories. In their home countries there was not too much freedom for students to decide by themselves. Students' voice was not valued. It seemed that there was no evidence to suggest that self-directed learning was part of classroom practice in the colleges in these participants' home countries. For example, one participant noted:

> In my home country, we don't have many opportunities to discuss in a class. The major way of teachers' instruction is lecture…In my English language class, we just follow teachers' English words and even when we don't understand we don't often question teachers in the class. —*Xi*

All participants in this study had been in the United States for at least 1 year. They reported that in their home countries, they were more likely to be in teacher-centered classrooms and were taught what to do step by step, but when they came to the U.S. classroom setting, and when they were no longer told what to do but had to manage resources, make decisions, and deal with problems, they could develop some characteristics of autonomous learning.

Effective Instructional Strategies

Scaffolding increases learners' independence and helps learners to know not only "what to think and do, but how to think and do," so that new skills and understandings can be applied in new contexts (Hammond & Gibbons, 2005, p. 10). Participants reported favorably on the role the teacher played in helping and supporting them. Scaffolding provided by teachers was perceived as effective instructional strategies that support these students' self-directed learning. They identified "models or examples," "activating or connection to background knowledge," and "interactions" as effective strategies for them to make progress in their self-directed learning. For example, participants noted:

> When I wrote paper or assignment, the professor will provide some examples, peer's projects and sometimes materials written in different countries and languages to let us understand how to write every section for a paper work. —*Ashraff*

> When the professor talked about one topic, he always asked me the situation that happened in China, and I can speak more about the topic. —*Pei*

> My professor provided simple example that is similar to our projects. I can use the similar method to solve my problem. Although the procedure may not be exactly the same, but it's helpful for me to familiar with the process and the knowledge that I should learn. —*Juan*

> I interacted and discussed a lot in the class and teachers provided a lot of opportunities for us to communicate with peers. —*Pei*

DISCUSSION

The findings of the study speak to a growing body of research literature (e.g., Lee & Macaro, 2013; W. Li, 2009; Lin, 2015) that reveals learners' translanguaging strategies and functions. Based on the evidence detailed in the Results section, a commonality across these NNES graduate students was their desire to autonomously learn English in academic courses while using and maintaining their native languages. Most of them valued the use of native languages in meaning making and self-direction. They considered translanguaging as functional and used different strategies to improve their English language ability and academic course learning. Languages were mixed in many contexts through which subject content was learned. Translanguaging pedagogical practices were productive in supporting students' academic development such as translanguaging-encouraging classwork and class environment. Translanguaging strategy use, including "teacher-directed translanguaging" and "student-directed translanguaging" could increase students' independence and promote students' ability of learning inside and outside of classroom. In the content area classes, mastery of content is most important, and if students need to make meaning in their native language, this should be encouraged (García et al., 2011). Even though one participant who had a more positive self-perception of his English proficiency mentioned languages other than English should not be valued in content area classrooms, other students used and valued multiple languages in their thoughts, writing, and speech. It is consistent with studies that show the benefits of translanguaging in developing learners' agency (Marshall & Moore, 2018; Martínez-Álvarez & Ghiso, 2017). Participants in the study demonstrated their self-management, motivation and persistence, and self-monitoring in their academic learning. When they encountered difficulties, they were more likely to persist in their learning, maintain their efforts, seek assistance and resources to solve problems, and achieve learning goals.

Students reported challenges from English academic language in their self-directed learning. Academic language requires greater mastery of the English language for NNES students (Bifuh-Ambe, 2009). These students may lack the linguistic and cultural background and experiences that are taken for granted by teachers. This mismatched expectation could be detrimental to these students' self-directed learning and academic performance. The barrier for these NNES graduate students' self-directed learning development may be related to the lack of language knowledge and linguistic resources. Translanguaging and its related practices could enhance classroom communication, respond to discourse and sense-making needs, and give freedom to students for meaning negotiation, which can be embedded in subject-matter content where communication is meaningful (García et al., 2011).

Translanguaging strategies reported in this study include searching reference literature in students' home languages, previewing/reviewing lecture materials by translating, and asking native peers for clarity, etc. Frequent peer support and teacher support were considered effective in negotiating meaning in particular. Students with more linguistic resources and stronger proficiency were more inclined to help their peers. Students spoke home languages for the purposes of learning English or academic course content. Anything useful to achieve the primary goal could be strategically employed. Switching was not an aim in itself, but a process or a strategy to facilitate communication or to get ideas across. Translanguaging is timesaving and when students are involved in communication, especially with native peers, they utter the word that first comes to mind and avoid thinking about its equivalent in English. It confirms the findings of Clegg and Simpson (2016) that translanguaging enables self-directed and group learning which in a strictly L2-medium education is almost impossible to accomplish in L2. But this study contributes more to the related research since it examined self-directed learning from the translanguaging perspective comprehensively, both from teacher-directed and student-directed translanguaging. Students reported translanguaging individually and collaboratively. Not all students or even the teacher may be able to read all these multiple languages, but having them available in a classroom conveys a strong message that all languages are valuable. Establishing a translanguaging-friendly environment is important and it creates a classroom where students' voices and inputs are legitimate and valued (García, 2011).

Moreover, some participants reported that they lacked self-directed learning experience in their home country classroom. The classroom participation patterns in these students' home countries were different from those in the United States. In their home countries, they lacked questioning experience, initiative, and critical or independent thinking. NNES students may lack the necessary information, resources, knowledge, skills, and confidence to undertake tasks totally independently (Braine, 2010; Cheung, 2010). However, when they are given opportunity, freedom, and are told how to perform, students can develop characteristics of self-directed learning, which may contrast with the conventional beliefs found by Z. Fang (2014) that Asians were less likely to be autonomous than Westerners. Participants reported they valued interactive classroom activities in the U.S. college, which encouraged students to take responsibility for their own learning. Students agreed that they benefitted from teacher and peer support in their self-directed learning development. Teachers allowed students to utilize translanguaging and transliteracy to clarify meaning and make personal applications to their own experiences. Clearly the focus here is on communication rather than the linguistic code itself. The findings provide evidence to support the assertion of Biggs and Watkins (2001), Jingnan (2011), and Littlewood (2001). Students need to feel that they have some control over what is being taught, and when they feel autonomous, they are more likely to be motivated and to persist in what they are learning.

Scaffolding was reported as an effective instructional strategy by most NNES graduate students in this study. Scaffolding is designed to "provide the assistance necessary to enable learners to accomplish tasks and develop understandings that they would not be able to manage on their own" (Hammond & Gibbons, 2005, p. 9). Teachers should scaffold learning to promote language acquisition and academic success (Maxwell et al., 2011). These effective guidance and instructional strategies help learners to become actually self-directed even after learners finish their formal studies.

Participants also identified the value of group work and participation in classroom discourse in the United States. This kind of class activity is crucial for NNES students, especially students from nonscience and nonengineering fields that usually require more oral classroom participation and thus may require more advanced English listening and speaking skills (Ferris, 1998). Students could learn more and explore and yield new ideas and valuable insights during groupwork or discussions with peers. In particular, the qualities and skills that are essential for graduate students to do research cannot be developed just from textbooks; development also requires advisors' guidance and communicating with others through research tasks. Teachers need to pay attention to the group size in arranging groups. Lohman and Finkelstein (2000) identified higher self-directed learning in small and medium groups but lower self-directed learning in large groups.

Additionally, students from STEM fields reported fewer classroom activities or discussions used by teachers. It seems true especially for NNES students in STEM fields since as Morrison and Anglin (2006) stated, the most common way of class delivery for NNES students in STEM fields was lecture, and STEM classes required hands-on experimentation in laboratory settings. The process of trial and error is an important part of science (Morrison & Anglin, 2006), thus less attention was paid to various class activities. In this case, translanguaging strategies may focus on enhancing academic literacy or abilities.

IMPLICATIONS AND CONCLUSION

This study identified that the participants valued self-directed learning and translanguaging practices in the U.S. university setting, and they developed the awareness and capability of self-management, motivation and persistence, and self-monitoring in their academic learning. Meanwhile, with the help of teacher support and peer support, students adopted different translanguaging strategies and sought resources to assist their English language and academic course learning. Two types of translanguaging strategies including teacher-directed and student-directed translanguaging were reported. Students translanguaged individually and collaboratively. The effective instructional strategies include scaffolding and collaborative learning.

Based on these findings, I suggest that teachers implement translanguaging pedagogies that encourage the development of the full range of students' linguistic resources and make the efforts necessary to get to know their students. Teachers may help students to feel more comfortable to translanguage across linguistic proficiency levels and devote themselves to creating a trusting, respectful, and collaborative context to make students enjoy a high degree of autonomy to achieve academic success. Making translanguaging a norm in classrooms would support student learning, and designing multimodal and multilingual projects enables students to share their stories and experiences. I also suggest that teachers help students to recognize the great linguistic resources they have and facilitate students' discussion through student-led activities. Teachers can recognize these practices as common across their multilingual students and help students value these practices. It is emphasized that through these practices, students' linguistic proficiencies and perspectives can be revealed, which in turn can lead to instructional shifts that responsively support them in self-directed and lifelong learning.

This study also implies that teachers should pay attention to the language they use in and out of class to ensure that NNES students can understand the class content completely. Teachers can provide cognitive or metalinguistic scaffolding for meaning making to accommodate students' needs; model learning strategies such as questioning and clarifying; engage students in the learning of content knowledge; enhance their responsibility for participation; and help them use English academic language appropriately in classroom work.

In particular, college administrators should also work closely with international organizations within NNES graduate students' communities to provide services for NNES graduate students to achieve identity, integrate into local communities, and minimize the influence of limited language proficiency on their academic success. I want to emphasize the importance of collaboration between students, teachers, and related organizations in the process of students becoming self-directed learners and proficient as lifelong learners.

The study has some limitations. First, this study discusses findings from 12 Asian NNES graduate students, and the findings are limited to one U.S. university context. Given the potentially varying scope and levels of linguistic diversity among different universities, the findings cannot be generalized to other contexts. In addition, as the study drew on interview data and some relevant documents, its findings may not be able to fully capture the participants' self-directed learning and translanguaging in real practice. Furthermore, further research is still needed for how to facilitate self-direction and how a self-directed learner becomes motivated in a given context where they do not have a great deal of power. The teacher perspective could be explored together with students' perspectives in classrooms to further meet the needs of NNES graduate students. Teachers' roles in shaping the quality of students' experiences should be examined to analyze teachers' influence on students' affective, cognitive, and behavioral abilities. Studies could further find ways to use students' varied home language practices as scaffolds for the development of NNES students' English and academic literacy.

Acknowledgments

This work was supported by Science Foundation of China University of Petroleum, Beijing (No. ZX20170005) and Beijing Outstanding Talent Training Foundation (No. 69J19009).

REFERENCES

Ade-ojo, G. (2005). The predisposition of adult ESOL learners in a FE college towards autonomy. *Journal of Further and Higher Education, 29*(3), 191–210.

Ariza, E. N. (2010). *Not for ESOL teachers: What every classroom needs to know about the linguistically, culturally, and ethnically diverse students* (2nd ed.). Allyn & Bacon.

Biancarosa, G., & Snow, C. E. (2004). *Reading next—A vision for action and research in middle and high school literacy: A report to Carnegie Corporation of New York* (2nd ed.). Alliance for Excellent Education.

Bifuh-Ambe, E. (2009). Literacy skills acquisition and use: A study of an English language learner in a U.S. university context. *Adult Basic Education & Literacy Journal, 3*, 24–33.

Biggs, J. B., & Watkins, D. A. (2001). Insights into teaching the Chinese learner. In D. A. Watkins & J. B. Biggs (Eds.), *Teaching the Chinese learner: Psychological and pedagogical perspectives* (pp. 277–300). Comparative Education Research Centre, the Chinese University of Hong Kong.

Bista, K. (2015). Asian international students' college experience: Relationship between quality of personal contact and gains in learning. *Journal of International & Global Studies, 6*(2), 38–54.

Braine, G. (2010). *Nonnative speaker English teachers: Research, pedagogy, and professional growth*. Routledge.

Brockett, R. G., & Hiemstra, R. (1991). A conceptual framework for understanding self-direction in adult learning. In *Self-direction in adult learning: Perspectives on theory, research, and practice*. Routledge.

Canagarajah, S. (2011). Codemeshing in academic writing: Identifying teachable strategies of translanguaging. *Modern Language Journal, 95*, 401–417.

Candy, P. C. (1991). *Self-direction for lifelong learning*. Jossey-Bass.

Casanave, C. P. (2005). *Writing games: Multicultural case studies of academic literacy practices in higher education*. Lawrence Erlbaum.

Casanave, C. P., & Li, X. (2008). Introduction. In C. P. Casanave & X. Li (Eds.), *Learning the literacy practices of graduate school: Insiders' reflections on academic enculturation* (pp. 1–13). The University of Michigan Press.

Cheung, Y. L. (2010). First publications in refereed English journals: Difficulties, coping strategies, and recommendations for student training. *System, 38*(1), 134–141.

Clegg, J., & Simpson, J. (2016). Improving the effectiveness of English as a medium of instruction in sub-Saharan Africa. *Comparative Education, 52*(3), 359–374.

Cohen, L., Manion, L., & Morrison, K. (2013). *Research methods in education*. Routledge.

Collier, C. (2011). *Seven steps separating difference from disability*. Corwin.

Cummins, J. (2000). *Language, power, and pedagogy: Bilingual children in the crossfire*. Multilingual Matters.

Davis, E. A., & Miyake, N. (2004). Explorations of scaffolding in complex classroom systems. *Journal of the Learning Sciences, 13*(3), 265–272.

Entwistle, N. J., & Peterson, E. R. (2004). Conceptions of learning and knowledge in higher education: Relationships with study behavior and influences of learning environments. *International Journal of Educational Research, 41*, 407–428.

Erichsen, E., & Bolliger, D. (2011). Towards understanding international graduate student isolation in traditional and online environments. *Educational Technology Research and Development, 59*(3), 309–326.

Fang, F. M., & Zhang, L. (2012). Teachers' roles in promoting students' learner autonomy in China. *English Language Teaching, 5*(4), 51–56.

Fang, Z. (2014). A discussion about college teachers' roles in English viewing, listening and speaking autonomous learning. *International Forum of Teaching and Studies, 10*(1), 50–55.

Ferris, D. (1998). Students' views of academic aural/oral skills: A comparative needs analysis. *TESOL Quarterly, 32*, 289–318.

García, O. (2009). Emergent bilinguals and TESOL: What's in a name? *TESOL Quarterly, 43*(2), 322–326.

García, O. (2011). *Bilingual education in the 21st Century: A global perspective.* Basil/Blackwell.

García, O., Flores, N., & Chu, H. (2011). Extending bilingualism in U.S. secondary education: New variations. *International Multilingual Research Journal, 5*(1), 1–18.

García, O., & Li, W. (2014). *Translanguaging: Language, bilingualism and education.* Palgrave Macmillan.

Garrison, D. R. (1997). Self-directed learning: Toward a comprehensive model. *Adult Education Quarterly, 48*(1), 18–33.

Gu, M. (2014). From opposition to transcendence: The language practices and ideologies of students in a multilingual university. *International Journal of Bilingual Education and Bilingualism, 17*(3), 310–329.

Hailu, T. E., & Ku, H. Y. (2014). The adaptation of the horn of Africa immigrant students in higher education. *Qualitative Report, 19*, 1–19.

Hall, N., & Webb, D. (2014). Instructors' support of student autonomy in an introductory physics course. *Physical Review Special Topics–Physics Education Research, 10*, 1–22.

Hammond, J., & Gibbons, P. (2005). What is scaffolding? In A. Burns & H. de Silva Joyce (Eds.), *Teachers' voices 8: Explicitly supporting reading and writing in the classroom* (pp. 8–16). National Center for English Language Teaching and Research, Macquarie University.

Hornberger, N. H., & Link, H. (2012). Translanguaging and transnational literacies in multilingual classrooms: A biliteracy lens. *International Journal of Bilingual Education and Bilingualism, 15*(3), 261–278.

Institute of International Education. (2019). *Open Doors Report on International Educational Exchange.* Retrieved November 18, 2019 from https://www.iie.org/opendoors

Jick, T. D. (1979). Mixing qualitative and quantitative methods: Triangulation in action. *Administrative Science Quarterly, 24*, 602–611.

Jiménez, R. T., David, S., Fagan, K., Risko, V. J., Pacheco, M., Pray, L., & Gonzales, M. (2015). Using translation to drive conceptual development for students becoming literate in English as an additional language. *Research in the Teaching of English, 49*(3), 248–271.

Jingnan, S. (2011). Autonomy in EFL education. *Canadian Social Science, 7*(5), 27–32.

Kember, D. (2000). Misconceptions about the learning approaches, motivation and study practices of Asian students. *Higher Education, 40*, 99–121.

Kim, E. J. (2012). Providing a sounding board for second language writers. *TESOL Journal, 3*(1), 33–47.

Kimchi, J., Polivka, B., & Stevenson, J. S. (1991). Triangulation: Operational definitions. *Nursing Research, 40*(6), 364–366.

Knowles, M. S. (1975). *Self-directed Learning*. Association Press.

Lee, J.-H., & Macaro, E. (2013). Investigating age in the use of L1 or English-only instruction: Vocabulary acquisition by Korean ESL learners. *The Modern Language Journal, 97*(4), 887–901.

Lewis, G., Jones, B., & Baker, C. (2012). Translanguaging: Developing its conceptualisation and contextualisation. *Educational Research and Evaluation, 18*(7), 655–670.

Lewis, W. G. (2008). Current challenges in bilingual education in Wales. *AILA Review, 21*, 69–86.

Li, W. (2009). Polite Chinese children revisited: Creativity and use of code-switching in the Chinese complementary school classroom. *International Journal of Bilingual Education and Bilingualism, 12*, 193–211.

Lim, J. M.-H. (2017). Writing descriptions of experimental procedures in language education: Implications for the teaching of English for academic purposes. *English for Specific Purposes, 47*, 61–80.

Lin, A. (2015). Conceptualising the potential role of L1 in CLIL. *Language, Culture and Curriculum, 28*(1), 74–89.

Littlewood, W. (2001). Students' attitudes to classroom English learning: A cross-cultural study. *Language Teaching Research, 5*(1), 3–28.

Lohman, M. C., & Finkelstein, M. (2000). Designing groups in problem-based learning to promote problem-solving skills and self-directedness. *Instructional Science, 28*, 291–307.

Marshall, S., & Moore, D. (2018). Plurilingualism amid the panoply of lingualisms: Addressing critiques and misconceptions in education. *International Journal of Multilingualism, 15*(1), 19–34.

Martínez-Álvarez, P., & Ghiso, M. P. (2017). On languaging and communities: Latino/a emergent bilinguals' expansive learning and critical inquiries into global childhoods. *International Journal of Bilingual Education and Bilingualism, 20*(6), 667–687.

Maxwell, R. J., Meiser, M. J., & McKnight, K. S. (2011). *Teaching English in middle and secondary schools* (5th ed.). Pearson.

McKinney, K., Vacca, K., Medvedeva, M. A., & Malak, J. (2004). Beyond the classroom: An exploratory study of out-of-class learning in sociology. *Teaching Sociology, 32*, 43–60.

Middelborg, J. (2005). *Highland children's education project: A pilot project on bilingual education in Cambodia.* UNESCO Bangkok.

Mitchell, E. S. (1986). Multiple triangulation: A methodology for nursing science. *Advances in Nursing Science, 8*(3), 18–26.

Moore, P. (2013). An emergent perspective on the use of the first language in the English-as-a-Foreign-Language classroom. *The Modern Language Journal, 97*(1), 239–253.

Morrison, G. R., & Anglin, G. J. (2006). An instructional design approach for effective shovel-ware: Modifying materials for distance education. *Quarterly Review of Distance Education, 7*(1), 63–74.

Mukminin, A., & McMahon, B. J. (2013). International graduate students' cross-cultural academic engagement: Stories of Indonesian doctoral students on an American campus. *The Qualitative Report, 18*, 1–19.

Overzat, T. (2011). *Counseling Asian international students: Ethnics, issues, and ideas.* Retrieved from http://counselingoutfitters.com/vistas/vistas11/Article_75.pdf

Palfreyman, D. M., & Al-Bataineh, A. (2018). 'This is my life style, Arabic and English': Students' attitudes to (trans)languaging in a bilingual university context. *Language Awareness, 3*, 1–17.

Pintrich, P. R. (2004). A conceptual framework for assessing motivation and self-regulated learning in college students. *Educational Psychology Review, 16*, 385–407.

Rojas-Drummond, S., & Mercer, N. (2003). Scaffolding the development of effective collaboration and learning. *International Journal of Educational Research, 39*, 99–111.

Samimy, K., Kim, S., Lee, J., & Kasai, M. (2011). A participative inquiry in a TESOL program: Development of three NNES graduate students' legitimate peripheral participation to fuller participation. *The Modern Language Journal, 95*(4), 558–574.

Sawtelle, V., Brewe, E., & Kramer, L. H. (2012). Exploring the relationship between self-efficacy and retention in introductory physics. *Journal of Research in Science Teaching, 49*, 1096–1121.

Wang, D. (2019). Translanguaging in Chinese foreign language classrooms: students and teachers' attitudes and practices. *International Journal of Bilingual Education and Bilingualism, 22*(2), 138–149.

Wei, L. (2020). Multilingual English users' linguistic innovation. *World Englishes, 39*(2), 236–248.

World Bank. (2005). *In their own language: Education for all.* http://documents1.worldbank.org/curated/en/374241468763515925/pdf/389 060Language00of1Instruct01PUBLIC1.pdf

Xue, M. (2013). Effects of group work on English communicative competence of Chinese international graduates in United States institutions of higher education. *The Qualitative Report, 18*(14), 1–19.

Zimmerman, B. J. (2002). Becoming a self-regulated learner: An overview. *Theory into Practice, 41*(2), 64–72.

HONG SHI, PhD, is a lecturer in the School of Foreign Languages at China University of Petroleum-Beijing. Her major research interests lie in the area of instructed SLA, foreign language teaching, English for academic purposes, and teaching materials assessment. Email: shihong2005sd@163.com

Peer-Reviewed Article

OJED
OPEN JOURNALS IN EDUCATION

© *Journal of International Students*
Volume 11, Issue 1 (2021), pp. 216-237
ISSN: 2162-3104 (Print), 2166-3750 (Online)
doi: 10.32674/jis.v11i1.1446
ojed.org/jis

Dilemmas and Coping Strategies of Chinese International Students' Mental Health Problems: The Parents' Perspectives

Lan Jin
Purdue University, USA

Lalatendu Acharya
Indiana University Kokomo, USA

ABSTRACT

Talking about mental health issues like depression with parents is a challenging exercise for Chinese international students (CISs) as well as their parents due to their cultural context and family hierarchical structure. This study engages with the parents of CISs to identify their dilemmas and coping strategies employed to discuss depression with their children studying in United States. Thirteen Chinese parents of CISs were recruited into in-depth interviews. A constant comparative method was employed for data analysis. The results revealed that the parents struggled with different dilemmas while talking about depression. Four coping strategies emerged: (a) communicating openly, (b) improving understanding through social media and shared experiences, (c) respecting, being sensitive, and not being judgmental, and (d) encouraging help-seeking and support-seeking. The findings provide crucial insights for mental health interventions involving parents of CISs.

Keywords: adjustment, Chinese international students, coping strategies, depression, mental health, parents

The number of international students has increased rapidly at American universities, from 582,996 in 2002 to 1,094,792 in 2018 (International Institute of Education, 2018). Research has identified that this process of moving and adjusting to an unfamiliar place creates stress for international students. Chinese international students (CISs), the largest international student population in the United States (33.2%; International Institute of Education, 2018), face tremendous stress in the process of transitioning into the American college. These stresses are associated with many health problems, such as depression, low self-esteem, headache, and heart diseases (Cheung, 2010). This population is at heightened risk of depression and anxiety (Bastien et al., 2018; Cheung, 2010), due to the challenges of acculturative stress (Han et al., 2013; Settles et al., 2012), language barriers (Han et al., 2013), academic difficulties (Han et al., 2013; Settles et al., 2012), sense of loneliness (Han et al, 2013; Settles et. al, 2012), weak social support network (Forbes-Mewett & Sawyer, 2016), and financial hardship (McCullough & Larson, 1999; Settles et al., 2012). Recent studies at different universities found a 32%–47% rate for depression symptoms among CISs (Acharya et al., 2018; Cheung, 2010; Wei et al., 2007).

The CISs utilize several positive coping strategies to tackle depression problems, such as informational social support, positive interpretation, and emotions venting and also negative ones such as denial and avoidance (Inman & Yeh, 2007; Sapranaviciute et al., 2013). Family support, traditional cultural beliefs, lack of knowledge about services, and perceived stigma toward depression complicates their coping process (Sapranaviciute et al., 2013). In the collectivistic Asian cultures, family plays a central role in people's lives and is assumed to be an important supportive system for young people (Inman & Yeh, 2007).

Although families function as key supporters for CISs, speaking with them about mental health issues can be challenging. Influenced by implicit communication styles rooted in Chinese culture and the hierarchical structure of traditional Chinese families, conversation about negative topics such as mental health issues may create various conflicts and dilemmas. Furthermore, geographical separation between CISs and their parents, as well as time difference, brings additional challenges to their conversation. This study employs a qualitative research design using in-depth interviews with parents of CISs and reports dilemmas that they faced when talking with their children about mental health problems, and identifies strategies they used to address these dilemmas. The study provides theoretical and practical implications for researchers, university administrators, educators, parents, and students to navigate mental health issues of international students.

LITERATURE REVIEW

Previous studies with Chinese student and family participants have outlined that communication about depression with family members (Gao et al., 1996; Leach & Braithwaite, 1996) and parents provided an important supportive system for young people (Chao, 1994; Inman & Yeh, 2007). Research with various student populations further shows that discussing depression with family can be an effective way to reduce the effects of depression, manifest the availability of emotional support, and assist with coping (Cohen & Wills, 1985; Ying et al., 2000).

However, talking about depression is a challenging exercise for CISs and their parents. For example, the relationship among family members strongly influences the patterns of family communication in China (Xing et al., 2010). Family members are regulated by obligation of different generations and ages. The basic principle in the Chinese family is that children should please, respect, and be subordinate to their parents (Hwang, 1999). Despite the importance of social support and interdependent relationships in Chinese families, there are conflicts between Chinese parents and children that affect their communication. When individual desires are in conflict with the construct of filial piety, the children tend to conceal personal interests and compromise (Hwang, 1999). Meanwhile, parents are expected to make all efforts to provide strong support, especially economic and informational, for the development of children, and thus have high expectations (Gao et al., 1996).

These cultural concepts in Chinese families complicate the context in which family communication occurs and make conversation about negative issues such as mental health problems difficult. The structure of a traditional Chinese family is hierarchical, in which an individual's interest, especially the younger generation's interest, is held inferior to the collective family interest (Zhang, 2007). Communication on a range of topics is thus limited. Family interactions emphasize harmony and interdependence of family members; therefore, conflicting discussions are usually avoided (Keating et al., 2013; Xu, 2012). For example, parents have the dominant power to make the decisions for the family, and the children are expected to show the desired subservient behavior (Wu & Chao, 2011). Chinese parents expect their children to perform well in academia, be successful, and be able to support them when they age. So, to achieve a harmonious atmosphere in the family, it is likely that CISs do not discuss their mental health problems, insecurities, and other issues, which they perceive as impediments to their parent's desires of success and harmony (Xu, 2012). This situation gives rise to competing goals (emotion or problem disclosure versus maintaining harmonious relationship) in the communication between Chinese parents and their children (Roscoe & Barrison, 2019).

In addition, parental sacrifices made for children's achievements create this cultural environment of high expectations, putting pressures on the children that manifest in the children's unwillingness to share negative experiences such as stress and depression (Liu, 2009). Parental sacrifice is regarded highly in the Chinese culture (Zhang, 2007). The parents work hard and provide financial support for the higher education of the child with the hope that their child will live a successful life and take care of the family. So, sharing information and communicating about depression could construe to parents that the children are not able to discharge their responsibilities properly, leading to more stress and a sense of guilt (Xu, 2012). In this case, disclosing emotions and maintaining harmonious relationship are competing goals, which poses challenges for parents and children to discuss depression. Further, the stigma surrounding mental health issues influences the family members' response and communication. Depression is often perceived as a stigma in the Chinese society, and thus disclosing their depression-like symptoms threatens the self-esteem of children and shames their families (Wang & Mallinckrodt, 2006). As a result, communication about depression between family members is purposeful but challenging in Chinese families. There are very few (negligible) studies that focus on examining family communication around depression in CISs. This gap and the fact that the CISs constitute the largest contingent of international students underlines the importance of this research. Furthermore, the mental health needs of the student community have grown over the years and Chinese students face significant stressors while studying internationally (Cheung, 2010). Our study emerged from this literature review and the personal experience of one of the researchers. It aims to examine the family communication processes among Chinese parents and their children studying as international students in the United States. This inquiry can greatly support the various mental health wellness activities at American universities targeted at the burgeoning Chinese student population. A review of different family communication studies indicated the normative theory of social support (Goldsmith, 2004) as a useful and efficient framework. The following section focuses on the normative theory of social support, which was used to guide the study.

Normative Theory of Social Support

Multiple goals theories assume that human communication is purposeful, pursuing multiple goals at the same time, with the goals often in conflict (Caughlin, 2010). Multiple goals theories are a group of interpersonal communication theories that examine multiple communication goals and resulting conflicts in interpersonal communication (Caughlin, 2010; Wilson & Feng, 2007). As one of the multiple goals theories, the normative theory of social support suggests that communication is undertaken to pursue instrumental, identity, and relational objectives and that these multiple goals may be conflicting (Goldsmith, 2004). The normative theory of social support has been widely used in the field of complex communication situations between family members (Goldsmith & Fitch, 1997; Roscoe & Barrison, 2019; Wilson et al., 2015). The theory posits that people pursue the competing instrumental, identity, and relational goals at the same time in their interpersonal interactions. Instrumental goals refer to outcomes having primary influence on the behavior of message receivers, such as reducing stress or promoting help-seeking actions. Identity goals are related to identity needs like maintaining harmony, autonomy, and dignity as per culture; relational goals influence both the message receivers and senders, such as managing the interpersonal relationship between the parent and child (Knapp & Daly, 2011). The normative theory of social support focuses on potential meanings associated with forms of interpersonal communication (Wilson et al., 2015). For example, a Chinese parent who suggests that her child seek mental health care could be interpreted as a way of caring, but also as indicating that the child was not meeting parental expectations. Goldsmith (2004) assumed that the meanings communicators attribute to their conversation influence whether the multiple and potentially conflicting objectives can be achieved. The normative theory of social support highlights that communication is based on achieving diverse and perhaps conflicting aims. This results in dilemmas for the communicators as they pursue multiple conflicting objectives, which can be interpreted as communicating incongruent meanings (Goldsmith & Fitch, 1997; Wilson et al., 2015). A dilemma is the situation where a set of competing purposes and conflicting outcomes occur (Goldsmith & Fitch, 1997). The normative theory of social support focuses on verbal and nonverbal features and strategies that communicators use to manage communication difficulties or dilemmas that emerge in conversations.

The normative theory of social support assumes that dilemmas are situated within a context. The specific sociocultural context may influence how the communicators interpret the meanings of the talk (Wilson et al., 2015). The effectiveness of communication is evaluated according to the extent to which the communicators accomplish goals while managing the context-specific dilemmas. Communicative practices, which are essential to managing dilemmas, are presumed to vary across specific sociocultural contexts (e.g., military culture, stigma etc.; Wilson et al., 2015). Effective communication strategies depend on the cultural context and can not necessarily be generalized, because multiple and competing goals and dilemmas manifest from specific meanings attached to the different types of talk. For example, in the context of talking about depression, the parents should balance instrumental goals of providing advice with the relational goal of conveying caring, as the CIS could be affected very negatively with interpretations of stigma or losing face. In this case, the parents might navigate the challenge through underscoring the validity of the CIS's negative emotions, such as sadness, anxiety, and stress. In particular, since the hierarchical power in Chinese families create pressure on the CIS, the parents can empower them with more sense of control and confidence by encouraging them, showing respect, and providing decision-making powers. Thus, this research proposed to address the following research questions guided by the normative theory of social support.

Research Questions

Despite the importance of family communication in coping with depression, very little research has focused on the parents' dilemmas regarding communication around depression of CISs (Wei et al., 2010). This study engages with CISs' parents to identify the dilemmas they face and coping strategies they employ discussing their child's depression. This exploration can inform future interventions in addressing depression of CISs. Thus, the first research question was:

RQ1: What are the dilemmas that parents of a CIS experience when discussing about depression with their child?

The normative theory of social support (Goldsmith, 2004) further assumes that coping strategies are used to manage the dilemmas that emerge during the discussion. Further, not all discussions happen face to face and the geographical distance between China and the United States and the intercultural context also complicate matters. Therefore, we proposed the second question:

RQ2: What are the coping strategies that parents of a CIS adopt to address dilemmas when discussing depression with their child?

METHOD

Participants

Thirteen Chinese parents whose children were studying in the United States were recruited through convenience sampling (age range of 43–63; $M = 53.54$, $SD = 5.32$). Sample eligibility was assessed by whether the parents had expressed concerns that their child was at risk of depression, and/or the child had experienced episodes of depression or persistent low mood in the United States. Data collection continued till sample saturation at 13 participants, as further interviews would not likely reveal any new theoretical insights (Strauss & Corbin, 1998). Therefore, we stopped sampling when the obtained data became repetitive and confirmed the resulting analyses.

Data Collection

We conducted thirteen in-depth face-to-face interviews with participants in China. We recruited the sample through a convenience sampling method in an urban community. We distributed flyers in the local community and advertised on an information-sharing website and social media, popular with many Chinese international students and parents. We made an appointment for an individual interview for those who responded. The first author, who is Chinese, conducted the interviews. The interviewing author explained the purpose, procedures, benefits, and risks of participating in the study to the participants before the interview. After reading and signing the consent form, we asked all participants to complete a demographic questionnaire. Then, we interviewed all participants and asked open-ended questions about their experiences of dealing with their child's depression and their communication and coping strategies around it. We audio recorded interviews and transcribed them verbatim immediately. Analysis informed the subsequent data collection and vice versa (Fram, 2013; Glaser & Strauss, 1967; Glaser, 1992). The major interview questions were the following: What are your expectations toward your child and the conversation about depression-like symptoms between you and your child? What difficulties/dilemmas have you encountered in the process? What were your strategies to cope with the difficulties you encountered when talking about depression-like symptoms with your child? In addition, we asked probing questions to clarify and expand on participants' responses. One of the researchers, who is a native Chinese speaker, translated the transcripts from Chinese to English. Her Chinese background allowed her to translate the documents in a way that was culturally sensitive and contextually rich (Turner, 2010). A second translator, who was a counselor from the Department of English who had grown up speaking both English and Chinese, further checked the translation. We resolved divergence in translation by further discussion and made modifications depending on agreements between the two translators (Turner, 2010). The second author guided the study design and analysis and manuscript preparation.

To answer the first research question, we identified dilemmas from the transcripts by examining the participant's communication for potentially contradictory goals (conflicts). The answers to the second question about coping strategies emerged from the themes coded from words/ phrases frequently used by the participants (Burck, 2005).

Ethical Consideration

The study was approved by the Institutional Review Board of the researchers' university. A local approval by a community leader in China was provided. The community leader was the head of a local public hospital. He was an expert in the field of health issues and familiar with local cultural and religious norms with experience of engaging with the community over 30 years. Confidentiality was maintained through the assignment of a code for each participant and the data obtained; and we use pseudonyms for the participants below.

Data Analysis

Based on interpretive framework, the study utilized a constant comparative method as an analytic strategy to analyze the data (Fram, 2013; Glaser & Strauss, 1967; Kolb, 2012; Strauss & Corbin, 1998). The constant comparative method is often used to analyze data in order to develop a grounded theory, which itself has evolved over time from its positivistic and postpositivistic beginnings to a more constructivist approach as led by Charmaz (2008). Over time, researchers have also used comparative analysis as a data analytic technique in descriptive or interpretive projects outside the purview of a grounded theory approach (Boeije, 2002; Fram, 2013; O'Connor et al., 2008; Thorne, 2000). We identified descriptive categories as soon as data collection had begun, through generating and comparing codes applicable to each category (Glaser, 1965). These categories influenced the development of interviews so that the emerging concepts might be explored more thoroughly (Boeije, 2002). The data in hand were constantly compared with the new data (Boeije, 2002; Glaser, 1965; Kolb, 2012).

We used open coding was followed by axial coding to develop categories from connecting data. We identified the core categories in the selective coding process (Strauss & Corbin, 1998). Additional data consisted of field notes and self-reflective notes/memos, which assisted in moving analysis to a more conceptual level (Strauss & Corbin, 1998).

RESULTS

We recruited 13 Chinese parents of CISs in the study. The demographic profile of the participants is reported in Table 1. The results indicated that the parents struggled with several dilemmas when talking about depression with CISs. Four coping strategies emerged from the dialogues. It is important to note that participants designated the term "depression" as "low mood," "sadness," or "emotional problems," rather than an indication of a formal diagnosis. The participants were concerned that these "low mood" conditions may lead to clinical depression diagnosis if they and their children did not address it well.

Table 1: Participant Demographics (*N* = 13)

Characteristics	*n*	%
Sex		
Male	6	46
Female	7	54
Education level		
High school graduate	1	8
Community college	1	8
Four-year college	11	84
Marital status		
Married	13	100
Years in the United States (child)		
6 mo–1 yr	3	23
2–5 yr	8	62
> 5 yr	2	15
Occupation		
Employed	10	77
Retired	2	15
Housework	1	8
Have a passport		
Yes	9	69
No	4	31
Have gone to the United States		
No	9	69
1–2 times	4	31
Monthly income		
¥5,000–9,999	6	46
¥10,000–14,999	7	54

Dilemmas of Talking About Depression with CISs

Data analysis revealed four dilemmas that the parents encountered when talking with their children regarding depression. In this study, dilemmas refer to potentially incongruent meanings that emerged in the family conversation connected to multiple and competing objectives (Wilson et al., 2015).

Dilemma 1: Expecting the Child to Explicitly Disclose Concealed Problems

The first dilemma dealt with the parents' expectation of the child to disclose their depression struggles explicitly, while at the same time expecting the child to deal with depression, keeping in mind the larger goal of succeeding. The parents expected their children to discuss depression, but they only talked about positive issues with their parents with reassurances that they can handle their problems by themselves. As Li (a father, 47 years old) described:

When I ask my daughter how she is doing, she often answers, "Don't worry; I am doing well; I can address the problems; I can solve it by myself." She has been there for three years. I know that it is difficult. Sometimes I can recognize through her tone and facial expression that she is very stressed or depressed. But she doesn't tell us explicitly.

The participants further explained that their children avoided disclosing because they wanted to prevent anxiety and worry:

Many children are not willing to talk with parents about the problems they encounter, or that they feel depressed, because the parents live far away from them. The children are afraid that their parents would take the problems too seriously if they tell the parents about the difficulties. They are concerned that the parents worry too much. They don't talk to the parents. —*Ying* (a mother, 50 years old)

The participants indicated that some children tended to conceal the difficulties or depression problems, or talked about their troubles passively. This was because they did not want to bother their parents and invalidate the parental expectations and sacrifice.

Dilemma 2: Expecting the Child to Disclose Problems While Being Unsure How to Support

Another dilemma participants faced is their expectation for their child to disclose problems, while being unsure if they as parents could provide any support. The parents expected open communication as one important goal and encouraged children to reveal their depression problems. They believed that open communication about depression and problems could provide them relief. For example, Fan (a mother, 45 years old) described:

We have a lot of conversation to prevent depression problems and reduce stress. We may not talk about depression directly, but talking with parents is very important to release their stress. They are staying abroad. They have no relatives and few close friends there. Hence, communication with parents is very crucial for the child to feel that they have strong support from us.

However, the participants were not sure if they could provide any other support besides the open conversation opportunity. Yang (a father, 60 years old) indicated:

Parents should have a deep conversation with the child. For example, what do you think about the context of the US? What do you think about people in your class and your office? What do you think about your major? These can deepen our understanding of her study and life. It is also beneficial for her personal development and inspiring her thoughts. But it is hard to have this kind of thorough conversation, and I don't know what I can do next to help her.

The parents found it tough to initiate and maintain this conversation, because they could not understand the U.S. cultural context and the problems that their child encountered. The lack of understanding came from their absence of direct experiences, inadequate knowledge about American college life and culture, and the intergenerational gap between the parents and child. This created obstacles to the conversation between the parents and child, and in addressing the depression problems. For example, Zhao (a father, 51 years old) narrated:

The children are situated in a context that parents don't know. We only get to know about America a little through our child's description, such as study environment, living situation, and natural environment. We can't experience what they have experienced. People's perception and behavior may change as the environment around them changes. We also have an intergenerational gap with the child. Our beliefs are not the same with them. We might have conflicting thoughts on some issues. So, the child may not accept your suggestions, or even reject strongly. This is our communication problem. We have different thoughts and ways to cope with problems. How can we help them without understanding?

Although the participants expected their children to reveal their depression problems, their lack of understanding of American culture and context placed barriers in family communication and provision of effective support.

Dilemma 3: Parents' High Expectations of Children – Being Successful and Happy

The parents expected the children to aim high, work hard, and at the same time, not feel stressed while achieving their desired goals and success. As the parents described, they had multiple expectations of their child. They expected their child to achieve high academic and career success, and at the same time to be happy. Bin (a father, 56 years old) said:

I hope that she could be an expert in the field that she is interested in, and improve herself. Also, I expect her to be excellent in the language. It is really important to be proficient in one language. In one word, I hope she is doing well in her study, and be happy as well.

However, the parents realized that high parental expectations may cause huge stress to the child. They understood that the process of pursuing goals can be tough, which may influence the child's mental health, but they still expected outstanding performance. For example, Yang indicated:

225

But on the other hand, the process of learning is difficult, and is suffering. No pain no gain. You must pay something to achieve your goal. So, in the process they might be stressed and depressed. I know that what I hope may bring pressure to my child. Sometimes my daughter just doesn't want to talk because I always say 'work hard' …we all expect our child to be outstanding.

The participants recognized that their conflicting expectations toward their child, of being happy and also prioritizing working hard to excel created a dilemma. Further, the parents' relentless emphasis on high academic performance impacted their communication. Qiu (a father, 55 years old) described his struggles communicating support to his son:

I hope that he has a feeling of happiness. It is easy to say, but hard to accomplish, right? On one side, you want to be happy; on the other side, you must make efforts and work hard, which is quite stressful. This is one conflict. You have to keep a balance between hard working and mental health. The child should be able to control his own life. I can't help with this. You need to work hard, but…you shouldn't only work. If you get too much pressure, you may be depressed. It is difficult to maintain the balance.

Dilemma 4: Communicating Care and Helplessness at the Same Time

The parents faced the conflicting goals of professing care and at the same time communicating their helplessness. The participants often highlighted that they were concerned about their child's life and depression problems in the United States, but at the same time professed that they may not be in a position to help. Meng (a father, 57 years old) described that he was concerned about his daughter's mental health state:

I am always worried that my daughter may be too stressed. I tell her that we are friends when we are talking. If you tell me about your difficulties or problems, I will not blame you. I will try my best to help you. I hope that she doesn't have the depression problems. I am very concerned about that. I think the most important thing in life is staying happy, but how can I help her?

Although the participants indicated that they cared about the child's problems, it was difficult for the parents to provide direct and effective help to the child.

The geographical separation also made it challenging to provide emotional and instrumental support, such as being available, providing an emotional hug, helping with housekeeping, and providing money. Additionally, the participants were of no help when dealing with academic problems. Juan (a mother, 48 years old) said:

We are not able to help with the specific approaches to address her depression and stress. On one hand, we (parents) are far away from the child. We can do nothing for her. If she is at home, we could comfort her by giving her a hug, or cook for her. We also don't have the ability to help her solve the problems, especially her academic problems. She can only rely on herself. We are merely able to encourage her to overcome the difficulties. Parents can't help. We don't know the language, the culture, or the context there. We know nothing. We are willing to help, but unable to do so.

The participants outlined the conflict created by their desire to care and support with their actual incapability that prevented them from offering effective support.

Furthermore, the participants disclosed their strong emotional feelings when talking about depression concerns. They felt anxious and sad while hearing about their children's problem or realizing that they were unable to help. Juan shared, "Actually parents are anxious and worried about the child when they have depression problems. We just do our best to let her know our experiences and thoughts. We hope that can help her.

We reflected in our journal notes:

The participant narrated her feelings and emotions while interacting with the child. When she realized that she could not help her child due to limited knowledge, she was anxious and guilty. On the other hand, if she found that her child accepted and appreciated her support and help, she was very happy with that. The parent's emotions were tightly connected to whether she could provide effective support to her child. The child expects support from the parents, and the parents expect that they can assist the child. The parents obtain feeling of satisfaction when providing support.

Meng described his struggles and strong emotions considering his child's problems in the United States. He said, "Sometimes I tell my child, thinking about your difficulties in the US, I feel teary. Why? Because I am not able to go there and help you." The participant indicated that he felt very sad when he realized that he couldn't help the child. Although Meng could understand that CISs may encounter various difficulties in the United States, it didn't make sense to him how difficult the problems were. He was struggling with the fact that he wanted to give everything he had to the child but he could not provide any direct help. These strong emotional expressions highlighted the importance of using coping strategies to address the participants' dilemmas and provide support to their children. Thus, we asked the participants about the various coping strategies that they used to address these dilemmas.

Coping Strategies

Participants used or suggested the following coping strategies to deal with the multiple communication dilemmas that they encountered when talking about depression and related mental health issues with their children studying in the United States.

Communicating Openly

Facing the challenge that the child was not willing to talk about depression actively, the participants emphasized that parents should establish an open conversation climate with the child. They believed that the whole family should work together to deal with depression. Depression of the CISs was a concern that required the efforts of all family members. For example, Jing said, "We address a problem through family talks. We exchange everyone's opinions. Combining everyone's perspectives, the problem can be solved effectively." Qiu (a father, 55 years old) indicated that the family empowered their child to achieve more effective communication,

> We help him to deal with depression or stress by conversations and negotiation. What we say is just one recommendation or suggestion…the children have the right to determine what they will do. I think this is effective communication. Parents should lead and guide children when they are young. But if you force the children to do something, it will not work. The children will not obey. So, the interactive way of communication is the best way. It is efficient.

Han (a mother, 55 years old) emphasized the necessity of open communication from parents' side,

> I think parents should keep communication channels open with the children, and contact them regularly. You can't leave them alone. If they are too busy to talk, leave them a message. At least, parents can be sensitive and be always available to maintain the children's mental health. It requires cooperation of the entire family.

Cooperation of family here means that the parents should take action to relieve the child's stress or depression through mutual discussion, empowering the child by providing them freedom to take major decisions, and actively keeping in touch with them.

Improving Understanding through Social Media and Shared Experiences

The participants stated that a better understanding of the intercultural context in American colleges and the lives of their children could be achieved through social media usage. CISs extensively use social media and update information about their social lives. Further, information is also shared through social media by communities like Chinese associations, parent associations, and international student organizations. The participants suggested that using audio visual features of social media like video chat can help the parents connect over long distance. Meng noted:

> My wife often uses social media like "WeChat" (a hugely popular social media application in China) to obtain rich information about the American college life, and talks with my daughter by video chat on "WeChat." That is very helpful and convenient, since we can see her facial expression and tell if she is happy or distressed.

In addition, the participants communicated a lot with other CISs' parents to learn from their experiences. Cai (a mother, 43 years old) stated:

> I have many relatives and friends whose children are also studying in the US. We often talk about each other's children; how they are doing, their difficulties, what they are interested in...The true experiences of relatives and friends make more sense. We can talk a lot about the children's experiences and problems, and exchange our thoughts.

Thus, social media and shared experience of other CIS parents were two main sources of information that the parents relied on to increase understanding of American culture and the college life of CISs.

Respecting, Being Sensitive, and Not being Judgmental

In order to provide relief to their children, the participants emphasized the significance of emotional support, such as reassurance, encouragement, and respect. Zheng, (a mother, 52 years old) stated: "I think parents should comfort the child, rather than emphasizing the expectations frequently. Don't put pressure on them... They are already highly stressed in the US. Give the children more space and reassurance (by)." Yang, noting a non-judgmental attitude, stated:

> As parents who are far away from their children, what we can do best is just to provide comfort, support and emotional encouragement...Parents should not judge their child's thoughts, behaviors, or decisions. If the child talks about depression, we can't say that it is bad or abnormal. We should show respect when we listen to them. Otherwise they won't talk or follow your suggestion.

Furthermore, the participants pointed out that they observed their child's mood cautiously and were sensitive to the emotional status of their child. Han noted:

> Sometimes I recognize that her voice on the phone is very low, and she may be unhappy. I ask her, "What happened; you do not seem happy." I keep asking, and then she reveals that she feels depressed because of her thesis and the communication problems with the professors. She won't tell me unless I notice her emotional change.

Hence the participants suggested that treating their children with respect, listening nonjudgmentally, and being sensitive to emotional changes could facilitate supportive family communication.

Encouraging Help-Seeking and Support-Seeking

The participants encouraged their children to seek help from peers who were more familiar with the American context, and could provide helpful suggestions. As Meng said:

> I always suggest to him to seek for help from friends, especially people who are international students too. They can help each other through communication and interaction. Many problems can be addressed…The international students have similar experiences. They can learn from each other. They feel comfortable and happy when talking with friends.

Fan described that she addressed her daughter's depression problems through comforting and encouraging help seeking. She shared:

> When she discloses that she is much stressed or has depression problems, I first comfort her; and then I tell her that speaking with friends could be beneficial. I also talk to my friends' kids who are international students, asking them to contact my daughter. Conversation with others can help her make sense of what the problem is, and gain knowledge about how to solve the problem. She can make friends with more people. It is a process of personal development.

Additionally, some participants encouraged their children to seek out professional mental health services, which were an efficient way to address depression. Han said:

> I suggested to my daughter to use the mental health services at her university when she feel too stressed. The parents should encourage their child to seek help from the mental health services. Depression is like your mind is getting a cold. It is not a shame. You should go when you need help. In particular, the US pays more attention on mental health than China does. It will be more effective to visit the psychiatrist and address your depression. They are experts. They are more professional than your friends and families. They can provide more professional help. Asking for help means you are mature and aware of your needs.

Ultimately, the participants often recommended their children to learn from the experience of their peers and utilize mental health services to address their depression issues.

DISCUSSION

Based on Goldsmith's (2004) normative theory of social support, the results of the study revealed the dilemmas parents encountered when talking about depression with their children and the coping strategies they used to deal with the dilemmas. The findings of the study were consistent with the existing research and they further expanded the normative theory of social support into the new context of international students communicating about depression with their parents. We discuss the theoretical and practical implications and limitations of the study.

Using the normative theory of social support, similarities and differences appear in the dilemmas that Chinese parents encounter when communicating about mental health with their children when compared with other populations studied. An example is the mental health concerns of military families (Wilson et al., 2015) and older couples talking about lifestyle changes (Goldsmith et al., 2006). Emphasizing "caring" and creating a meaning of "it is normal" to have this problem in different contexts is presented in all the three studies. However, in this study, dilemmas resulted from "implicit communication" (e.g., "I expect you to disclose but you conceal"), which is unique to the communication style in Chinese culture. This implicit communication style as a key feature of Chinese culture has been echoed by other studies as well (Gao et al., 1996; Jin & Acharya, 2016). These findings support a key assumption of the normative theory of social support (Goldsmith, 2004) that conversational dilemmas are situated in contexts and diverse meanings are formed in different cultures (Roscoe & Barrison, 2019). Furthermore, this study suggested that families reframe the identity (i.e., beneficial to personal development) and relational meaning (i.e., connecting to social network, conveying care) of seeking help as they develop coping strategies. However, our study stresses more on collaborative coping styles than Wilson's et al. (2015) study.

Regarding theoretical implications, our study applies the normative theory of social support in a new cultural context and further supports the assumptions. The normative theory of social support (Goldsmith, 2004) assumes that a high quality of communication depends on the degree to which speakers can achieve multiple and potentially contradictory expectations while managing meanings related to conversation topics and speakers' relationships. The parents' attempts to pursue expectations can be interpreted as communicating conflicted meanings (e.g., expecting the child to disclose versus inability to understand the child's disclosure; hoping the child prioritizes working hard versus being less stressed), and thus the parents must manage multiple goals in the process of purposeful communication (Caughlin, 2010). Being a parent, the participants believed that they had the responsibility to provide the support that the child needed. In this sense, communication was necessary to make support efficient. However, parents noted that their child tended to avoid mentioning depression issues. They realized that it was necessary to encourage and perform bidirectional communication— that is, not only to encourage their child to talk, but also to open themselves up to proactive and frequent communication with their children. The children's passive communication with their parents is potentially rooted in the traditional Chinese culture of "listening-centered" (*tinghua*) communication where speaking is tied to seniority and hierarchy (Fang & Faure, 2011; Gao et al., 1996). Children are thus expected to listen more and speak less. So, to operate in this context, it is very important for the parents to keep open and regular communication, and look for verbal and nonverbal indicators of depressive symptoms in their child. For example, the participants in the study pointed out that they made efforts to be sensitive to the child's emotions. This suggests that Chinese parents who are worried about their child's mental health should look out for depressive symptoms such as avoiding conversation, low voice, reduced eye contact, other nonverbal behaviors like unhappy facial expressions, etc. (Fossi et al., 1984).

The participants utilized several approaches to improve their understanding of the cultural context in the United States and made efforts to engage in active conversation with their children. Perceived understanding is related to feelings of connection and confirmation in family relationships (Reis, 2007). The participants identified that it was difficult to understand their child's depression issues without any experience of the context or conditions, so it made sense that the parents tried to connect with and understand the child's experience through different means, such as talking with other parents and using social media.

Furthermore, the participants recommended that parents should endeavor to show unconditional and nonjudgmental caring, support, and commitment to the CISs to reduce their stress and other environmental pressures. Furthermore, verbalizing high parental expectations in conversations will lead to increased stress and should be avoided. Many participants also suggested being respectful to their children and not rushing to conclusions. By practicing nonjudgmental listening, the parents create more scope for their children to share negative experiences of depression. Also, the act of being respectful to the children's experiences would prevent the emergence of negative meanings of depression.

Additionally, as the participants encountered difficulties in providing meaningful assistance due to the long distance and inadequate cultural understanding of the United States context, they advocated various sources of help for their children. The participants suggested seeking professional help and peer support, which was beneficial to the CISs' personal development. The strategies attempted to reduce societal stigma by reframing the meaning of seeking help (e.g., it is a process of development or a sign of maturity). Thus, the participants endeavored to manage the negative meanings associated with depression, aiming to redefine the context through communication. In addition, the coping strategies included connecting the CISs to a social network where peers come together to help each other.

In terms of practical implications, it was encouraging that many participants in our study recognized the importance of destigmatizing mental illness to encourage help seeking by the CISs through utilizing professional mental health services and asking for help from a social network. When they struggled with the dilemma of "I care about you but am not able to help," they attempted to use other ways to address the dilemma, and therefore reshaped the meaning of seeking help (e.g., "it is not abnormal but good for your growth"). Given the active role that parents play in dealing with CISs' mental health problems, health campaigns or university initiatives should also target families, especially parents, as the study indicates that the CISs' parents often encourage them to talk with other peers or seek help from professionals.

Several limitations in the study should be noted and addressed in future research. First, the study did not include a number of low-income participants. Being a low-income parent might have a different impact on specific difficulties when talking about depression with their children. For example, students in a low-income family may hesitate to disclose their financial problems with the parents, as the parents would already be under financial stress by sending their child abroad. Also, the study only interviewed parents of CISs. Future research could explore dilemmas and coping strategies experienced by other family members, such as spouses or significant others, and investigate how family members cooperate to provide social support to the CIS. Future studies could also plan to increase and diversify the number of participants. Future studies could also replicate this with other international student communities.

CONCLUSION

Families are important entities in which we exhibit our needs through emotional expression and seek support. Understanding the communicative practices and coping strategies to deal with depression and mental health issues warrants further investigation. The findings suggest insights for campus wellness programs to promote supportive and effective social support for CISs and to engage families and parents in mental health promotion programs. The parents are vital stakeholders in the depression issue for CISs. Psychological service providers, residence assistants, university administrators, and educators who implement mental health promotion interventions need to value the role of family support. In addition, the coping strategies that emerged in the study underline some important issues that should be considered in communication about depression in practical settings, such as open and active talk, utilizing social media, and avoiding the emphasis of high expectations. In addition, communicative practices about mental health concerns may vary depending on the cultural contexts and meanings of mental health. The findings can also be transferred to mental health communication approaches across multiple contexts beyond international students, such as among minorities and cross-cultural populations.

REFERENCES

Acharya, L., Jin, L., & Collins, W. B. (2018). College life is stressful today—Emerging stressors and depressive symptoms in college students. *Journal of American College Health, 66*(7), 655–664. https://doi.org/10.1080/07448481.2018.1451869

Bastien, G., Seifen-Adkins, T., & Johnson, L. R. (2018). Striving for success: Academic adjustment of international students in the U.S. *Journal of International Students, 8*(2), 1198–1219. https://doi.org/10.32674/jis.v8i2.143

Boeije, H. (2002). A purposeful approach to the constant comparative method in the analysis of qualitative interviews. *Quality and Quantity, 36*(4), 391–409. https://doi.org/10.1023/A:1020909529486

Burck, C. (2005). Comparing qualitative research methodologies for systemic research: The use of grounded theory, discourse analysis and narrative analysis. *Journal of Family Therapy*, *27*(3), 237–262. https://doi.org/10.1111/j.1467-6427.2005.00314.x

Caughlin, J. P. (2010). A multiple goals theory of personal relationships: Conceptual integration and program overview. *Journal of Social and Personal Relationships*, *27*(6), 824–848. https://doi.org/10.1177/0265407510373262

Chao, R. K. (1994). Beyond parental control and authoritarian parenting style: Understanding Chinese parenting through the cultural notion of training. *Child Development*, *65*(4), 1111–1119. https://doi.org/10.1111/j.1467-8624.1994.tb00806.x

Charmaz, K. (2008). Constructionism and the grounded theory. In J. A. Holstein & J. F. Gubrium (Eds.), *Handbook of constructionist research* (pp. 397–412). Guilford.

Cheung, P. T. A. (2010). *Depressive symptoms and help-seeking preferences among Chinese (including Mainland China, Hong Kong, and Taiwan) international students* (Publication No. 3424290) [Doctoral dissertation, University of Houston]. ProQuest Dissertations & Theses Global.

Cohen, S., & Wills, T. A. (1985). Stress, social support, and the buffering hypothesis. *Psychological Bulletin*, *98*(2), 310. https://doi.org/10.1037/0033-2909.98.2.310

Fang, T., & Faure, G. O. (2011). Chinese communication characteristics: A Yin Yang perspective. *International Journal of Intercultural Relations*, *35*(3), 320–333. https://doi.org/10.1016/j.ijintrel.2010.06.005

Forbes-Mewett, H., & Sawyer, A.M. (2016). International students and mental health. *Journal of International Students*, *6*(3), 661–677. https://www.ojed.org/index.php/jis/article/view/348

Fossi, L., Faravelli, C., & Paoli, M. (1984). The ethological approach to the assessment of depressive disorders. *Journal of Nervous and Mental Disease*, *172*(6), 332–341. https://doi.org/10.1097/00005053-198406000-00004

Fram, S. M. (2013). The constant comparative analysis method outside of grounded theory. *The Qualitative Report*, *18*(1), 1–25. https://nsuworks.nova.edu/tqr/vol18/iss1/1

Gao, G., Ting-Toomey, S., & Gudykunst, W. B. (1996). Chinese communication processes. In M. H. Bond (Ed.), *The handbook of Chinese psychology* (pp. 280–293). Oxford University Press.

Glaser, B. G. (1965). The constant comparative method of qualitative analysis. *Social Problems*, *12*(4), 436–445. https://doi.org/10.2307/798843

Glaser, B. G. (1992). *Emergence vs. forcing: Basics of grounded theory analysis*. Sociology Press.

Glaser, B. G., & Strauss, A. L. (1967). *The discovery of grounded theory: Strategies for qualitative research*. Aldine.

Goldsmith, D. J. (2004). *Communicating social support*. Cambridge University Press.

Goldsmith, D. J., & Fitch, K. (1997). The normative context of advice as social support. *Human Communication Research, 23*(4), 454–476. https://doi.org/10.1111/j.1468-2958.1997.tb00406.x

Goldsmith, D. J., Lindholm, K. A., & Bute, J. J. (2006). Dilemmas of talking about lifestyle change among couples coping with a cardiac event. *Social Science & Medicine, 63,* 2079–2090. https://doi.org/10.1016/j.socscimed.2006.05.005

Guba, E. G., & Lincoln, Y. S. (1994). Competing paradigms in qualitative research. In N. K. Denzin & Y. S. Lincoln (Eds.), *Handbook of qualitative research* (pp. 105–117). SAGE.

Han, X., Han, X., Luo, Q., Jacobs, S., & Jean-Baptiste, M. (2013). Report of a mental health survey among Chinese international students at Yale University. *Journal of American College Health, 61*(1), 1–8. https://doi.org/10.1080/07448481.2012.738267

Hwang, K. K. (1999). Filial piety and loyalty: Two types of social identification in Confucianism. *Asian Journal of Social Psychology, 2,* 163–183. https://doi.org/10.1111/1467-839X.00031

Inman, A. G., & Yeh, C. J. (2007). Asian American stress and coping. In F. T. L. Leong, A. G. Inman, A. Ebreo, L. Yang, L. Kinoshota, & M. Fu (Eds.), *Handbook of Asian American psychology* (2nd ed., pp. 323–340). SAGE.

Institute of International Education. (2018). Open Doors Report. Retrieved September 29, 2019, from https://www.iie.org/Research-and-Insights/Open-Doors/Data/International-Students

Jin, L., & Acharya, L. (2016). Cultural beliefs underlying medication adherence in people of Chinese descent in the US. *Health Communication, 31*(5), 513–521. https://doi.org/ 10.1080/10410236.2014.974121

Keating, D. M., Russell, J. C., Cornacchione, J., & Smith, S. W. (2013). Family communication patterns and difficult family conversations. *Journal of Applied Communication Research, 41*(2), 160–180. https://doi.org/10.1080/00909882.2013.781659

Knapp, M. L., & Daly, J. A. (2011). *Handbook of interpersonal communication* (4th ed.). SAGE.

Kolb, S. M. (2012). Grounded theory and the constant comparative method: Valid research strategies for educators. *Journal of Emerging Trends in Educational Research and Policy Studies, 3*(1), 83–86.

Leach, M. S., & Braithwaite, D. O. (1996). A binding tie: Supportive communication of family kinkeepers. *Journal of Applied Communication Research, 24*(3), 200–216. https://doi.org/10.1080/00909889609365451

Liu, M. (2009). Addressing the mental health problems of Chinese international college students in the United States. *Advances in Social Work, 10*(1), 69–86. https://doi.org/10.18060/164

McCullough, M. E., & Larson, D. B. (1999). Religion and depression: A review of the literature. *Twin Research and Human Genetics, 2*(2), 126–136. https://doi.org/10.1375/136905299320565997

O'Connor, M. K., Netting, F. E., & Thomas, M. L. (2008). Grounded theory: Managing the challenge for those facing institutional review board oversight.

Qualitative   Inquiry,   14(1),   28–45.
https://doi.org/10.1177/1077800407308907

Reis, H. T. (2007). Steps toward the ripening of relationship science. *Personal Relationships,   14*(1),   1–23.   https://doi.org/10.1111/j.1475-6811.2006.00139.x

Roscoe, L. A. & Barrison, P. (2019). Dilemmas adult children face in discussing end-of-life care preferences with their parents. *Health Communication, 34*(14), 1788–1794. https://doi.org/10.1080/10410236.2018.1536946

Sapranaviciute, L., Padaiga, Z., & Pauzienė, N. (2013). The stress coping strategies and depressive symptoms in international students. *Procedia - Social   and   Behavioral   Sciences,   84*(9),   827–831. https://doi.org/10.1016/j.sbspro.2013.06.655

Settles, B. H., Sheng, X., Zang, Y., & Zhao, J. (2012). The one child policy and its impact on Chinese families. In C. Kwok-bun (Ed.) *International handbook of Chinese families* (pp. 627–646). Springer.

Strauss, A. L., & Corbin, J. M. (1998). *Basics of qualitative research: Techniques and procedures for developing grounded theory* (2nd ed.). SAGE.

Thorne, S. (2000). Data analysis in qualitative research. *Evidence-Based Nursing, 3,* 68–70. http://dx.doi.org/10.1136/ebn.3.3.68

Turner, D. W. (2010). Qualitative interview design: A practical guide for novice investigators.   *The   Qualitative   Report,   15*(3),   754–760. https://nsuworks.nova.edu/tqr/vol15/iss3/19

Wang, C.-C. D., & Mallinckrodt, B. (2006). Acculturation, attachment, and psychosocial adjustment of Chinese/Taiwanese international students. *Journal   of   Counseling   Psychology,   53*(4),   422–433. https://doi.org/10.1037/0022-0167.53.4.422

Wei, M., Heppner, P. P., Mallen, M. J., Ku, T. Y., Liao, K. Y. H., & Wu, T. F. (2007). Acculturative stress, perfectionism, years in the United States, and depression among Chinese international students. *Journal of Counseling Psychology, 54*(4), 385–394. https://doi.org/10.1037/0022-0167.54.4.385

Wei, M., Liao, K. Y.-H., Chao, R. C.-L., Mallinckrodt, B., Tsai, P.-C., & Botello-Zamarron, R. (2010). Minority stress, perceived bicultural competence, and depressive symptoms among ethnic minority college students. *Journal of Counseling Psychology, 57*(4), 411–422. https://doi.org/10.1037/a0020790

Wilson, S. R., & Feng, H. R. (2007). Interaction goals and message production: Conceptual and methodological developments. In D. R. Roskos-Ewoldsen & J. L. Monahan (Eds.), *Communication and social cognition: Theories and methods* (pp. 71–95). Routledge.

Wilson, S. R., Gettings, P. E., Hall, E. D., & Pastor, R. G. (2015). Dilemmas families face in talking with returning US military service members about seeking professional help for mental health issues. *Health Communication, 30*(8), 772–783. https://doi.org/10.1080/10410236.2014.899659

Wu, C., & Chao, R. K. (2011). Intergenerational cultural dissonance in parent–adolescent relationships among Chinese and European Americans. *Developmental   Psychology,   47*(2),   493–508. https://doi.org/10.1037/a0021063

Xing, X.-Y., Tao, F.-B., Wan, Y.-H., Xing, C., Qi, X.-Y., Hao, J.-H., Su, P.-Y., Pan, H.-F., & Huang, L. (2010). Family factors associated with suicide attempts among Chinese adolescent students: A national cross-sectional survey. *Journal of Adolescent Health, 46* (6), 592–599. https://doi.org/10.1016/j.jadohealth.2009.12.006

Xu, J. (2012). Filial piety and intergenerational communication in China: A nationwide study. *Journal of International Communication, 18*(1), 33–48. https://doi.org/ 10.1080/13216597.2012.662466

Ying, Y. W., Lee, P. A., Tsai, J. L., Yeh, Y. Y., & Huang, J. S. (2000). The conception of depression in Chinese American college students. *Cultural Diversity and Ethnic Minority Psychology, 6*(2), 183–195. https://doi.org/10.1037/1099-9809.6.2.183

Zhang, Q. (2007). Family communication patterns and conflict styles in Chinese parent-child relationships. *Communication Quarterly, 55*(1), 113–128. https://doi.org/10.1080/01463370600998681

LAN JIN, PhD, is an Intercultural Research Specialist in the Center for Intercultural Learning, Mentorship, Assessment and Research (CILMAR) at Purdue University. Her major research interests lie in the area of intercultural competence development, program design and evaluation, and mental health of international students. Email: jin124@purdue.edu

LALATENDU ACHARYA, PhD, is an Assistant Professor in the Department of Allied Health Science at Indiana University Kokomo. Dr. Acharya's research examines the different pathways to influence health behavior and address disparities through participatory health communication, health promotion and marketing interventions. Under this thematic area, he works on addressing health behavioral issues and disparity outcomes in the fields of mental health and environmental health, especially in adolescents, college students and vulnerable communities. E-mail: lacharya@iu.edu

Peer-Reviewed Article

© *Journal of International Students*
Volume 11, Issue 1 (2021), pp. 238-250
ISSN: 2162-3104 (Print), 2166-3750 (Online)
doi: 10.32674/jis.v11i1.1710
ojed.org/jis

OJED
OPEN JOURNALS IN EDUCATION

Diversification of International Student Base: A Misplaced Effort

Wei Liu
University of Alberta, Canada

ABSTRACT

Underlying the goal of diversifying the sources of international students in post-secondary education is a naive logic: The portfolio of international students is controlled by the recruitment efforts of host countries and universities. Given this logic, the host countries and universities decide on where their international students are from and how diverse their international student population is. The logic results in an overestimate of the value of recruitment efforts by host countries and universities. It tends to overlook a whole range of other macro factors that determine international student mobility more significantly than recruitment efforts. Most notably, certain macro factors are beyond the control of host countries and universities, and thus their diversification efforts are futile and a waste of resources.

Keywords: diversification, international student, macro factors, mobility, recruitment

International student enrollment has become a key revenue source for host universities and a growing export industry for host countries. However, the high percentage of Chinese students in the total international student body, and thus the over-reliance on one country for international enrollment, has been perceived as a risk factor by major host countries and universities. There appears to be a unanimous strategy adopted in Anglo host countries and universities to diversify the base of international students. Will this effort succeed in diversifying away from Chinese students? This article is an attempt to answer this question.

The Dominance of Chinese International Students

In the 21st century, Chinese students have become the largest group of international students in major countries where English is the primary language—that is, Anglo countries. By 2015, more than 40% of student visas (600,000) in the United States were issued to students from mainland China (Schrager, 2018). The United Kingdom is the second most popular study-abroad destination worldwide for international students. As of 2017–2018, 106,530 of the 458,520 international students attending universities in the United Kingdom were Chinese, representing 23% of the total international student body, second only to the European Union's 30% (Study in UK, 2019). With Brexit completing, the United Kingdom might lose the big international student number from the European Union, making Chinese students the number one group. China is also the largest source country of international students in Australia, at 40% of total international student enrollment (Tran & Forbes-Mewett, 2019). Likewise, in Canada, the number of international students at all education levels reached 494,525 in 2017, with 40% of this population being Chinese (Canadian Bureau for International Education, 2019).

In all Anglo countries, international student education has become a key export industry. International students contributed $42 billion to the U.S. economy (Institute of International Education, 2019), £25 billion to the U.K. economy (Universities UK, 2019), $34.9 billion to the Australian economy (Study International, 2019), $12.8 billion to the Canadian economy (Government of Canada, 2017), and NZ $4.28 billion to New Zealand's economy (ICEF Monitor, 2017a) per year. International students' tuition has also become a very important source of institutional income. In the United States, international students constituted 12% of the total student population in 2015, but their tuition fee accounted for $9 billion of revenue to American public universities, or 28% of total annual tuition revenue (Loudenback, 2016). In Canada, international student fees amounted to $2.75 billion, which represents 35% of all fees collected and 9.3% of total institutional revenue (Usher, 2018). Some major public universities in Anglo countries receive more revenue from international students' tuition fees than from their provincial or state governments. For example, in the 2018–2019 school year, the University of Toronto reported 30% of its operating budget was generated from international students' tuition, while the provincial grant only amounted to 25% of the same budget (University of Toronto, 2019).

Diversification as Risk Management

It was once good news that public universities in the West could find new sources of revenue in the context of declining operating grants from governments. However, major host countries and universities of international students are becoming increasingly concerned about the fact that students from a single country, China, constitute the majority of the international student base. Host countries have been asking the "what if" question: What if something happens to significantly alter the current scale of outbound student mobility from China?

(ICEF Monitor, 2015). One clear result of this happening is that many major host universities would plunge into financial difficulty, given the large portion of the institutional revenue contributed by international student fees. How can major host universities of Chinese students manage such a potential risk?

As a strategy for risk management, Brown University in the United States has taken the lead in purchasing insurance to protect itself against the potential loss of international student tuition revenue, with $424,000 paid since 2017 in premiums for coverage up to $60 million if there's a 20% drop or more in revenue from Chinese students in a single year following "triggering events," such as visa restriction, a pandemic, or a trade war (Schrager, 2018). The three "triggering events" seem to be real threats. At the height of the Trade War between the United States and China in 2019, the Chinese Ministry of Education issued a study abroad alert, warning Chinese students about the visa delays, denials, and other risks they might encounter in their applications for U.S. schools (Skinner, 2019). The 2020 COVID-19 world pandemic has significantly decreased international student mobility from mainland China and Hong Kong, as health and safety have become a major concern for students and their families (see Mok et. al, 2021).

A more common strategy adopted by many countries and universities has been to diversify the source countries of international students by shifting recruitment efforts. For example, in the Canadian International Education Strategy (2019–2024), one of the three major goals is "to diversify the countries from which international students come to Canada" (Ministry of International Trade Diversification, 2019). Similarly, Australia aims to diversify its international student population to reduce its reliance on China (Walker, 2018). Institutions and schools have also aimed to diversify beyond China (and India) in their recruitment strategies (see e.g., ICEF Monitor, 2017b). It is risky to put too many eggs in only one basket, which is common sense. But how risky is China as a basket? What exactly are the risk factors for the Chinese basket? One typical approach in predicting international student mobility is to examine the "pull" and "push" factors (Altbach, 1998). In this context, students are pulled by more favorable conditions in host countries and pushed by unfavorable conditions at home. So what are the pull and push factors for Chinese students?

The Pull Factors

One most important historical pull factor for Chinese students' decision to pursue overseas study has been the technological advancement in the West through the large-scale industrialization that took place almost two centuries before China. As a result of the Western industrialization,

> ...(a) few countries dominate global scientific systems, the new technologies are owned primarily by multinational corporations or academic institutions in the major Western industrialized nations, and the domination of English creates advantages for the countries that use English as the medium of instruction and research. (Altbach, 2015, p. 7)

After China's repeated defeats in military encounters with Western invaders that landed on China's shores since the late 1930s, the Qing government (1644–1912) finally realized they needed to end their closed-door policy and start learning from the industrialized West. In 1872, the Qing government sent the first group of 30 young teenagers to study in the United States. In order to establish China's own navy, many Chinese soldiers were sponsored to study the navy in Europe. This is considered the first wave of overseas studies by China (Shu, 2011).

In 1911, the Republican Revolution, led by Sun Yat Sen, overthrew the last dynasty in China and started the Republican era. Sun and his party were mostly educated in Japan, the first industrialized Asian country. Accordingly, during his leadership (1911–1927) there were many Chinese students studying in Japan. This became the second wave (Shu, 2011). In 1927, Jiang Kai Shek led a coup and seized power from the Nationalist Party. Jiang was pro-Western and pro-American. During his leadership, he introduced the American educational system in China and declared Chinese medicine witchcraft. During his rule (1927–1949), many young people studied in the United States, which was the third wave (Shu, 2011). During Mao's leadership (1949–1965), China was isolated by the West; China turned to Russia as its central international ally. During this time, Russia was also the only destination for Chinese students studying abroad. This was considered the fourth wave of Chinese overseas study (Shu, 2011).

The fifth wave, also the current wave, started after the Cultural Revolution (1966–1976). The new Chinese leader, Deng Xiaoping, adopted a more pragmatic approach in China's social and economic development. His "Reform" initiative introduced market principles and entrepreneurship in running the economy domestically. His "Open-up" policy encouraged Chinese businesses and people to reengage with the West and learn from the West. In 1985, China put forward a very clear policy on Chinese citizens studying overseas: "Support students' efforts to study overseas; encourage them to come back upon completion; free to go and free to return." (Biao & Shen, 2009, p. 515). The same policy continues to be in force today. The economic success China has had in the past few decades is to a large extent due to China's trade and engagement with the West. Actively learning from the West has helped China speed its catch-up with the West. Such Western exposure and reference may have taken the form of both Western-trained Chinese scholars returning to work in China and the "Brain Circulation" (Saxenian, 2005) of Chinese scholars working overseas.

Another important pull factor, as pointed out by Altbach (2015), is the dominance of English as a world language. The status of English as a foreign language in Chinese school curriculum might be one of the highest in the world, if not the highest, carrying the same curriculum weight as Math and Chinese language art (Liu & Lin, 2019). English, while serving as the world's first language in business, is also intertwined with economic factors. A breakdown of the percentages of world gross domestic product (GDP) by language shows that English accounts for 20.77% of the world GDP, though Chinese is closing the gap, accounting for a little less than 20% (19.64%) of world GDP, as of 2018 (see Alexika, 2018). Even if the Chinese-speaking world can surpass the English-speaking world as the number one GDP generator, English will remain a very important language to learn, with instruction in English continuing to be the advantage of higher education in Anglo countries. Within China, students' achievement in English as a school subject has very high stakes both for their educational advancement (from elementary school all the way to graduate programs) and their future employment, in a very competitive environment (Liu & Lin, 2019). For Chinese parents, even if the quality of education in a certain subject area in an overseas university is equivalent to a domestic Chinese university, being able to master the English language alone would make their children's overseas study a worthy investment.

The Push Factors

The push factors in China that drive students' outbound mobility may include the fierce competition for admission into top Chinese universities, the perceived lower quality of higher education at home in second- and third-tier institutions, and the increasing number of middle class families enabled by the robust economic growth in the past few decades (Liu, 2016). The Chinese open-door policy was adopted since the late 1970s, as mentioned above. However, the number of students studying overseas from China in the 1980s and 1990s was small, and most of them were government-sponsored students (www.eol.cn, 2020). The number grew quickly since 2000 at about 25% each year, and over 90% of the growth was driven by self-sponsored students (see Figure 1).

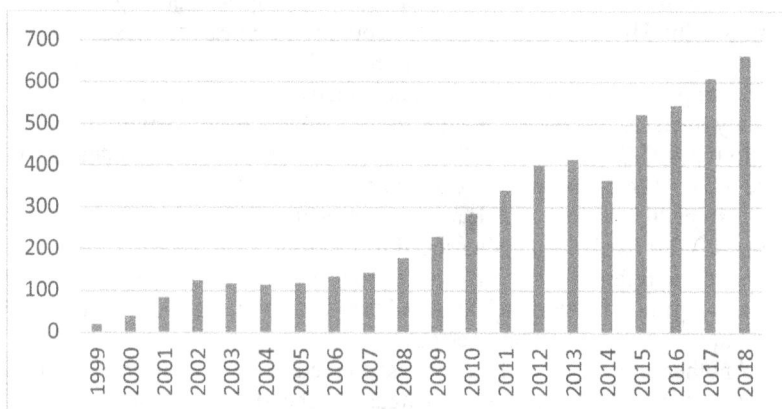

Figure 1: Number of Chinese Students Studying Overseas (in thousands) (based on www.eol.cn, 2020)

The general trend of Chinese students' outbound mobility, despite some small fluctuations, matches the trend of Chinese GDP per capita growth perfectly in the past 20 years, which speaks to the force of Chinese economy as a push factor (see Figure 2). There are many doomsayers in the West about the Chinese economy, forecasting that China will face economic crisis, if not in one already (see e.g., Pesek, 2019; Rapoza, 2019; Schuman, 2019). In spite of such negative views toward Chinese economic growth and the heightened uncertainty regarding a trade war with the United States, the Chinese economy still grew over 6% in 2019 (Reuters, 2019). China's economy also performed well in 2020, after effectively managing the COVID-19 pandemic. Whoever argues for the imminent bust of the Chinese economy thinks against the bigger trend of Asia as a whole returning to the historical norm of leading world economic growth (Mahbubani, 2018). The Chinese economy may not be able to grow at 10% annually in the future, but the large scope as a world's second largest economy today makes each small percentage increase a large increase in absolute terms.

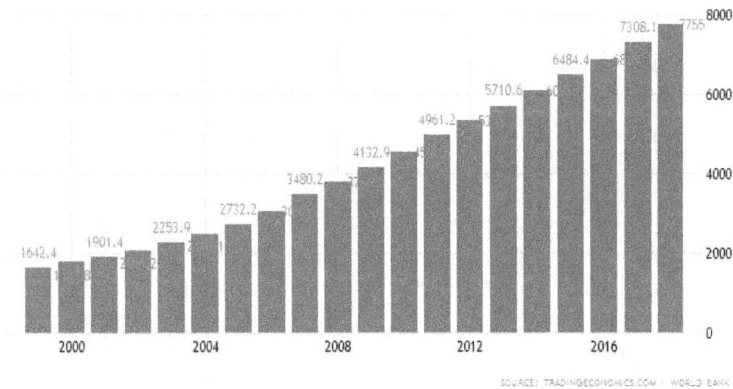

Figure 2: The Gross Domestic Product Per Capita in China (U.S. Dollars, 2000 to 2020) (https://tradingeconomics.com/china/gdp-per-capita)

The strong Chinese economy is a necessary condition for Chinese students' outbound mobility, but it is not a sufficient condition. People prioritize differently in their spending. In addition to economics, Liu (2016) suggested that the Chinese educational culture is the most important push factor for Chinese students' international mobility. The Chinese education-first culture encourages parents to try to send their children to the best institutions of higher learning possible, as far as they can afford. The Chinese saving culture makes Western tuition fees affordable to many middle-class Chinese families. Additionally, the Chinese extended-family culture makes one student's higher education a priority for the whole extended family. These features of traditional Chinese culture, together with economic growth, will continue to serve as push factors and drive the outbound mobility of Chinese students for a few decades to come.

The Political Factors

From the above analysis on the major pull factors and push factors, the Chinese basket as a source of international students does not seem to be such a risky basket. However, the risk analysis of China as a major source country of international students has been predominantly a political analysis. In a *Washington Post* article, Andreson and Svrluga (2019) posited that the accusation of the Chinese-sponsored Confucius Institutes as an espionage threat to the Western countries may potentially result in the retaliation of the Chinese government and thus the loss of Chinese students. A *Global News* (2019) article stated that Canadian universities would face a cash crunch if Canada's diplomatic difficulty with China over the arrest of a Huawai executive resulted in the world's most populous nation pulling its students from Canadian schools. Such politically oriented analyses boil down to the view that the Chinese government is an authoritarian oligarchy and it is by nature unpredictable. Worse yet, it is repressive and can exert power to inhibit its citizens' international mobility and travel. This seems to be the number one risk factor perceived by the host countries and universities of Chinese international students. But is such fear well founded?

In the first place, as we discussed above, China has viewed international education more as an opportunity than as a risk since the late 1970s (Li & Bray, 2007). In this sense, the concern over the Chinese government's obstruction of Chinese students' outbound mobility is unwarranted. The Chinese government believes in the benefit of Chinese citizens' overseas study, and China has had consistent policies to encourage Chinese citizens to study overseas over the past few decades. In the second place, political freedom and personal freedom are two different issues in the Chinese context, and China allows significantly more personal freedom to its people than the West has acknowledged. Every year, according to Mahbubani (2018), over 150 million Chinese travel overseas. If the Chinese government is as repressive as perceived by the West, would this many of its people be able to travel overseas? Additionally, once they are out of country, would they return to their country of origin? The China we have today is fundamentally different from the China during the Cultural Revolution, a point that most Westerners don't seem to get.

The Economic Factors

If one is still not convinced that China is a safe source of international students, and thus a safe basket to keep our eggs in, here is another question that needs to be considered: Are there other baskets to put our eggs in? The top contributing countries to the world economic growth from the developing world today are China, India, Indonesia, Russia, and Brazil (see Figure 3; Tanzi & Lu, 2019). According to the breakdown in Figure 3, for every $100 of new wealth generated in the world today, $28 is generated in one country—China, followed by India ($13.7). So India is the other sizable recruitment market for international students, right next to China. But it would be still concerning to many people to have only two baskets. If these two baskets are still risky, are we able to create additional baskets in other parts of the world through our recruitment efforts? Based on the breakdown again, the other baskets are small—Indonesia $3.4; Russia $2.1; Brazil $2.0—and thus the return for our recruitment efforts in these markets would be low. This is the economic reality we need to consider if we want to get the most out of our recruitment dollars.

Another crucial question in the economic analysis we need to ask here is whether the international student market today is a buyer's market or a seller's market. A seller's market would happen when major host countries and universities do not have enough capacity to take on the number of students who want to study there. A buyer's market happens when there are fewer students, and there is a competition among host countries and universities for the limited number of students. The current international student market seems to be a buyer's market in the sense that international students have choices and they can shop around a little. The many host countries and universities are competing for a limited number of students. In a buyer's market, we will need to pay more attention to the pull factors, very much like we need to make our house look more attractive if we want to sell it when there is a big inventory of houses on the market. We cannot afford to be picky about who the buyer is and where they are from. We sell our house to the highest bidders, students with the best grade point averages, no matter where they are from.

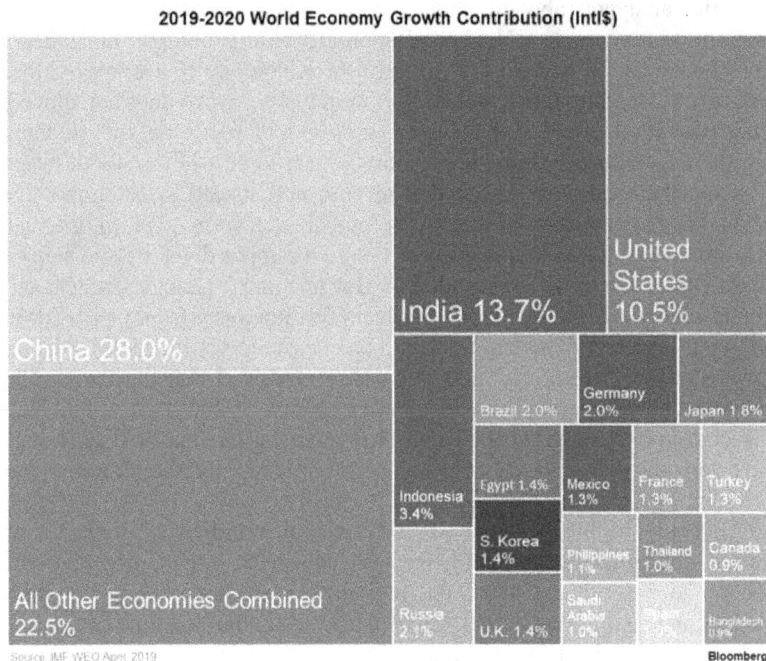

2019-2020 World Economy Growth Contribution (Intl$)

China 28.0%

India 13.7%

United States 10.5%

Brazil 2.0%

Germany 2.0%

Japan 1.6%

Indonesia 3.4%

Egypt 1.4%

Mexico 1.3%

France 1.3%

Turkey 1.3%

S. Korea 1.4%

Philippines 1.1%

Thailand 1.0%

Canada 0.9%

All Other Economies Combined 22.5%

Russia 2.1%

U.K. 1.4%

Saudi Arabia 1.0%

Bangladesh 0.9%

Source: IMF WEO April 2019

Bloomberg

Figure 3: Country Contributions of World Economic Growth

The push factors as discussed above are largely out of the control of the host countries and universities. As such, diversification efforts expended in low-yield markets is a misplaced effort. It does not make economic sense. It is not putting eggs in different baskets; it is throwing eggs on rocks, an unaccountable way to spend the limited resources. Underlying the goal of diversifying the sources of international students is a purely naive and wrong logic, and the logic is: The mobility of international students is at the whim of host countries and universities' recruitment efforts. Given this logic, the host countries of international students can decide where their international students are from and not from. If I can use another metaphor, recruitment in low-yield markets with poor push factors is like milking dry cows, thinking if we milk harder, milk will come out. Using the real estate example again, diversification effort in non-yield or low-yield markets is like trying to change the minds of potential buyers who don't have the desire or cannot even afford to buy your property. The effort is misplaced again.

The Ethical Consideration

Internationalization worldwide is increasingly motivated by profits rather than by either government policy or goodwill (Yang, 2002). International education has been taken in the West as a driver of local economy, as a platform to recruit good-quality immigrants (Liu & Lin, 2016). Admittedly, the whole economic analysis above equates international students as commercial commodities, and such a Neoliberal approach to international education is by nature unethical. In addition, a diversification strategy is a common business practice to try to enter into a new market or industry, which does not sit well with higher education either. Ethical education should focus on the students and students' development. Some universities appear to be still shy about discussing international education as a source of revenue and instead focus on the diversity line in open discourses to stress the global education goal in international education—that is, international students enrich campus diversity and help expose domestic students to different cultures. But imagine a Chinese student on your campus who overhears the policy of diversification away from China (or India). How would she feel? The feeling would be uneasy, to say the least. If the student is aware of the "Head Tax" and "Chinese Exclusion" that the earlier Chinese immigrants once experienced in history (e.g., Kenneth, 2007), she might make the connection and feel utterly offended. The diversification rhetoric could potentially send a very unwelcoming message to Chinese students and their families, verging on racism.

After all, the push factors for international mobility, as discussed above, create a generalized interest in overseas education but do not give specific direction to individuals, while the pull factors are specific to potential host countries and institutions (Davis, 1995). To put it another way, the concern should not be the demand for international education from international students. The concern should be the quality of supply and the competition between the suppliers of international education in the West. More serious effort should be made within host institutions in Anglo countries to improve the quality of education and services to international students to make sure that they stay as a more desirable choice for future international students, no matter where they are from. This is the only wise thing to do and the ethical thing to do. One Chinese saying goes to the following effect: "If your liquor smells good, you would not need to worry that customers won't find you in the deep alley." If an analogy can be drawn here, the major host countries and universities of international students should focus on providing the best educational experience, and customers from far and near would find their way to you.

CONCLUSION

The diversification strategy of international students is based on unwarranted political fear and is a misplaced effort. It is unwarranted because the economic rise of Asia, an undoubted trend, will continue to supply international students who desire the perceived high quality post-secondary education in English. Diversification efforts are misplaced, as efforts should instead be channeled toward ensuring better quality education and services to international students in order to remain well placed in the competition among major host countries.

REFERENCES

Altbach, P. (1998). *Comparative higher education: Knowledge, the university, and development.* Ablex Publishing.

Altbach, P. (2015). Perspectives on internationalizing higher education. *International Higher Education, 27,* 6–8. https://doi.org/10.6017/ihe.2002.27.6975

Alexika. (2018). *Top business languages of the world for exporters in the global marketplace in 2018.* Retrieved from https://alexika.com/blog/2018/11/29/top-business-languages-of-the-world

Andreson, N., & Svrluga, S. (2019, June 3). *Universities worry about potential loss of Chinese students.* The Washington Post. https://www.washingtonpost.com/local/education/universities-worry-about-potential-loss-of-chinese-students/2019/06/03/567044ea-861b-11e9-98c1-e945ae5db8fb_story.html

Biao, X., & Shen, W. (2009). International student migration and social stratification in China. *Journal of Educational Development, 29*(5), 513–522. https://doi.org/10.1016/j.ijedudev.2009.04.006

Canadian Bureau for International Education. (2019). *International students in Canada.* https://cbie.ca/wp-content/uploads/2018/09/International-Students-in-Canada-ENG.pdf

Davis, T. (1995). Flows of international students: Trends and issues. *International Higher Education, 1,* 2–4. https://doi.org/10.6017/ihe.1995.1.6167

Global News. (2019, February 7). *If China orders international students home, some Canadian schools face money trouble: agency.* https://globalnews.ca/news/4937419/canadian-universities-china-students-moodys/

Government of Canada. (2017). *Economic impact of international education in Canada—2017 update.* https://www.international.gc.ca/education/report-rapport/impact-2017/index.aspx?lang=eng

ICEF Monitor. (2015, March 3). *The China challenge: Diversification and managing risk in international education.*

https://monitor.icef.com/2015/03/china-challenge-diversification-managing-risk-international-education/

ICEF Monitor. (2017a, February 1). *New Zealand: Economic impact of international education up 50% since 2014.* https://monitor.icef.com/2017/02/new-zealand-economic-impact-of-international-education-up-50-since-2014/

ICEF Monitor. (2017b, December 20). *A roadmap for building more diversity in your international enrolment.* https://monitor.icef.com/2017/12/roadmap-building-diversity-international-enrolment/

Institute of International Education. (2019). *Economic impact of international students.* Retrieved January 18, 2021, from https://www.iie.org/Research-and-Insights/Open-Doors/Data/Economic-Impact-of-International-Students

Kenneth, M. H. (2007). A history of Chinese immigration in the United States and Canada. *American Review of Canadian Studies, 37*(2), 150–160. https://doi.org/10.1080/02722010709481851

Li, M., & Bray, M. (2007). Cross-border flows of students for higher education: Push–pull factors and motivations of mainland Chinese students in Hong Kong and Macau. *Higher Education, 53,* 791–818. https://doi.org/10.1007/s10734-005-5423-3

Liu, W. (2016). The international mobility of Chinese students: A cultural perspective. *Canadian Journal of Higher Education, 46*(4), 41–59. https://doi.org/10.47678/cjhe.v46i4.186143

Liu, W., & Lin, X. (2016). Meeting the needs of Chinese international students: Anything we can learn from their home system? *Journal of Studies in International Education, 20*(4), 357–370. https://doi.org/10.1177/1028315316656456

Liu, W., & Lin, X. (2019). Family language policy in English as a foreign language: A case study from China to Canada. *Language Policy, 18,*191–207. https://doi.org/10.1007/s10993-018-9475-5

Loudenback, T. (2016, September 16). *International students are now 'subsidizing' public American universities to the tune of $9 billion a year.* Business Insider. https://www.businessinsider.com/foreign-students-pay-up-to-three-times-as-much-for-tuition-at-us-public-colleges-2016-9

Mahbubani, K. (2018). *Has the West lost it? A provocation.* Allen Lane.

Ministry of International Trade Diversification. (2019). *Building on success: Canada's international education strategy (2019–2024).* https://www.international.gc.ca/education/strategy-2019-2024-strategie.aspx?lang=eng#figure1

Mok, H. M., Xiong, W., Ke, G., & Cheung, J. (2021). Impact of COVID-19 pandemic on international higher education and student mobility: Student perspectives from mainland China and Hong Kong. *International Journal of Educational Research, 105.* https://doi.org/10.1016/j.ijer.2020.101718

Pesek, W. (2019, November 11). *China's economy is in more trouble than markets think.* Nikkei Asia. https://asia.nikkei.com/Opinion/China-s-economy-is-in-more-trouble-than-markets-think

Rapoza, K. (2019, July 26). *How close is China to a financial crisis?* Forbes. https://www.forbes.com/sites/kenrapoza/2019/07/26/how-close-is-china-to-a-financial-crisis/#35de3bfd73f3

Reuters. (2019, September 4). *Citing trade tensions, IMF cuts China's 2019 GDP growth forecast to 6.2% from 6.3%.* https://www.reuters.com/article/us-china-economy-imf/citing-trade-tensions-imf-cuts-chinas-2019-gdp-growth-forecast-to-6-2-from-6-3-idUSKCN1T60MP

Saxenian, A. (2005). From brain drain to brain circulation: Transnational communities and regional upgrading in India and China. *Studies in Comparative International Development, 40,* 35–61. https://doi.org/10.1007/BF02686293

Schrager, A. (2018, December 7). *A US university is buying insurance in case Chinese students stop coming.* Quartz. https://qz.com/1486345/universities-are-insuring-against-a-china-shock/

Schuman, M. (2019, January 17). *Forget the trade war. China is already in crisis.* Bloomberg Businessweek. https://www.bloomberg.com/news/articles/2019-01-17/forget-the-trade-war-china-is-already-in-crisis

Shu, X.C. (2011). *Modern Chinese study abroad history* [in Chinese]. Shanghai Bookstore Press.

Skinner, M. (2019, December 17). *The financial risk of overreliance on Chinese student enrollment.* World Education News + Reviews. https://wenr.wes.org/2019/12/the-financial-risk-of-overreliance-on-chinese-student-enrollments

Study International. (2019, March 19). *International students boost Australia's economy, but are locals happy about it?* https://www.studyinternational.com/news/international-students-boost-australias-economy-but-are-locals-happy-about-it/

Study in UK. (2019, August 29). *International student statistics in UK 2019.* https://www.studying-in-uk.org/international-student-statistics-in-uk/

Tanzi, A., & Lu, W. (2019, May 6). *Where will global GDP growth come from over the next year.* Bloomberg. https://www.bloomberg.com/news/articles/2019-05-06/where-will-global-gdp-growth-come-from-over-the-next-year

Tran, L., & Forbes-Mewett, H. (2019, August 27). *How to attract a desirable mix of international students.* University World News. https://www.universityworldnews.com/post.php?story=2019082708492496

Universities UK. (2019, August 29). *International students now worth £25 billion to UK economy—new research.* https://www.universitiesuk.ac.uk/news/Pages/International-students-now-worth-25-billion-to-UK-economy---new-research.aspx

University of Toronto. (2019, August 26). *Budget report 2018–19 and long range budget guidelines 2018–19 to 2022–23.* http://www.planningandbudget.utoronto.ca/Assets/Academic+Operations+Digital+Assets/Planning+$!26+Budget/budget201819.pdf

Usher, A., (2018). *The state of post-secondary education in Canada, 2018.* Higher Education Strategy Associates.

Walker, A. (2018, July 24). *Australia aims to diversify its international student population.* Bachelorstudies. https://www.bachelorstudies.com/news/australia-aims-to-diversify-its-international-student-population-2496/

www.eol.cn. (2020, Feb 24). The 2019 report on Chinese study abroad trends. https://www.eol.cn/html/lx/report2019/yi.shtml

Yang, R. (2002). *Third delight: The internationalization of higher education in China.* Routledge.

WEI LIU, PhD, works at the University of Alberta International, managing the Global Academic Leadership Development (GALD) Program. His major research interests lie in the area of Foreign Language Education and International Education. Email: weidavid@ualberta.ca

Study Abroad Reflection

© *Journal of International Students*
Volume 11, Issue 1 (2021), pp. 251-256
ISSN: 2162-3104 (Print), 2166-3750 (Online)
doi: 10.32674/jis.v11i1.2564
ojed.org/jis

OJED
OPEN JOURNALS IN EDUCATION

Adding an International Student's Voice to the Pandemic Discourse as Thinkers, not Subjects: Reflections on Power, Stillness and Humanness

Sarah Jane D. Lipura
University of Auckland/Ateneo de Manila University
New Zealand/Philippines

ABSTRACT

As of this writing, the impact of the COVID-19 pandemic on international higher education is continuously being documented, drawing enough, if not too much, attention towards international students. However, the voices of international students remain muted such that much of what has been said about their experience do not directly come from them but from those who claim to speak on their behalf. In this essay, I attempt to add an international student voice to the pandemic discourse by shifting attention to international students not as subjects but as thinkers and co-producers of knowledge in their own right, in hope of also contributing to the broader conversation about ethics and responsibility surrounding international education and international student mobility research and practice. I do so by sharing my own reflections on the crisis and its critical relation to power, stillness and humanness

Keywords: COVID-19 pandemic, ethics, international education, international student, knowledge study abroad

As of this writing, the impact of the pandemic on international higher education is continuously being documented, drawing enough, if not too much, attention towards international students. As an international doctoral student whose research focusses on international student mobility and education migration, this documentation of the pandemic has offered me a unique opportunity to observe first-hand how the world views international students through the sudden transnational cross conversations among international education pundits, providers and policymakers, as if animating the spectrum of frameworks used to represent them in extant literature. As researcher, I was drawn to how the mobility of disease has mobilised the many times competing and other times overlapping approaches and lenses applied in the exploration, analysis and interpretation of international student mobility (Bista, 2019; Lipura & Collins, 2020). However, while the global health crisis has afforded these frames to converge around common questions that address the vulnerability of international students (see Raghuram & Sondi, 2020), the questions are largely probed in connection with the vulnerability of countries, industries and institutions dependent on them (see Bothwell, 2020). This very much reveals what views remain dominant in reality, such that attention is skewed towards international students as 'departing consumers' and 'exit and reluctant investors', critical in revenue generation for universities to survive (Ghazarian, 2014; Pham, 2020) and more broadly, for international education industry to thrive (Lo, 2018). Indeed, the importance of bringing the vulnerability issue to the fore in an unprecedented time cannot be downplayed but in ongoing conversations about the pandemic's present impact and future implications, much of what has been said about international students do not directly come from the students themselves such that locating them within the pandemic discourse may be easy but hearing them is not.

INTERNATIONAL STUDENTS AS THINKERS?

In general, the lack of 'active' international student voice has been acknowledged in recent literature. Waters (2018), for instance, illustrates how economic agenda has dominated the framing of international students rather than them being viewed firstly as individuals (p. 1474). This resonates broadly with the calls to rethink international student mobility research in relation to ethics (Yang, 2019) and responsibility (Madge et al., 2009). But even in the context of "thinking responsibly for and caring about international students" (Madge et al., 2009, p. 35), international students remain as 'subjects'. This prompts me to ask whether this view may be unsettled by shifting attention towards international students as 'thinkers' and co-producers of knowledge. With the pandemic both as a backdrop and subject of thought, I query the following: while international students are widely talked about, what do students think and say about their own situation and the crisis per se? Will not international students' unique educational experiences and everyday lives as social actors potentially generate critical yet emphatic perspectives to inform, as well as mobilise, both thinking and action around the pandemic? If so, is it unethically ambitious to treat international students as thinkers in their own right, and to thus encourage them to express their views? Or would it be self-serving to do so especially in time of crisis?

I partially approach these questions while acknowledging the potential limits and pitfalls of my own subjectivities arising out of my multifaceted self as an international student, researcher and ordinary human. In articulating my views, I expose my own need, vulnerability and effort to cope while in a position that is spatially, economically and socially 'privileged' by being geographically and politically located where international students are considered a "part of the community" more vocally than other places; by having the means to be able write this reflective piece while embracing the state of stillness; and by being connected to a community locally and globally in a time of physical isolation. In exercising this privilege, I recognise the tension between the tendency to be opportunistic and the accountability attached to such privilege. With this in mind, my intention remains focused on contributing to and possibly shaping a discourse where international students can emerge from being subjects to thinkers with a voice to express one's imaginings such as on what may be considered critical issues emerging from the pandemic, namely, power, stillness and humanness.

REFLECTION

Power

I was born in the so-called Global South, where many countries have been battling one of the world's deadliest diseases even long before the arrival of COVID-19, namely, tuberculosis (TB). Coming from a high TB incidence country, part of my visa requirements prior to my departure as international student was to submit proof that I do not have TB. According to a recent article published in The Lancet, a leading journal in medicine, tuberculosis is mainly associated with poor countries and people with poor living conditions (Wingfield et al., 2020). In contrast, COVID-19 has struck major powers with China, UK, US and other major European countries switching places as the pandemic's epicentres (Wingfield et al., 2020). Along with the marginalised, power wielders at the upper tiers of global and local hierarchies are suddenly shaken by COVID-19. Power seems to be overturned not in the sense that there was a reversal of circumstances between the powerful and the powerless, but in the sense that status quo was destabilised, upsetting and unsettling at the same time what and who holds power. COVID-19 and the absence of vaccine also leaves the powerful, vulnerable and the stable, disturbed. This claim, however, should not be taken to mean that the pandemic bears a homogenising effect for all. On the contrary, the impacts of coronavirus, as in any crisis or calamity, are widely discriminating with the marginalised most adversely affected. What makes the difference, however, is the unsettling of power that has placed those who thought were sitting invincible atop their economic, social and professional comfort zones pre-COVID on a condition of uncertainty. Unlike in the case of TB where stakes are mostly exclusive to those who cannot afford immunity and medication, coronavirus and the absence of vaccine has exposed everyone to risk and uncertainty – the degree being nonethelesss differential across individuals and societies.

A discussion on COVID-19's impact on the complex structures of power may be reserved for another piece but fundamentally, the disturbing of power should be interrogated as it can be transformatively positive or dangerous. On the one hand, power can be brought to a level of consciousness about the unevenness of our world and be converted into positive action that brings communities together to respond to the crisis. On the other hand, power, when shaken, can be reinforced to restore the 'status quo' of inequality or a create worse version of it. Because the pandemic has made life more difficult 'to control', claims to vulnerability are increasingly compounded coming even from groups who used to sit comfortably on their stable positions. Caution against rhetoric should thus be exercised, so that the plight of the marginalised are not taken advantage of or obscured by a disguised agenda. This becomes extra critical when vaccine becomes available and hopefully COVID-19 does not end up as another tuberculosis – a problem enduring only at the margins.

Stillness

The global spread of coronavirus is said to have paralysed our interconnected, hypermobile physical world (Xiao, 2020) as countries were pushed to go into lockdown. However, I argue that while the pandemic has discouraged and limited physical movements, it equally encouraged 'hyper-connectedness', accelerating formal and informal meetings online that transcend the barriers of time and distance. Spatial absence is replaced by virtual presence, allowing, if not compelling people to be readily accessible and available. Likewise, the pandemic has triggered a parallel acceleration of different types of mobilities such as of corporeal bodies through cross-border exodus of tourists, international students, migrants and citizens back to where they consider 'home' or where they have been recalled; of information and images circulating virtually about the crisis; of aid and resources being sought and provided; of ideas and ideologies moving political actions; and of the virus itself and the disease it carries. Emerging from these movements, however, is 'stillness', which I describe not as the opposite of mobility or a condition of immobility, but as a state of contemplativeness and introspection re-energised by the pandemic.

Amidst my transnational and mediated experiences of the crisis arising out of my status as a cross-border student, I was drawn to the sense of stillness in different forms. First is the experience of stillness as a conscious pause for reflection – something I thought we have robbed ourselves of as a generation due to our undivided and excessive attention towards 'having' or 'doing'. Such stillness prompted us to think about our 'being' – how it was affected by our previous normal and how it is being shaped by the new one. Stillness is also awareness. Despite the pandemic not really slowing us down as we continue to be overwhelmed and preoccupied with the hustle and bustle of the every day, it has made us aware of our own situation in relation to things around us that we had never before noticed or had chosen to ignore. Appreciation, for instance, is better expressed than before, but more particularly for those whose work we now consider 'essential'. Or that our attention was drawn to the realities of and impossibility of social distancing in urban poor communities, where life operates in restricted and condensed spaces. Even more perhaps is the awareness not of change per se, but of sudden change – that the lives we are used to can change overnight. But in stillness also comes restedness, when our agencies become fully pensive and accepting of the here and now. I contrast stillness with the obsession with the future, specifically of the 'post-COVID' future, a new language, if not mindset, that we start to embed in our everyday. Stillness as restedness is not equal to despair, neither is it being oblivious about what lies ahead nor being passive about the future. If, as what it seems, COVID-19 is a real war, then stillness means embracing the here and now in order to go past it. Surely, the pandemic puts our humanity to test but just like trees that transform in stillness, we, too, can embrace this season with restedness and prudence.

Humanness

If there is any area where we feel the impact of the pandemic the most, that, I would argue, is our humanness. Humanness has many aspects but here I focus on two – our inclination towards humanities and our rootednesss in a shared humanity. On humanities, it is worth noting how the crisis has inspired the sudden unleashing of human creativities in forms we have so easily disregarded due to 'lack of time' – music, poetry, philosophy or simply reading or engaging in a conversation. The big irony is that as we wait for Science and Medicine to invent a cure, we turn to Humanities – the most devalued in academia – to keep us sane and living. In the same way, the pandemic has shaped our sense of belongingness, restoring and strengthening relationships for some, but also triggering exclusion and even displacement for others. But at the end of the day, it served as a great reminder that wherever we are, whether moving or not, here or there, our rootedness is in our humanity that we all share.

CONCLUSION

While not explicitly on cross-border education, this piece encourages critical and empirical attention towards ethics and responsibility surrounding international student mobility research and practice, where students can be treated as thinkers and co-producers of knowledge. This reflection also offers a critical example of how a student's own voice and imagining may contribute to a particular discourse, such as on the pandemic.

REFERENCES

Bista, K. (2019). Exploring the field: Understanding the international student. In K. Bista. (Ed.), Global perspectives on international experiences in higher education: Tensions and issues (pp. 1-16). Routledge.

Bothwell, E. (2020, March, 26). *Coronavirus: global student flows to suffer 'massive hit' for years.* Times Higher Education. March 26. https://www.timeshighereducation.com/news/coronavirus-global-student-flows-suffer-massive-hit-years

Ghazarian, P. G. (2014). Actual vs. ideal attraction: Trends in the mobility of Korean international students. *Journal of International Students,* 4(1), 89-103.

Lipura, S. D. & Collins, F. (2020). Towards an integrative understanding of contemporary educational mobilities: A Critical agenda for international student mobilities research. *Globalisation, Education and Societies,* 18(3), 343-359, https://doi.org/10.1080/14767724.2020.1711710.

Lo, W. Y. (2018). Beyond competition. A comparative review of conceptual approaches to international student mobility. *Globalisation, Societies & Education*, 17(3), 261-273.

Madge, C., Raghuram, P. & Noxolo, P. (2009). Engaged pedagogy and responsibility: A postcolonial analysis of international students. *Geoforum*, 40(1), 34-45.

Pham, L. (2020). Capabilities and the 'value' flows of international graduate returnees and their networks. *Journal of International Students 10(2),* xii-xv.

Raghuram, P. & Sondhi, G. (2020 May 11). Stuck in the middle of a pandemic: are international students migrants? *Open Democracy.* https://www.opendemocracy.net/en/pandemic-border/stuck-middle-pandemic-are-international-students-migrants/

Waters, J. (2018). International education is political! Exploring the politics of international student mobilities. *Journal of International Students,* 8(3), 1459-1478, doi:10.32674/jis.v8i3.66.

Wingfield, T., Cuevas, L. E., MacPherson, P. Millington, K. A. & Squire, S. B. (2020). Tacking two pandemics: A plea on World Tuberculosis Day. *The Lancet Respiratory Medicine, https://doi.org/10.1016/S2213-2600(20)30151-X*

Xiao, M. (2020, April 20). *Regimes of (im)mobility in the time of pandemic.* Compas. https://www.compas.ox.ac.uk/2020/regimes-of-immobility-in-the-time-of-pandemic/

Yang, P. (2019). Toward a framework for (re)thinking the ethics and politics of international student mobility. *Journal of Studies in International Education,* 102831531988989. doi:10.1177/1028315319889891

SARAH JANE LIPURA is a final year doctoral student at the University of Auckland and a faculty member (on leave) of Ateneo de Manila University. Her major research interests lie in the areas of international student mobility, migration and Korean Studies. Email: slip932@aucklanduni.ac.nz

Study Abroad Reflection

© *Journal of International Students*
Volume 11, Issue 1 (2021), pp. 257-265
ISSN: 2162-3104 (Print), 2166-3750 (Online)
doi: 10.32674/jis.v11i1.1272
ojed.org/jis

OJED
OPEN JOURNALS IN EDUCATION

Becoming an Intercultural Doctoral Student: Negotiating Cultural Dichotomies

Tram-Anh Bui
Brock University, St. Catharines, Canada
Ho Chi Minh City University of Foreign Languages
and Information Technology, Vietnam

ABSTRACT

International students experience both challenges and possibilities when they situate themselves in new sociocultural environments. The process of intercultural learning affects their self-formation and construction of their multiple identities. This self-reflective paper examines my experience as an international doctoral student transitioning from a Vietnamese cultural background to Canadian culture. By using concentric storying to deconstruct my journal entries, I found recurrent themes of conflicts and tensions emerging through different dialectical processes in my journey of becoming an intercultural doctoral student. My intercultural learning exposed my vulnerable selves while I searched for my core values and beliefs. This journey has brought profound changes in making meaning of my adventure in transnational space. My story may shed light on the understanding of life in transition and provide direction for other international doctoral students seeking to enhance their intercultural competence in a similar educational landscape.

Keywords: concentric storying, intercultural competence, intercultural learning experience, international doctoral students, self-reflexivity

---

"We do not learn from our experience. We learn from reflecting on experience."
(Dewey, 1933, p. 78).

From East to West

Coming from the East
Going to the West
Looking for a bright future
Everything is new to me here
Leaving home with purpose and mission
But sometimes still wondering why I am here
How can I fit in?
How can I be recognized?
Where do I belong?
Life in between cultures
Is not easy
Encountering tensions and conflicts
My community of selves is exposed
Seeing different parts of me
Exploring my core values and beliefs
Continuing to be
Keeping reflections
To make meaning of my life
The life in transnational space
The life with different on-going intercultural experiences.
(Bui, journal entry, October 2019)

This poetic fragment is the frequent personal dialogue I have had with myself since my husband and I landed in Canada for my doctoral study in 2016. I dreamed of experiencing a different language environment in an advanced, internationally recognized educational system that could help me create a better future. Fortunately, all my hard work paid off when I got a chance to further my education in Canada. Three months after getting married, with excitement and four suitcases my husband and I took a nearly 20-hour flight from Vietnam to Canada. Our whole new journey began (Bui, journal entry, June 10, 2016). My personal goals and expectations for my career and family created a situation of intercultural learning readiness when I entered the host culture in Ontario, Canada. In this reflective paper, I focus on the intercultural learning process as a profound personal change involving perspective transformation.

Some studies indicate intercultural experience is a transformational learning process, leading sojourners to embark on a journey of personal growth and development (Morgan, 2010; Savicki, 2008; Taylor, 1994). Intercultural adaptation is the process of intercultural learning in transforming international students' knowledge of self and awareness of others (Gill, 2007). With constant reflection on the new reality and lived experience, new knowledge is scaffolded and co-constructed. This self-reflective process can be regarded as a way of being and a process of personal development to obtain insights into one's own learning experience in different cultural and academic practices (Mezirow, 1991).

Furthering my academic study in Canada was a turning point in my life; this was the first time I set foot in the 'Western world.' I position myself as a person learning about Western paradigms and the multicultural values of other cultures in the host country through the lens of a female Vietnamese doctoral student. While I understand that my way of knowing about the host country might not thoroughly reflect the experiences of other international students, my experiences may help other international graduate students in their self-exploration process to make meaning of their cross-border journeys.

I have learned that the journey of becoming interculturally competent is also a journey of becoming more mature and more independent in self-development and personal growth (Bui, 2019). Sojourners like me need to acquire new skills to understand the culture in the host country, to overcome intercultural stress, and to develop psychological well-being (Kim, 1988; OECD, 2019, 2020). My intercultural learning has also exposed my vulnerable selves through different tensions in my search for my core values and beliefs to make meaning of my adventure in Canada (Drake, 2010).

Clandinin and Connelly (2006) taught me that

People shape their daily lives by stories of who they and others
are and as they interpret their past in terms of these stories. Story ...
is a portal through which a person enters the world and by which his
or her experience of the world is interpreted and made personally meaningful.
(p. 477)

In this context, I learned that one way to understand my intercultural learning experience in Canada was to inquire into my experiences in constructing multiple identities as a newcomer, a doctoral student, an emerging researcher, and a new bride. In this piece, I reflect on my intercultural learning experience and how I have negotiated cultural differences through different dichotomies.

I have employed concentric storying (Drake & Elliot, 1999) to analyze my journal entries of my experiences since arriving in Canada; this enables me to tell and retell stories with a structured path to meaning-making and transformational learning. Through this process of deconstructing stories and story parts, I have discovered recurrent themes, conflicts, and tensions (Drake & Elliot, 1999; Gibbs, 2018). I asked myself whether the parts suggest a similar theme. Was there a recurrent conflict? Did I play a similar character in each story? I identified and examined my basic beliefs and values. Implicit core values became explicit. This resolution led to the first steps in transformation and ways of being in the world. When revisiting all the stories I wrote down, I recognized the recurrent themes of my stories associated with my new life in Canada. They are about tensions I have encountered as I have adapted to a new social and academic environment.

I used different platforms to journal. I have physical notebooks and electronic journals in Word, OneNote, and apps on my phone. Some of my entries were in the form of short paragraphs; some were in the form of stories with a title, beginning, body, and ending; and some entries combined poetry and photos to express my way of being. These ways of journaling paved the way for me to learn more about my inner selves and others. Chronicling my experiences in a cross-border circumstance has widened my understanding of the tensions and dichotomies I have encountered (Chang, 2008).

NEGOTIATION OF CULTURAL DIFFERENCES THROUGH DIFFERENT DICHOTOMIES

Traditional Methods Versus Modern Methods: A Passive Learner Versus an Active Learner

One of the emerging tensions that challenged me was the difference between the traditional methods of education in my home country and the new ones in the host country. As a person growing up in a teacher-centered educational system in Vietnam (a Confucian heritage country), I learned that teachers had the power to decide what and how students should learn. The role of each student in class was as a receiver passively obtaining the information of the lesson, mainly through teachers. I was always mindful of my role: I felt I had to accept without question the information I received from teachers and other authoritative people. The passive learning approach was more familiar to me than the more active approach of asking, discussing, and providing feedback to instructors. Vietnamese cultural norms were embedded in all my endeavour, helping to maintain harmony in relationships and avoiding conflicts in my inquiry for knowledge. But they also prevented me from expressing my views openly (Hofstede, 2003; Stole, 1998; Subramaniam, 2008; N. T. Tran, 1999; Nguyen, 1989). In my first doctoral course in Canada, I twice skipped writing exit cards commenting on my instructors' teaching because I did not know what to write. When I tried to put words on the card, I was apprehensive about writing something that might make them unhappy or that might put me in a vulnerable position (Bui, journal entry, July, 2016).

Acceptance Versus Rejection: Approval Versus Disapproval

Acceptance and rejection are other conflicts that I encountered. In my journal entries, I recorded my discomfort at not obtaining employment like other graduate students who spoke English as their first language. To make ends meet, I looked unsuccessfully for a job in a local outlet mall. This was a challenging time for me because I felt marginalized. I felt that my social and academic achievements in Vietnam were undervalued, and I was questioning why I was here on this challenging journey. It was the feeling of not belonging and not being accepted in the new academic environment. What I had achieved in Vietnam was juxtaposed with how Canada seemed to reject my accomplishments. Embarking on my doctoral journey in transnational education led me to experience a change in my professional identity. Dang and Tran's work (2017) resonated with me because of this. They shared that leaving the country of origin meant leaving all of the familiarity behind, in my case, my home institution, my teaching position, and my connectedness with beloved colleagues and students. Transitioning from being known and recognized by many others to "being no one and [being] known by nobody" (Dang & Tran, 2017, p. 80) was a challenge for me since I always felt homesick, lonely, and powerless. My experience correlates with Leung's (2017) research, which points out that professionals often encounter significant obstacles in practicing their profession. Migrants' qualifications and competencies are often not recognized or accredited.

Dependence Versus Independence and Distance Versus Intimacy: A Doctoral Student and a New Bride

A turning point in my academic journey is my story as a young married woman encountering the dilemma between distance and intimacy with my husband and my doctoral study. My husband could not find any employment opportunities suitable for him to further his profession in St. Catharines where my university is located. He searched for other opportunities in different cities across Canada and finally found a position in another province that aligned with his experience in Vietnam. This meant I was standing in the dichotomies of whether I should move there to support his career or stay in St. Catharines for my doctoral study. As a doctoral student, I needed to be close to my university campus. As a married woman, it was necessary to be with my husband to support him in his career in a new province. The only one who I could think of to ask for advice was my "supervisor at the time". I asked him whether I could move to a new place with my husband and simultaneously commit to progressing with my doctoral work. My supervisor, however, did not agree and chose to drop me as a mentee when I most needed supervisory support. I chose to go to a new province with my husband for a few months and support him set up a new life there. Then, to maintain my commitment to my studies, I decided to go back to St. Catharines alone.

Reflecting on this story, loneliness was my experience when my husband and I lived far away from each other. I became a caretaker of my soul to make my husband and parents feel that I was fine to be alone. I started to empower myself to create positivity in my life through meditation and involvement in voluntary work. Taking my experience as the foundation of this paper has made me understand life in transition "as a process; composed over time, in place, and in different relationships" (Clandinin et al., 2013, p. 220).

Integration Versus Assimilation: East Meets West

I could see the conflict within me when I was struggling to find my way to integrate into a new environment. Some inner dialogues explicitly showed my feeling of being an outsider in a new culture. As I began to improve my language and build reliable relationships with my professors and cohort, I recognized some cultural differences among us. I constantly asked myself these questions: How could I understand them better? How could I have a sense of belonging to this new culture? I also asked myself whether I was integrating or assimilating into this new culture. I began to appreciate the differences among us and nurture a sense of diversity. I found that I could keep my own distinctive cultural values while accepting cultural differences and saw myself as a tessera in the Canadian cultural mosaic. In other words, I felt more confident that with my own cultural heritage I could contribute to its diversity, allowing me to embrace more than one identity.

I believe that my intercultural identity is evolving, but I still want to maintain my national identity and feel proud of it. Interestingly, what I have experienced in Canada has helped me understand more about myself and my cultural values (Cranton, 2008; Pusch, 2009). I recognize that whatever I do will reflect my identity as a Vietnamese person. Whatever I say not only reflects my characteristics but also my cultural heritage. I consider my pride in my heritage as the major driving force in all of my efforts. The more I become interculturally competent, the more I recognize my own national identity. People might not remember my name, but they will refer to me by saying "she is from Vietnam" or "she is Vietnamese." That is also one of my motivations to strive for excellence— to shape a positive impression about Vietnamese people. I also have a desire to reconnect with my homeland and contribute to my country as well as the host country's Vietnamese community.

CONCLUSION

Becoming an intercultural doctoral student has enabled me to engage in self-reconstruction, self-formation, and identity redefinition (L. T. Tran, 2012). This reflexive process has given me the opportunity to explore my core values, beliefs, and the factors contributing to my thoughts from my past to my future. I have learned to navigate my personal, academic, and professional selves from a familiar culture to a new one by reviewing my own experiences and shaping multiple identities of becoming more competent in adapting to the new culture. Navigating my doctoral work is related to my self-negotiation of being Vietnamese, being a sojourner, and being an intercultural doctoral student in a North American university. My multiple identities as an autonomous learner, a new bride, a caretaker of my own soul, and an intercultural doctoral student have become the core aspects underlying my personal and professional growth. I feel thankful for the hardships that I have experienced during my doctoral study and my magic helpers (Drake, 1991) who supported me to achieve my goals. This journey has allowed me to gather my courage and enhance my grit, perseverance, and determination. These values will always be part of my package, for every new adventure to wherever this life takes me.

My story might help students understand more about their intercultural experience and be aware of this learning process. Intercultural learning is a recursive process repeated continuously as students transfer to a higher level of intercultural competence. Cultural disequilibrium in this learning process tends to happen continually throughout the time international students spend in the host culture, even though it could be lessened in intensity over a period of time as they become more interculturally competent (Taylor, 1994; Kim, 2000). They could also play different roles in this intercultural experience and engage themselves in critical reflection to explore their own values and beliefs to make meaning of their adventure; for example, they could learn to be an observer, a participant, and a friend to build up authentic intercultural relationships when adapting to a new cross-border life (Taylor, 1994; Deardorff 2009, 2020). By understanding students' tensions, relationships between international graduate students and their faculty advisors or course instructors may be improved (Soong et al., 2015) and "a dialogical pedagogic model for mutual adaptation can be developed between international students and academics" (Tran, 2011, p. 79). Perhaps colleges and universities in the host countries need to create intervention strategies to show empathy and support for international doctoral students.

REFERENCES

Bui, T. A. (2019). *Becoming an intercultural doctoral student: Negotiating identities through different dialectical processes* [Paper presentation]. *AERA, Division J,* Toronto, Canada.

Chang, H. (2008). *Autoethnography as method.* Left Coast Press.

Clandinin, D. J., & Connelly, F. M. (2006). Narrative inquiry. In J. L. Green, G. Camilli, & P. B. Elmore (Eds.), *Handbook of complementary methods in education research* (pp. 477–488). Lawrence Erlbaum.

Clandinin, D. J., Steeves, P., & Caine, V. (Eds.). (2013). *Composing lives in transition: A narrative inquiry into the experiences of early school leavers.* Emerald Publishing.

Cranton, P. & Wright, B. (2008). The transformative educator as learning companion. *Journal of Transformative Education, 6*(1), 33–47.

Dang, T. X., & Tran, T. L. (2017). From "Somebody" to "Nobody": International doctoral students' perspectives of home-host connectedness. In L. T. Tran & C. Gomes (Eds.), *International student connectedness and identity: Transnational perspectives* (pp. 75–91). Springer.

Deardorff, D. K. (2009). Synthesizing conceptualizations of intercultural competence: A summary and emerging themes. In D. K. Deardorff (Ed.), *The SAGE handbook of intercultural competence* (pp. 264–269). SAGE.

Deardorff, D. K. (2020, November 13). *Student mobility and their intercultural development: Developing habits for an intercultural lifestyle* [Keynote address]. Online Internationalisation: Meeting the Challenge of Student Mobility in a Global Pandemic. Virtual Conference, the University of Hong Kong, Hong Kong. https://www.cetl.hku.hk/vconf2020/programme/

Dewey, J. (1933). *How we think: A restatement of the relation of reflective thinking to the educative process.* Henry Regnery.

Drake, S. (1991). The journey of the learner: Personal and universal story. *The Educational Forum, 56*(1), 47–59.

Drake, S. (2010) Enhancing Canadian teacher education using a story framework. *The Canadian Journal for the Scholarship of Teaching and Learning, 1*(2). http://dx.doi.org/10.5206/cjsotl-rcacea.2010.2.2

Drake, S., & Elliott, A. (1999, April). *Concentric storying: A vehicle for professional development in teacher education* [Paper presentation]. 1999 AERA Annual Meeting, Montreal, Quebec.

Gibbs, G. R. (2018). *Analyzing qualitative data* (2nd ed.). SAGE.

Gill, S. (2007). Overseas students' intercultural adaptation as intercultural learning: A transformative framework, *Compare, 37*(2), 167–183. https://doi.org/10.1080/03057920601165512.

Hofstede, G (2003). *Cultures and organizations: Software of the mind.* Profile Books.

Kim, Y. Y. (1988). *Communication and cross-cultural adaptation: An integrative theory.* Multilingual Matters.

Kim, Y. Y. (2000). *Becoming intercultural: An integrative theory of communication and cross-cultural adaptation.* SAGE.

Leung, W. H. M. (2017). Social mobility via academic mobility: Reconfigurations in class and gender identities among Asian scholars in the global north. *Journal of Ethnic and Migration Studies, 43*(16), 2704–2719.

Mezirow, J. (1991). *Transformative dimensions of adult learning.* Jossey-Bass.

Nguyen, K. (1989). On the historical role of Confucianism. *Vietnamese Studies, 94*(4), 67–72.

Morgan, D. A. (2010). Journeys into transformation: Travel to an "other" place as a vehicle for transformative learning. *Journal of Transformative Education, 8*(4), 246–268.

Organisation for Economic Cooperation and Development. (2019). *PISA 2018 Assessment and Analytical Framework* [Annual report]. PISA, OECD Publishing. https://dx.doi.org/10.1787/b25efab8-en.

Organisation for Economic Cooperation and Development. (2020). *Learning to live together. PISA 2018 Results (Volume VI): Are students ready to thrive in an interconnected world?* [Annual report]. PISA, OECD Publishing. https://doi.org/10.1787/d64c458c-en.

Pusch, M. D. (2009). The interculturally competent global leader. In D. K. Deardorff (Ed.), *The SAGE handbook of intercultural competence* (pp. 66–84). SAGE.

Savicki, V. (2008). *Developing intercultural competence and transformation: Theory, research, and application in international education.* Stylus Publishing.

Soong, H., Tran, L. T., & Pham, H. H. (2015). Being and becoming an intercultural doctoral student: Reflective autobiographical narratives. *Reflective Practice, 16*(4), 435–448.

Stole, W. H. (1998). Destiny and determination: Psychocultural reinforcement in Vietnam. In W. H. Stole & G. A. Devos (Eds.), *Confucianism and the family* (pp. 311–328). State University of New York Press.

Subramaniam, G. (2008). Confronting Asian concerns in engaging learners to online education. *International Education Studies, 1*(4), 10–18.

Taylor, W. E. (1994). Intercultural competency: A transformative learning process. *Adult Education Quarterly, 44*(3), 154–174.

Tran, L. T. (2011). Committed, face-value, hybrid or mutual adaptation? The experiences of international students in Australian higher education. *Educational Review, 63*(1), 79-94, DOI: 10.1080/00131911.2010.510905.

Tran, L. T. (2012). Transformative learning and international students negotiating higher education. In S. Sovic & M. Blythman (Eds.), *International students negotiating higher education: Critical perspectives* (pp. 124–141). Routledge.

Tran, T. N. (1999). *Cơ sở văn hoá Việt Nam. [The fundamentals of Vietnamese culture]*. Education Publisher.

TRAM ANH BUI is a Ph.D. candidate in Educational Studies at Brock University, Canada and a lecturer at Ho Chi Minh city University of Foreign Languages and Information Technology (HUFLIT), Vietnam. Her major research interests lie in the area of student mobility, international student leadership, intercultural competence, EFL teacher education, and mindfulness in qualitative inquiry. E-mail: tb15qg@brocku.ca

Book Review

© *Journal of International Students*
Volume 11, Issue 1 (2021), pp. 266-269
ISSN: 2162-3104 (Print), 2166-3750 (Online)
doi: 10.32674/jis.v11i1.3344
ojed.org/jis

OJED
OPEN JOURNALS IN EDUCATION

A Transdisciplinary Approach to International Teaching Assistants: Perspectives from Applied Linguistics

Stephen Daniel Looney & Shereen Bhalla (Eds.), Multilingual Matters, 2019. 200pp. Paperback. ISBN-13 978-1-788-92553-2

Reviewed by Heidi Fischer, *Old Dominion University, USA*

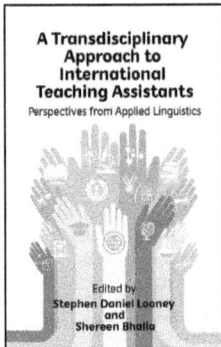

A Transdisciplinary
Approach to
International
Teaching Assistants
Perspectives from Applied Linguistics

Edited by
Stephen Daniel Looney
and
Shereen Bhalla

In the Fall 2018 semester, almost 30% of graduate teaching assistants at U.S. higher education institutions (HEIs) were international students. Moreover, of the HEIs that hired international teaching assistants (ITAs), 41% enrolled 50 or more ITAs and approximately one third enrolled 100 or more ITAs (U.S. Department of Education, 2018). These statistics alone warrant a closer look at the practices, preparation, and evaluation regarding ITAs on college campuses. The editors of *A Transdisciplinary Approach to International Teaching Assistants: Perspectives from Applied Linguistics* also make the case for the intentional intersection of research and practice on the topic of ITAs so that research can impact ITA practices.

The edited volume situates ITAs as "multilingual, skilled, migrant professionals who participate in and are discursively constructed through various participant frameworks, modalities and activities" (p. 13). Viewed through an applied linguistics lens, the chapter authors highlight their contribution to a transdisciplinary approach to the study of ITAs and review extant literature on the topic, before sharing results of studies with ITA participants. The volume as a whole makes the case for why conducting explicitly transdisciplinary research on the topic is essential to better understanding the complexities of ITA identities.

The editors lament the fact that so much of the discourse surrounding ITAs among undergraduate students, parents, and ITA policy developers has been deficit-oriented: ITAs fail to be understood in the classroom. In fact, much of the literature on the topic is dated and lacks theoretical support. Furthermore, the editors argue, research regarding ITAs must go beyond pronunciation and grammar to include ITAs' interactional skills and identity development through participation in various communities of practice.

The book contains three sections in addition to an introductory and concluding chapter. The structure of the book matches that of its paradigmatic lens: second language acquisition (SLA). SLA consists of three components: micro, which includes semiotic factors; meso, which refers to sociocultural factors; and macro, which contains ideological factors. Combined, these three components produce SLA viewed through a transdisciplinary lens and shape the identity of ITAs. The three chapters in the micro section of the book explore verbal and nonverbal communication and social interactions among ITAs who were observed in lecture halls, laboratories, and during office hours. The chapters conclude with calls for paradigm shifts of research on ITA communication. First, researchers and practitioners alike should consider ITAs as co-participants in discourse along with their students. Second, there is a need to understand classroom interaction and embodied communication to effectively prepare ITAs for their roles. Finally, ITA studies should be placed in the context of intercultural education, as authority is exercised and understood differently in different cultures.

At the meso level, the book explores ITAs' social identities and social contexts. One chapter in this section advocates for a World Englishes approach to ITA assessment, moving away from testing for "Inner Circle English." The authors also make the case for positive structured interactions between U.S. undergraduates and ITAs who are embedded into courses or existing workshops, such as orientation programming. Enhancing the undergraduate students' interactions with and their affect toward ITAs is a valuable first step for HEI practitioners. This step can be enhanced by a deeper understanding of ITAs' identity creation and navigation of their various communities of practice.

The two chapters that consider the macro level of SLA examine recruitment practices for international students and ITA instructional planning, thus situating ITAs in foreign policy and higher education studies. This section of the book recommends that HEIs explicitly describe in their policies the value that ITAs add to the institution. This value should not only reflect ITAs' contributions at the institutional level, but also at the national level. Examples include the diversity and cultural knowledge ITAs bring to the classrooms of students who may have limited interactions with people outside their home society. Furthermore, the authors make the case for using course logic to evaluate the input factors and outcomes of ITA preparatory courses.

The book concludes with a call for ongoing institutional support structures for ITAs as well as an urging for researchers and practitioners to act as change agents who advocate for ITAs against monolingual ideologies. Practitioners must recognize that ITAs have individualized experiences based on their involvement in communities of practice. The curriculum to support these international students should be shaped as ongoing professional development, moving beyond linguistic remediation to supporting ITAs as the multilingual professionals they are.

Programming to support ITAs must involve undergraduate students and the ITAs themselves where possible. Future research should contribute toward a national standard for ITA preparation, beginning with an updated textbook. Finally, the authors insist that the TOEFL and its monolinguistic ideology be revisited, and that ITAs be placed on the agenda for advocacy at relevant national organizations.

Throughout the book, the authors frame their conversation about ITAs with a positive regard toward the international students' abilities and expertise. Yet, by referring to ITAs as "immigrants" (p. 23) and "foreign" (p. 76), the authors inadvertently contribute to the dated and value-laden discourse about teaching professionals who are first and foremost international students. Further, although the introductory chapter seems to indicate that the book will take a North American approach to the topic of ITAs, the vast majority, if not all, of the studies included in the volume were conducted at U.S. HEIs.

A second edition of the volume would benefit from an additional chapter on intercultural competencies in the micro section of the book. A transdisciplinary view of SLA must include this essential concept that impacts verbal and nonverbal communication alike. Intercultural competence is defined as "the ability to communicate effectively and appropriately in intercultural situations based on one's intercultural knowledge, skills, and attitudes" (Deardorff, 2004, p. 194). ITAs have to navigate an intercultural context on a daily basis, and their ability to effectively communicate with their undergraduate students, colleagues, and supervisors is critical to their success.

Nonetheless, this is an important read during the time of a global pandemic, as ITAs who are already studying abroad make an even more significant contribution to campus internationalization while outbound mobility is curtailed. The book will be a beneficial read for practitioners who work with international students at the graduate level and who want to understand the challenges of working in an ITA capacity. *A Transdisciplinary Approach to International Teaching Assistants* not only adds to the sparse literature on ITAs, but it also provides practical suggestions for HEI administrators who work with ITAs and who seek to implement preparatory programming and evaluation procedures. The editors recommend that ITA practitioners and supervisors engage with ITAs in their institutional communities of practice. This engagement entails faculty and staff who work with ITAs having a comprehensive understanding of ITAs in their classrooms and laboratories, research teams, and departments. ITAs would benefit from the resulting fruitful relationships between ITA administrators and supervisors that might lead to a thoughtfully co-constructed training curriculum. Perhaps a novel recommendation of the book is for these administrators to engage with ITAs through their student organizations. This engagement would support a holistic understanding of international student perspectives, which would ideally lead to a more enriching experience for international students who serve as ITAs.

REFERENCES

Deardorff, D. K. (2004). *The identification and assessment of intercultural competence as a student outcome of internationalization at institutions of higher education in the United States* (Order No. 3128751). ProQuest Dissertations & Theses Global. (305165880).

U.S. Department of Education, National Center for Education Statistics, Integrated Postsecondary System. (2018). *Graduate teaching assistants by race/ethnicity: Fall 2018*. https://nces.ed.gov/ipeds/datacenter/

HEIDI FISCHER is a Ph.D. candidate in the Higher Education program at Old Dominion University (ODU) in Norfolk, Virginia. Originally from Germany, Heidi completed her higher education in the U.S. South. She previously worked in the education abroad field, advising hundreds of students on education abroad opportunities. Throughout her career, Heidi also created and managed dozens of exchange partnerships with universities abroad, and oversaw the annual planning of short-term, faculty-led programs. Currently, she works as a Graduate Research Assistant in the Department of Educational Foundations and Leadership at ODU. Her research interests include critical discourse analysis, narrative inquiry, campus internationalization, education abroad outcomes, and community colleges. Email: hfisc002@odu.edu

Book Review

© *Journal of International Students*
Volume 11, Issue 1 (2021), pp. 270-273
ISSN: 2162-3104 (Print), 2166-3750 (Online)
doi: 10.32674/jis.v11i1.3233
ojed.org/jis

The Oxford Encyclopedia of Global Perspectives on Teacher Education

Jo Lampert (Ed.), Oxford University Press, 2019. 1568pp. ISBN-13 978-0190670221

Reviewed by Yang Gao, *Dalian Maritime University, China*

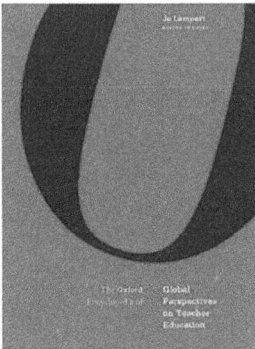

Jo Lampert, as the Editor-in-Chief, did a phenomenal job in collecting and editing works on teacher education for this book. I was hesitant to review the book at first, as I believed an encyclopedia (as the book title indicates) would require tons of effort to read and thus make the task challenging. However, having read the book, I am proud of myself as a reader who hasn't missed this contribution to the literature and even more proud of the authors who have contributed both classic and avant-garde works to the field. I would synthesize the book's benefits into two main categories: perspectives and availability. In terms of the perspectives, the book provides the reader with an assortment of views on teacher education; some are innovative and inspiring, some are combined and synthesized, and some are updated and newly developed from canonical works. As for availability, all collected works appear online as part of the *Oxford Research Encyclopedia of Education*, which makes access convenient.

As the book is not organized in chapters or sections, I frame this review through my classification of the perspectives. Specifically, my classification includes some paired, dichotomic perspectives with overlapping tenets. This review refers to exemplar articles from the book, rather than all contributions, given the abbreviated nature of a book review.

The first type of perspective is the dichotomy between theory-based and practice-based works. For example, some works focus on complexity theory (e.g., Mártin et al.); postcolonial theory (e.g., Viruru & Persky); disability critical race theory (e.g., Migliarini & Annamma); and sociolinguistic theory, including systemic functional grammar (e.g., de Oliveria & Smith) and translanguaging theory (e.g., Espana et al.), presenting how these theories are related to teacher education. Some of the theoretical frameworks may also relate to certain methodological, inquiry-based paradigms, including ethnographic inquiry (e.g., Rivas-Flores) and heuristic inquiry (e.g., Fogelgarn) in teacher education. Different from these theory-based contributions, several of the collected works are practice-based. For example, Cahnmann-Taylor and Sanders-Bustle offer an article on art-informed pedagogies in teacher preparation; Yang and MacLeod on blended-learning pedagogies; Gist et al. on culturally responsive pedagogy; and Hobbs et al. on trauma-informed pedagogy.

The second type of perspective is the dichotomy between canonical and emerging works. The encyclopedia includes quite a number of the former, some of which might be a revisiting or extended version of the existing literature. For example, Grenfell contributes an article guiding us to revisit Bourdieu and education, which offers lasting insight to teacher educators. Noddings' article on care in teacher education addresses how caring and being cared for are essential concepts in the field. Masny devotes an article to Deleuze and Guattari and teacher education but extends the line of inquiry with modes of thought to "problematize, conceptualize, and challenge normativity" (Masny, 2019, p. 1). On the other hand, some articles contribute to newly developed, innovative methods or consider how postmodernism has made contemporary teacher education different from previous versions. For example, there are quite a few articles discussing how the digitalized world has informed teacher education. Keengwe provides a chapter on globalization, digital technology, and teacher education in the United States; Kelly discusses how "networks make use of the capabilities of the internet and related technology to better support teachers" (p. 1). Additionally, Niess contributes a chapter on teachers' knowledge for the digital age.

The third type of perspective among the collected works is the dichotomy between indigenous and international perspectives. Some authors focus on indigenous teacher education, typically in developed, western countries. For example, Phillips pens a chapter on indigenous Australian studies with a proposal on how the indigenist standpoint pedagogical framework is inherently "reformative, relational, and critically reflexive" in supporting and facilitating students to re/intake indigenous knowledge (p. 1). There are also contributions in the collection that seek to broaden the scope of teacher education by using an international lens. For example, Panda contributes an article analyzing international standards and benchmarks among teacher training programs in different sample countries. Through the analysis, Panda recommends that standards and benchmarks should be flexible and dynamic.

One of the most important contributions that the book has made is the focus on "Global South" perspectives, which differ from previous publications in the field that typically stem from an American or European perspective. Specifically, the book includes myriad articles addressing the Asia Pacific region (e.g., Cheng; Forlin), including Japan (e.g., Nagashima) and Singapore (e.g., Chong & Gopinathan; Loh & Hu). It also includes teacher education perspectives from

Russia (Valeeca & Kalimulin), Mexico (Hamann et al.), and South Africa (Soudien & Sayed). All of these included perspectives make the book valuable indeed for the global reader.

Another type of perspective is the dichotomy between concept-orientation and stage-oriented articles. Specifically, a considerable number of core concepts or models have been (re)visited and extended through the collected works to probe their impacts on and relations with teacher education. These concepts include agency (Flessner & Kandel-Cisco), reflection (Korthagen & Nuijten), accountability (Mayer), teacher beliefs (Fives et al.; Tatto), teacher identity (Martínez-de-la-Hidalga & Villardón-Gallego), teacher leadership (Frost), spiritual development (Mohanty), and well-being (Gustems-Carnicer & Calderon). In addition, there are works focused on providing staging insights on teacher education. For example, some works highlight initial teacher education programs or teacher preparation programs (e.g., Sharplin et al.; Solomon; Zygmunt et al.), some teacher development (e.g., Jones & Ellis; Madalińska-Michalak), and some teacher quality and assessment (e.g., Beck et al.; Deluca & Braund; Polly).

While the book contributes to the field of teacher education with unique, innovative, and comprehensive perspectives, it might be even better if the editorial team had assembled clear-cut sections. The current format might cause the reader, especially one new to the field, to spend extra time in selecting their focal points. It is also worth mentioning that some of the collected works might be adapted versions (e.g., Burnett & Lampert) or reprinted versions (e.g., Mayer; Mayer et al.) of previous, classic works (e.g., Lampert & Burnett, 2016). In sum, this publication may serve as a stimulus to those interested in exploring the field of teacher education, as well as to those wanting to understand varied perspectives within teacher education.

REFERENCES

Kelly, N. (2019). Online networks in teacher education. In J. Lampert (Ed.), *The Oxford Encyclopedia of Global Perspectives on Teacher Education*. Oxford University Press. https://doi.org/10.1093/acrefore/9780190264093.013.416

Lampert, J., & Burnett, B. (2016). *Teacher education for high poverty schools* (Vol. 2). Springer. https://doi.org/10.1007/978-3-319-22059-8

Masny, D. (2019). Deleuze and Guattari and teacher education. In J. Lampert (Ed.), *The oxford encyclopedia of global perspectives on teacher education*. Oxford University Press. https://doi.org/10.1093/acrefore/9780190264093.013.374

Phillips, J. (2019). Indigenous Australian Studies, indigenist standpoint pedagogy, and student resistance. In J. Lampert (Ed.), *The Oxford Encyclopedia of global perspectives on teacher education*. Oxford University Press. https://doi.org/10.1093/acrefore/9780190264093.013.257

YANG GAO, PhD, is an associate professor at Dalian Maritime University (DMU). Before his appointment at DMU, he taught at San Jose State University and Kent State University in the United States. Yang does research in TESOL and ESL teacher education. Email: gaoyang666@dlmu.edu.cn

Book Review

© *Journal of International Students*
Volume 11, Issue 1 (2011), pp. 274-277
ISSN: 2162-3104 (Print), 2166-3750 (Online)
doi: 10.32674/jis.v11i1.3258
ojed.org/jis

OJED
OPEN JOURNALS IN EDUCATION

Critical Pedagogy in Hong Kong: Classroom Stories of Struggle and Hope

Carlos Soto, Routledge, 2019. 176pp. ISBN-13: 978-1-138-61180-1.

Reviewed by Huili Han & Luo Zhang, *Central South University, China*

CRITICAL PEDAGOGY
IN HONG KONG

CLASSROOM STORIES OF STRUGGLE AND HOPE

Carlos Soto

Critical Pedagogy in Hong Kong: Classroom Stories of Struggle and Hope is a book about pedagogy. However, the book is not only a collection of educational views, it is also more narrative and dramatic, fascinating and with extremely strong readability. This is a work of enlightenment and rebirth. Many ideas in this book are exactly what readers think, feel, and wonder. Many real thoughts buried by teachers and students come out on paper, providing abundant educational resources for researchers, educators, and both pre-service and in-service teachers.

The book is both theoretical and practical. One focus of the book is on the nuances of the historical development of critical pedagogy, including its goals and deficiencies. Soto also discusses the existence and development of two dimensions of critical education—teaching and learning—in an exam-oriented environment at two research sites, New Territories Schools (NTS) and Industrial Secondary Schools (ISS). Soto applies critical pedagogy theory to the inequitable educational environment in Hong Kong through a hopeful "field" story. Throughout the book he explores the limitations and possibilities of empowering minority students through the practice of critical pedagogy in Hong Kong.

The author divides the book into seven parts. The first part examines how the struggles and needs of students in emerging markets are framed from a demographic perspective. The second part provides a literature review and theoretical framework. In this section, the author narrows the theoretical framework to the main ideas of the late Brazilian educator Freire, and introduces and defines important concepts, such as banking education, critical consciousness, generative theme, dialogue, empowerment, etc. The third part summarizes and demonstrates the critical ethnographic approach used in this study from an ethical perspective. The fourth part is an overview of the author's year-long ethnographic work at NTS, the first study site. It explains how Soto implemented curriculum guidelines at NTS, and how he generated the topics and developed the participation tools. The fifth part is an overview of the author's work at the second research site, ISS. This part mainly discusses how the curriculum should be developed under the guidance of critical pedagogy from the perspective of tool development. The sixth part focuses on the dialogue and behavior of ISS students related to the practice of critical pedagogy in daily life. The seventh part responds to the research question, advocating the deconstruction of oppressive social conditions and school practices, and constructing a new critical pedagogy theory and practice. The first and second parts clarify the key terms and lay a solid theoretical foundation; the third, fourth, fifth, and sixth parts discuss the generative theme, participation tools, course materials, student dialogue, and action in turn. Each part is supported by "on-the-ground" examples; thus, the book makes the content, teaching process, and results of the critical education method tangible.

One of the most substantial features of this book is the authenticity of it, drawing directly from the experiences of pre-service teachers and students. The authenticity also comes from the critical pedagogy ideas that the author expresses and has tried to implement. For example, one idea is that many students suffer from self-abuse or self-harm during adolescence and cut their bodies; there are also many adolescent students suffering from love. Soto uses a series of participatory tools such as film, literature and philosophy to help students look at themselves with a new perspective, inspire themselves, understand their own problems, and connect with the greater cultural conflict and historical struggle. In addition, Soto clearly explains that teachers at the surveyed sites felt helpless in the area of banking education, an area with a strictly prescribed teaching method that must be used in the classroom given various external pressures. These include the pressure of the high stakes and high academic level exams in Hong Kong, schools trying to improve reputation and promote freshmen enrollment, and parents feeling that their hard-earned money has been wasted. These various pressures are causing teachers to have less choice in course materials. This kind of pressure is also a disaster for students, because under banking education, "filling in the blanks" is the main form of learning, which lacks the channels and opportunities for students to fully express their opinions.

This book examines critical educational theory and practice in Hong Kong. Soto does not blindly praise critical education theory. Instead, he holds a dialectical point of view to describe the shortcomings of critical pedagogy. The first weakness he identifies is the lack of precision and transparency; the second weakness is the lack of tangible and clear tools and materials as a support; and the third weakness is that it is easy to fall into the critical dilemma of blindly deconstructing oppressive conditions and neglecting construction of social conditions suitable for critical pedagogy. Furthermore, critical education overemphasizes the heroic role of teachers in repressive schools. Influential researchers argue that the hegemony of dominant structures creates a false sense among people that they cannot collectively challenge the status quo. What we have not taken into account, however, is that many of those researchers substitute one form of hegemony for another. That is, they do not really question their understanding of the social world but advocate that the oppressed replace their own "original consciousness" with the researcher's own "constructed consciousness."

Critical Pedagogy in Hong Kong: Classroom Stories of Struggle and Hope speaks what many people want to say but dare not say and does what many people want to do but dare not try. The author explores the significance of being an analytical teacher and researcher and is constantly reborn in this process. Education should represent the hope to deconstruct current inequality and oppression, and then to construct new social conditions. It should be the main force to promote social change. For teachers and students under the oppression of an unequal education environment, this book can instigate their rebirth. Because school education has a natural sense of alienation from students that is not influenced by nationality or race, it is important to understand that any real teaching practice requires a commitment to social change in the unity of subordinate and marginalized groups. The book advocates for students, teachers, and school leaders to break with traditional education ideas, and supports students and educators in having a firmer goal of a future, fair education system. Isn't that what the education revolution is all about? Hopefully, readers will find insight from the story to help them embark on their own journey of challenging existing systems and rebuilding new systems based on equality.

REFERENCES

Soto, C. (2019). *Critical pedagogy in Hong Kong: Classroom stories of struggle and hope.* Routledge.

HUILI HAN, PhD., is an associate professor at Central South University in P. R. China and a visiting scholar at The George Washington University in the U.S. She is on the review board for the Human Science and Technology Award in China and is a peer reviewer of the Journal of Comparative & International Higher Education in the U.S. She presided over a project for the Ministry of Education and participated in a number of provincial and national level research projects. Her book was published by a national, first-level publishing house in China, and she has also translated three books. Her major research interests lie in the area of national governance, online education research, higher education research, and multiculturalism. Email: huilihan2018@hotmail.com

LUO ZHANG is a graduate student at Central South University in P. R. China. She is pursuing a Master of Law degree. Her major research interests lie in national governance, college students' career planning, and multiculturalism. Email: 1816034963@qq.com.

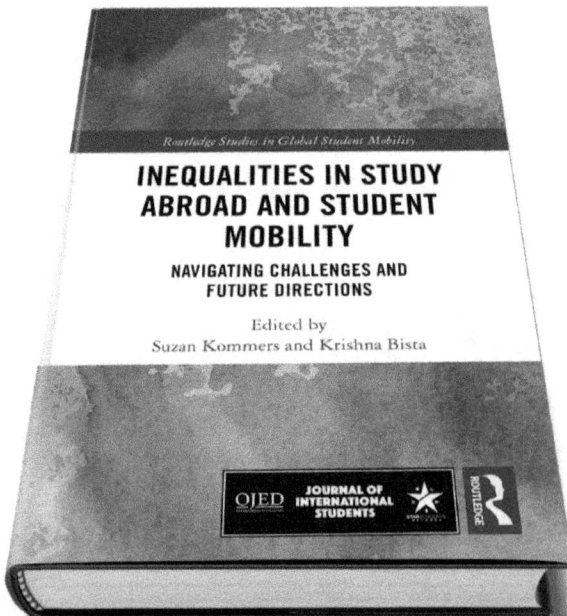

www.ingramcontent.com/pod-product-compliance
Lightning Source LLC
Chambersburg PA
CBHW052122270326
41930CB00012B/2724